Alternative Lithography

A printmaker's guide to working with foil, wood, lino, paper and polyester

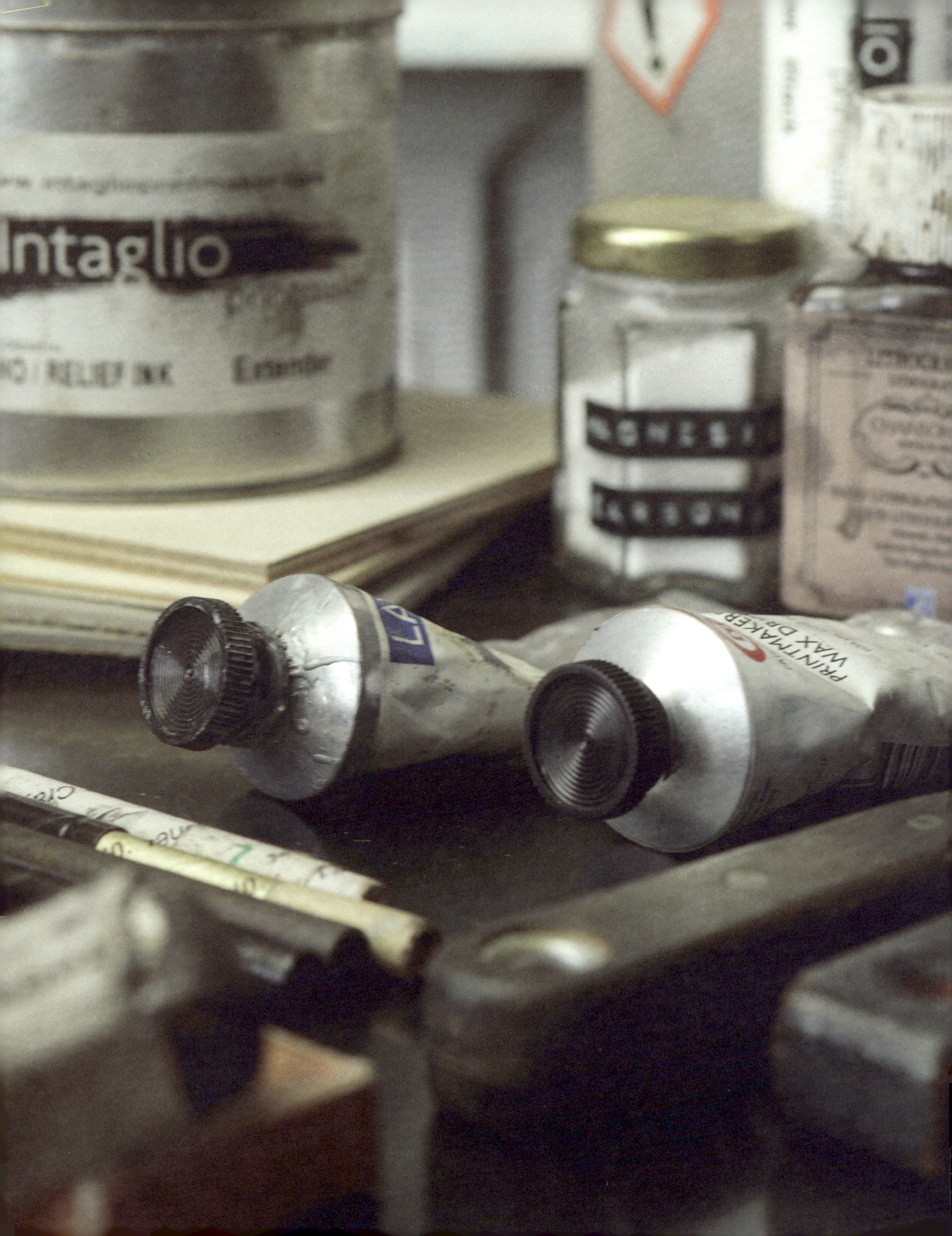
Intaglio
RELIEF INK
Extender
PRINTMAKER
WAX

Alternative Lithography

Scarlett Rebecca

A printmaker's guide to working with foil, wood, lino, paper and polyester

THE CROWOOD PRESS

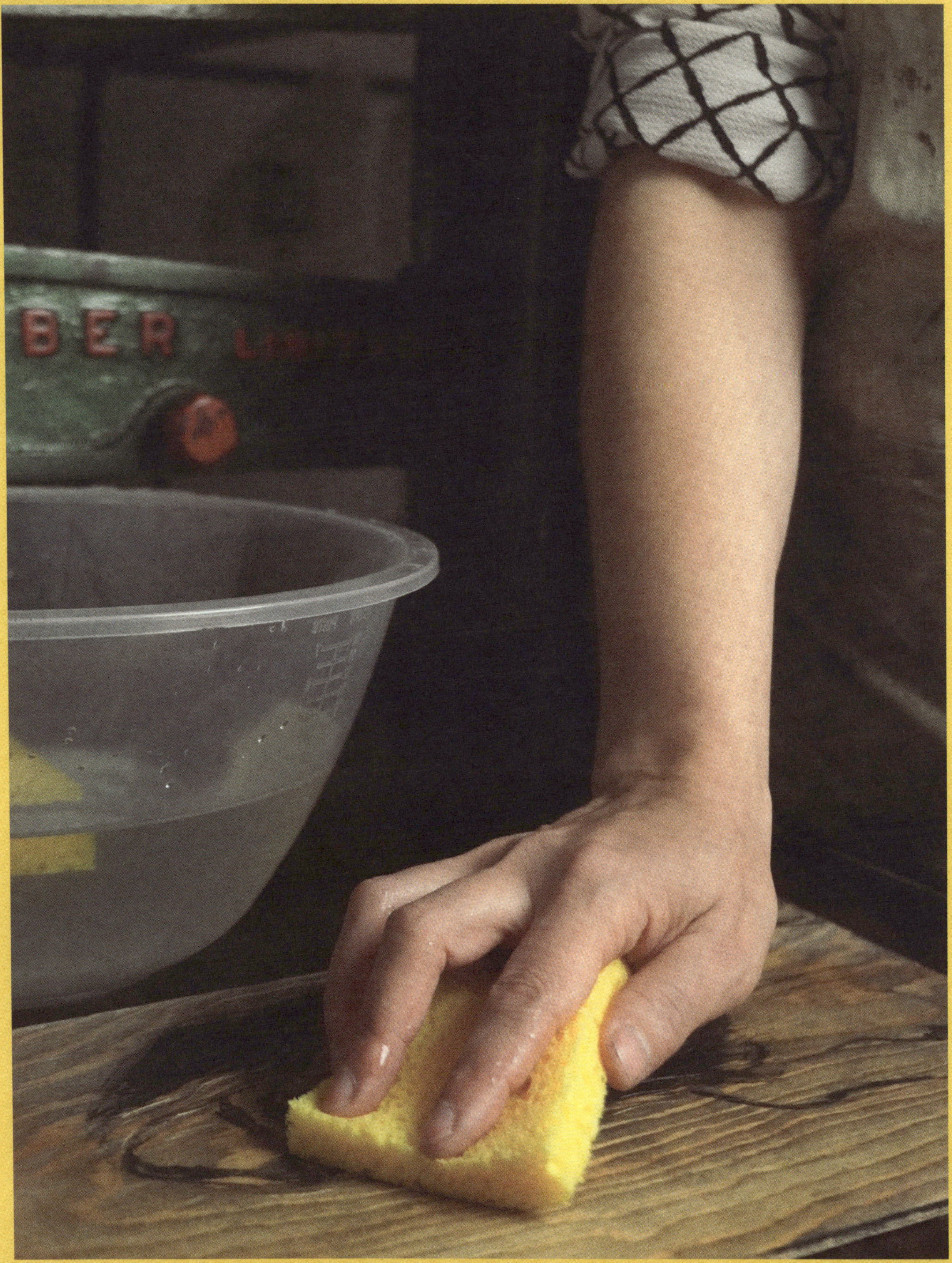

CONTENTS

Introduction

CHAPTER 1 | What is lithography? *11*

CHAPTER 2 | Materials and equipment *18*

CHAPTER 3 | Preparing to print *28*

CHAPTER 4 | Foil lithography *36*

CHAPTER 5 | Wood lithography *64*

CHAPTER 6 | Lino lithography *88*

CHAPTER 7 | Paper plate lithography *112*

CHAPTER 8 | Polyester plate lithography *134*

CHAPTER 9 | Developing your prints *156*

CHAPTER 10 | Advanced processes *168*

CHAPTER 11 | Cleaning up *176*

CHAPTER 12 | Professional practice *182*

Suppliers 188 | Workshops 189 | Featured artists 189 | Index 190 | Acknowledgements 192

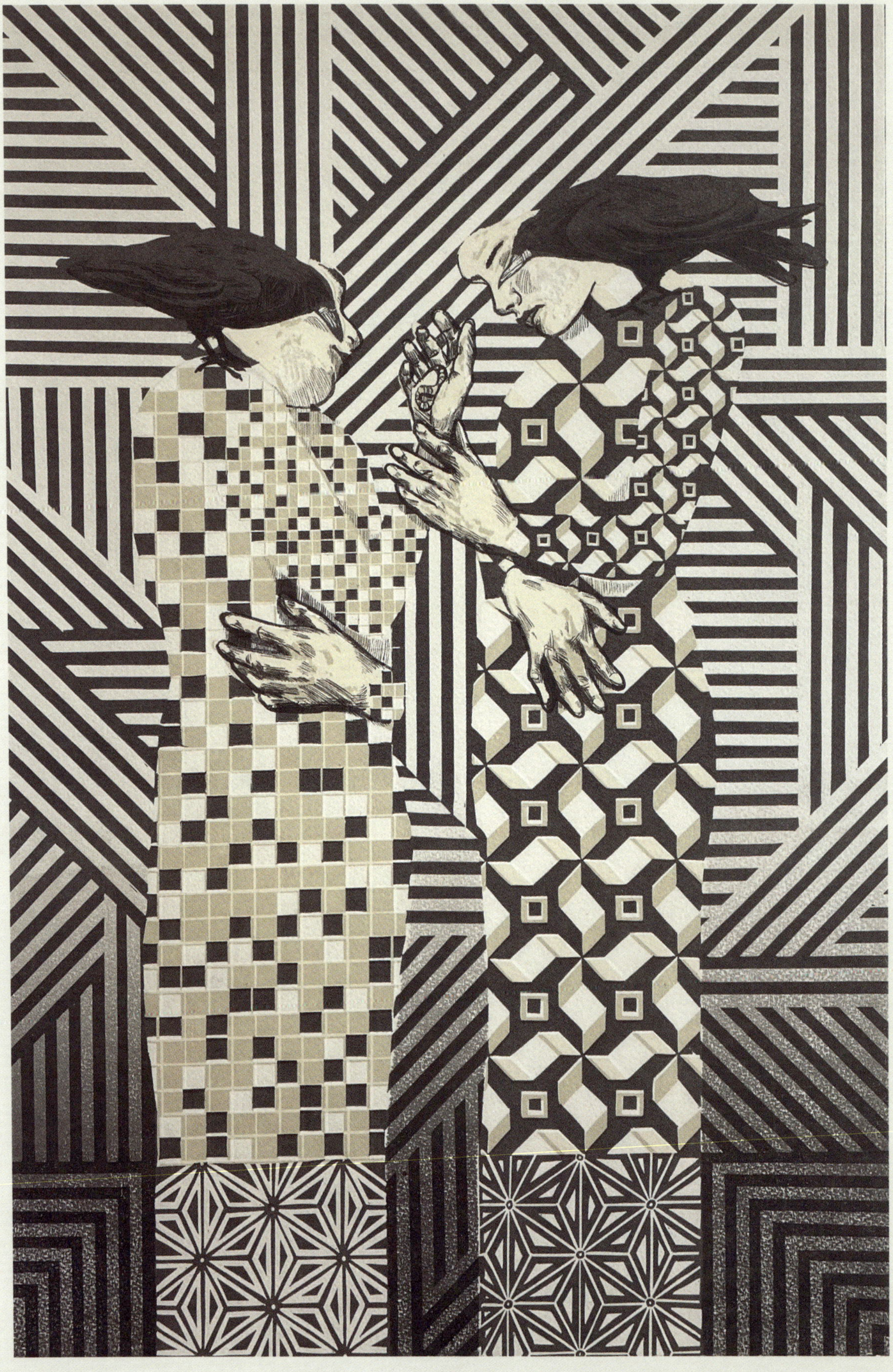

Introduction

This book will introduce you to the versatility of lithographic printmaking and show you why it is such an exciting medium to work with.

Lithography enables you to produce prints with an unparalleled range of tonality and mark making. There is a freedom to working on the lithographic surfaces that cannot be achieved in other printmaking processes. When carving a linocut or engraving a drypoint, for example, we must adopt a prescriptive way of working, whereas lithography provides the most seamless transition from drawing and painting into printmaking. The lithographic plates/surfaces easily replace the page or canvas, with little disruption to our approach to drawing. When we are making a lithographic print we can use delicate washes alongside bold brush marks, we can combine detailed pen and ink drawings with loose crayon marks, and we can employ photographic imagery; all on the same plate. The material you choose for the lithographic plate will also have an impact on the print; if you use lino you can carve into the surface as you would with traditional linocut; if you choose plywood as your lithographic surface the woodgrain will show through in your print. All of these factors compounded are the reason why I fell in love with lithography, and why it remains my favourite form of printmaking.

FACING PAGE
Scarlett Rebecca,
Forgetting, a moment, my place on the menu.
Linocut with polyester plate lithography and monotype,
37.5 x 50cm, 2023.

The aim of this book is to introduce you to an exciting form of printmaking and to give you the skills to make ambitious prints to a high standard, no matter where you are working; whether it's from a professional printmaking workshop or from your kitchen table. The development of the alternative lithographic methods included in this book make lithography an affordable and accessible form of printmaking, no longer limited by specialist equipment and materials.

All the processes demonstrated in this book can be followed without the use of a press, or they can be adapted for use in the workshop. Joining a printmaking workshop can feel intimidating to a beginner, but by following the instructions in this book, you will be able to enter the workshop confident in your own printmaking skills.

How should you use this book?

I want to encourage you to learn the rules of lithographic printmaking before you break them. Learn the processes by exploiting their idiosyncrasies; explore, test, play and make mistakes. As a printmaker it is important to understand what is happening at each stage of a process in order to troubleshoot the problems that will occur. As you familiarise yourself with the processes you will recognise the cause of each problem. Don't be scared to make mistakes; you will learn so much from each failure. Each mistake you learn from, or problem you overcome, will enable you to develop your skills and ultimately improve the quality of your prints.

Once you know the process and you can anticipate the outcomes you can start to be adventurous; act on the curiosity that makes you wonder 'what will happen if I do *this*?' or 'will it work if I try *that* instead?'. The developments in lithography featured in this book were born out of curiosity and experimentation, so you never know, you could invent the next lithographic process.

Alongside each lithographic process in this book, I have included the work of a selected contemporary artist working in the field of fine art printmaking. Their inclusion in this book is intended as an example of how each process can be used at a professional standard. Their interpretation of each process, and their invaluable insights are intended to inspire your thinking around lithography.

By the end of this book, it is my hope that lithography will take its place as your favourite form of printmaking, and you too will become a champion of lithographic printmaking.

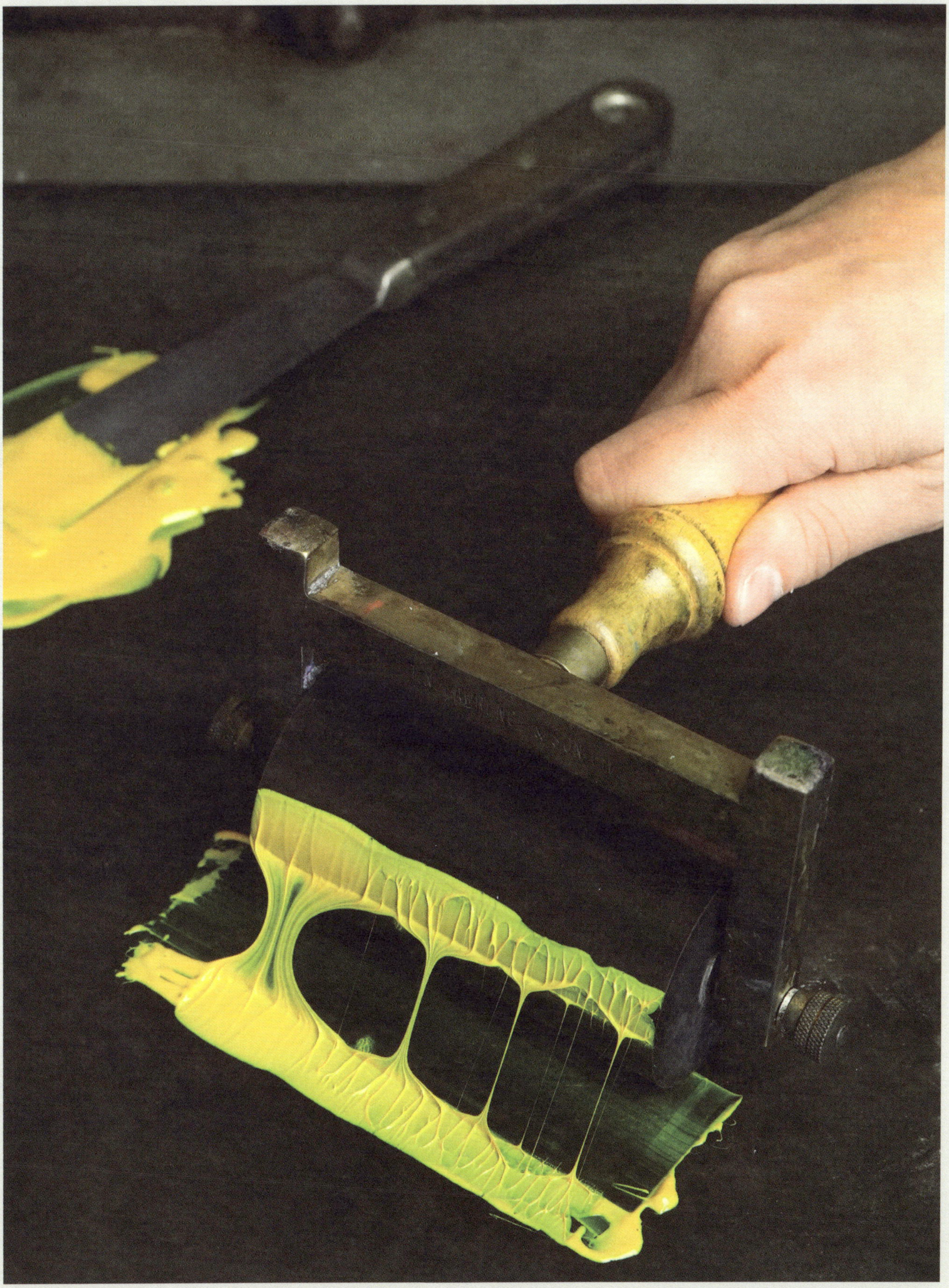

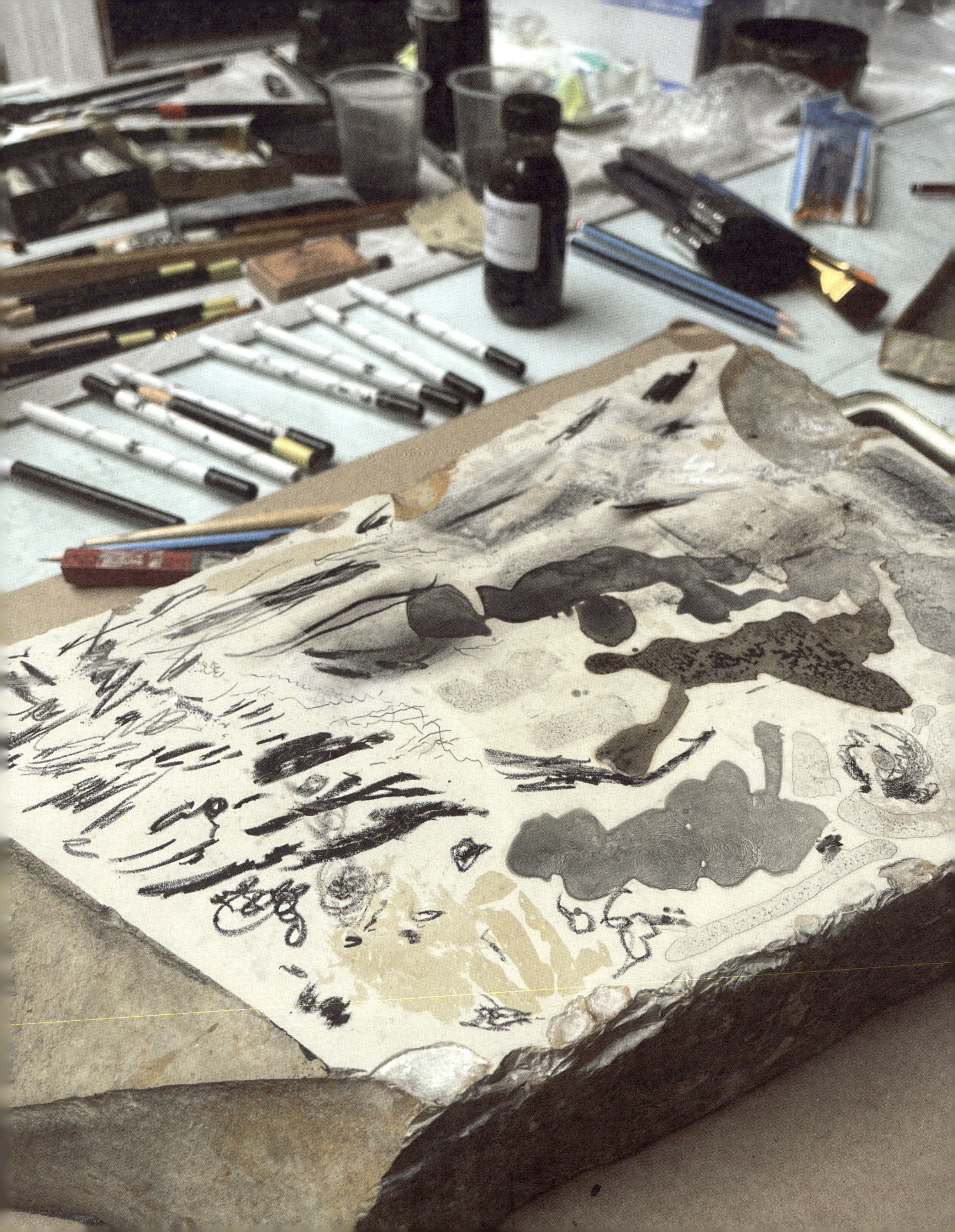

CHAPTER 1

What is lithography?

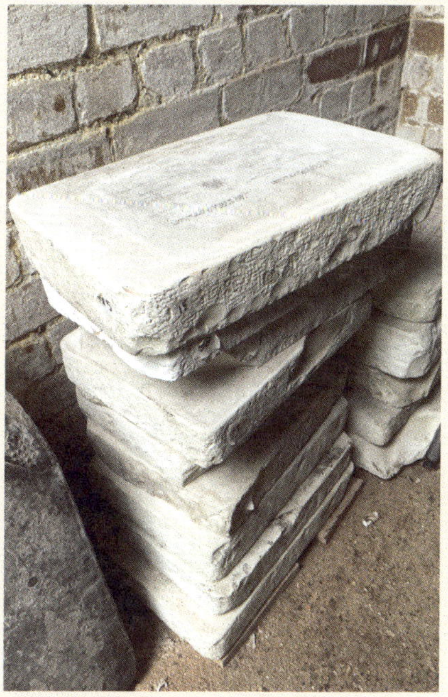

A selection of lithographic stones which were used for printing commercial labels, some with the old images still on them.

Lithography was developed by Alois Senefelder, around 1798 in Bavaria, Germany, making it one of the youngest forms of printmaking. Great heavy slabs of limestone are used as the matrix (the surface the image is made on) within lithography. The term 'lithography' comes from the ancient Greek: líthos for 'stone' and gráphō meaning 'to write'. Lithography was devised as a process to mass produce Senefelder's music scores, which then expanded commercially to include posters, etc. Metal plate lithography was developed in the mid-1800s as a cheaper and easily transportable alternative for use in commercial printing. The term 'lithography' has been retained within the industry to encompass all materials used with the lithographic process (stone, metal, wood, etc.) even though stone is no longer the primary material.

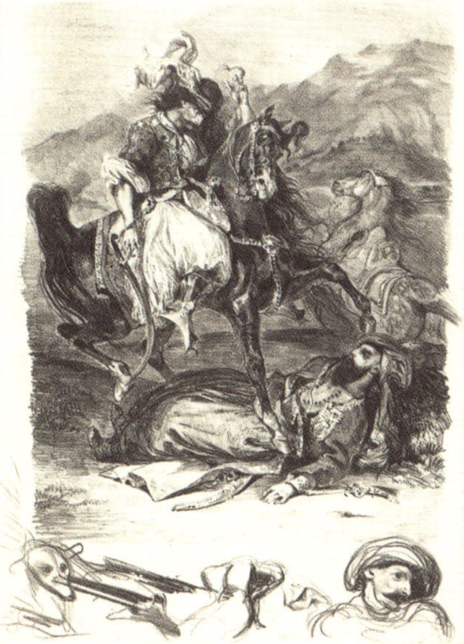

Combat du Giaour et du Pacha (The battle of the Giaour and the Pasha), Eugène Delacroix, lithograph, 1827.

Artists worked with commercial printers from early in the development of the process, and it saw multiple periods of unpopularity and revival. Lithography was established as a fine art process around the turn of the twentieth century. Renowned artists, such as Odilon Redon, Henri de Toulouse-Lautrec, Eugène Delacroix and, later, Käthe Kollwitz, Marc Chagall, Helen Frankenthaler and Robert Rauschenberg, worked collaboratively with master printers. The Curwen Studio, established in 1958 by master printer Stanley Jones MBE, is the UK's most renowned fine art lithographic publisher. The Curwen Studio has worked with Barbara Hepworth, Paula Rego, David Hockney, Elisabeth Frink and many others, and is still publishing prints today.

FACING PAGE
A range of crayons and tusche washes tested on a slab of limestone at Belfast Print Workshop.

RIGHT
Le Polype Difforme Flottait sur les Rivages, Sorte de Cyclope Souriant et Hideux (The deformed polyp floated on the shores, a sort of smiling and hideous Cyclops), Odilon Redon, lithograph,1883.

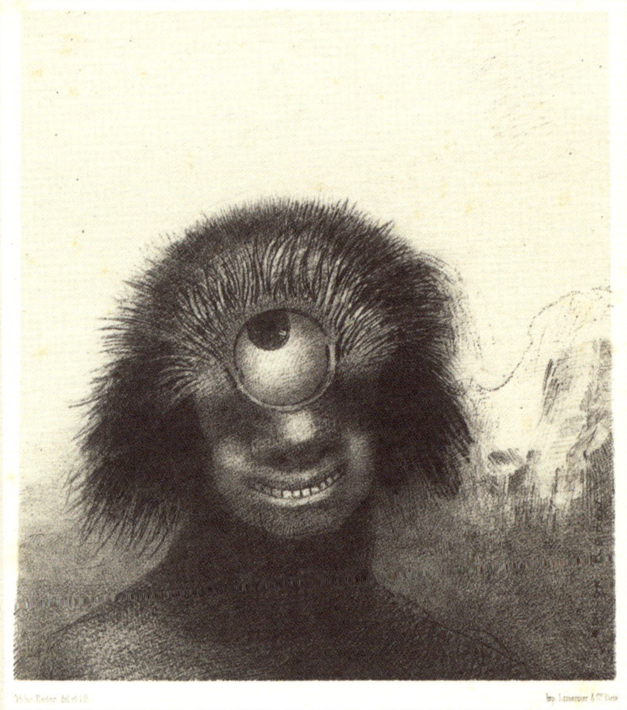

BELOW
Cover for *L'Estampe Originale*, Henri de Toulouse-Lautrec, six-colour lithograph, printed by Edouard Ancourt, 1893.

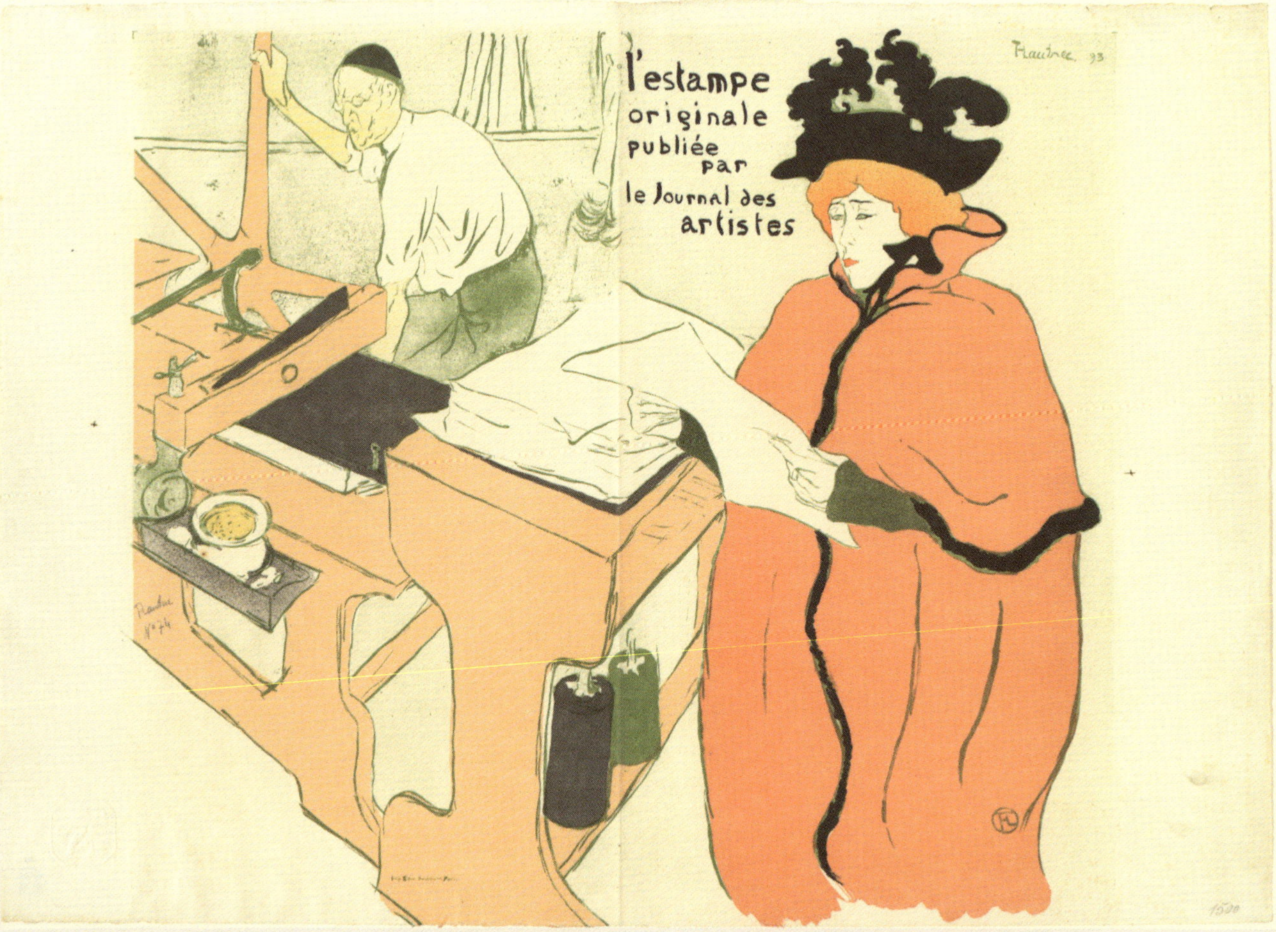

Lithography today

Commercial lithographic printing is still ongoing with most newspapers, publications, greeting cards, etc. being printed on large scales with automated lithographic presses. Stone lithography is deemed as an endangered craft in the UK by Heritage Crafts (2024) with few printmaking workshops in existence. Many workshops and universities have made the decision to stop their provision of stone lithography due to the space, time and cost that traditional stone and plate lithography demands. Stone lithography is an especially rare print form for individuals as it requires very specialist equipment, a large investment of time and a high level of energy and able-bodied capability.

However, thanks to institutions such as The Tamarind Institute of Fine Art Lithography in New Mexico, established in 1960 by artist June Wayne, and the generous nature often found within printmakers, I believe lithography is far from endangered but is instead seeing a resurgence in popularity. The culture of collaborative printmaking, where artists work with master printers, is still surviving and artists are still seeking out the expertise of lithographers. Lithography will always be the underdog of the printmaking world, but it will also always be sought after as the lithographic process is the closest to magic that an artist can get.

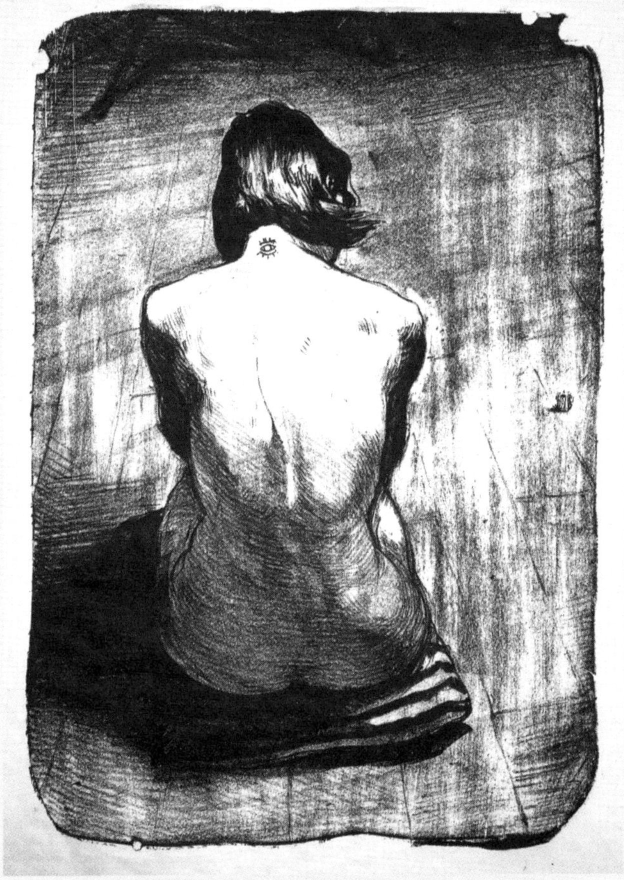

RIGHT
Jake Spicer, *Sophia*, 2018. Lithograph incorporating the edge of the stone.

The lithographic process

Lithography sits within the planographic printmaking family wherein the print is transferred from a matrix with a flat surface. The image is held on the matrix temporarily, as with monotype, or it is held permanently, through chemical intervention, as with lithography. This is different to relief printmaking, like linocut or woodcut, where the ink is held on the raised surface of the matrix, and to intaglio printmaking, like drypoint engraving or etching, where the ink is held in the recesses or burrs of the matrix.

The principle of all lithography relies on the fact that water and oil repel each other. An image is created in greasy materials on the stone and is treated with an etch to separate the image area from the non-image area. This is different to intaglio etching where the acid corrodes the exposed area of the metal as the strength of the etch within lithography is much weaker. After the stone has been etched the non-image area will become hydrophilic (water-attracting) and the image area will remain oleophilic (grease-attracting). The matrix is kept damp so that the oil-based ink on the roller will be rejected by the water in the non-image area but will be attracted to the greasy image.

Stone lithography process

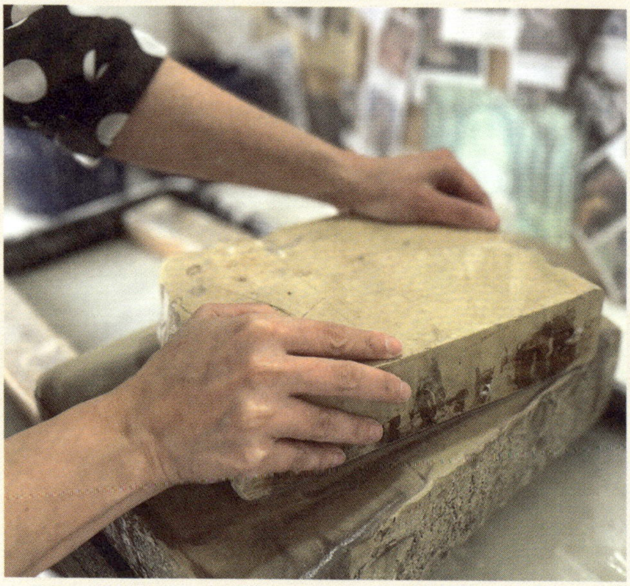

1. Stones are ground with a levigator (a hardened disc of steel) or against one another, using carborundum grit in different grades of coarseness. The stones are ground flat and smooth, creating a fresh drawing surface, free from impurities.

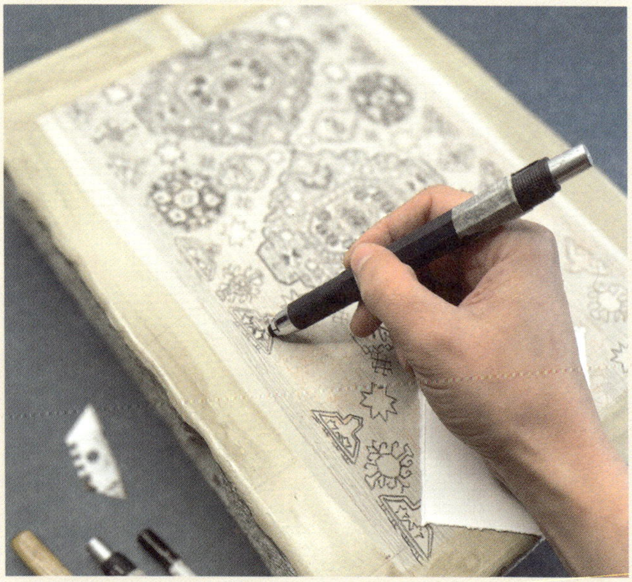

2. Images are drawn directly onto the stone using specialist grease-based crayons and inks. Each layer requires a separate stone. The image is drawn in reverse as it will be reflected when printed.

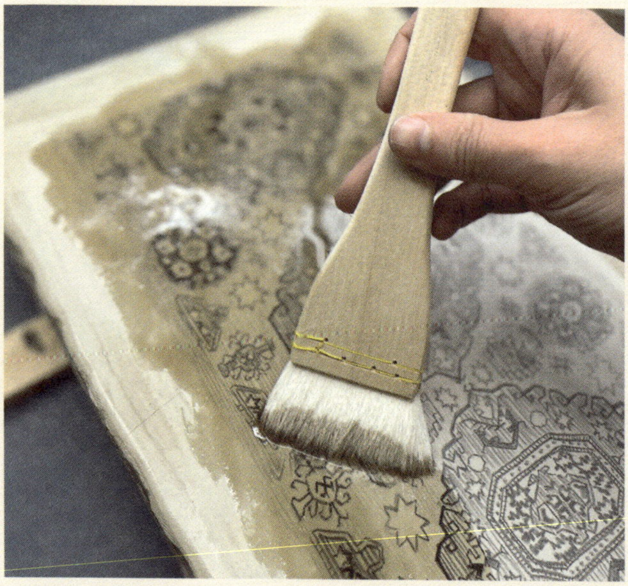

3. To adhere the image to the stone an acidified gum etch is applied to the stone. This reinforces the greasy drawing and establishes a water-attracting gum film on the non-image areas of the stone.

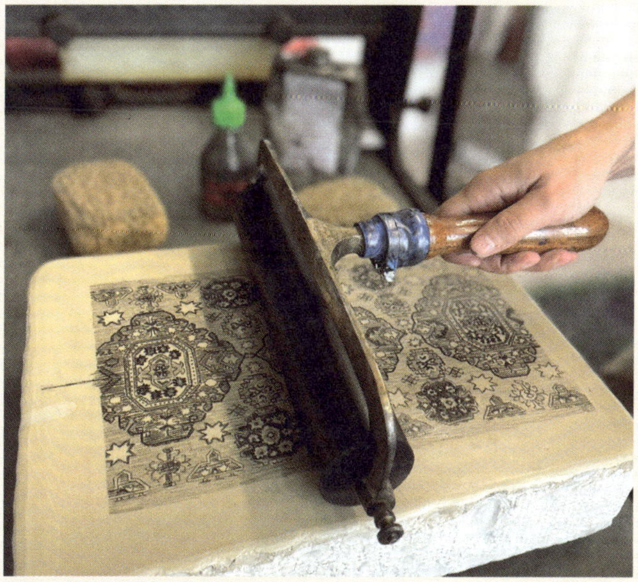

4. When inking the stone ready to print, the stone is dampened to create a protective layer of water on the non-image of the stone; the oil-based ink will then reject the water and only attach to the image area.

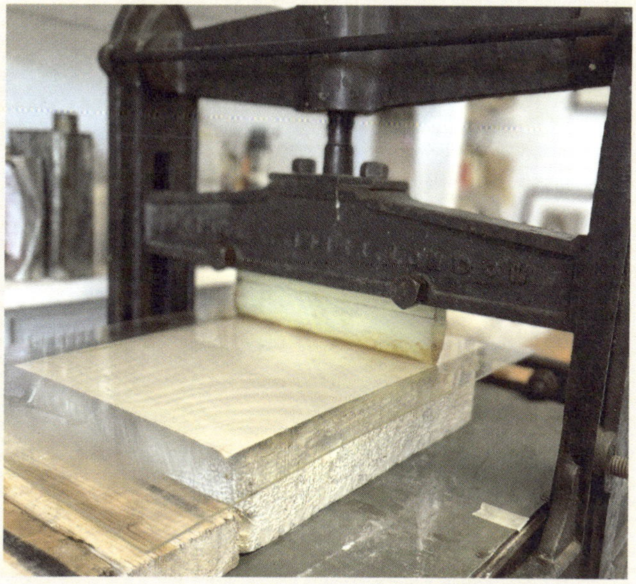

5. Prepared paper is laid over the stone and a protective tympan put on top of this. The stone is then run through the press which employs strong, flat pressure where the stone and scraper bar make contact.

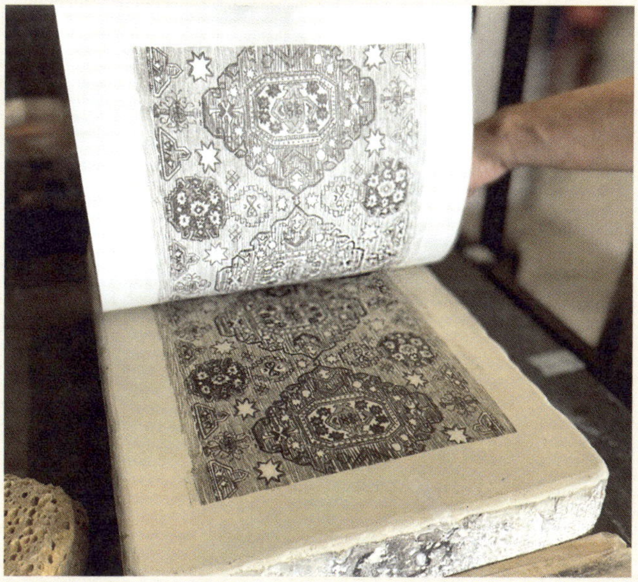

6. The print retains the exquisite details of the drawing on stone incredibly faithfully. The stone can be dampened and inked again to print large scale editions. Additional layers require multiple stones.

Alternative lithography

This same principle of lithography is at the heart of all the alternative processes contained within this book. Instead of using stone as the matrix, we will be exploring alternative materials such as foil, wood and lino. The methods of treating the matrix so that it becomes both oil-attracting and water-attracting differ slightly between the alternative processes. However, the printing aspect of all the included processes remains the same.

Accessible, affordable and eco-friendly versions of lithography are in continual development, and many alternative lithographic processes are employed in workshops, universities and homes throughout the world. I believe that the current revival we are seeing in lithography is due to the developments in these exciting alternative processes.

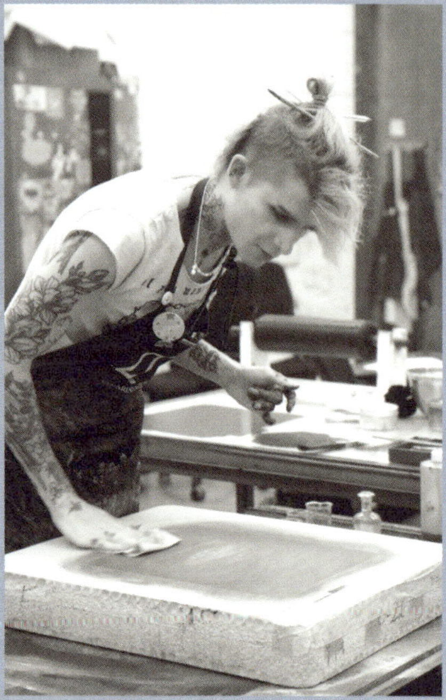

Brian Wagner (USA)

hedgebitch.com

Brian Wagner is a lithographer and book artist, whose work focuses on queer existence and memory. They attended the world-renowned Tamarind Institute of Fine Art Lithography and are a trained Collaborative Printer and Lithographer.

My densely-layered and rendered lithographs explore the tenderness, loneliness, acceptance, and gentle anger of queerness, grief, and healing. These prints and writings consider the physical and emotional spaces of love, hurt, trauma, and remembrance of relationships in the forms of drawn landscapes and queer symbolism of the day-to-day life of a queer person. The emphasis on rural landscape, bird flocks, and fragmented spaces is a nod to the migratory nature of queer life and love and the act of taking up space but never as much as queer people need, constant movement for a partner or self-preservation, and the trauma of queer love inherently impacted by external and internal forces. It's easy for queer people to get used to resilience and ignore the trauma that is experienced every day, even from the community and partners, and it's my hope that these spaces can offer solace to someone who has faced the same.

With the use of lithography, I utilise the process and its ability to hold soft, gentle tones and deep transparent colours overlapping to create these spaces. Stone lithography specifically lends itself well to my work with its aptness for drawn detail and subtlety. Labour intensive and requiring patience, the process can be long and daunting but the respect and care towards each print are an important factor in my work. Drawing slowly and working from photographs, sketches, or pure memory of these locations and domestic spaces, lithography requires careful consideration of each line and mark made. While formal, my lithographic process is treated as a 'sketchbook' or 'journaling' of sorts, as a selection of thoughts, imagery, and personal experience. Text is often incorporated as a connection to the lived, day-to-day life of a queer person.

FACING PAGE
Brian Wagner, *Grantsburg, WI; Jan. 1st, 4:45pm*, six-colour stone lithograph, 20 x 18in.

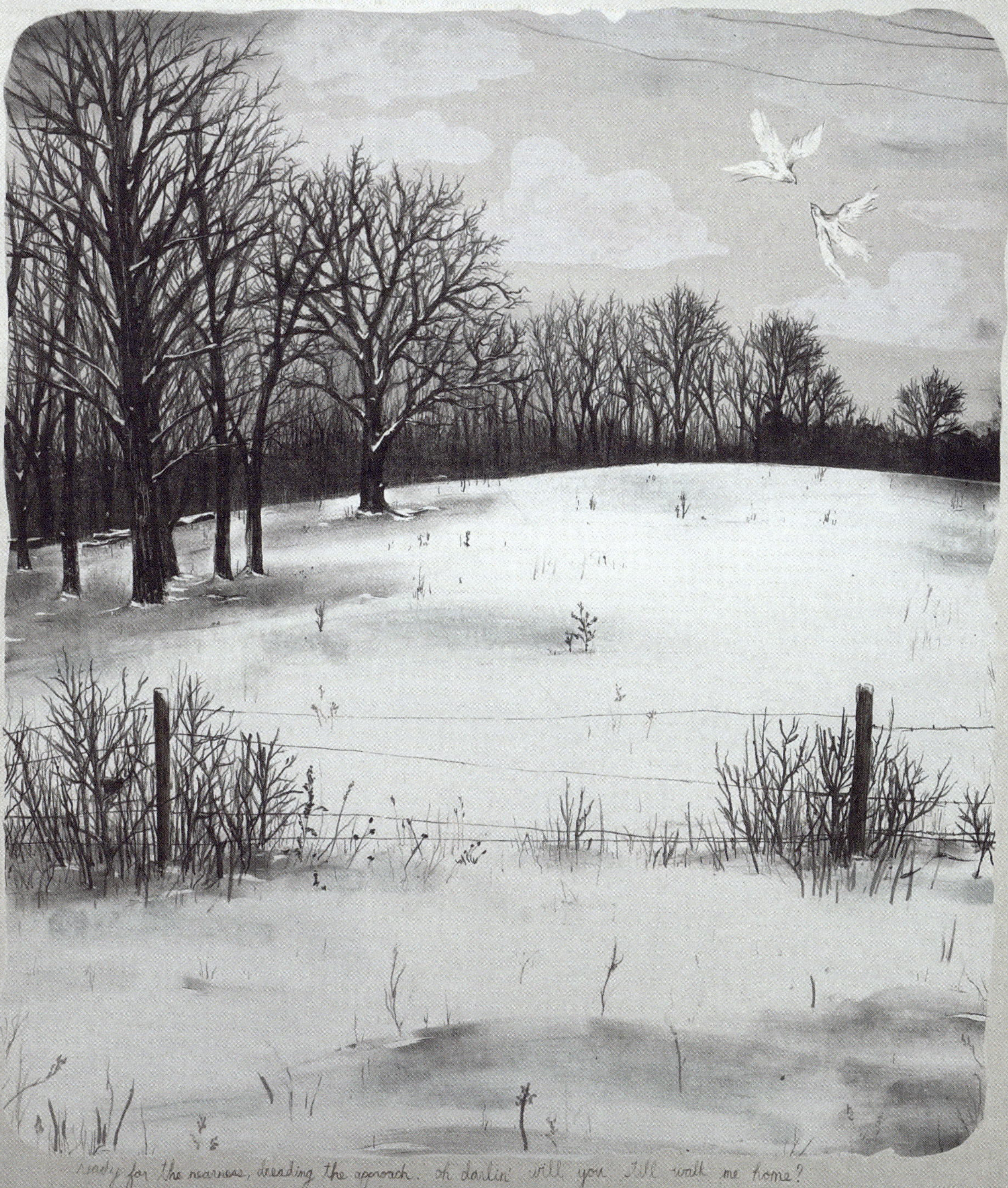

ready for the nearness, dreading the approach. oh darlin' will you still walk me home?

CHAPTER 2

Materials and equipment

In the UK we are fortunate to be spoilt for choice when it comes to printmaking brands and shops. Some of the materials you will need for lithography will be found in specialist printmaking shops, but many of the necessary materials can be found in general art stores. You don't need to spend a fortune on materials; the humblest of art materials can produce fantastic quality prints when handled correctly. Specialist lithographic drawing materials, inks, modifiers and papers can be very expensive nowadays, but alternatives can be used. However, some of these alternatives can be a useful stop gap while you're testing, but they may affect the archival quality and longevity of your final printed editions.

When it comes to equipment, I recommend spending a little bit more and investing in good quality tools and taking good care of them. It is said that a bad worker blames their tools, and it's true, a good printmaker can produce quality prints with poor equipment, but the standard of their work will be limited by the poor quality tools. This is especially true for printmaking rollers. Lithographic print uses a flat surface as the matrix and requires complete contact between roller and matrix, to transfer ink to all the fine details. So, a dented or warped roller will make inking your matrix difficult and limit the amount of detail that will be reproduced in the print.

FACING PAGE
Rollers, inks and sundries used for lithographic printmaking in Scarlett Rebecca's studio.

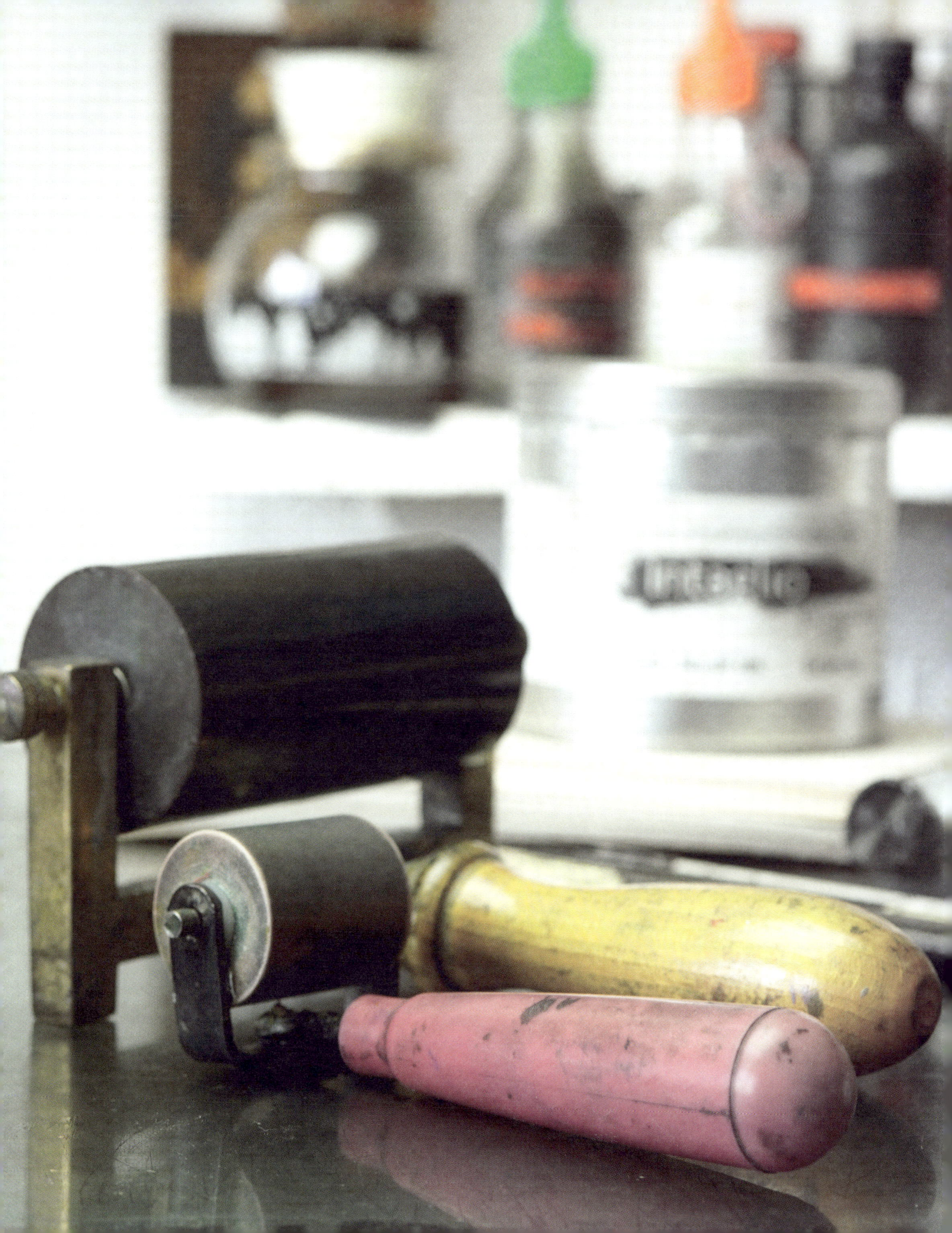

Drawing materials

Dry media

Lithographic drawing materials need to contain grease/wax/oil, to attract the oil-based ink and repel the gum. Lithographic crayons are available in a variety of hardnesses which denote the amount of grease in them. The more grease, the darker the image will be.
Alternatives: *wax crayons, oil pastels, chinagraph pencils and chocolate.*

Wet media

Lithographic tusche is a mixture of grease and pigment suspended in water. When tusche dries the particles of grease will settle like tide marks, forming the recognisable lithographic reticulated washes. Tusche can be bought in liquid form or in a stick where you must mix your own dilution of ink. It is difficult to simulate these effects with other drawing materials.
Alternatives: *toner particles suspended in water, waterproof Indian ink, and printing ink diluted with solvent.*

Other drawing materials used in this book include permanent markers, stopping out varnish, photocopy transfer with acetone (nail polish remover), ballpoint pens, dip pens and gum arabic.

A selection of specialist lithographic crayons from a variety of makers from across the globe, with a litho drawing chopstick designed by Lee Turner.

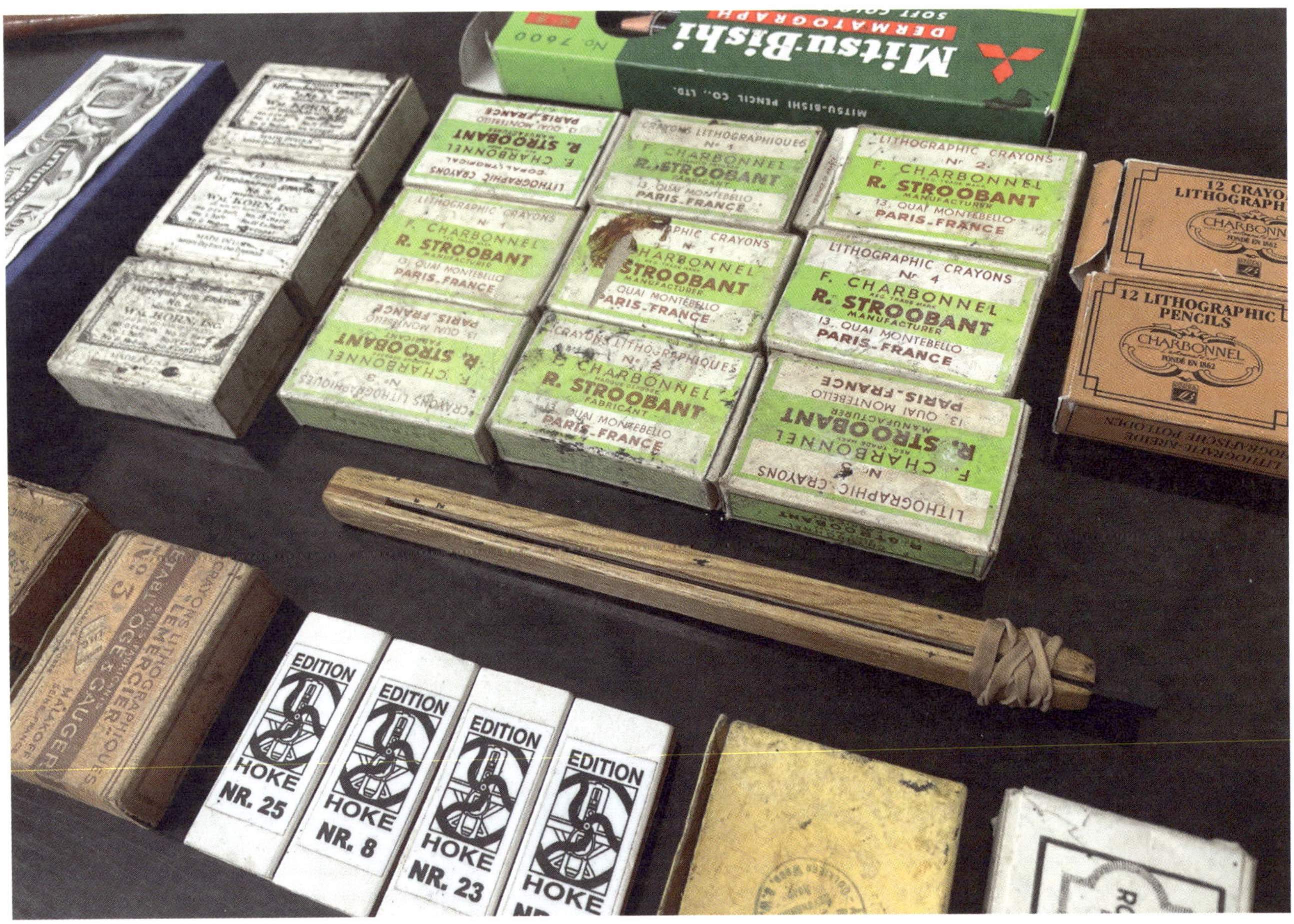

Matrices

Aluminium foil, traditional grey lino, side grain wood/plywood, photocopies/laser prints, and polyester lithography plates.

Printing inks

Traditional hand lithography inks are greasier and stiffer than other printmaking inks and may require modifying for use with alternative lithographic processes to loosen them.

Offset lithography inks are designed for commercial use. They are very highly pigmented so they can be mixed with a large ratio of extender. Offset inks are tackier than hand lithography inks and are not reliably archival or lightfast.

Relief printmaking inks can be used interchangeably with lithographic inks for alternative lithographic processes. Intaglio inks are not designed for lithographic purposes but can be used with the correct modifiers.

Transparent ink/extender will disperse the pigment of another ink in a clear printing base, brightening the colour and allowing colour blending when overlaid. The transparency of the ink will also allow the paper colour to have more effect on the ink colour.

Opaque white ink will increase the opacity of an ink, allowing it to be less affected by base layers; it will also lighten a colour.

Safe-wash or water-based printing inks are *not suitable* for lithography as they are immiscible in water.

Modifiers

Plate oil/linseed oil is used to reduce the tackiness of ink and to make ink more fluid. Alternative: *vegetable oil.*

Tack reducer is used to reduce the tackiness/stickiness of the ink but not affect the viscosity. This will help with the transfer of ink from plate to paper.
Alternative: *petroleum jelly.*

Magnesium carbonate is used to stiffen inks that are too loose, with no effect on the colour or transparency of

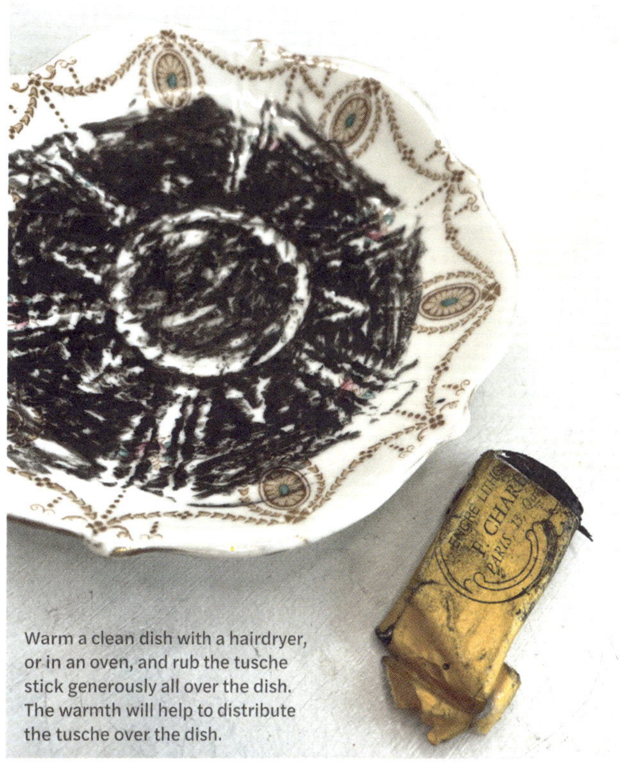

Warm a clean dish with a hairdryer, or in an oven, and rub the tusche stick generously all over the dish. The warmth will help to distribute the tusche over the dish.

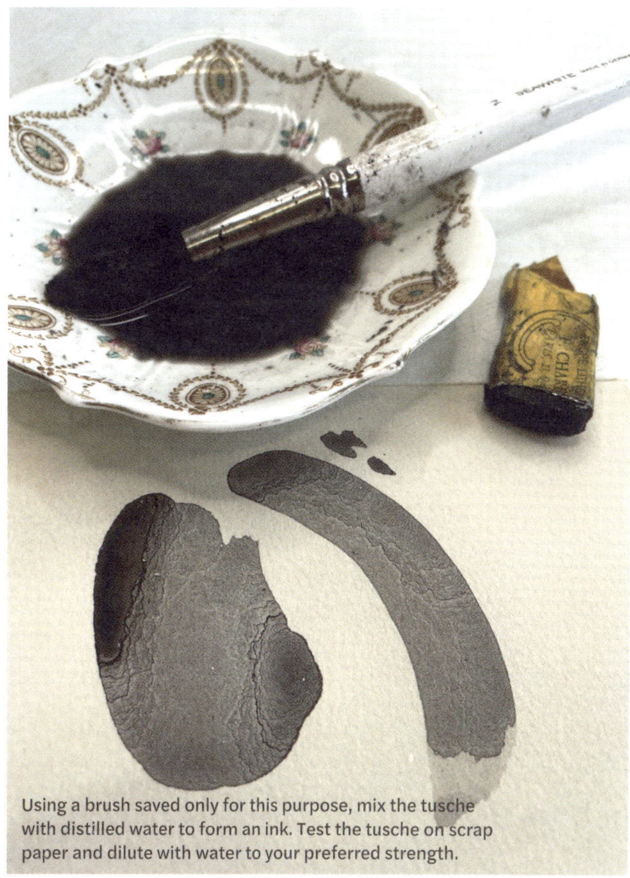

Using a brush saved only for this purpose, mix the tusche with distilled water to form an ink. Test the tusche on scrap paper and dilute with water to your preferred strength.

the ink. It will also speed up the drying time of the ink. Alternatives: *talc, French chalk, cornflour.*

Driers will speed up the drying time of the ink. Cobalt driers will dry the ink from the surface downwards, causing the ink to become shiny. Wax driers will have less effect on the appearance of the dried ink. Do not store inks with driers added to them.

Retarder will slow down the drying of the printing ink, to make it workable for longer periods of time.

Printmaking papers

Lithography can be used with a variety of weights and textures of printmaking papers and can be printed onto both dry and dampened papers. There are a few things to consider when selecting your papers:

Archival/acid free

Archival quality papers are strong, pH-neutral or slightly alkaline papers that will not discolour over time, disintegrate or affect the longevity of your image. This will mean your prints will remain in a good condition for decades, which is good news for your buyers. They will be more expensive than other papers so you may not want to use them for trial/test prints.

Mould-made and machine-made papers

These papers are made from cotton or wood pulp, or a mixture of the two. Mould-made papers will have a deckle edge on at least two sides whereas machine-made papers like cartridge papers will have a cut edge. They will contain size, which strengthens the paper by binding the fibres together. These papers can be dampened, which is an important consideration for many alternative lithographic processes. Machine-made papers can be hot or cold pressed, meaning their surface has been treated in production to smooth their surface and calendar (stretch) the paper.

Surface quality

Lithographic printing requires absolute connection between plate and paper for full transference of ink. Smooth papers are recommended, because textured papers will retain less ink, as the textured surface can prevent full contact with the plate. When printing onto dry papers, commercial coated papers designed for offset printing can be used. These papers will have a coating that will increase the smoothness and shine of the paper.

Eastern papers

Traditional papers produced in China (Xuan paper) and Japan (Washi paper) are thin, strong and flexible. They are usually made from long-fibred plant material and can come in a variety of weights and finishes. They are used for calligraphy, stationery, painting, crafts and printmaking and they are perfect for hand printing as they require less exertion to burnish compared to machine-made or mould-made papers.

Hand burnishing vs using a press

The weight and softness of a paper will affect the amount of pressure needed when printing and therefore, the amount of energy needed to burnish by hand. The softness of the paper will also need to be considered if any embossing is desired during printing, or if it is to be avoided. Transference of ink is improved when a paper is dampened so if you are intending to hand burnish your prints you will have more success with papers that can be dampened, whereas if you are using a press you will be able to improve transference with increased pressure. Textured papers can lose their textured appearance when calendared or printed in a press. Handmade papers can often be uneven or contain elements that can damage a press or blanket. This can be avoided by selectively hand burnishing.

FACING PAGE
Lithographic printing ink comes in tubes, cartridges and tins. Offset lithographic inks are most commonly found in large tins for commercial printing. A printer will often have a preference for a brand of ink.

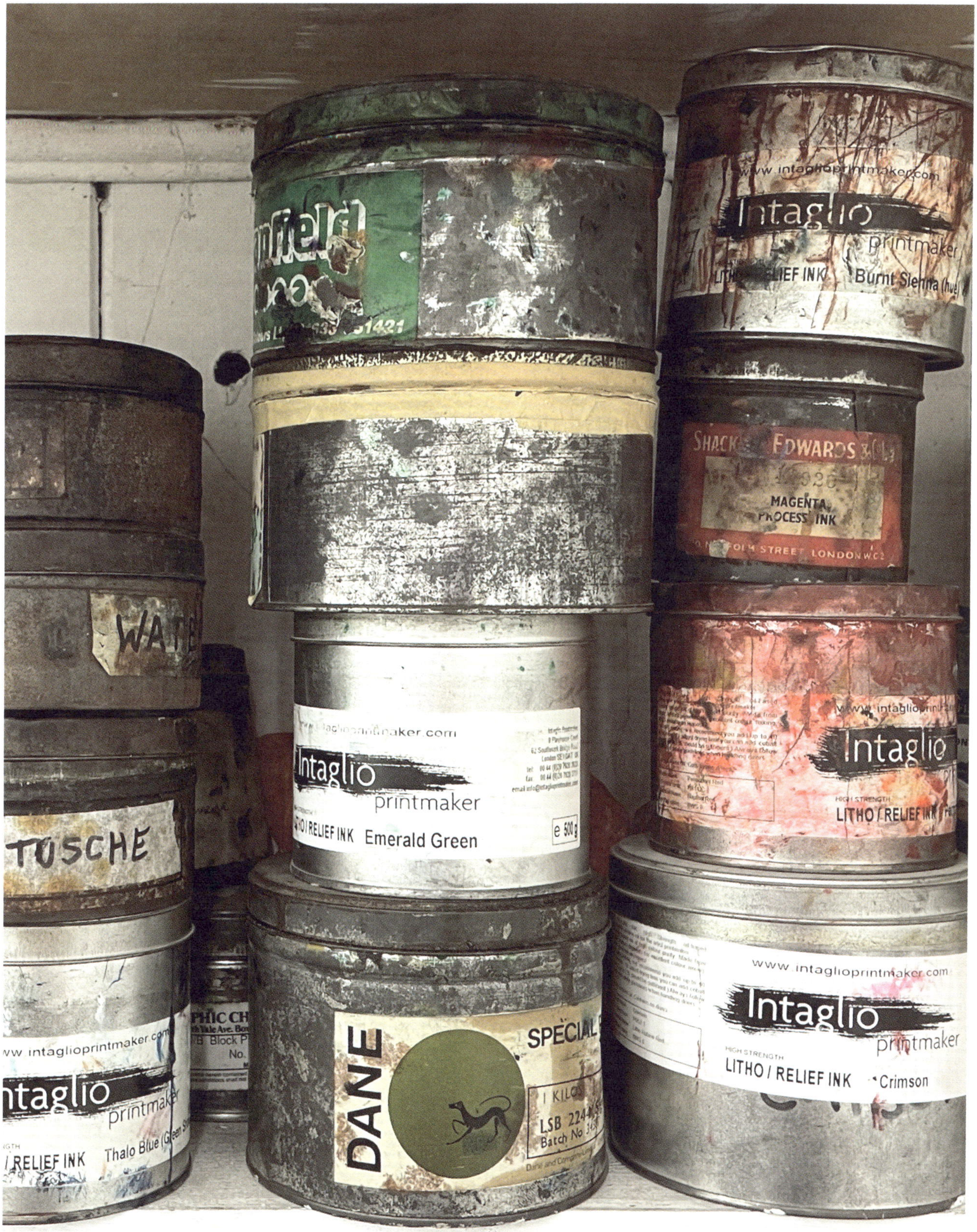
www.intaglioprintmaker.com
Intaglio
printmaker
Burnt Sienna (hue)
MAGENTA
PROCESS INK
WATE
TOSCHE
Intaglio
printmaker
Emerald Green
500 g
HIGH STRENGTH
LITHO / RELIEF INK
www.intaglioprintmaker.com
Intaglio
printmaker
Thalo Blue
DANE
SPECIAL
www.intaglioprintmaker.com
Intaglio
printmaker
HIGH STRENGTH
LITHO / RELIEF INK
Crimson

Other papers

Newsprint is a cheap, thin and very smooth paper which is ideal for proofs. It is not archival as it is not acid-free, and it will discolour very quickly.

Tissue paper is useful for interleaving between your drying prints, protecting your blankets when printing on a press and for storing prints. Avoid using glazed tissue paper.

Glassine is a strong archival paper likened to a blend of tissue paper and tracing paper, used for storing prints.

Papers used in this book

- Fabriano Artistico
- Fabriano Rosaspina
- Fabriano 5
- Somerset Satin
- Somerset Velvet Newsprint Grey
- Canaletto Bianco
- Seawhite Cartridge
- Awagami Bamboo Select, Washi
- Awagami Kozo, Washi
- Pei Zei, Xuan
- Photocopy paper 120gsm

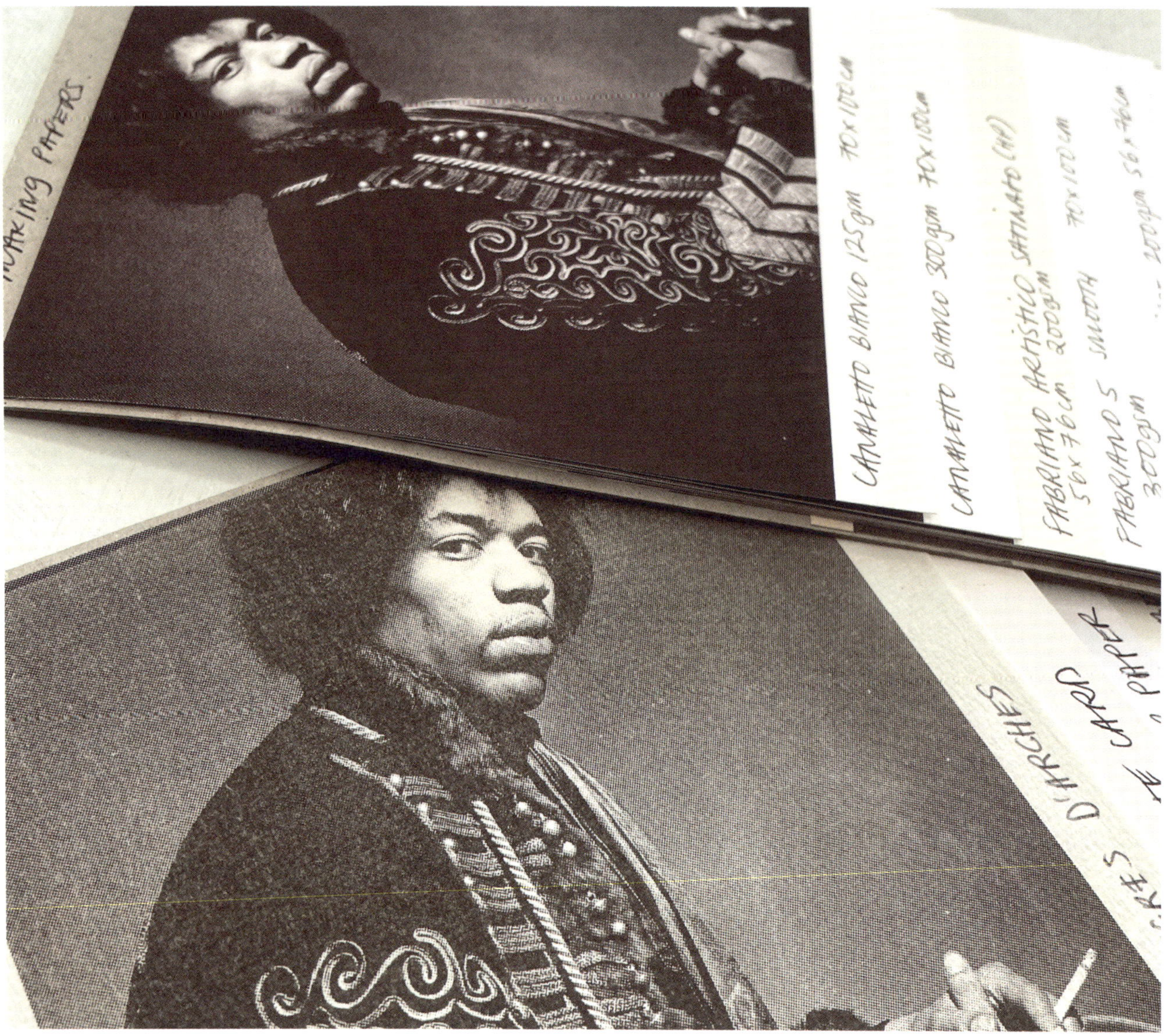

The qualities of a paper will affect how a lithograph will look when printed. A textural quality of a paper can dull an image, and a very smooth paper can enhance the vibrancy of the image.

Presses

Traditionally lithographs will have been printed on a specialist lithographic press designed for use with limestones. The presses needed to be strong enough to carry the weight of the stone. The press bed will travel under a scraper bar which will distribute firm, flat pressure against the paper on the stone, producing a reflected image. An offset press has two beds, one for the stone or plate and one for the paper. The offset press has a cylindrical rubber blanket which travels over the stone or plate, collecting the ink in reverse; it then transfers the ink onto dry paper the correct way around. This makes drawing the image much easier as you don't need to allow for the image to be reversed on the print.

However, specialist lithographic presses are not common, so alternative lithographic processes have been developed to use the much more readily available roller/etching press. All the alternative lithographic processes in this book have been printed using a roller press/etching press and by hand.

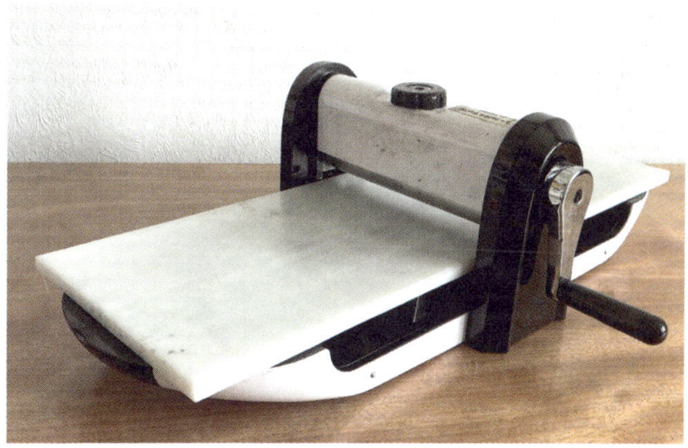

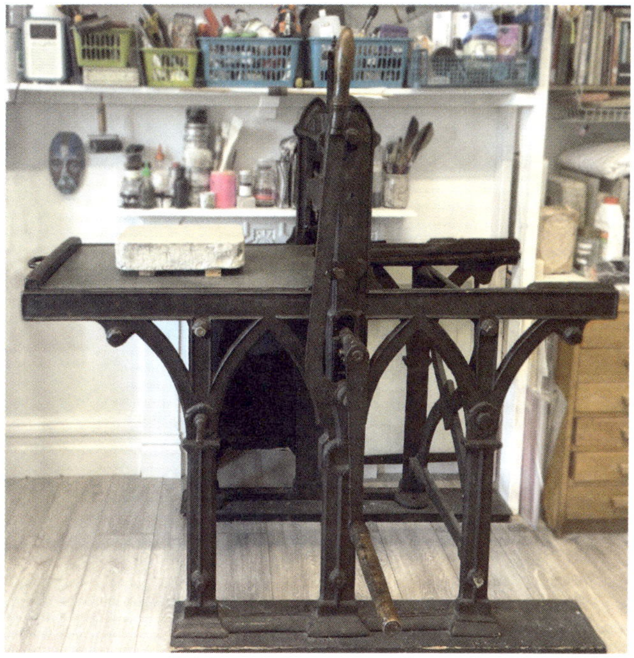

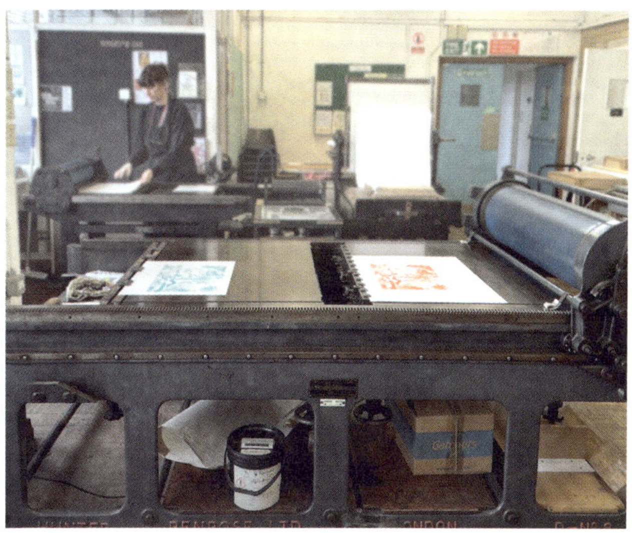

TOP
I used this Xcut Xpress die cut machine converted into an etching press for all the lithographs printed using a press in this book.

MIDDLE
Hughes and Kimber direct press in Scarlett Rebecca's studio.

BELOW
Deffa offset proofing press at Brighton University.

Rollers

The material, shore (hardness), and size of a roller are all factors to consider before purchasing a roller. The roller will need to be larger than the image to be inked to avoid lines from the edge of the roller, so consider the size of plate you will regularly be working with. Hard rollers may not be flexible enough to make full contact with the flat plate when inking up, so medium hardness rollers are recommended for their flexibility. No matter the cost of the roller, it is important to take good care of it. Keep your rollers propped up on their stands, never leave your rollers covered in ink for long periods when not in use, and avoid using solvents to clean them where possible. Whatever you use to clean your rollers, give them a wipe down with a lightly oiled rag afterwards to remove all traces of ink and cleaning fluids. Foam rollers are used to mimic the qualities of the traditional lithographic leather roller. The foam roller helps to keep the plate damp for longer and transfers the ink more delicately, where a rubber roller can be too forceful. Foam rollers can't be cleaned so you will need a roller for each colour you print with. If ink dries on the surface of the foam it renders it useless; to prevent this, wrap the roller heads in cling film and keep them in the freezer when not in use.

Hand printing

A sheet of greaseproof paper should be used to protect the back of a print when hand burnishing. A baren will apply distributed pressure; however, a wooden spoon (or similar) is more appropriate for applying the concentrated pressure needed for hand burnishing a lithograph.

Protective equipment

Alternative lithographic processes don't require PPE for protection of health as the materials are all low- or non-toxic, but cleanliness is important. Lithographic ink is highly pigmented and slow to dry, so protective measures are recommended, especially when working from a home environment. Wear gloves (rubber gloves are preferred rather than disposable gloves), and wear an apron.

A selection of hand rollers of varying size and hardness. The smallest rollers here cost between £5 and £15 whereas the large beautiful green durathene roller costs almost £200.

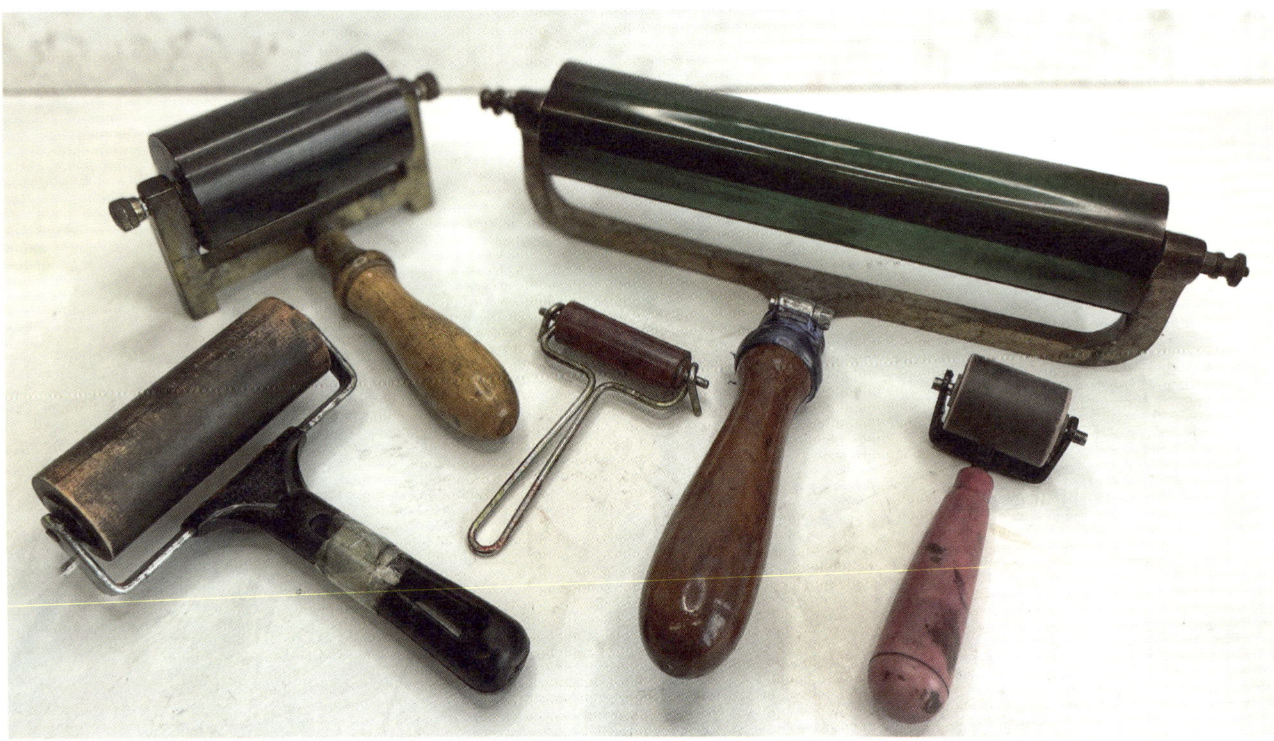

Sundries

Clean bowls for your dampening water. You need to have light-coloured bowls so that you can see when the dampening water gets too dirty. You will need one bowl for the clean dampening water, and another bowl to catch your dirty water, this is where you will squeeze out your sponge when it's getting dirty.

Cellulose sponges (*not plastic*) are used for dampening plates. Cellulose sponges are softer and more absorbent than plastic, and they can also be composted. Plastic sponges are scratchier and can damage the image.

Gum arabic is essential as it is used in every lithographic process featured in this book. It is used to protect your plate and create a water-attracting layer on the plate. It is used in liquid form but can also be purchased in crystal and powder form.

French chalk/talcum powder is used to break the surface tension on the plate when the gum is applied; it allows the gum to adhere closely to the drawing material on the plate.

Push knives are ideal for mixing, distributing ink and clearing up ink.

Solvents (low odour white spirit, citrus cleaners, etc.) can be useful for cleaning up stubborn ink. They are also useful for diluting printing ink to use as a drawing material. Ensure you are wearing gloves and the space you are working in is well ventilated when using solvents.

Working area

A flat, smooth, clean, wipeable surface large enough to fit your roller in both directions, is needed for rolling out ink. Use either a sheet of hardened glass, a sheet of acrylic or similar smooth and non-porous surface, or tape a piece of foil to a flat surface for a temporary inking area. (Clean the ink off the foil after using it and then recycle the foil.)

For drying prints made on dry paper a peg system can be used or a drying rack. Protect the prints from any dirt/ink on the pegs with pieces of scrap paper. Prints made on dampened paper will need to be interleaved between sheets of tissue paper and placed under heavy boards to dry flat.

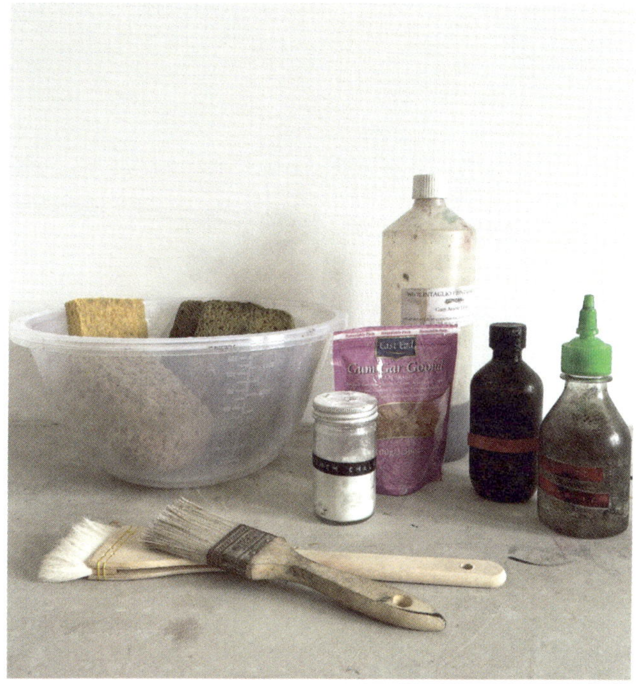

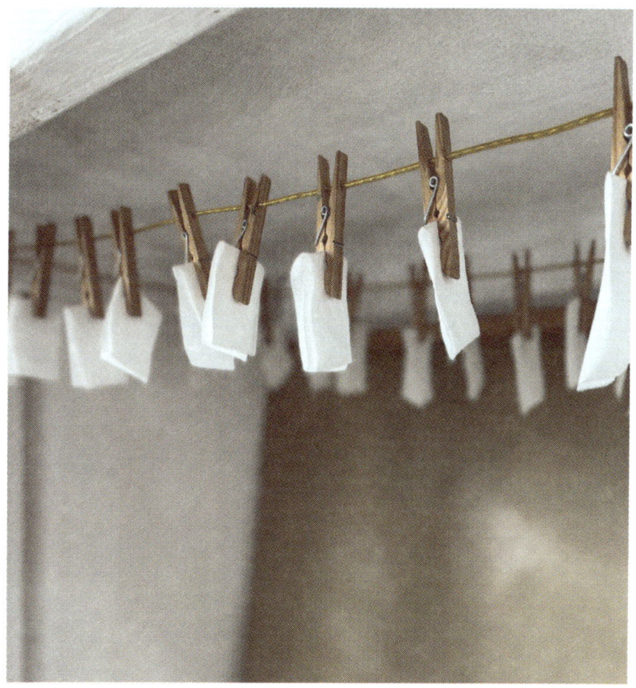

TOP
The essential equipment for most lithographic processes: cellulose sponges, bowls, gum arabic, brushes, cleaning materials, etc.

BELOW
A peg drying system is good for small spaces when printing on dry paper, use with pieces of scrap paper to protect prints from ink transfer.

CHAPTER 3

Preparing to print

Preparation is key for a successful session of printing. Making sure your space is clean and set up to work in, your materials are ready, and you've got a hot cup of tea, all help towards an enjoyable and stress-free printing experience. When you're not fully prepared, or you're rushing around, you're more likely to make mistakes and you won't be in the right mindset to tackle problems when they occur.

When you're working in a shared studio or public workshop you will want to make the most of the time you have, so it's useful to prepare some things, like tearing down your paper, before you come to print. It's important to get into good habits, especially when sharing a space; good preparation will save on waste in terms of materials, cost and time.

Preparing for printmaking is a skill in itself; it requires getting to know your materials and the properties you need in them. It requires a familiarity with your materials, so you should allow more time for trial and error when working with new materials or new equipment. Preparation can sometimes take just as long as the printing, so always allow yourself plenty of time; you don't want to find yourself rushing a print or having to awkwardly tear down paper with inky hands.

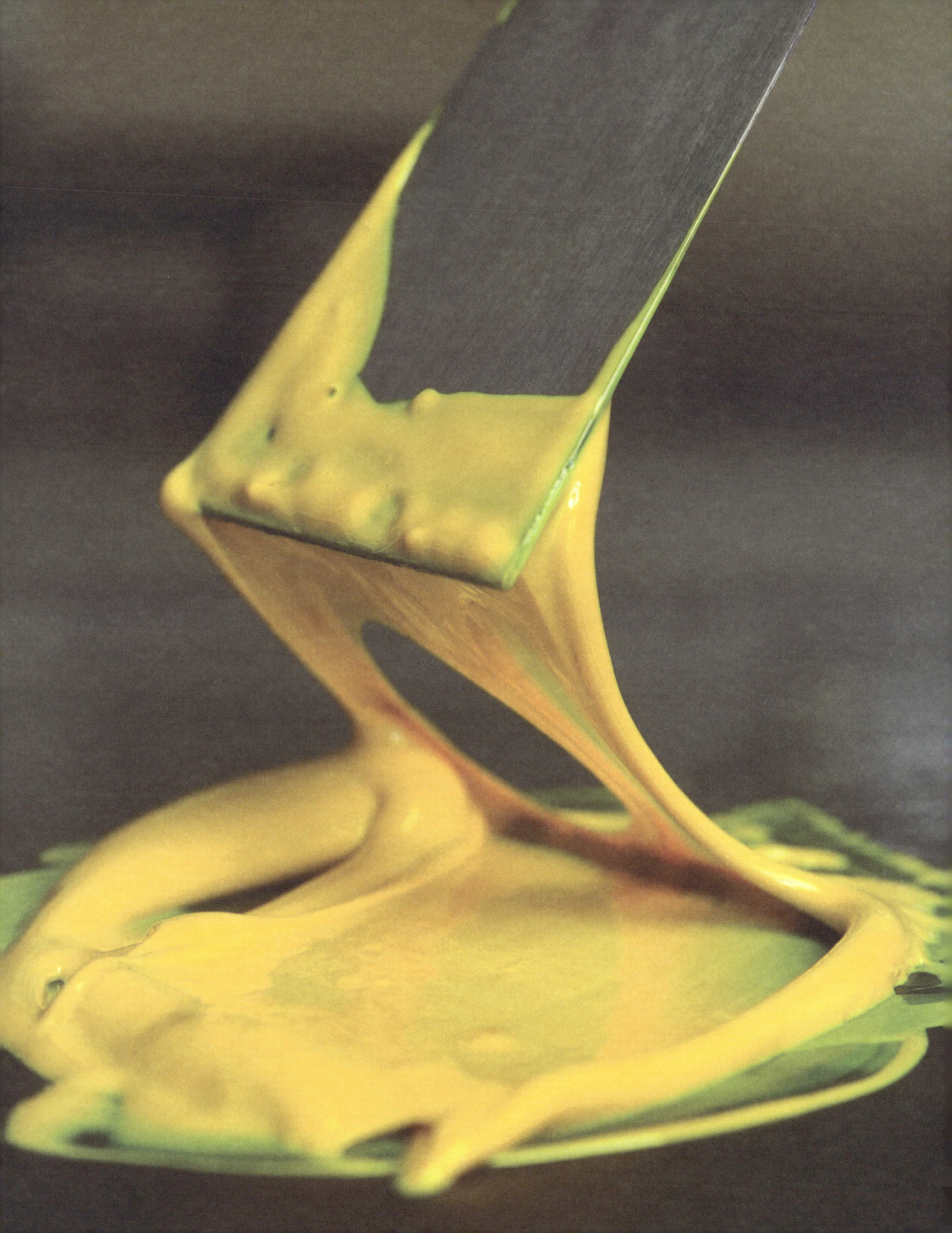

Preparing your printing space

Your first steps for lithographic printmaking will involve setting up a dedicated printing space. If you're working in a temporary space such as a kitchen table, you will need to be adaptive in your approach, and your printing space will be something you can easily set up and put away again. This set-up can become part of the process of mentally preparing to print. Your printing space will evolve as you start to use it and as you discover better ways of managing your areas.

You will need to section off a dedicated clean area of your workspace. This area will be for tearing paper, drying prints and burnishing your prints if you're not using a press. Alongside this you will need a dedicated dirty area for rolling out your ink and inking up your plates. Wipeable surfaces are recommended to ensure continued ease of cleanliness throughout.

Preparing your printing inks

Printing inks taken straight from the tube or tin need to be coaxed into a printable state. They will need to be moved around with a push knife to warm them and loosen them up. Before adding any modifiers to your inks, mix the colour you're aiming for and then check the viscosity. Different ink colours will have different properties – some will be sticky, some will be more fluid – so you can only judge the state of the ink once you're happy with the colour.

To test your ink's consistency, flatten your push knife onto a small amount of the ink and then raise it up to see how the ink falls in response. If the ink is very stringy/sticky then it will need tack reducer. If it's very dribbly it will need stiffening with magnesium powder. If the ink is very stiff it will need a little oil to loosen it. The standard optimum ink consistency is similar to that of Marmite: it will flow easily off the knife but not dribble, it will have enough body to hold its position in the pile of ink but still be soft enough to manoeuvre.

It is better to make slow, considered modifications of an ink while it is in use, rather than have to clean up and replace a rushed, poorly modified ink. Spend the time to get to know your inks and before you try adding any modifiers, *test your unmodified ink with a process first*, as it may work just fine as it is and not need modifying at all.

Lithographic printmaking requires a thin coating of ink on the roller, much less than for inking a linocut, for example. The ink should look velvety on the roller. If it looks orange-peel like, there is too much ink; if it looks very dull, with no shine, there isn't enough ink. When you're rolling out your ink you should be listening out for the tell-tell 'shushing' sound of the roller. If the rolling sounds sticky there is too much ink, and if there is little sound, there is not enough ink. The sound and appearance of the ink on the roller should be monitored while you're printing so you can maintain the same level of ink in each print of an edition.

Rolling the ink

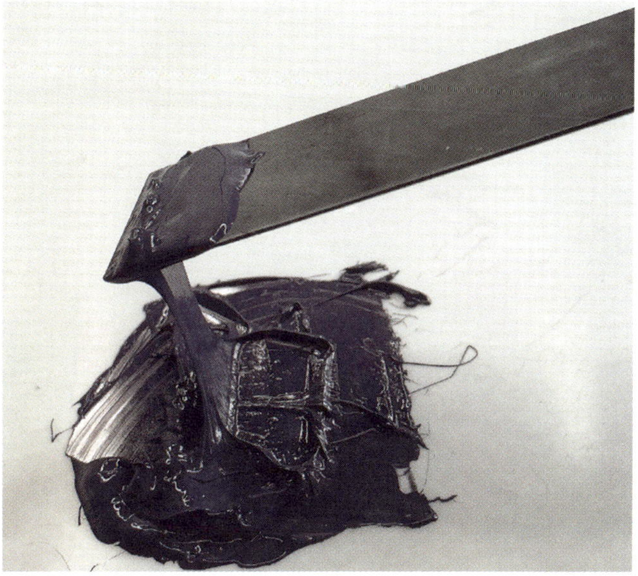

1. After taking your ink out of the tin or tube, move it around to loosen it and warm it. Once you have mixed your desired colour you can judge whether you need to add any modifiers to the ink.

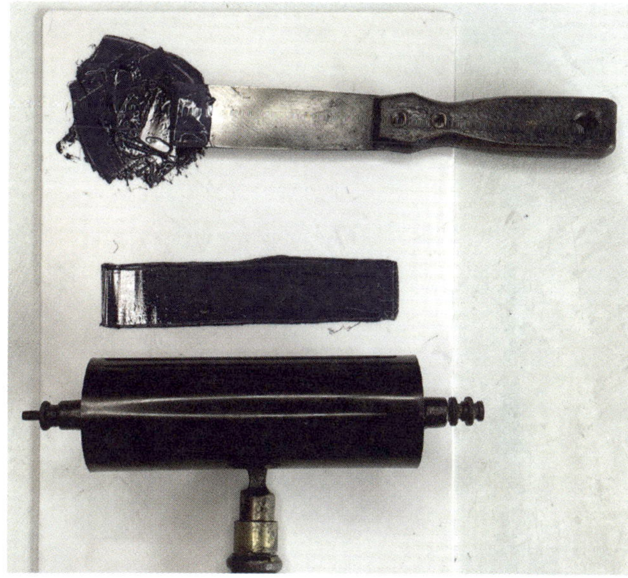

2. Use a push knife to spread a small bead of ink across your inking surface to the size of your roller. Try to stay away from the edge of the inking area so it is easier to control the spread of ink when you're cleaning up.

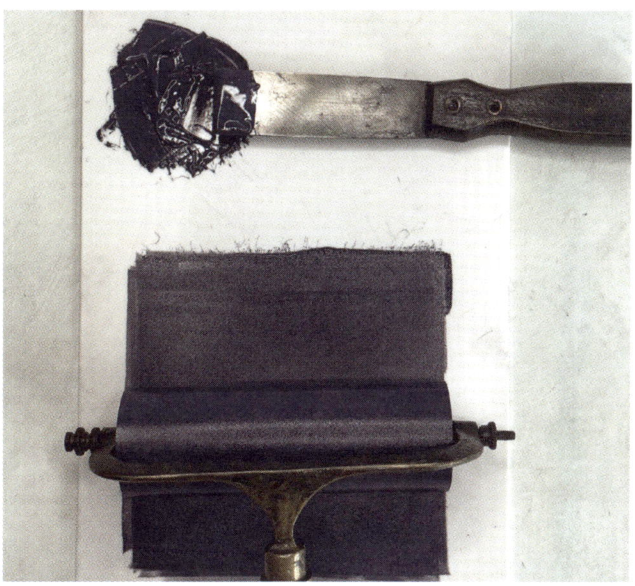

3. Roll out your ink into a square the size of your roller. Roll from top to bottom then lift the roller back to the top, to evenly coat the roller. Don't just roll back and forth without lifting and turning the roller as you won't evenly coat the entire roller.

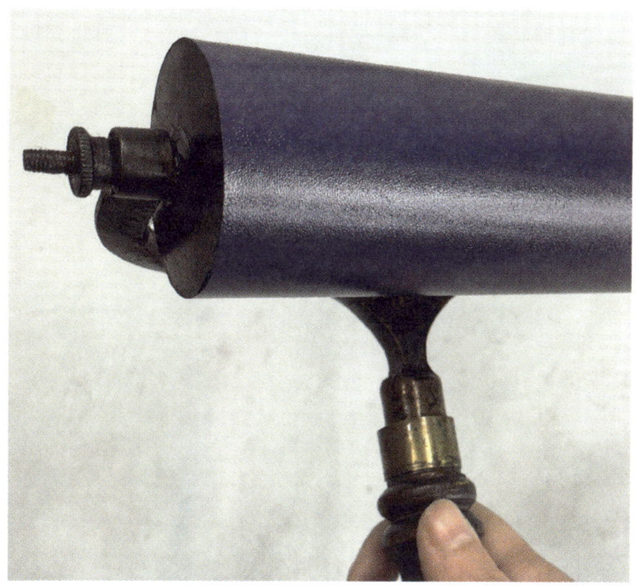

4. The ink should appear velvety on the roller with a slight shine. If it looks orange peel-like there is too much ink, and if it looks dull you need slightly more ink. Take the time to get this right, it should make a nice 'shushing' sound.

Preparing your paper

Working in your clean area, and with a sheet of clean newsprint protecting your printing paper, trim your papers to a workable size, either by cutting them with a knife for a straight edge or tearing the papers for a rough edge. When considering your registration, it is easier to register paper with a cut edge than it is with a deckled or torn edge. It is advisable to allow extra space than is needed in the margins of your print. This way you can tear down your paper after printing and remove any dirty marks or fingerprints. If your printing paper has a watermark, then you will need to take this into consideration to avoid printing over it. Some papers will have a working side, a side which is intended for printing on, often denoted by a watermark. Hold your paper up to the light; if the watermark reads the correct way, then you are looking at the working side of the paper. Once you have trimmed down your paper you may not be able to tell which side of the paper you're looking at, so put a small mark on the back of the paper to remind yourself.

If you're printing a multi-layered print on a press, it is good practice to calendar your paper before printing to avoid misregistration. Your paper will stretch and flatten when it goes through the press, meaning that it will be a slightly different size afterwards. Calendaring ensures that this stretch doesn't affect your printed image.

To calendar, run the paper through the press a couple of times in the direction of printing to stretch the fibres of the paper in that direction. Protect the papers with newsprint or tissue paper. Some papers have been calendared in their manufacturing process, but I often calendar them again anyway, just in case, as there is nothing more frustrating than the waste of misregistered prints.

Some alternative lithographic processes will require the printing paper to be dampened in order for it to pick up the full details of a print. If your printing paper is heavyweight or highly textured, dampening it will soften it and make it easier to be pushed in full contact with the plate. As we don't need to soften the paper to the extent that it needs to be pushed into any recesses of the plate, like with intaglio printmaking, the paper only needs to be soaked for a few minutes, surface-dampened with a sponge, or sprayed with water.

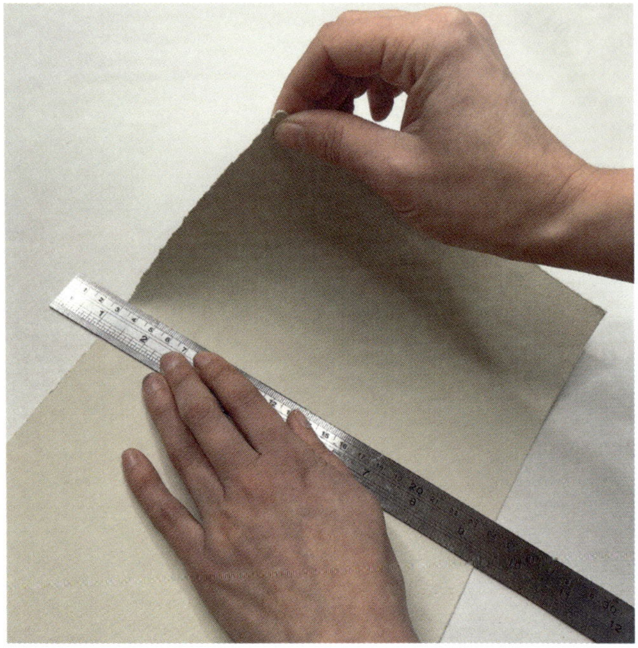

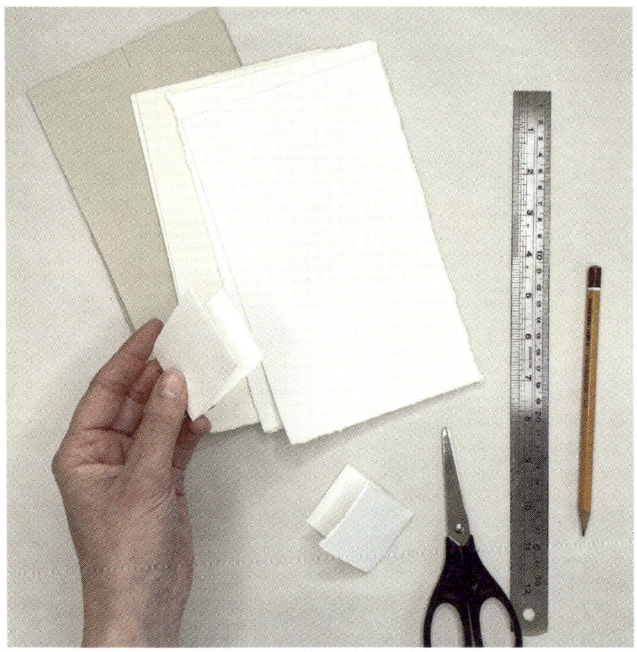

TOP
Use a straight edge, tear bar or a metal ruler to tear your paper against. Apply pressure to the straight edge to keep it in place and pull the paper towards it. Always tear your papers from behind.

ABOVE
Keep any scraps of paper, or offcuts after tearing down, to use as paper cuffs when handling your papers in the printing process. These will protect your prints from the inevitable inky fingers you will get while printing.

Dampening the paper

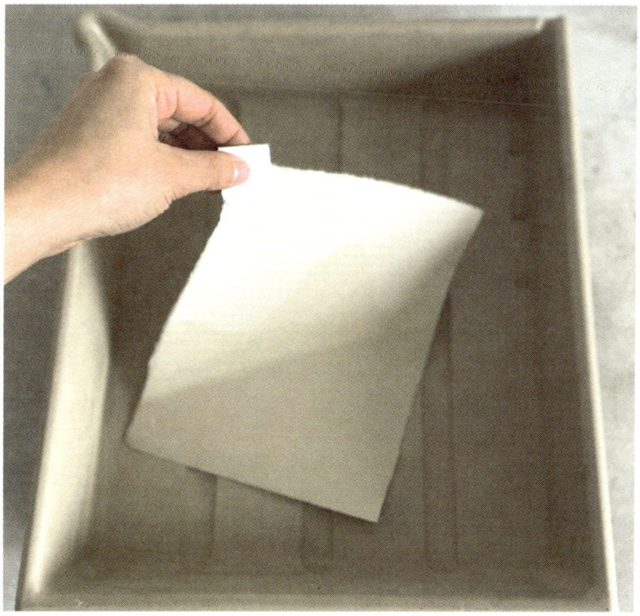

1. Submerge your paper in a tray of cold water and allow to soak for a few minutes. Different weights of paper will need less time than others and may only require surface dampening, unless an emboss is desired.

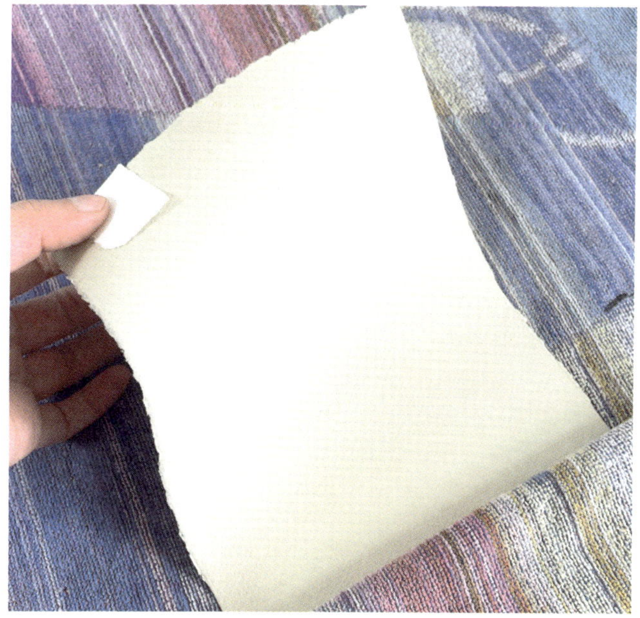

2. Remove from the water and allow the surface water to drip off. Blot in between layers of blotting paper, or a clean lint-free towel. Ensure there are no shiny areas of water left. The paper should feel flexible.

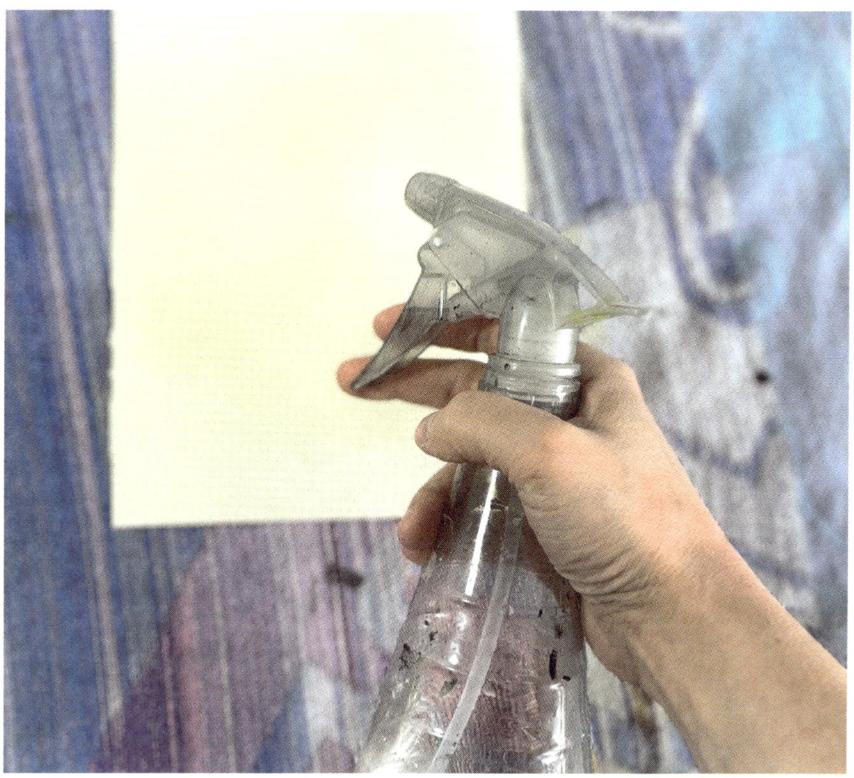

3. Alternatively, you can use a water mister to generously spray both sides of the paper and leave it to sit for a few minutes uncovered. Then blot off any excess water as in the previous method.

Registration

It is always good practice to register your prints and your proofs. It saves on paper wastage and allows for registration of future layers, even if that is not initially intended. In the 'T and bar' method of registration, two markers are drawn on the back of the printing paper, aligned in a straight line through the centre. The 'T' marker is drawn on the leading edge of the paper which will travel through the press first. Corresponding markers are drawn onto the plate or onto a registration guide. When printing, the leading edge of the paper is aligned to the registration guide and held in place with one hand, with the opposite end raised. The far edge of the paper is then lowered down in place, in alignment.

When printing multiple layers without a press, punch/pin registration can be used. As many of the alternative lithography processes featured in this book use thin plates, these pins are not suitable for printing on a roller/etching press as they can damage the press and blankets.

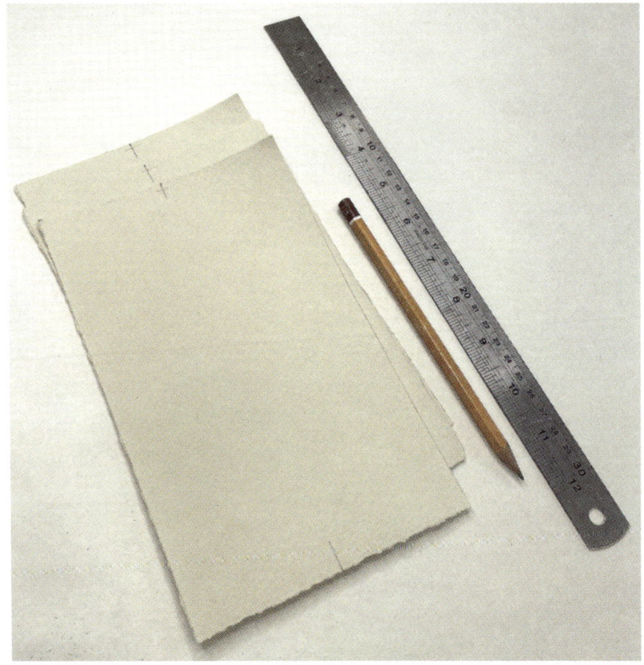

Registration marks on the back of the printing paper, showing the T mark along the top edge of the paper, and corresponding mark along the centre of the opposite edge.

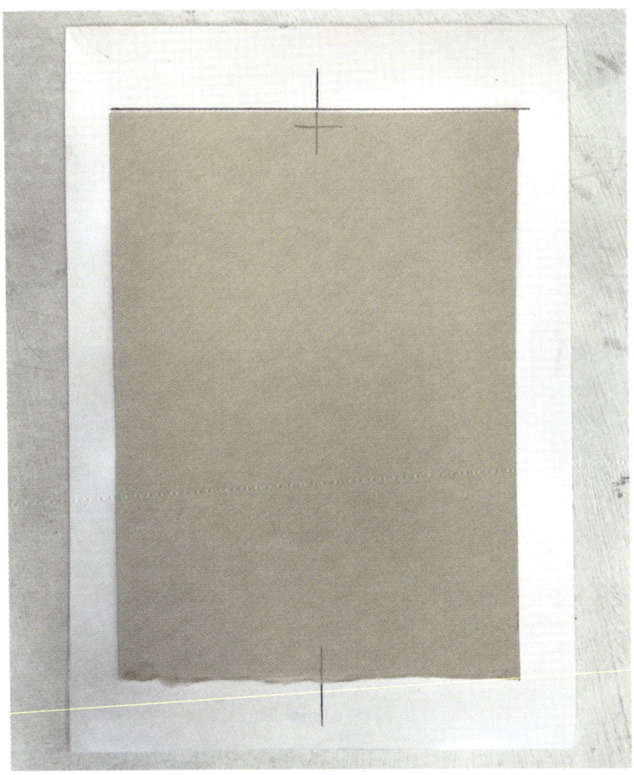

When the plate is larger than the printing paper, the registration lines can be drawn directly onto the plate, shown here on a polyester plate, with paper in register.

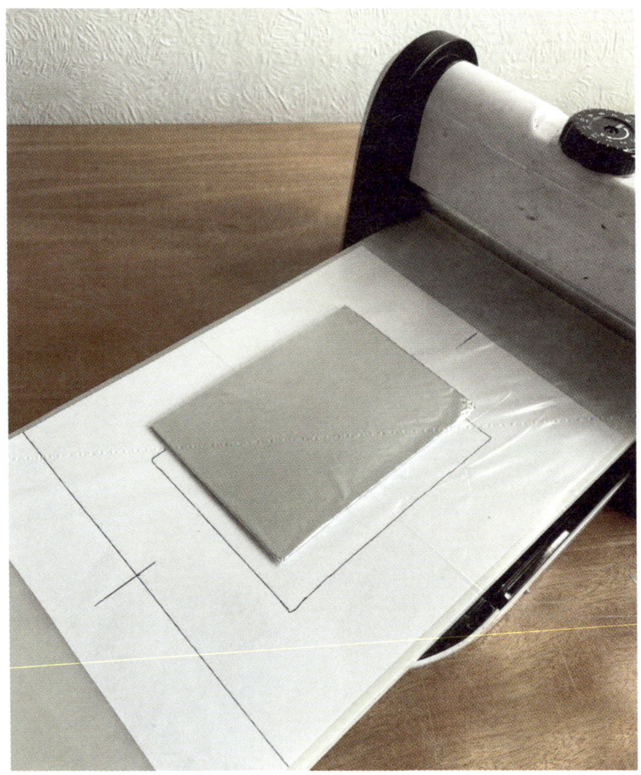

When the printing paper is larger than the plate, a registration guide can be attached to a press bed with plate registration markings.

Using a press

When printing a planographic print, absolute contact between the plate and the paper is vital. Only a thin film of ink is held on the flat surface of the plate and so the paper must be in full contact to transfer the ink. When the pressure is correct your plate will make a slight embossed marking on the printing paper. The paper doesn't need to be forced into the recesses of the plate like with intaglio printing, so the pressure needed is less in comparison. Conversely, as there is less ink to transfer compared to relief printing, more pressure and smoother paper is needed than when printing a relief print. However, some of the lithographic processes included in this book can combine elements of the intaglio and relief methods within the same matrix.

Ensure the press bed is clean or place a sheet of tissue paper beneath the plate. Place another sheet of tissue paper on top of your damp printing paper to stop the transference of size from the paper to your blankets. Over time the size can harden your blankets and reduce their working life. For some processes a blanket may not even be necessary.

Always print in the same direction so that the paper fibres are stretched in the same direction, otherwise misregistration can occur.

When printing lino or plywood, you may need runners of the same height as the plate either side of the plate on the press bed. These will ensure the pressure is engaged throughout and that the paper won't get knocked when the pressure engages with the plate.

With planographic printing as you don't need huge amounts of pressure there isn't too much difference in the results between prints from a press and hand-burnished prints.

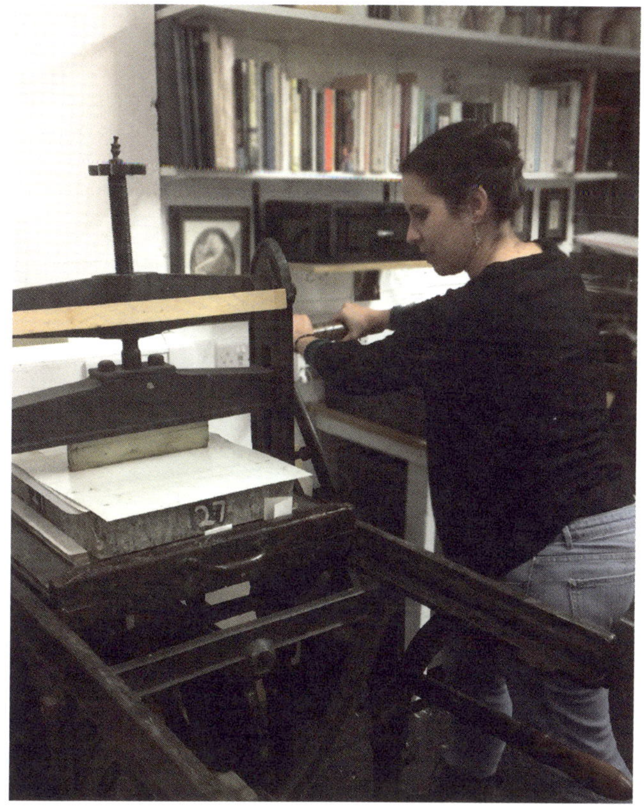

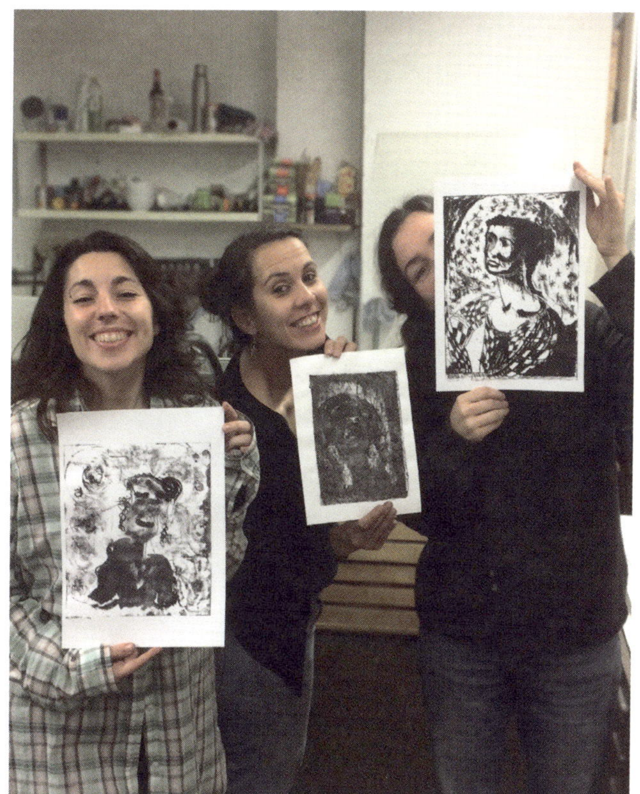

TOP
Printing a foil lithograph on a direct lithography press.

BOTTOM
Happy workshop participants with their foil lithographs.

CHAPTER 4

Foil lithography

Foil lithography, also known as kitchen lithography, was developed by French artist Émilie Aizier as a low-toxic alternative to stone and plate lithography. Foil lithography is the most accessible form of lithography as it predominantly uses humble materials you would find in your kitchen. The only specialist equipment you need for this process is a roller and some oil-based printing ink.

As you now know, the principle for lithography lies within the fact that water and grease repel each other, and the process involves the use of greasy drawing materials and an acidified etch. Foil lithography works in the same way, mimicking traditional metal plate lithography: the aluminium plate is reproduced using aluminium foil; phosphoric acid, which is traditionally used to etch aluminium plates, is found in cola. Our greasy drawing material becomes oil pastels, wax crayons and chocolate.

The marks you can achieve in foil lithography can be incredibly varied – bold and delicate. If well controlled, you can print good-sized editions before the plate deteriorates. We are also working with cheap and easily found materials, which means that the act of making shouldn't feel inhibiting. If you don't like your drawing or you mess up part of the process, it's OK! Just clean the ink off your plate, put that foil in the recycling and start again.

FACING PAGE
Etching the foil lithography plate by pouring cola over the entire plate.

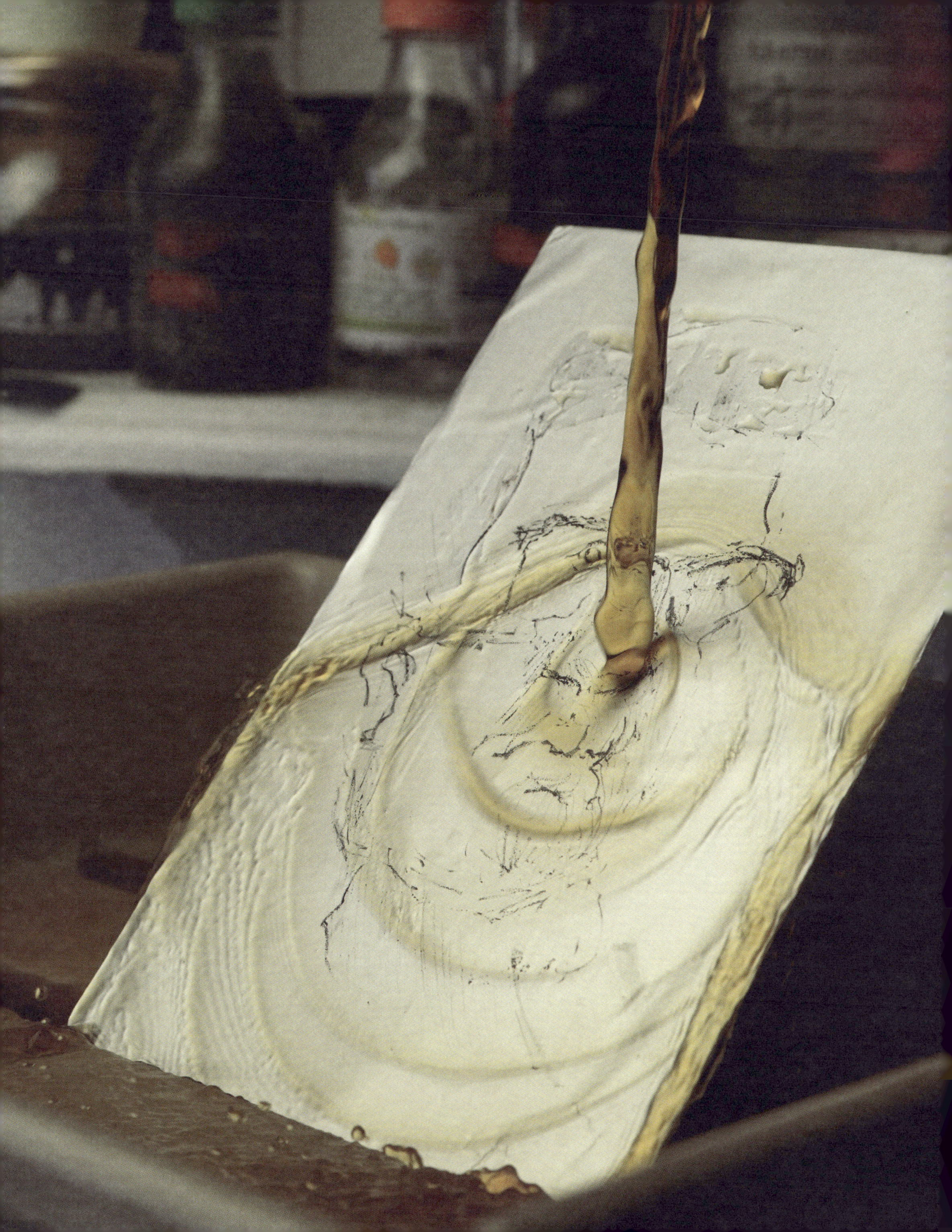

You will need to be very careful and methodical when producing your foil lithography plates. Ensure each stage of the process has been successful before continuing to the next stage. It's important that you don't accidentally transfer grease from another surface, or from your hands onto the plate, or you'll contaminate your plate right from the beginning. I have found this to be the trickiest and most temperamental type of lithography in this book, so we're jumping in at the deep end!

Ultimately, foil lithography is fast and fun. You can be spontaneous with your mark-making, and you're only limited by the size of the foil you can find in the supermarket.

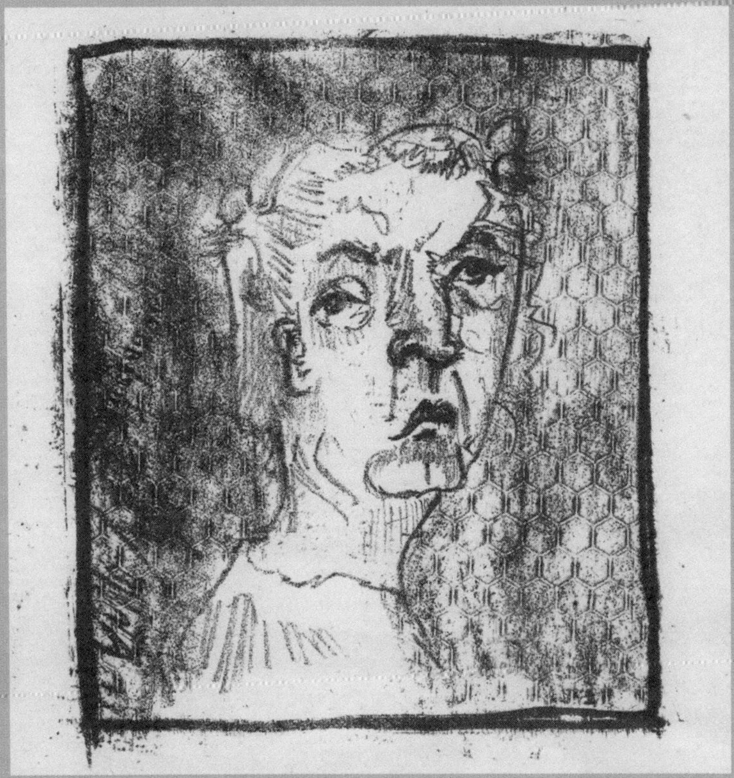

ABOVE
Some foils have a hexagon pattern on them which can interrupt the drawn mark when using crayons; however this can be incorporated into the design.

BELOW
Portrait in foil lithography by Scarlett Rebecca, sketched during a life drawing class, with a visible tape border on the plate which picked up ink and transferred to the print.

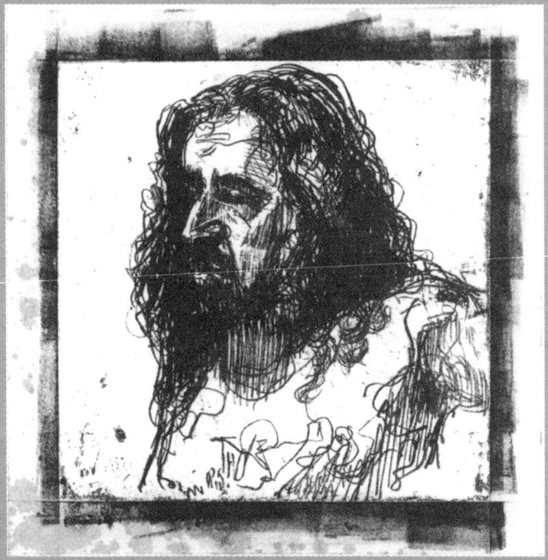

Preparing your plate

Prepare a clean surface to work on; you don't want any rogue grease contaminating your plate. Avoid using foil with a hexagonal pattern on it as this can interrupt your drawn marks. Any aluminium foil will work – it doesn't need to be extra strong or extra thick, although thickness will help to protect your plate from accidental scratches and holes. The dull side of the foil is our working surface as it has a slight roughness to it that will hold the detail of the drawing material better than the shiny side.

MATERIALS

- Foil
- Smooth backing plate
- Tape
- Cola
- Oil
- Clean rags or kitchen towel
- Water bowls for dampening water
- Cellulose sponge
- Printing ink
- Paper
- Chocolate
- Chinagraph pencil
- Oil pastel
- Indian ink
- Permanent marker

The materials needed for the foil lithography process.

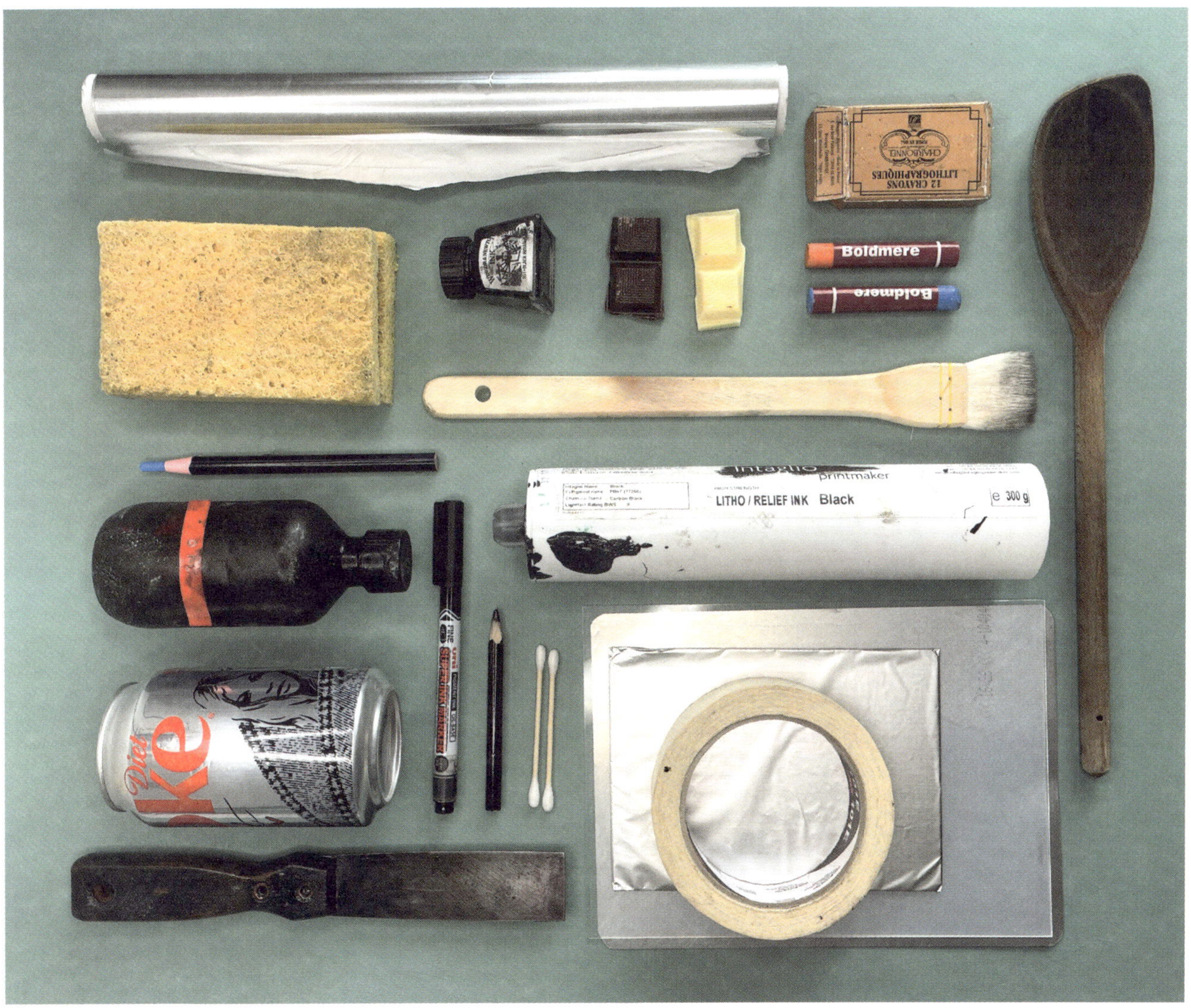

Preparation of plate *(continued)*

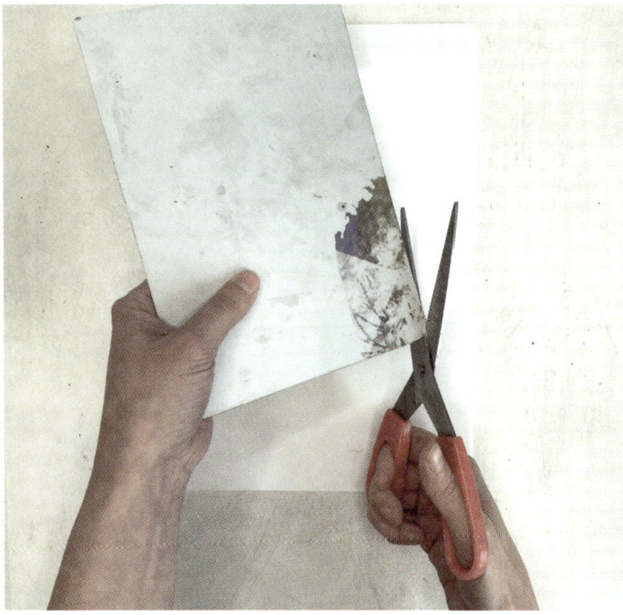

1. Round off the corners of any plates you're using with a pair of scissors or sandpaper. Sharp corners can easily pierce a hole in your foil if you're not careful.

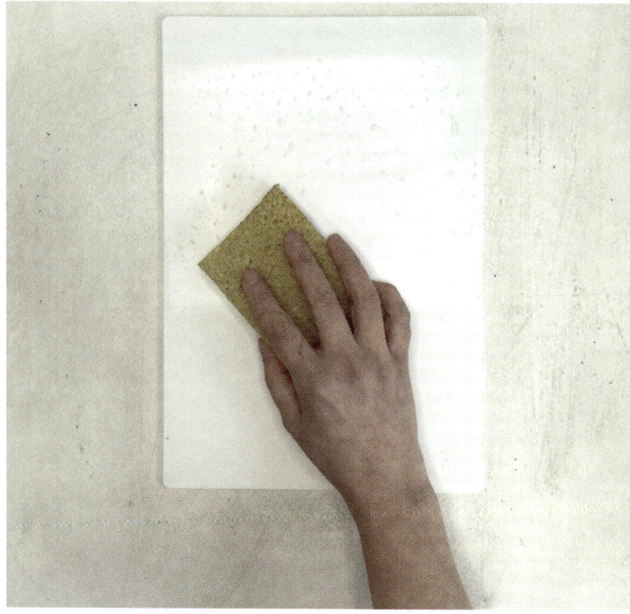

2. We don't need to glue the foil to the surface of the plate. Dampening the plate a little with some water helps the foil to stay in contact with the plate and prevents air bubbles.

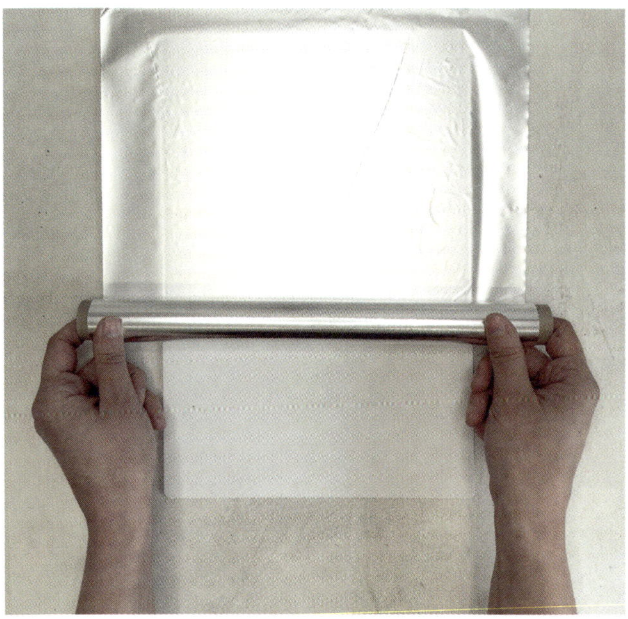

3. Roll your foil over the plate, shiny side down. Avoid the urge to smooth the foil out with your hands as you'll contaminate the plate. Don't worry about little creases in the foil. Cut the foil from the roll.

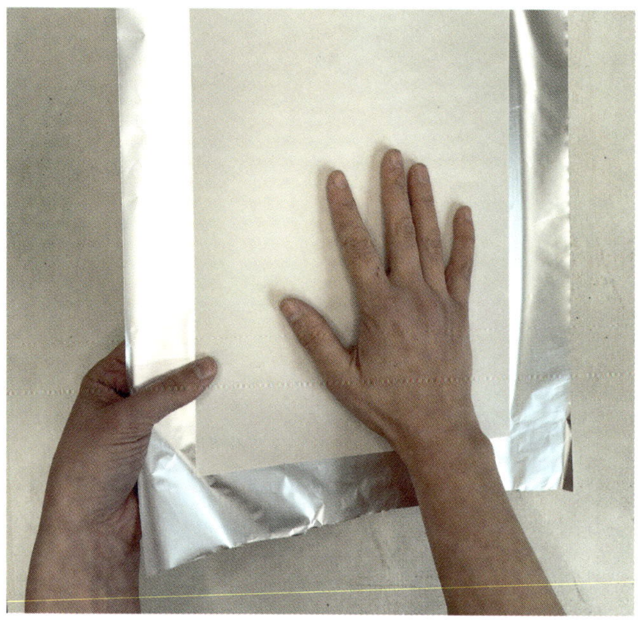

4. Use a clean scrap piece of paper to protect the front of the plate and flip the plate over. It doesn't matter if you touch the foil on the reverse of the plate so you can be unrestricted when handling the foil here.

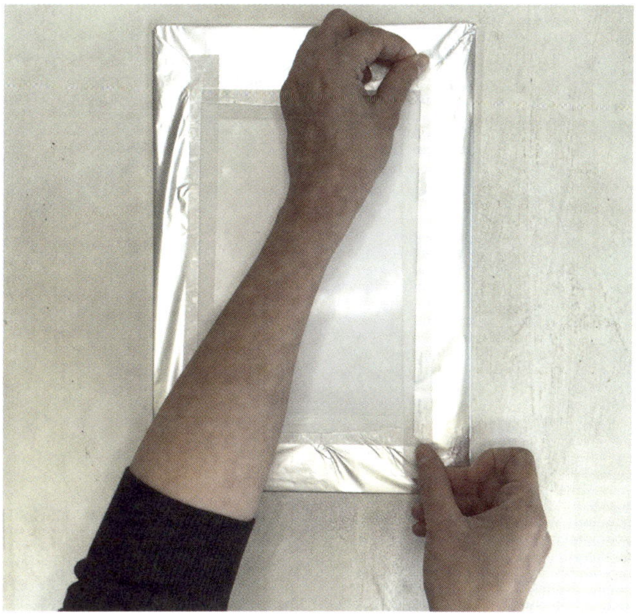

5. Tape the foil onto the back of the plate. Try to cover up any holes that cola could get into, or it can leak out while you're printing and leave a brown mark on your paper.

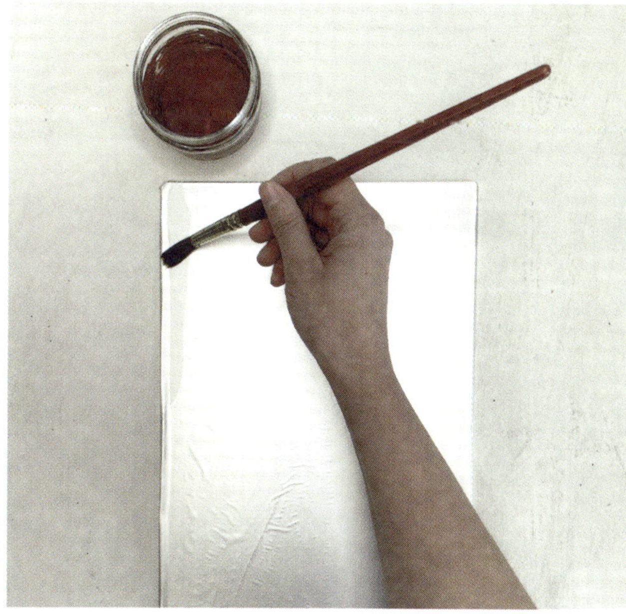

6. To protect the edges of your plate from greasy fingerprints while you're handling it, paint on a border of cola. The cola will desensitise the plate in that area and stop any grease from creating image area.

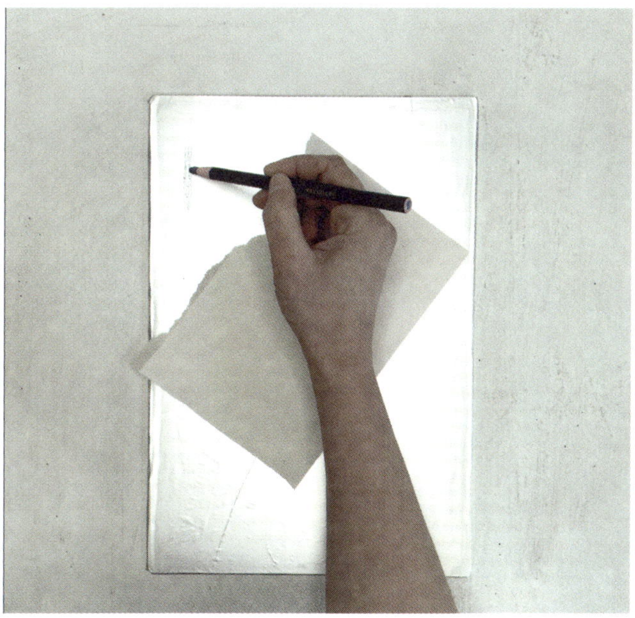

7. If you tend to rest your hand on the surface while you're drawing, then put a piece of clean scrap paper under your hand. This will stop any transference of oils from your skin onto the plate.

Drawing your image

I always recommend producing a test plate, a sacrificial plate, before you move on to create a more detailed image. Test all the drawing materials you have and see what range of marks you can achieve. You will also be testing the entire process with this first plate so don't risk an image you are invested in as it's quite likely that your first print will go wrong in some way.

Right from the beginning, do not touch the plate with your bare hands. The grease on your fingers will leave marks on the plate that will become the image area. Because there's no pigment in our finger grease you won't see these marks until you come to ink up your plates later. You will get a perfectly reproduced fingerprint on your plate, so you'll know how that mark got there.

Aluminium foil is relatively compliant and grease-receptive, and with the right care it can hold incredibly detailed drawings. When drawing with a pencil on paper you can vary your pressure and build up the image in layers of pencil to achieve varying tones. In foil lithography a lightly applied mark will print as dark as a heavily applied mark, so in order to achieve your tonal variation, you need to consider the size of your marks. When you want a lighter tone, you can use less pressure when drawing because it will deposit the grease in a smaller mark. Consider varying your line weight and distribution of marks and use hatching and stippling effects to achieve tonal variation.

This is the same for when using Indian ink with foil lithography; Indian ink can't be diluted for lighter tones. The diluted Indian ink will attract the printing ink in a solid dark area the same as un-diluted Indian ink, but, if it has been made too dilute, it won't attract the printing ink at all.

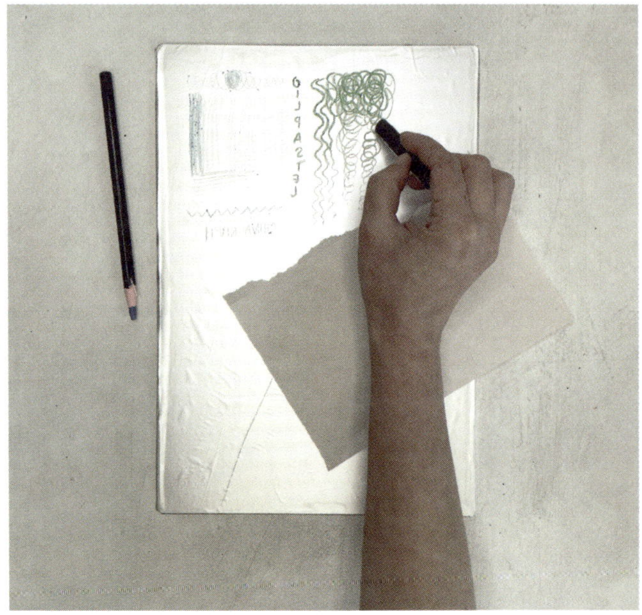

1. Chinagraph pencils/china markers create a pencil-like mark which inks up very faithfully. Vary the size of your marks with litho crayons and oil pastels to create a range of tones.

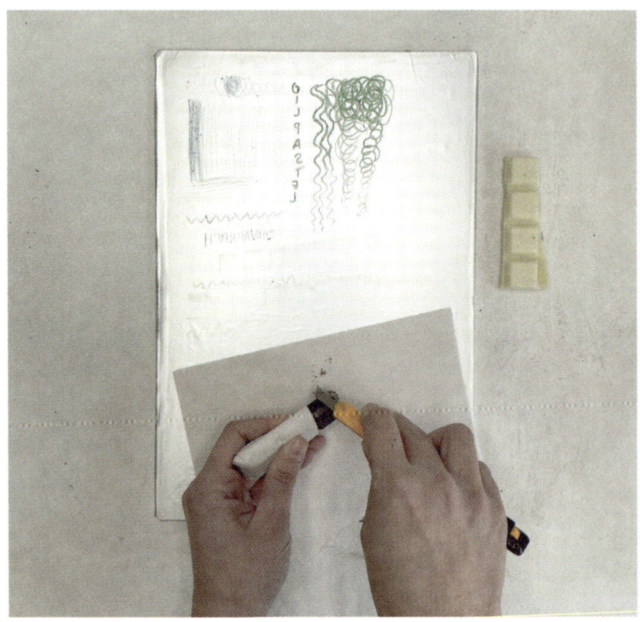

2. Dark chocolate will create fine, light marks while white chocolate, which contains more oils, will create solid, darker marks. Keep chocolate in the fridge so it doesn't melt in your hands and sharpen it with a knife.

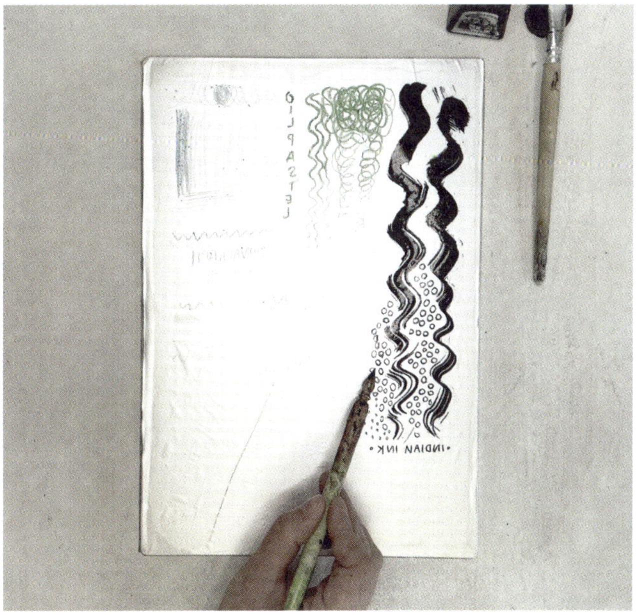

3. Use a variety of brushes or a dip pen with Indian ink for interesting textures. Make sure it's fully dry before you etch it, or it will wash away. Be careful with a dip pen not to pierce the foil.

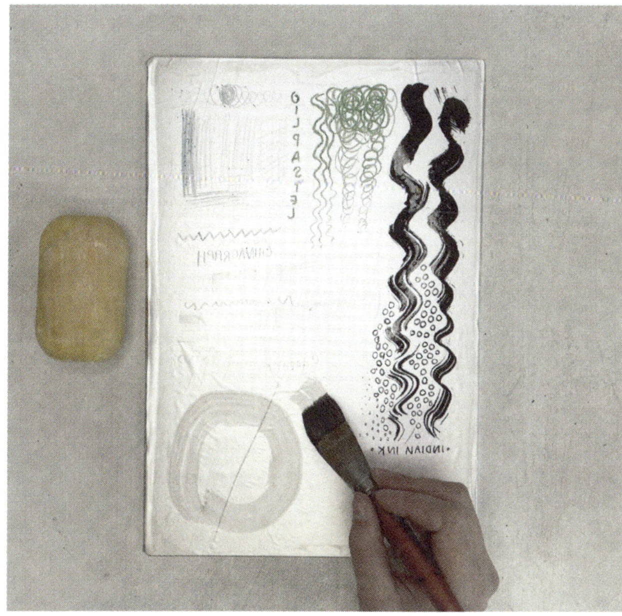

4. Soap can be a contrary drawing material which acts unpredictably but can create interesting marks. Use it dry like a crayon or with a brush and a little water. Be cautious when etching soap drawings.

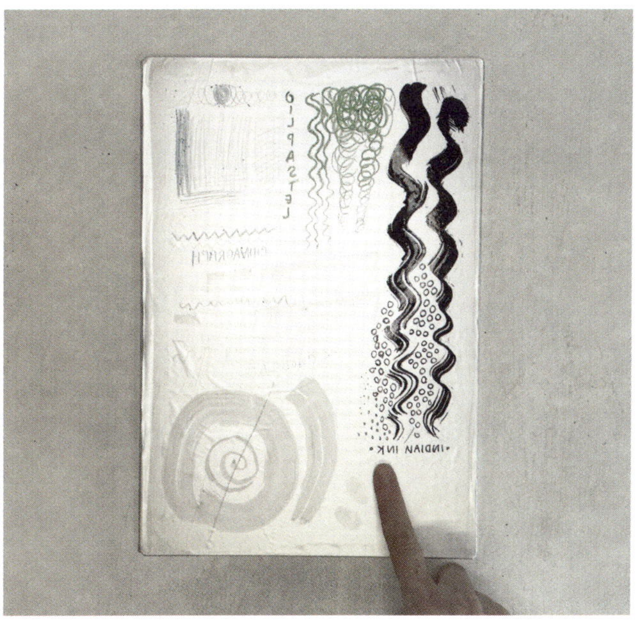

5. You may get accidental fingerprints on your plate but you can also add them intentionally and use your hands as a drawing tool. Anything greasy will leave a mark, so try to think outside the box.

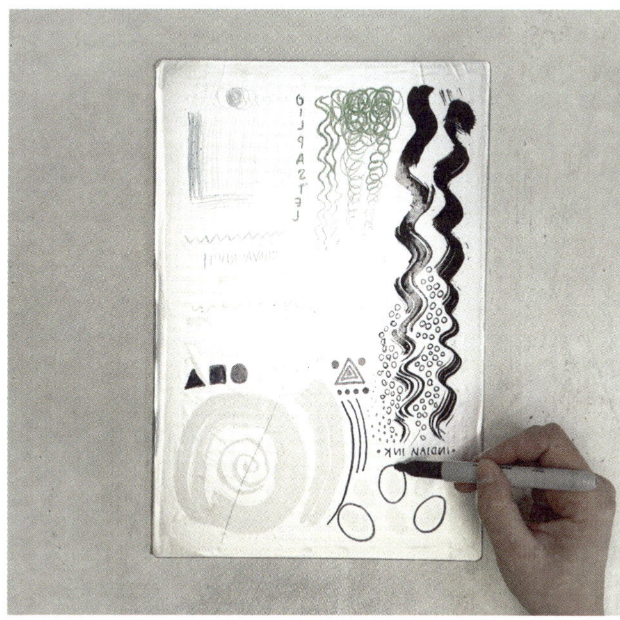

6. Permanent markers are useful because you are able to actually see them on the plate, when other materials are less visible. Draw with them slowly for a solid mark and remember to vary your mark making.

Drawing your image *(continued)*

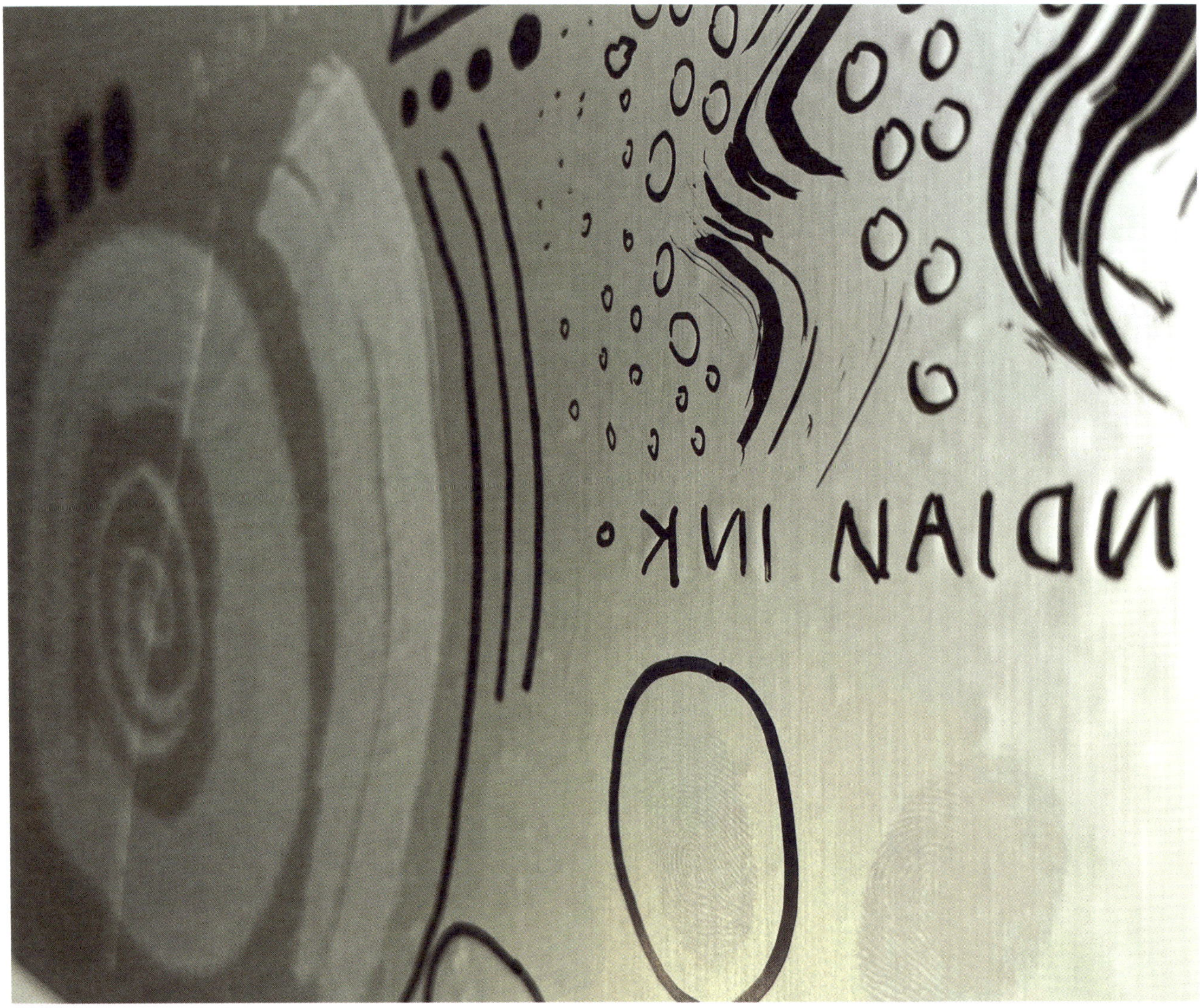

7. You will need to turn your plate in the light to be able to see some of your drawn marks on the plate. Some marks can seem very subtle at this stage but will appear much darker later on.

You will find that many drawing materials can be difficult to see on the plate while you're drawing so keep tilting the plate in the light to see what you're doing. Permanent markers and Indian ink have shellac and solvents in them that resist the etch and are brilliant because you can actually see what you're drawing onto the plate. Don't bother using any specialist lithographic tusche as it will fill in and print as a solid mark; use Indian ink, soap or printing ink diluted in solvent for painterly marks. Save the expensive tusche for another lithographic process in this book where its special qualities will be able to be reproduced.

Processing the plate

Cola has a pH value of around 3.4, making it quite acidic and a great etch for foil lithography. Diet cola is slightly more acidic too, so it is preferable to use. It's not the carbonated aspect of the cola that etches the plate but the phosphoric acid within its ingredients. So, you can use old, flat cola and store the cola in the fridge to use again and again until it becomes exhausted or contaminated. If you don't like to use cola, you can also use citric acid/lemon juice in the same way.

USING COLA

It is the phosphoric acid in the cola which has the etching effect on the plate, not the carbonated aspect of the cola, so old flat cola still works. Store used cola in the fridge and use it multiple times.

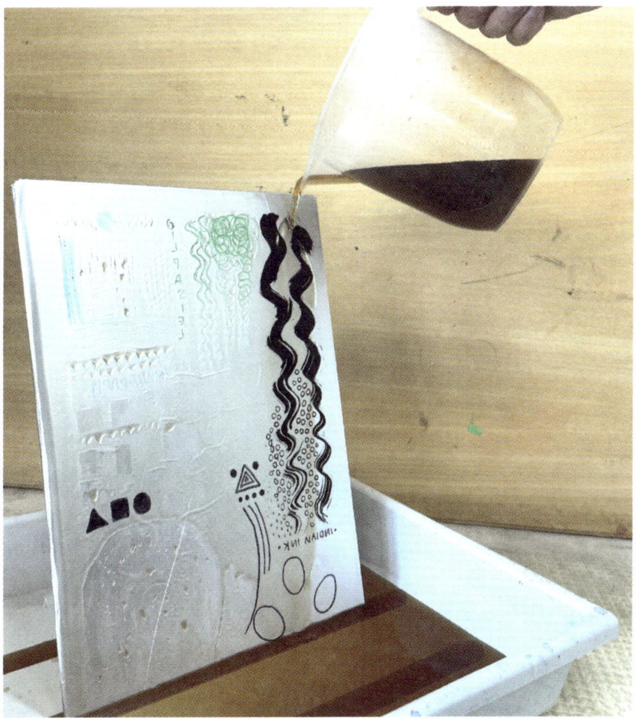

1. Prop up your plate in a tray and methodically pour cola over your entire plate. If you're using soap, start pouring the cola from bottom to top, to prevent any soap from dripping down the plate and creating image area.

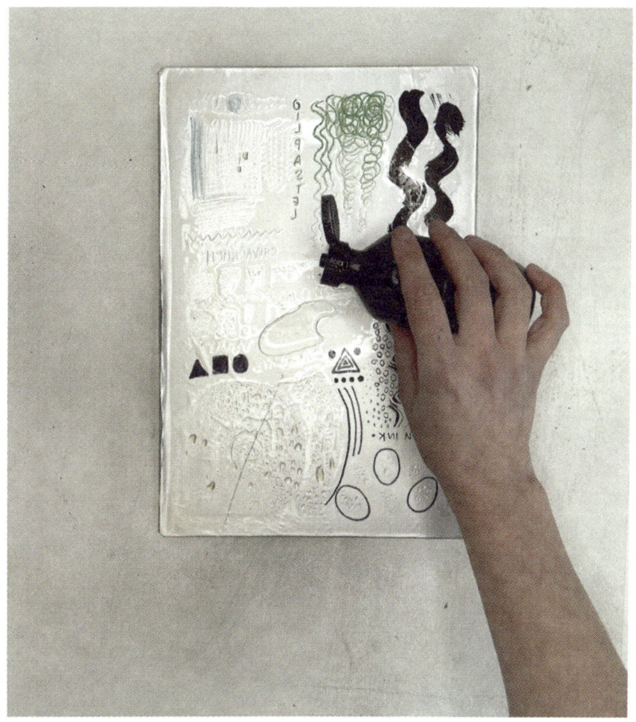

2. Rinse off the cola with water and make sure the water is sitting smoothly in your non-image areas and is rejecting the greasy areas. This is an important check point in the process.

Processing the plate *(continued)*

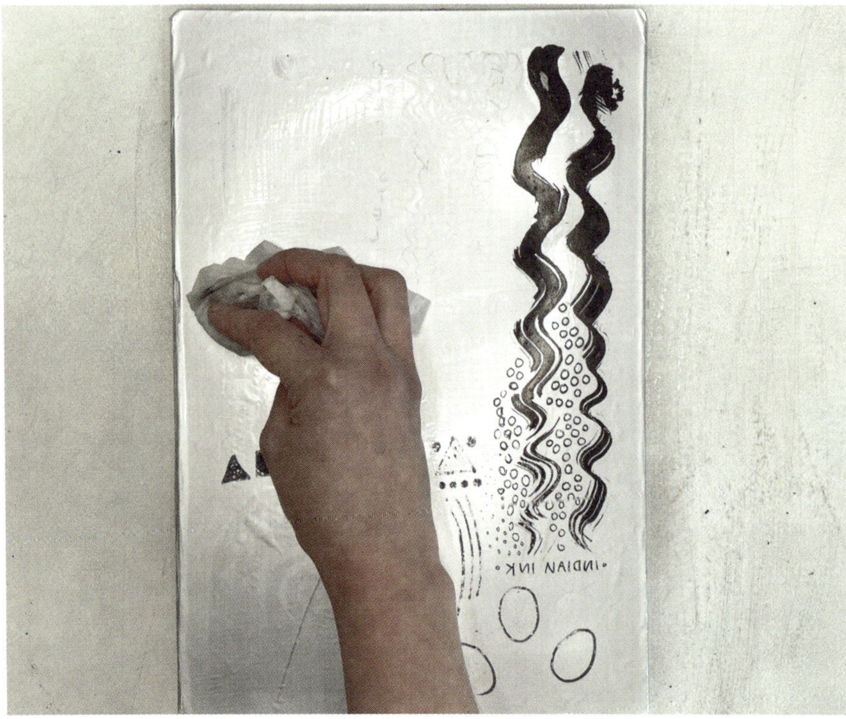

3. Using a little oil and a damp cloth, gently remove the non-permanent drawing materials. Ensure the plate stays damp and make sure to remove all traces of oil with a damp cloth afterwards.

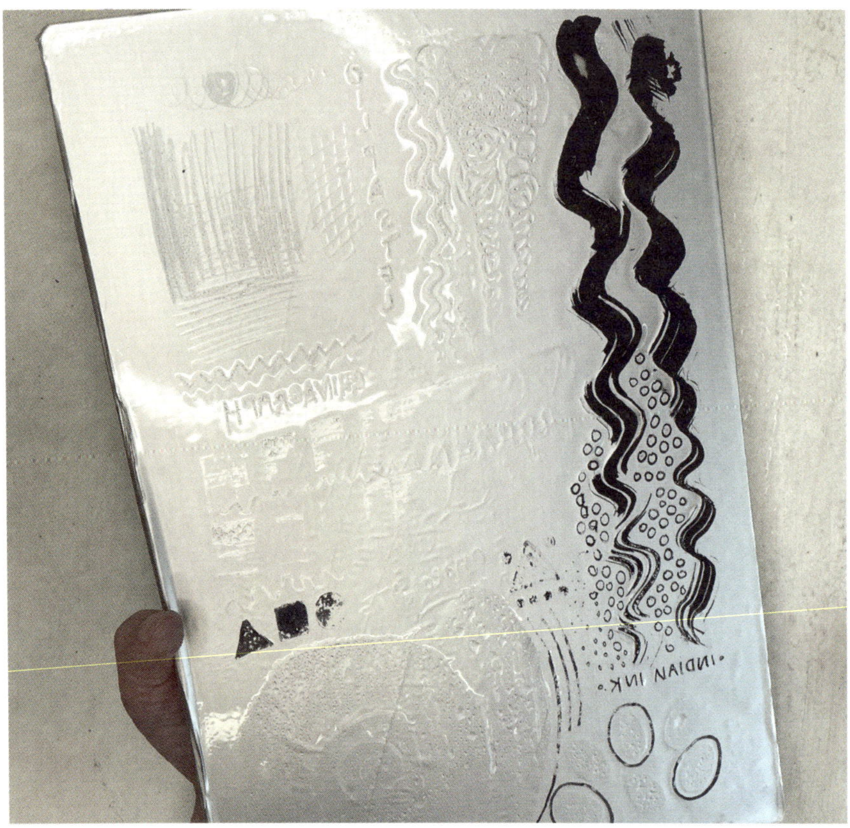

4. This is another check point: make sure the water on the plate is still sitting evenly in your non-image areas and rejecting your greasy drawing. Indian ink and permanent marker will remain on the plate.

Printing a foil lithograph

Make sure you follow the instructions for rolling out ink for lithography in Chapter 2 of this book. You won't need to make any modifications to your ink specifically for this process. It may feel counterintuitive inking up a damp plate but it's imperative for the water to act as a resist to the oil-based ink in your non-image areas.

Inking up a foil lithograph for the first time can take a few rolls; it's best not to recharge your roller too much as you can easily quickly overload your plate with ink. You'll know your plate has enough ink when you can *see* your whole image and your darkest areas look rich and velvety like your roller did. Make sure you finish inking after a roll not after a sponge-wipe or you'll end up with water droplets on your image and they'll come through onto your print.

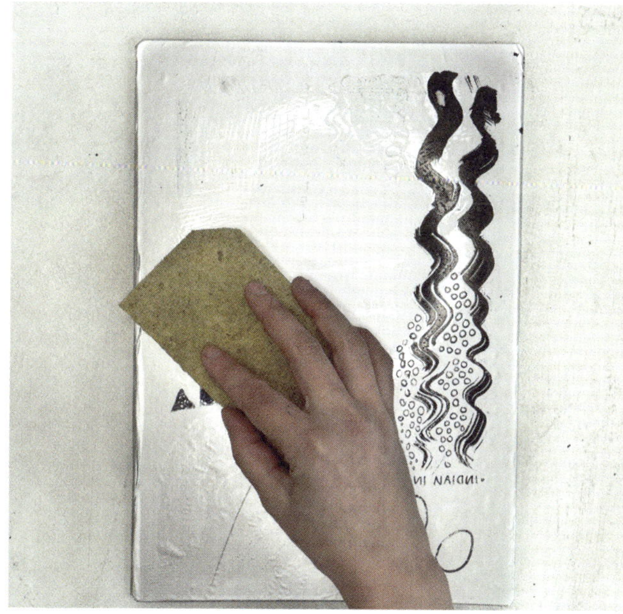

1. Using your cellulose sponge, dampen the plate with a little water. Too much water on the plate will make the ink bleed and too little water on the plate will mean it will dry too quickly.

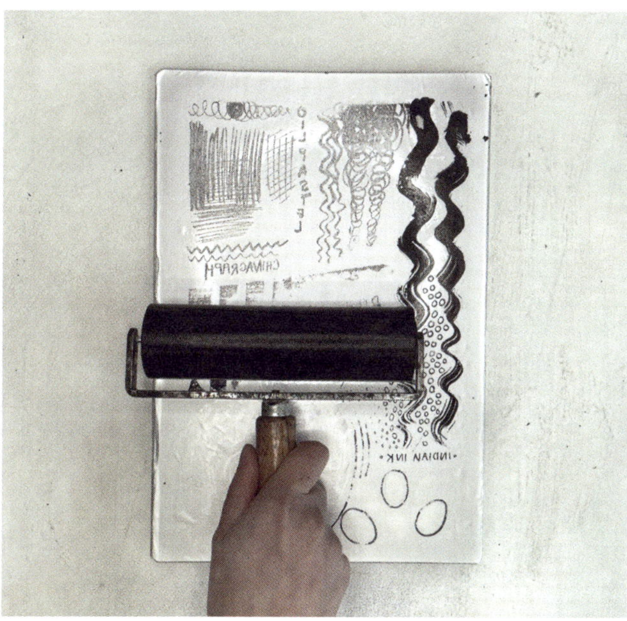

2. Using a very lean roller, quickly ink up the damp plate. The plate will darken slowly. Some areas will collect ink faster than others so you may need to selectively ink some areas.

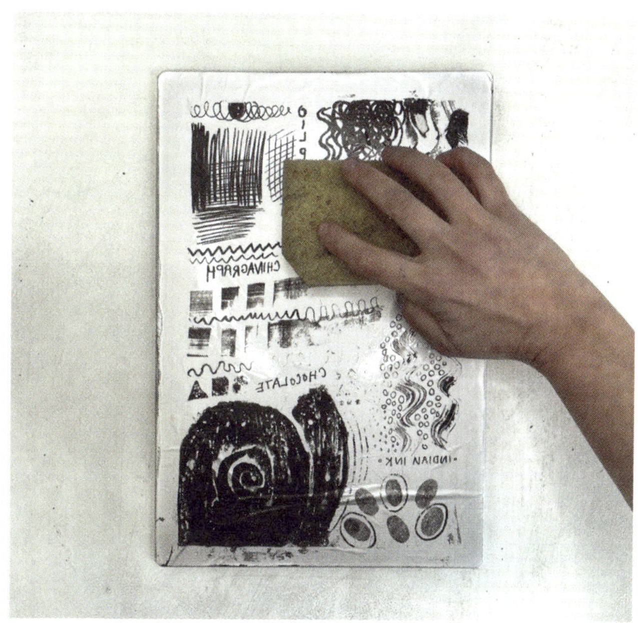

3. Do not let the plate dry. After a few passes with the roller, re-dampen the entire plate with your sponge. Always dampen the whole plate so no areas are accidentally left dry.

Processing the plate *(continued)*

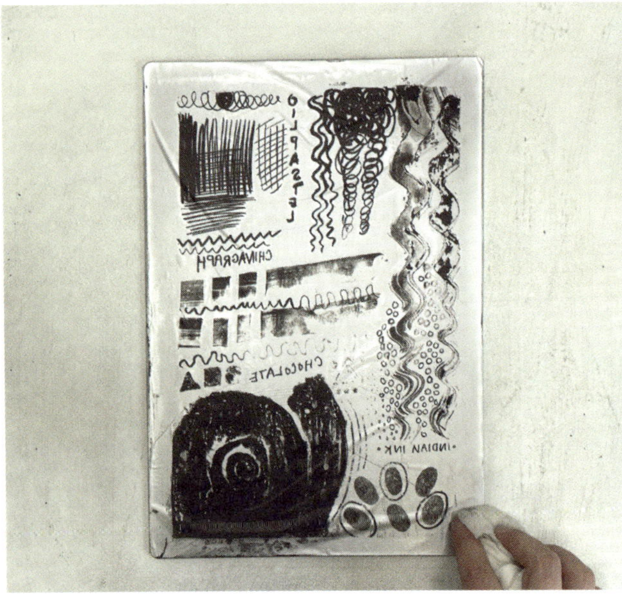

4. You may have areas of unwanted ink in places around the plate, especially the edges. Clean the ink off these areas with a damp cloth or damp cotton bud. They will return the next time you ink up.

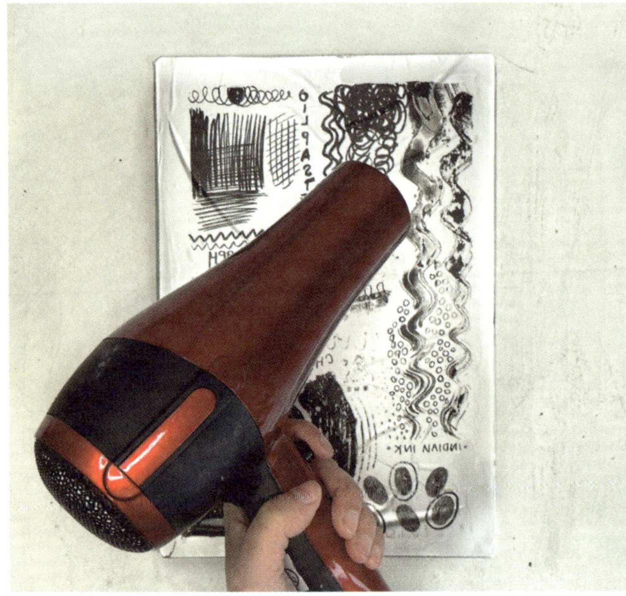

5. Before you print, dry the plate with a cold hairdryer or use a fan. This is the only time during the printing process that the plate will need to be dry. If you print with a wet plate the print will look blurry.

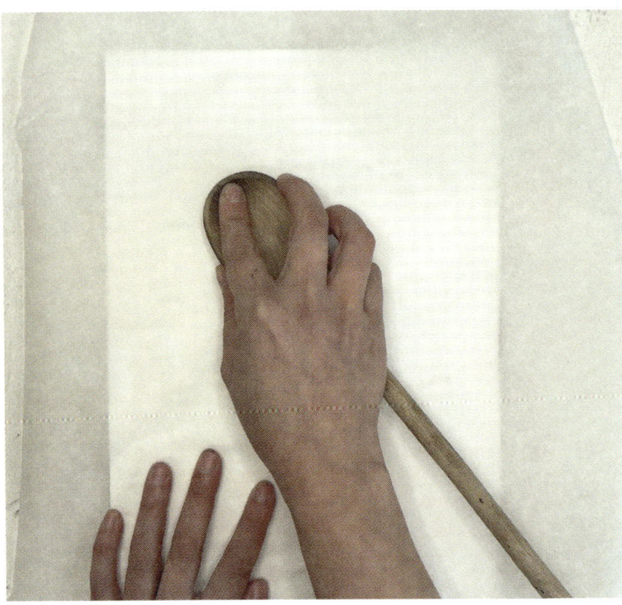

6. Place your printing paper on top of the plate, and a sheet of greaseproof paper on top of that, and burnish all over the plate in small circles. Use firm pressure with a wooden spoon or similar tool.

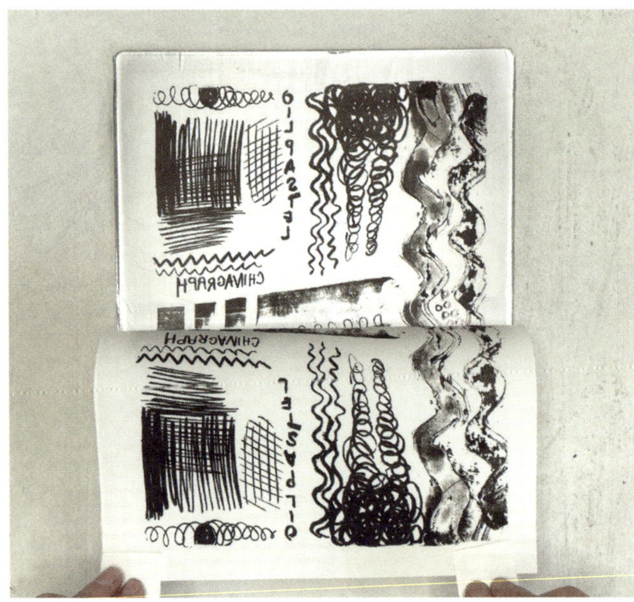

7. You can carefully peek at the print to see if you need to burnish further. Keep a hand on the print to stop the paper slipping. When fully burnished, slowly pull back the paper from the plate to reveal the print.

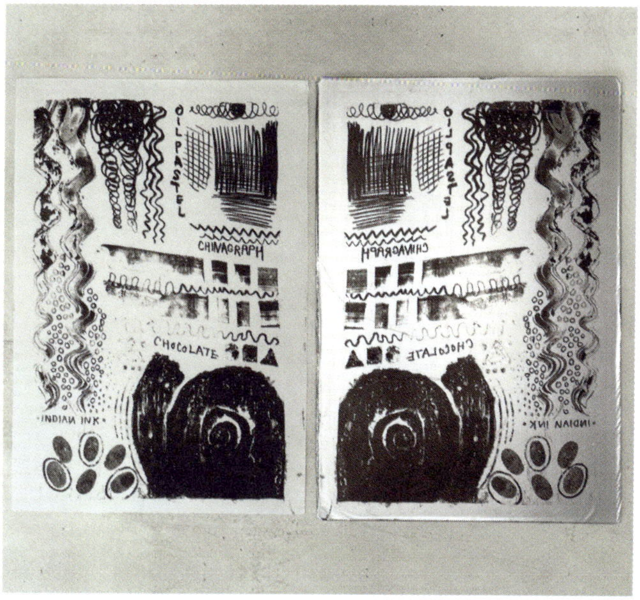

8. Print and plate comparison after the first print. The first print is always lighter and far crisper than the subsequent prints, so it's not recommended to use this print as a reference for an edition.

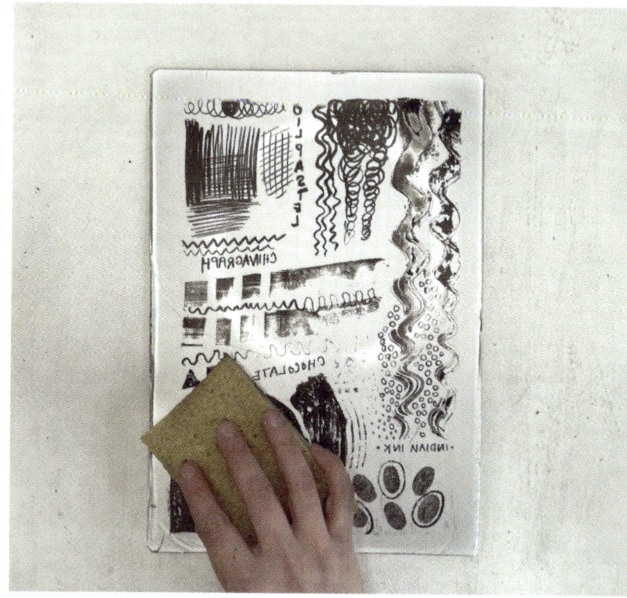

9. Dampen the plate again and ink up for the second time. The plate will collect ink much faster this second time so be wary. Consider inking up with less ink on your roller, for more control.

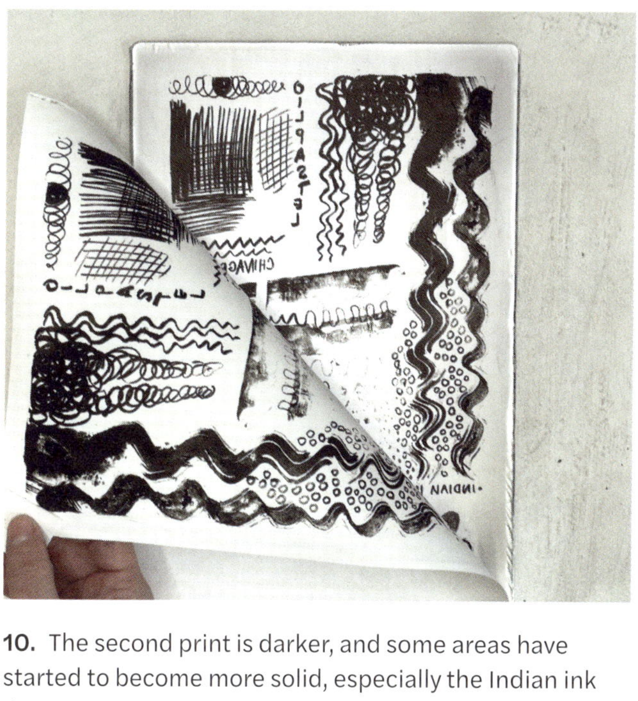

10. The second print is darker, and some areas have started to become more solid, especially the Indian ink drawing. Repeat your inking pattern for each subsequent print for a reliable edition.

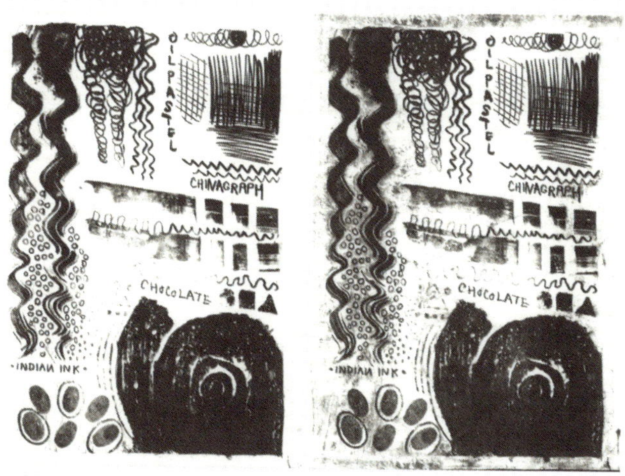

11. Comparison of an early print with a later print after the plate has seen much use, showing the progression of deterioration of the plate. A lot of scumming has occurred (ink collecting in unwanted areas of the plate and establishing new image area).

Making more ambitious prints

Once you've made your test plate and you are comfortable with the process you can start to become more adventurous with your prints and work closer to the way you normally draw, to see how the process translates your marks and affects your normal drawing habits.

If the thought of working straight onto a blank plate fills you with trepidation you may want to transfer an existing drawing onto the plate. You can do this using a sheet of carbon paper, or by creating your own form of transfer paper by covering a sheet of greaseproof paper in oil pastel or chocolate. Place the sheet of carbon paper/homemade transfer paper face down onto the plate and draw on top of it. The quality of whatever drawing implement you use will transfer onto the plate, so if you choose a sharp pencil, you'll get crisp fine lines, and if you choose a blunt or softer grade pencil, you'll get wider, softer lines. Be careful when using carbon paper, as anywhere you apply pressure to will transfer grease to the plate, so still be careful where you touch it and don't lean on it with your hands while you're drawing.

Working outside

All the lithographic processes in this book can be produced outside in some form. The plates themselves can be transported and drawn on outside of the studio in any setting, whether that be in the garden, on the train, or at a life drawing class. It may feel safe to stay in the reliable security of the home or studio, but working outside, or outside of your normal studio, can allow for a sense of immediacy that will help capture the moment in time of making. When drawing from photographs there is a barrier between you and the subject, you are forced to see your subject through a dulled and narrow lens of the camera, without all the external influences of the context to affect your drawing. When working from life you can select your own focus and let the sounds, smells and changing light affect how you work.

Due to the sensitive nature of the foil lithography plate, it will need an additional step added to the process to ensure that the plate can survive unaffected during transportation after etching outside. The addition of gum arabic forms a protective layer on the non-image area of the plate and stops the image area from deteriorating after etching. The application of gum arabic also means the plate can be stored after printing, to print again another time. Although the image on the plate will not be as well defined when printing the second time, it can still print successfully if handled well.

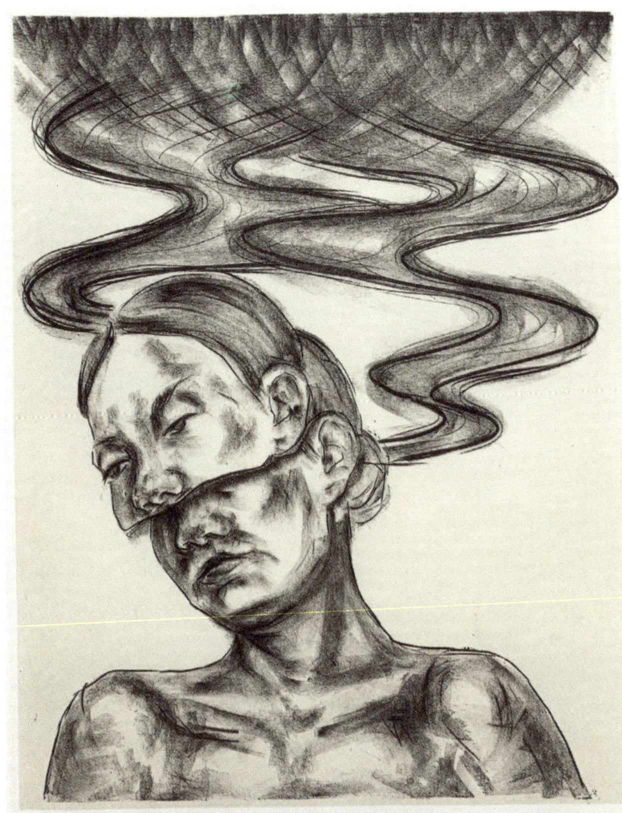

Valerie Syposz, *Embers*, foil lithography on gampi paper, backed on BFK Rives. 69 x 54cm, 2023.

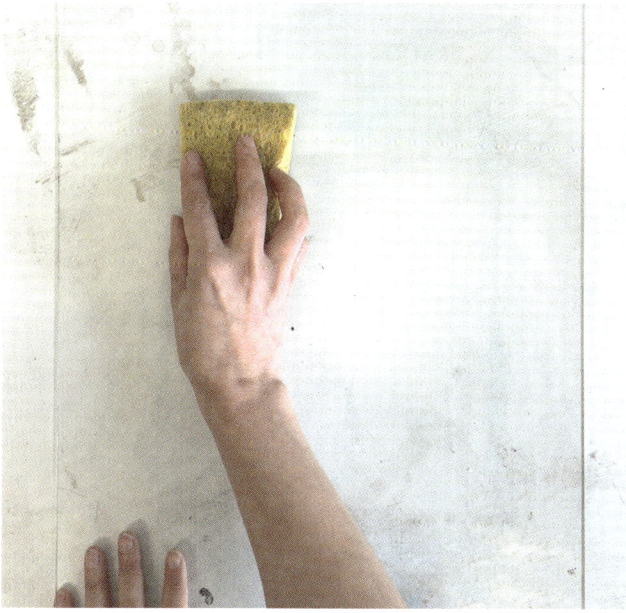

1. Dampen a surface large enough to hold the foil. It will need to be strong and rigid enough to carry around on location and have a desirable surface to draw on.

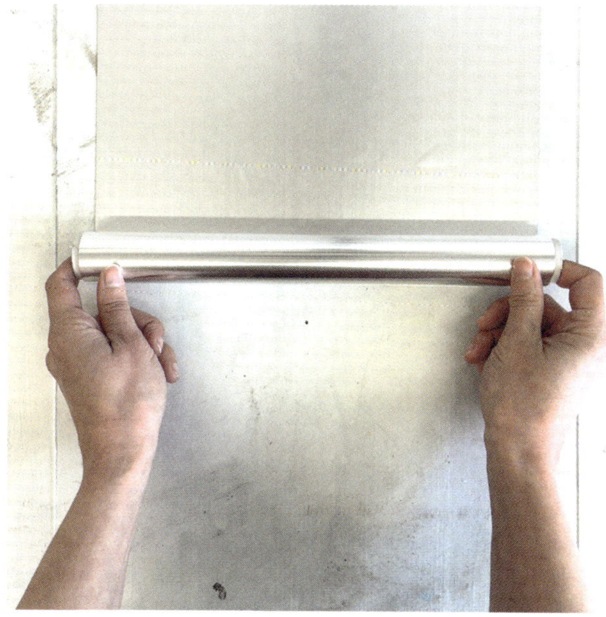

2. Roll the foil over the plate, cut the roll from the foil and tape the edges of the foil to your drawing surface. Try to avoid creating creases in the foil.

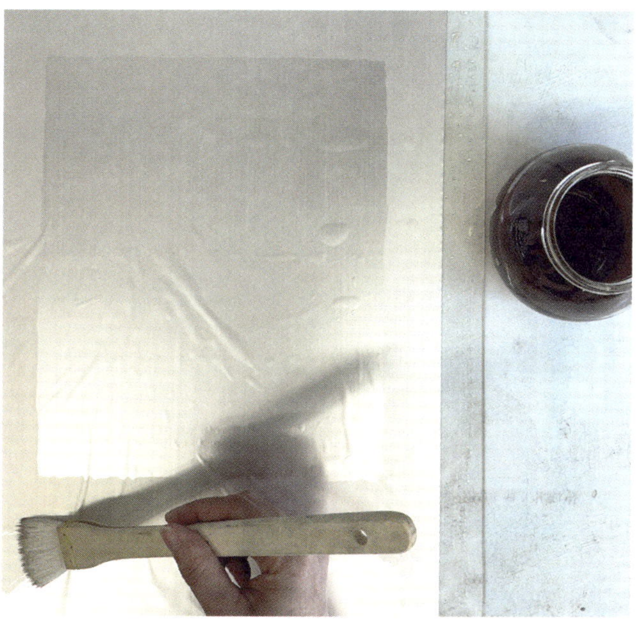

3. Use cola and a clean brush, saved only for this purpose, paint on a border of cola to desensitise that area, allowing space for hands to touch the edges of the plate when holding it.

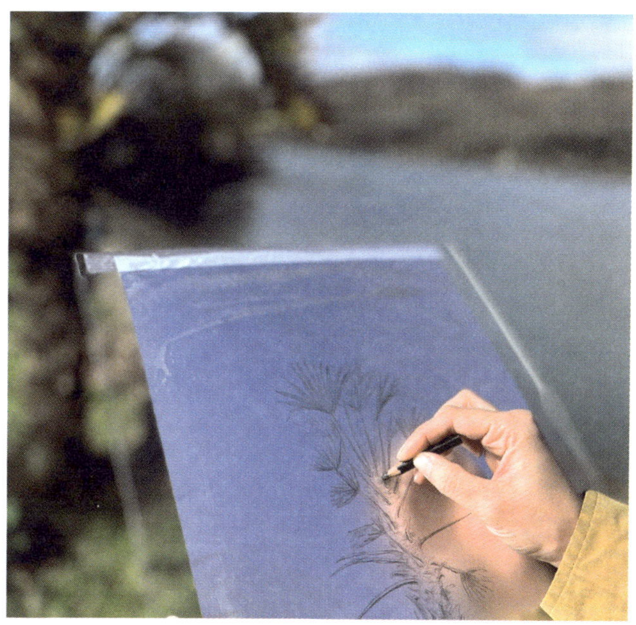

4. Your location and the weather will affect your material choices; try to avoid very hot, sunny places as this can make your greasy drawing material harder to handle.

Drawing outside *(continued)*

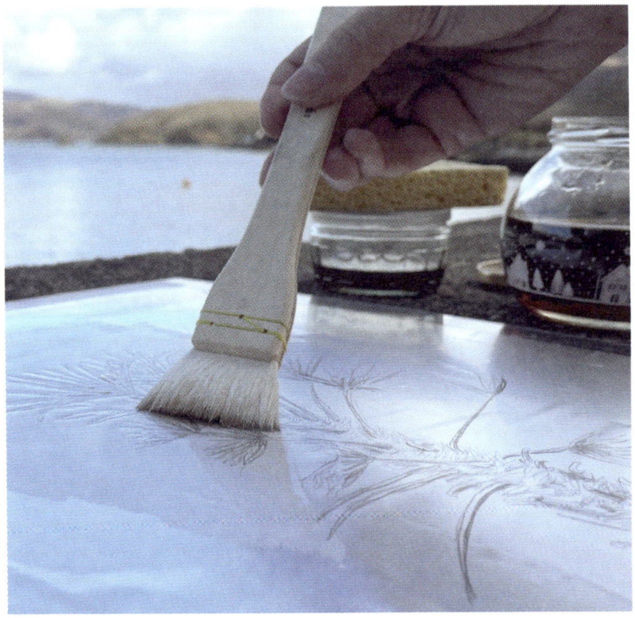

5. Again, using your clean, soft brush, which holds plenty of liquid, gently brush the cola over the plate, taking care not to smudge or carry grease over the rest of the plate.

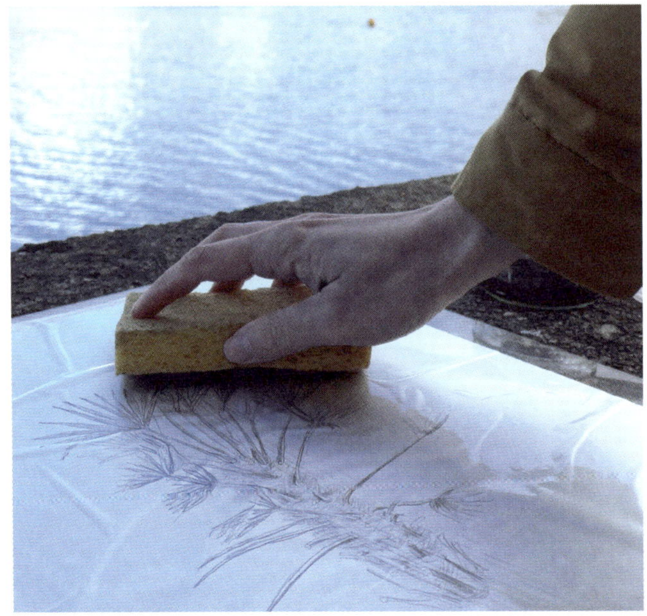

6. Using a sponge, apply a thin layer of gum arabic to the surface of the plate and allow it to dry. The gum will create a protective layer on the non-image area of your plate.

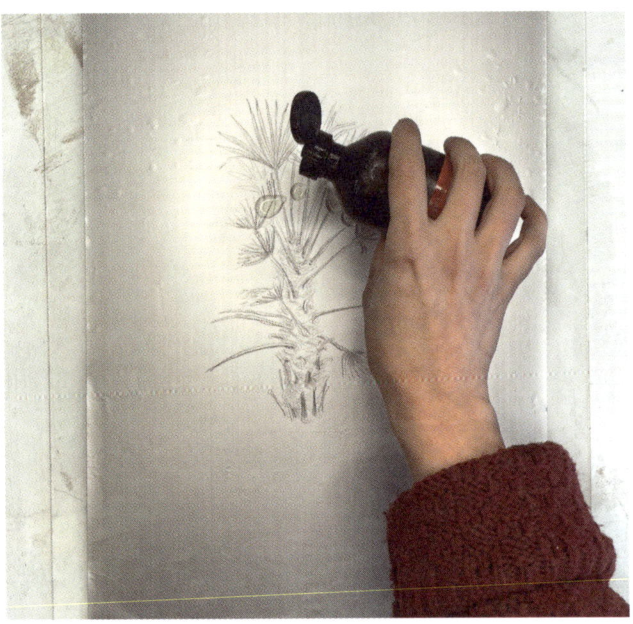

7. When back in the studio, using a little vegetable oil and dry cotton wool or a soft dry cloth, gently massage the plate to remove the non-permanent drawing material.

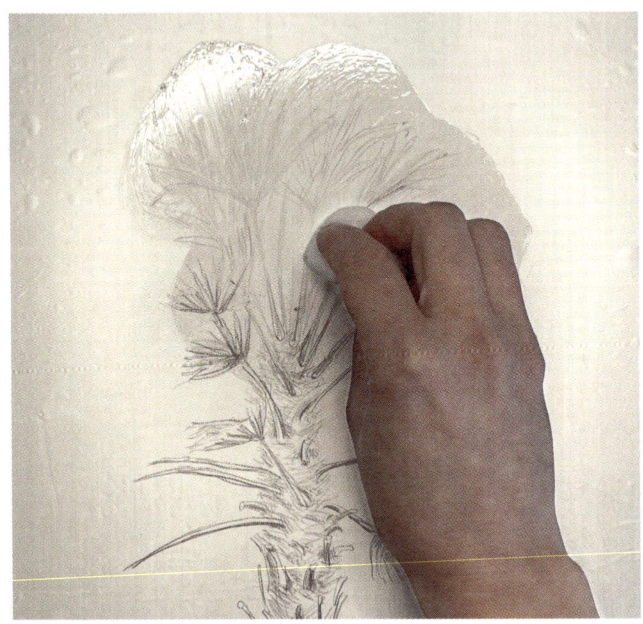

8. The gum arabic will protect the non-image area from the oil as the water did in the previous process example. Remove all traces of oil with the cotton wool.

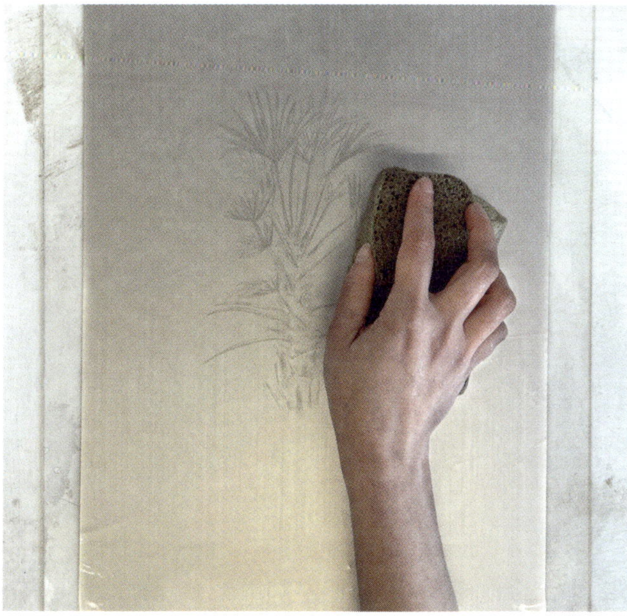

9. Dampen the plate with your sponge to remove the gum arabic layer. It may feel a little slimy with the remaining gum on it. Ink up the plate as normal.

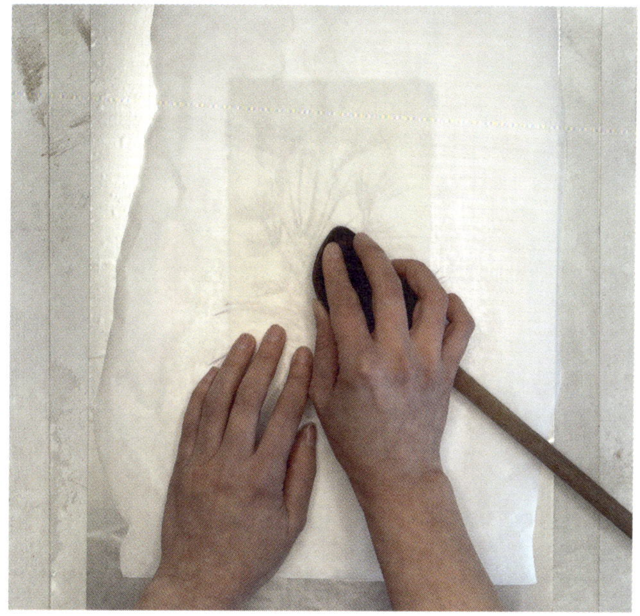

10. After inking up and drying the plate, print by hand using a wooden spoon to burnish. If your press is big enough, and your drawing surface strong enough, you can run it through a press.

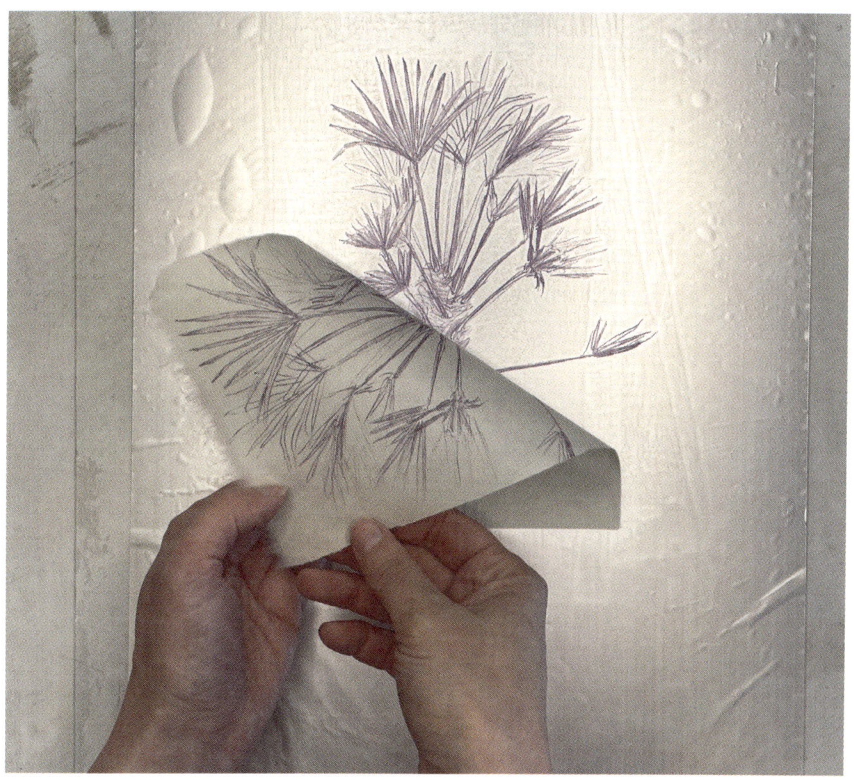

11. Slowly peel back your paper to reveal your print. In this example I am using a thin Japanese paper, which doesn't require dampening, but which needs firm hand burnishing.

Exploring monotype

When you have etched a drawing onto your plate you can start to develop it with monotype. Monotype is a planographic process wherein ink is applied directly to the plate in a painterly way. The ink is held on the plate temporarily and is removed when the print is taken, producing one distinct print. The plate is then cleaned and a fresh image is produced on the plate. The image can be produced additively, by painting/applying ink to the plate, or it can be produced reductively, where the plate is fully coated in ink and then the ink is wiped away using rags to produce the light areas of the image. Or the monotype can be produced using a combination of both methods. Monotype can be used as a process on its own to create a print or it can be used in combination with other processes like foil lithography, where the ink is applied to the lithographic plate.

Scarlett Rebeca, *Portrait of Xin with Fish*, monotype, 10 x 15cm, 2022.

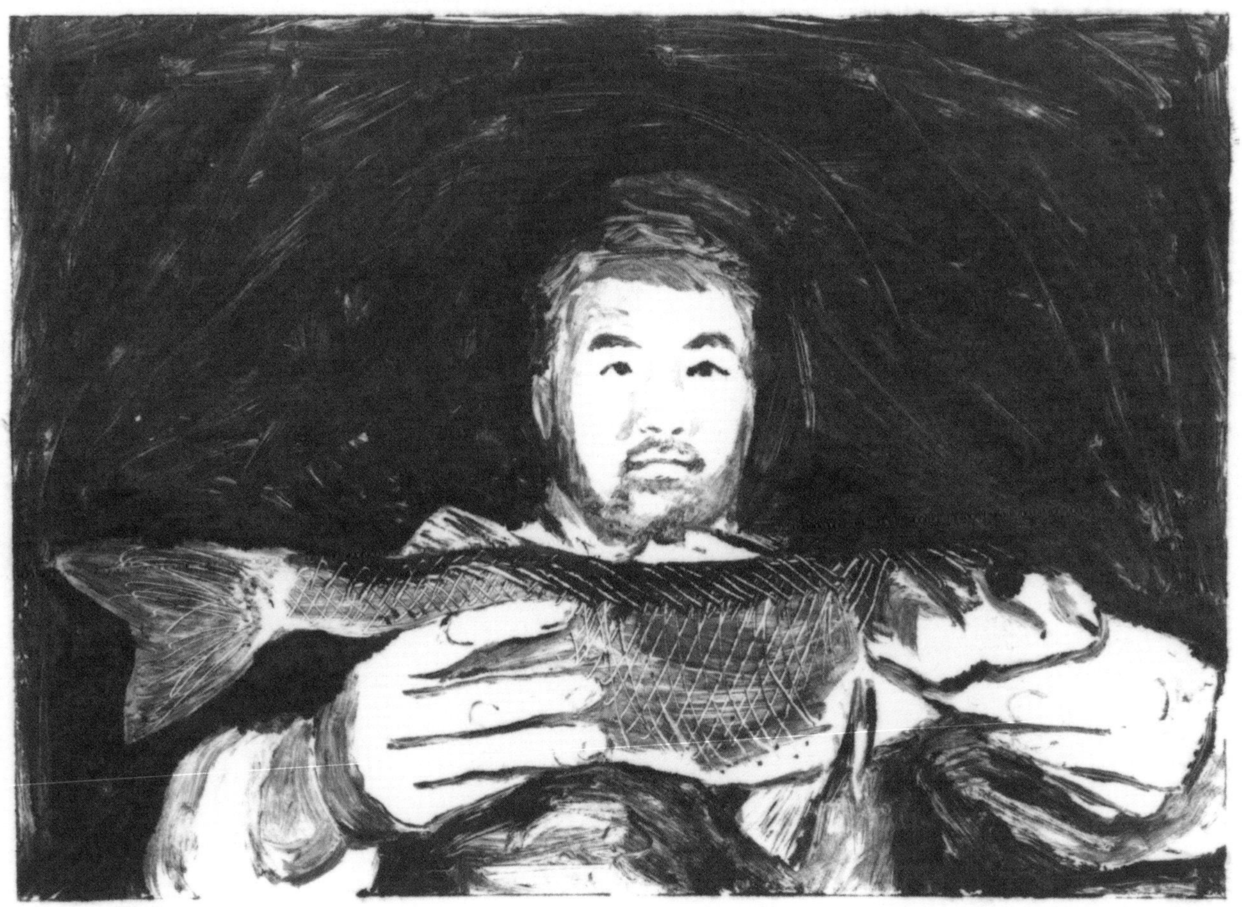

Exploring monotype

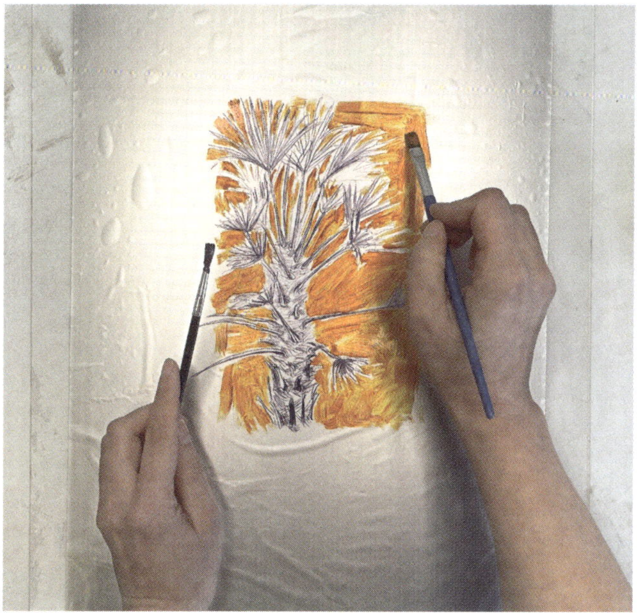

1. After inking up the plate normally, it must be dried. Paint the monotype elements onto the plate with printing inks loosened with tack reducer or oil. Avoid touching the lithographic areas as this can blur those areas.

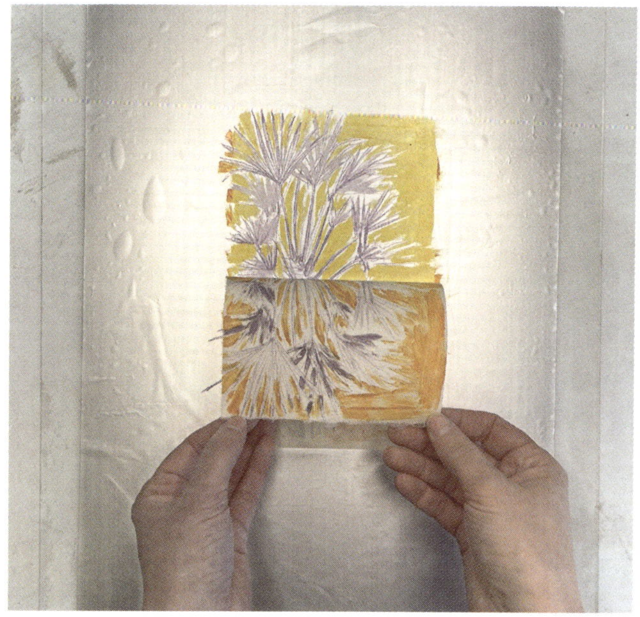

2. The ink on the plate will appear darker than it will on the print and will be lighter than the same colour ink used for the lithographic elements. This creates a wonderful range of tones.

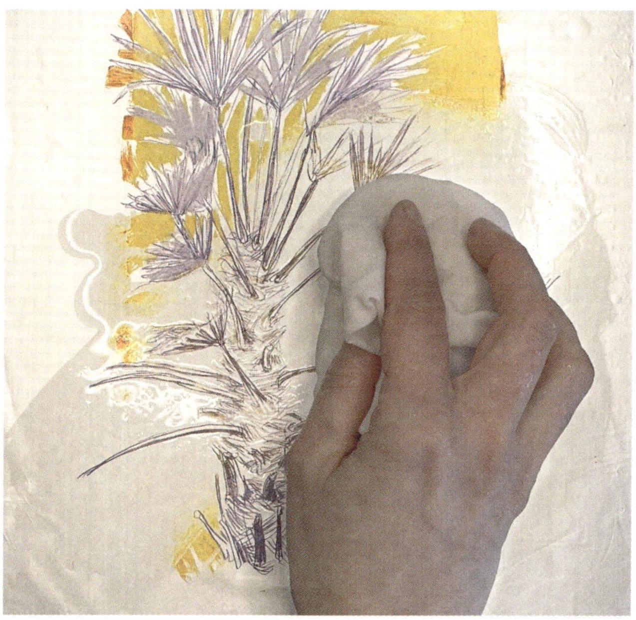

3. Use a damp cloth to collect the left-over ink on the plate after printing, before inking up again in the normal lithographic way. Some monotype ink may stick to the lithographic image area and muddy the colour.

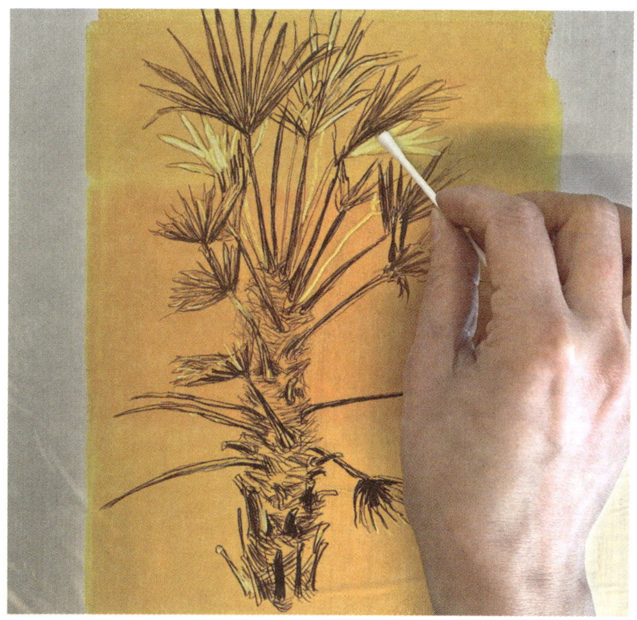

4. Using a looser viscosity ink, with oil added to it, roll ink straight over the lithographic image when the plate is dry. This ink will sit on top of the existing ink. Wipe away areas to bring back the light.

Exploring monotype *(continued)*

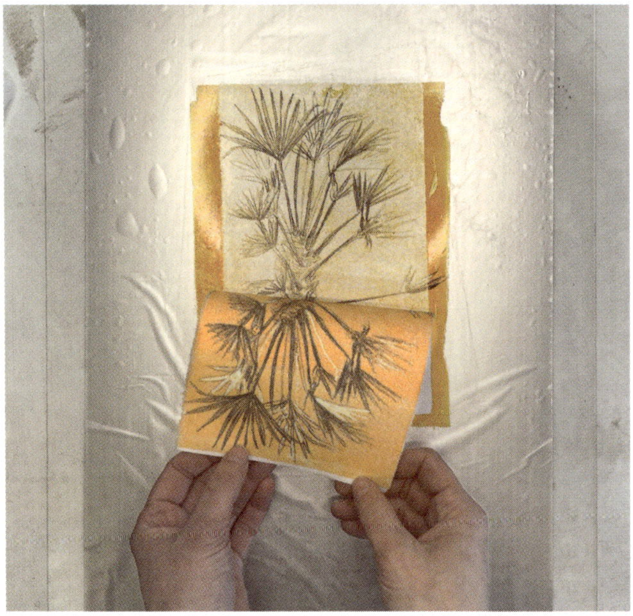

5. In this print reveal you can see how the purple layer of lithographic drawing now appears to be more of a brown hue with the addition of the overlaid orange layer.

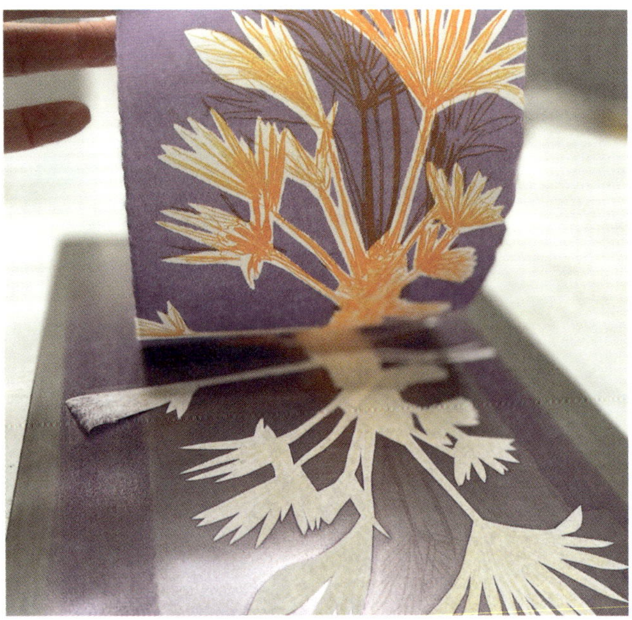

6. You can use an additional plate solely for a separate monotype layer without including lithographic elements. Use paper masks to selectively choose where the monotype layer will transfer.

Any monotype marks you make on the plate will be removed when you dampen your plate again, so you get a chance to test out a variety of different marks alongside a permanent image. By changing different elements of your prints, you can create images with completely different atmospheres to them. These prints can be created as finished works in themselves or they can be used as studies, as a way of experimenting with elements of the image before developing a final print.

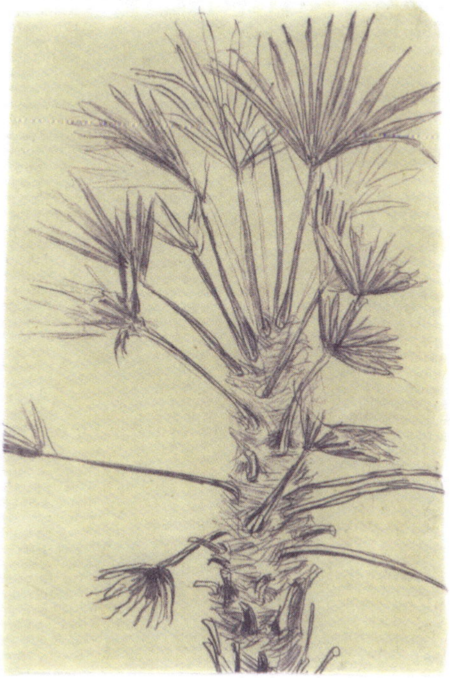

Foil lithograph in purple printed onto light green Japanese paper.

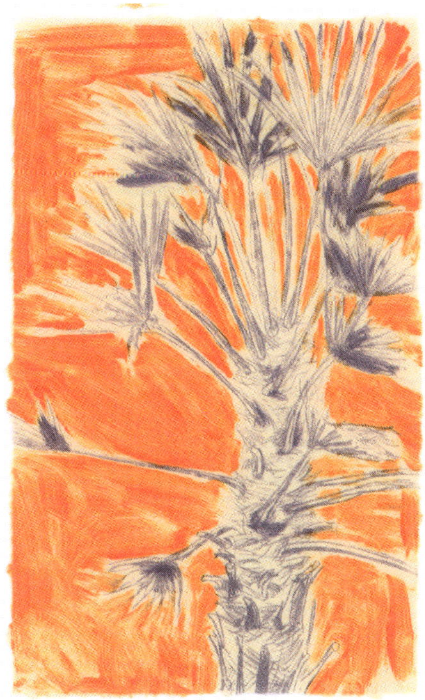

Foil lithograph in purple, with orange and purple monotype elements added with a paintbrush to the lithographic plate.

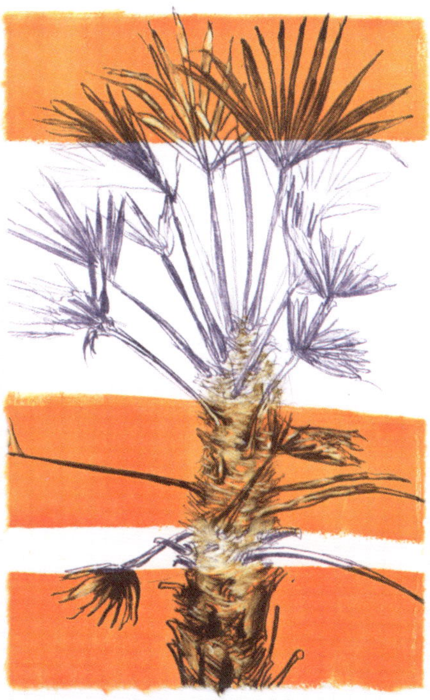

Foil lithograph in purple, with modified orange ink selectively rolled over the lithograph plate, with some areas removed with cotton bud.

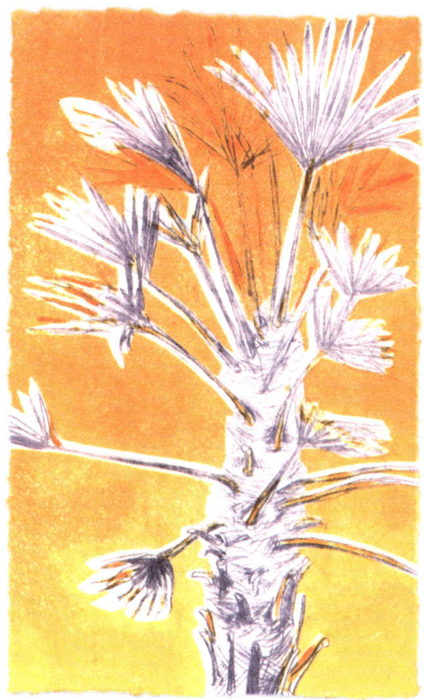

First layer: purple lithograph with added orange monotype. Second layer: monotype plate with orange blend roll, and paper mask.

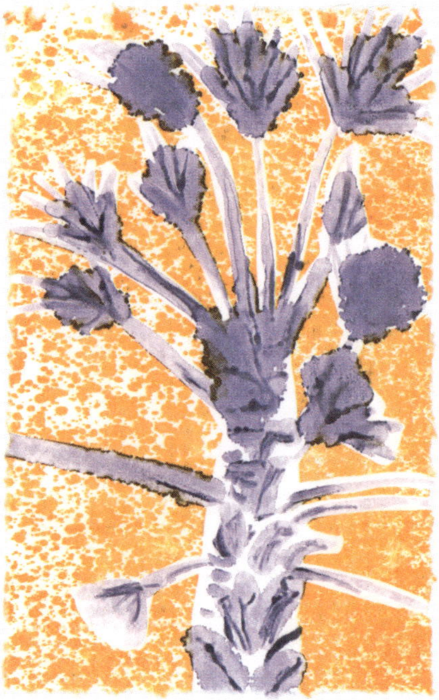

Splatter effect lithographic image in orange ink, with additional purple monotype details in purple ink mixed with solvent. Note the bloom of the solvent in the ink.

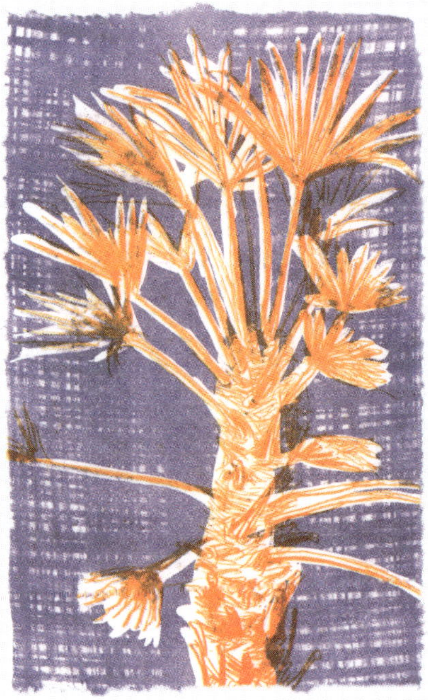

First layer: foil lithograph drawing printed in orange. Second layer: foil lithograph pattern drawing printed in purple.

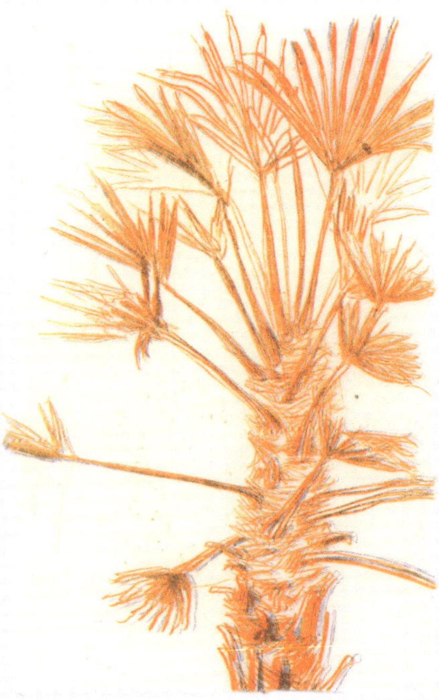

First layer: foil lithograph drawing printed in purple. Second layer: same foil lithograph plate printed offset in orange.

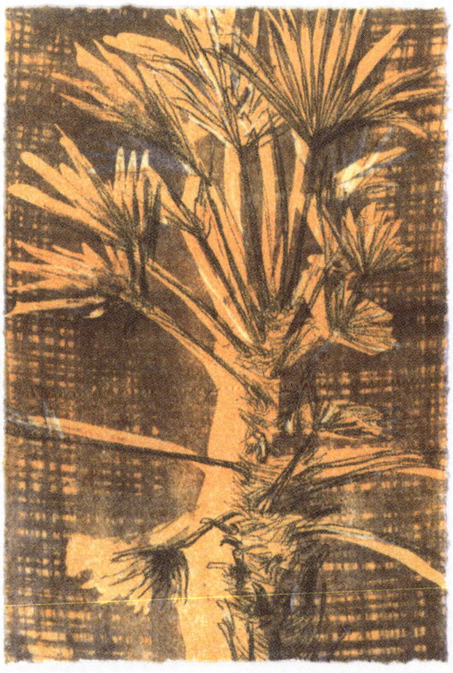

First layer: foil lithograph drawing printed in purple. Second layer: foil lithograph pattern drawing in purple, monotype layer in orange rolled over the plate.

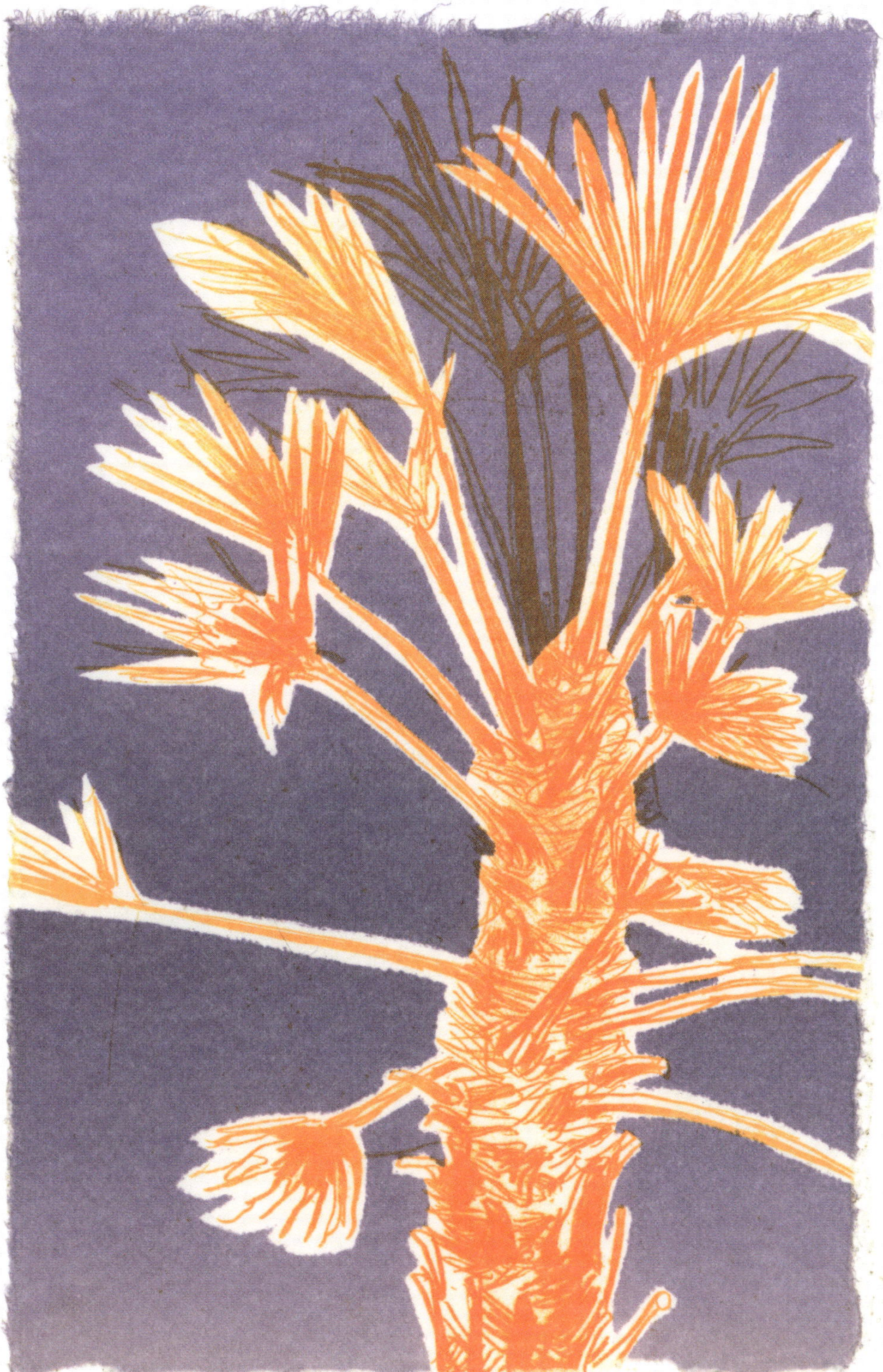

First layer: foil lithograph drawing printed in orange. Second layer: monotype plate with purple blend roll, and paper mask.

TROUBLESHOOTING

Accidental dry roll

The most common mistake that everyone makes with all lithography is inking up the plate without dampening it first. Without the protective layer of water, this will coat the whole plate in ink. But don't panic! You will be tempted to try to wipe off the ink with the sponge but **don't** do that. You'll just end up getting the sponge inky and contaminated and it won't last as long. The plate is smart and if you act quickly, it will remember which areas want to hold water and which ones want to hold ink.

To fix this mistake, cover the whole plate in water using a spray bottle or squeeze water from the sponge onto the plate. Roll back and forth over the plate with your roller, spreading the water over the plate, the unwanted ink will stick to the roller and slowly clear from the plate. If there is any ink left on the plate that won't come off, you'll just need to carefully wipe it away with a damp rag.

If your plate has been left too long in this state, with ink all over it, it can be difficult to clean it completely by just rolling over it. Instead use a little oil and a damp rag to remove all the ink. Wipe off all traces of oil with a clean damp cloth and then ink up the plate again carefully.

Soap

If you are using soap as a drawing material you can sometimes get streaky marks, or unusual marks. Soap is unpredictable; the best thing to do when using soap is to etch from the bottom of the plate to the top. That way when the soap streaks down on the plate when it's being etched, it will come into contact with desensitised areas and won't spread the marks.

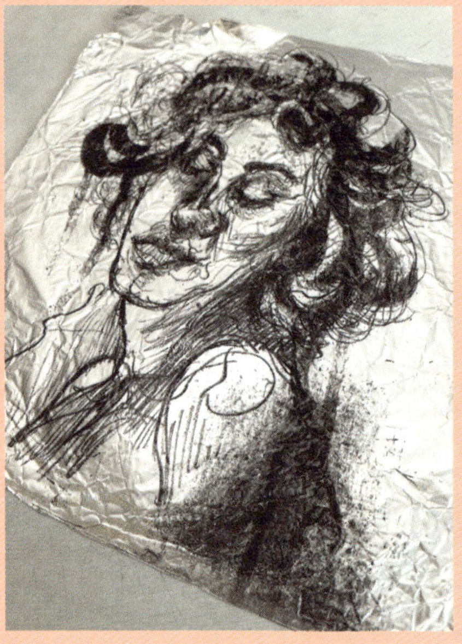

Soap drip marks on a foil lithograph plate, made by the cola when etching.

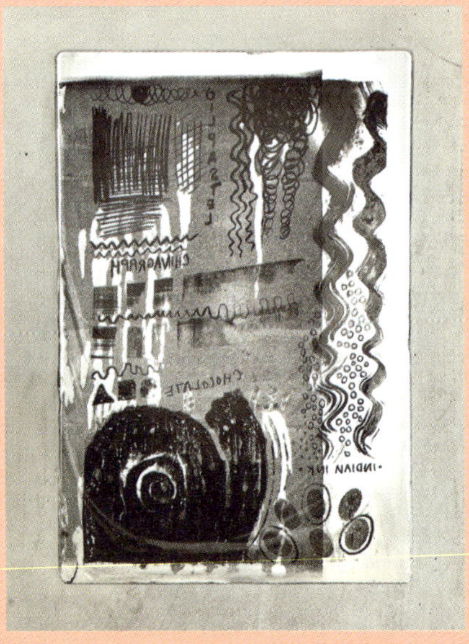

Ink will stick to the entire plate if a foil lithograph plate is inked up while it's dry. It needs the layer of water to act as a barrier between the plate and the ink.

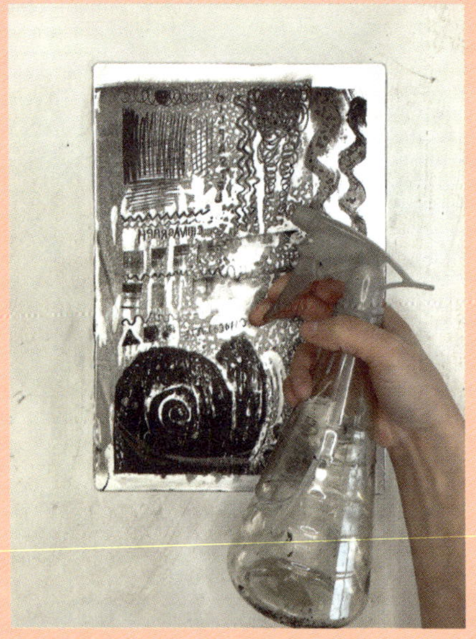

Do not attempt to collect the ink with your sponge as you will just contaminate your sponge. Generously spray water onto the plate.

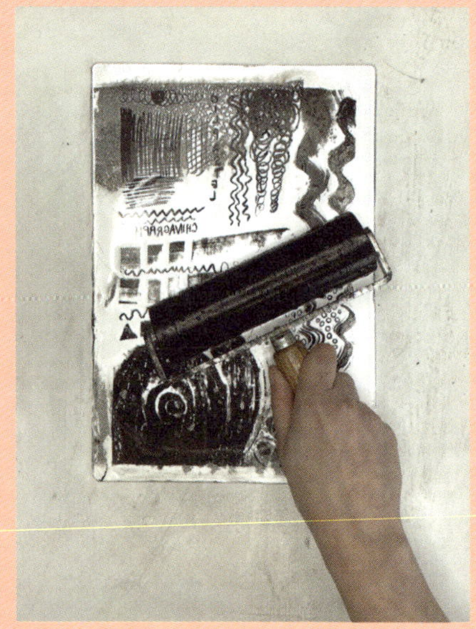

Use your roller to collect the ink. Quickly roll back and forth, spreading the water over the plate; the ink on the plate will attach to the roller instead.

Print too light

If your print is too light then you may not have added enough ink to your plate, your paper could have been too dry, or, if printing by hand, you didn't burnish with enough pressure.

Print too dark

If your print is too dark and you are losing detail then you have probably over-inked the plate, so try inking it with fewer rolls next time. Double-check your inking surface and roller, make sure the ink rolled out is velvety and not like orange-peel. Try removing some ink from the ink slab and roll the ink out more thinly. You may also need to replace your cola: if you have used it a few times it may have become contaminated or exhausted and won't be as effective. Remember too that it is unavoidable that your print will get darker and start to fill in over time.

If you are having problems with dark images and you can't work out why, try inking up your image without removing the drawing material with vegetable oil. The plate will ink up much darker all over if the oil isn't completely removed, or if the plate has been cleaned too vigorously, damaging the non-image area. Skip the cleaning step and ink up straight on top of the drawing material.

Paper sticking to plate

If your paper is coming away onto the ink of the plate then you may have oversoaked your paper or not blotted it dry enough, thus making it weaker. Or it could be a problem with the tackiness of your ink. If the ink is too tacky it won't want to let go of the plate and the paper. You will need to modify your ink slightly to reduce the tackiness. Scrape up your ink on your inking slab and mix in a tiny amount of tack reducer/petroleum jelly/oil and then roll it out fresh.

Greasy foil

If you're having problems with your plate that you can't work out the reason for, then test your foil. Sometimes if your foil is old, or it's getting towards the end of the roll then it won't work correctly with this process. You need to remember that this is just kitchen foil we're using – it hasn't been made for a printmaking process – so it may have been contaminated during the production process or from lying around the kitchen.

Test the foil by tearing off a piece of foil, don't worry about backing it to a plate, and pour cola over it. Rinse it under the tap and then try to ink it up. In theory, you haven't drawn onto the foil with anything greasy so there shouldn't be anything on the foil to attract the ink. If the foil does start to darken and pick up ink then you know that the foil is contaminated. Buy yourself a new roll of foil.

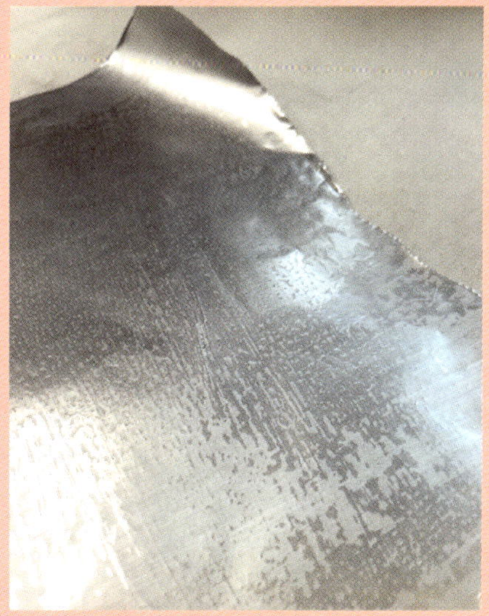

Water droplets sitting on a test piece of foil, showing that it is contaminated and not suitable for foil lithography.

NOTES ON CLEANING UP

Aluminium foil is easily recyclable and can be recycled numerous times, so it's a great material to use when you're considering your environmental impact. Clean off all the ink from your foil using a damp oily rag and remove the tape. Collect up all your foil into a ball no smaller than a tennis ball. You should then be able to put it in your recycling but do check your local government recycling regulations if you're not sure.

You can also carefully cut the foil off the backing plate and keep it – but do watch out as it will take a long time to dry.

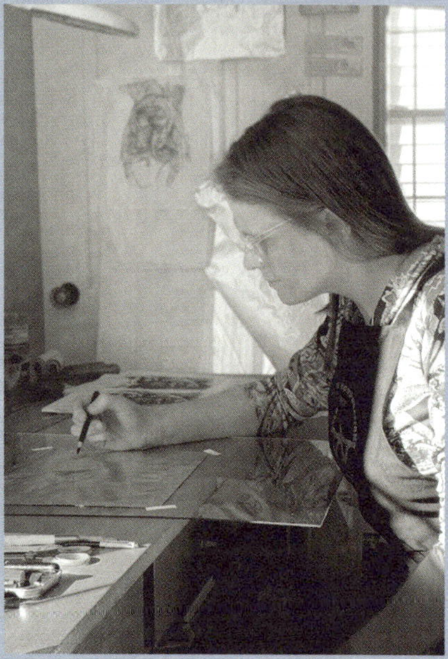

Valerie Syposz (Canada)

valeriesyposz.com

Valerie Syposz is a Canadian printmaker specialising in lithography and relief print. She received an MFA in printmaking at Tokyo University of the Arts in 2010, concentrating on ball-grained plate lithography. Valerie works from her home studio and exhibits internationally.

I love the entire process of printmaking – planning, preparing plates, printing, problem-solving: the craftsmanship involved. I think there is something very special about indirect art techniques, where the plates and blocks you spend hours, days, even weeks carving, drawing, and etching are not the finished product. All the extra steps required make the final artwork ever more rewarding.

I came to kitchen lithography at a time in my life where it seemed like creation was impossible. I had been working from home, printing by hand for several years. However, the wood engravings and woodcuts that were central to my craft required an immense amount of time and focus. Time and focus were luxuries I could no longer afford as parent and primary caregiver to two young children. Therefore, instead of struggling to continue the same creative process, I decided I needed to radically change my approach to art. It was at this point I first tried foil lithography, and I was instantly hooked.

There are a few factors that drew me to foil lithography. First off, I can print at home – something necessary for my current situation. Second, there is a directness to the medium, and accordingly, it can be a fast process. This has allowed me to fit printmaking into a difficult schedule, where I may only have one hour on any given day to focus on art. Most importantly, the possibilities for mark-making are endless. The experimental aspect of kitchen lithography has reawakened a sense of play and joy of exploration in my creation.

I have also changed the way I approach an image with foil lithography. Whereas previously I had the entire composition and colour scheme planned out, I now start with a simple sketch and a semi-formed idea of what the final print will look like. I work with multiple layers of foil, building up tones and gradation, bit by bit. After printing, I examine what is needed further, and adjust the next layer accordingly. The convenience and affordability of the material means I can experiment freely.

FACING PAGE
Valerie Syposz, *Dreamscape II*, foil lithography on calligraphy paper, backed on BFK Rives, 42 x 36cm, 2023.

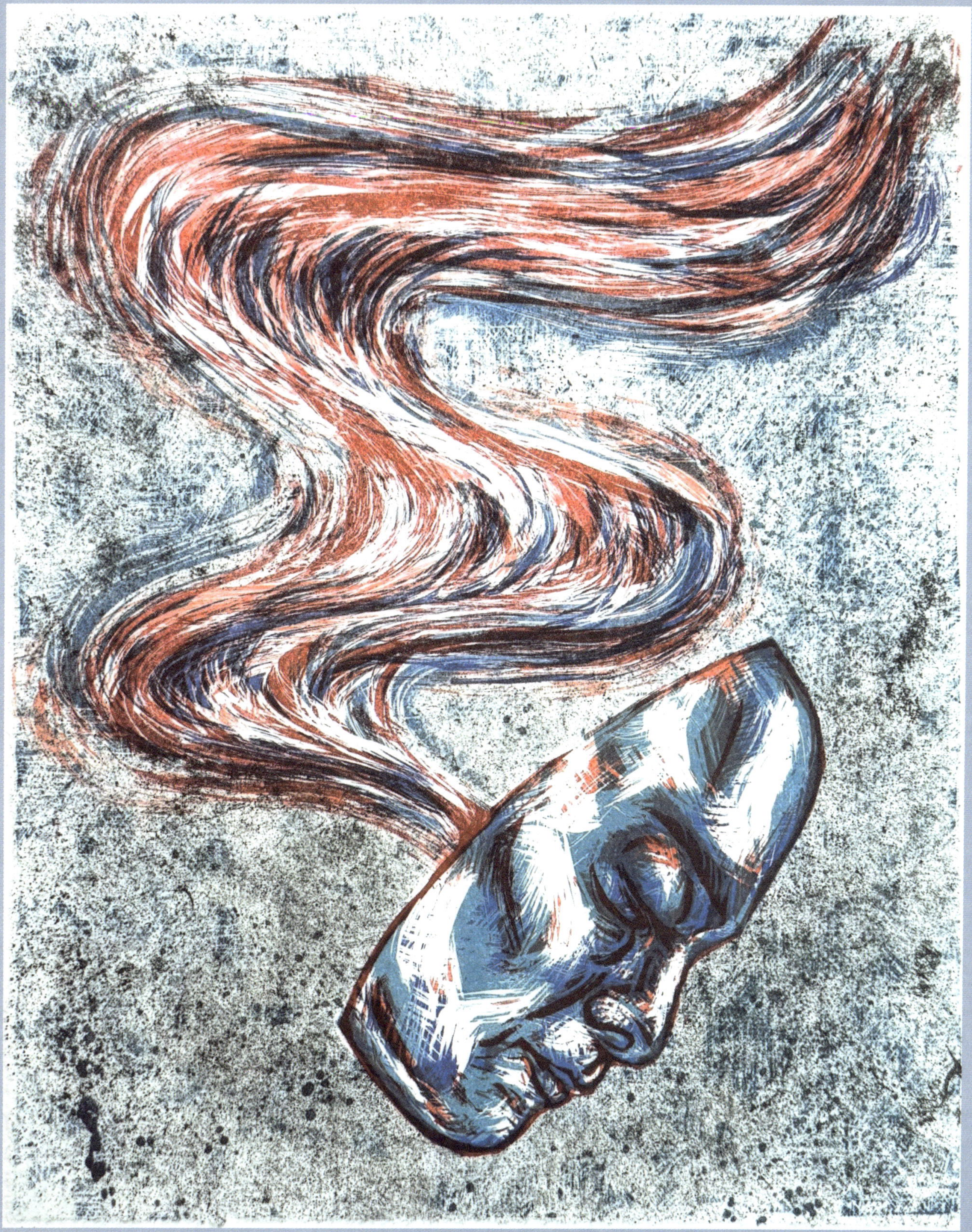

CHAPTER 5

Wood lithography

Wood lithography uses side grain wood, wood cut along the grain, as the lithographic matrix. Wood lithography is a fantastic development of the lithographic process that incorporates the beautiful and inimitable marks of the wood grain of the plate. You will also hear wood lithography being called Mokulito as it was developed in Japan in the 1970s by artist Ozaku Schisi. Mokulito translates from Japanese as *moku* – wood, *lito* – lithography. This process has also recently been popularised and further developed by Polish printmakers Ewa and Josef Budka.

The image-making within the planographic print family is very autographic; we draw onto the wood in the same way we would draw on a piece of paper. But with wood lithography the plate itself has an impact on the image as the wood grain gradually becomes more and more prominent as we print. The type of wood we choose for the matrix will impact the finished image.

One of the most exciting factors of the wood lithography process is that it straddles both planographic print and relief print. As we are using a piece of plywood as our lithographic plate, we can incorporate relief print principles and carve into the wood.

Once again we are considering the immiscibility of oil and water, as with foil lithography in the previous chapter, but the process is slightly different.

FACING PAGE
Inking up a wood lithography plate using a soft foam roller.

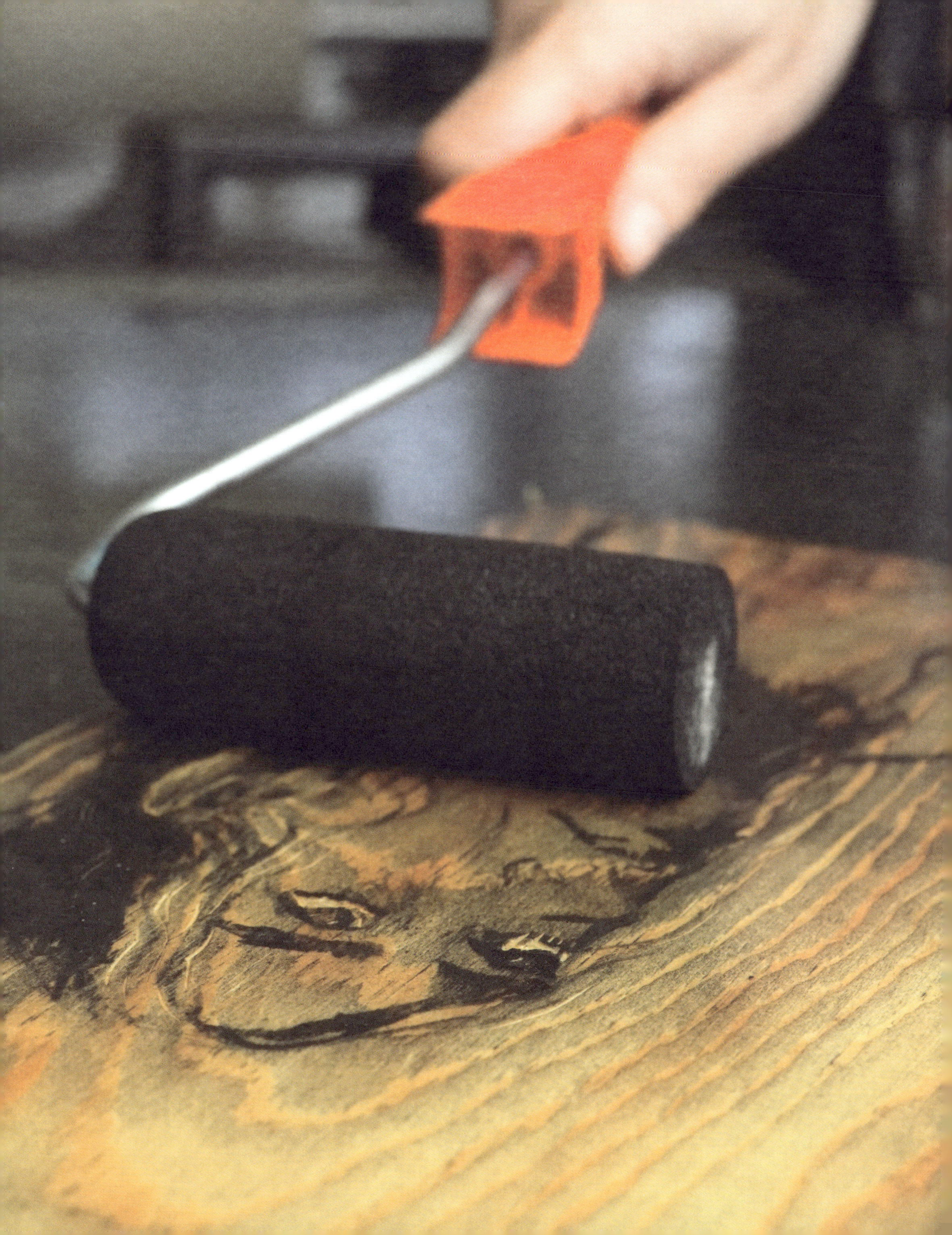

We will be drawing onto the plywood plate with greasy drawing materials, to attract the oil-based ink, and then we will coat the porous wood surface with gum arabic. The gum will create a hydrophilic (*water-attracting*) layer, which will attract and hold the water, which in turn repels the ink. Eventually, through the wear and tear of inking and printing, the gum layer will break down and the oils in the wood, combined with the oil-based printing ink will inevitably overpower the print.

Printing a wood lithography plate can feel like a race against time, with each print being slightly different from the last. This process is a brilliant gateway to thinking about your printmaking in a non-traditional way where making an exact edition is not the goal. Wood lithography will give you a varied edition where each print retains an aspect of the original drawing, but through a spectrum of subtle changes from light to dark. Each print within the variable edition will have its own unique qualities, while still being faithful to the edition, and you may find it difficult to choose your favourite.

Scarlett Rebecca, *Portrait of Esme*, wood lithography. Wood lithograph plate, alongside the first and last print in the edition of ten.

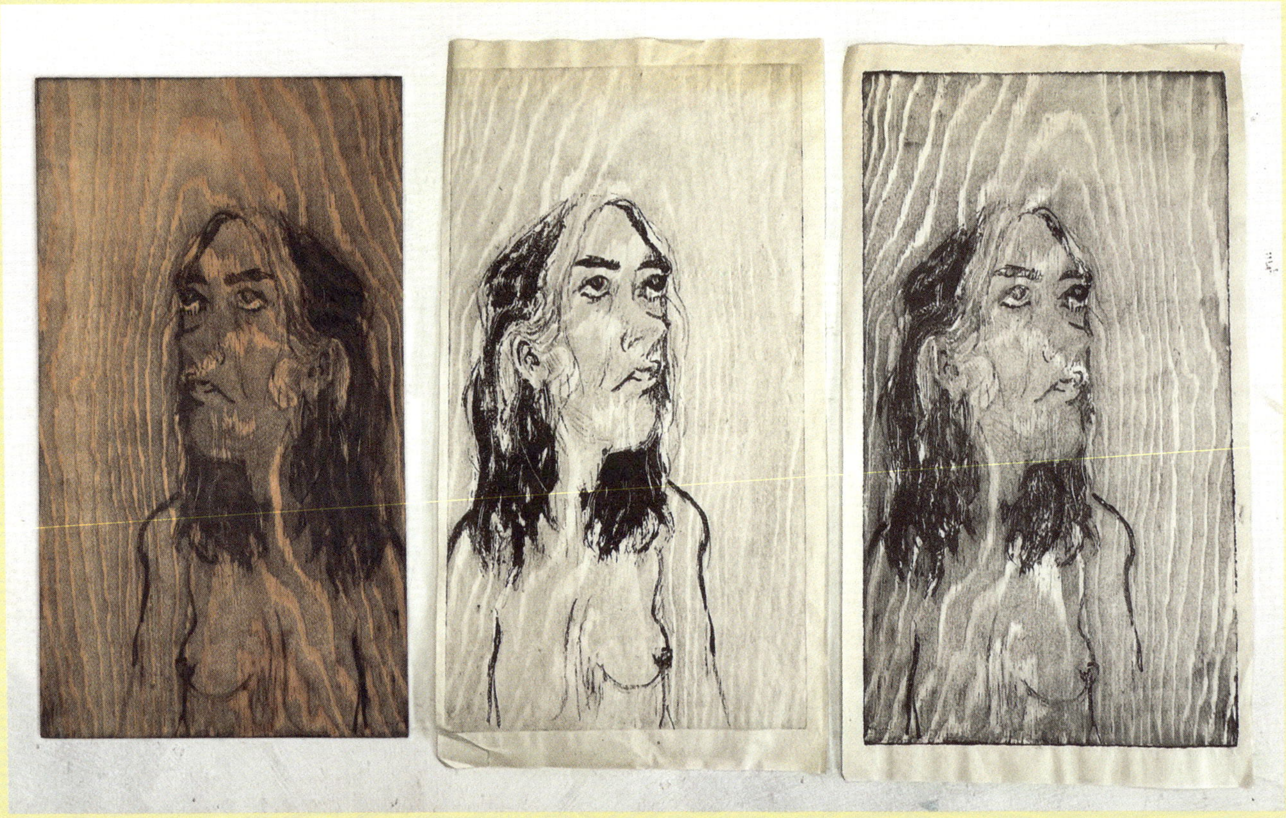

Which wood to choose

Hard plywood is best to use for wood lithography – maple, birch, beech, or whatever is available to you. The resin content in softer plywood can speed up the darkening of the plate or just make it unusable. Close-grain woods will be smoother, and wider-grain woods, or faster grown tropical plywood, can have an uneven surface even after sanding, which means they will be harder to draw onto, but they will create a prominent grain marking.

Use plywood that is at least 4mm thick. Anything thinner can bend and warp after it's gummed and when it gets wet, which will create a nightmare for registration. If you're using a press, you will be able to mitigate some of this bending through the pressure of the press.

The preparation, storage, and handling of the wood before it gets to you is difficult to account for and this can affect how the wood prints. Different types of wood will show through the woodgrain in varying strengths so it's a good idea to test a range of plywood types until you have found a supplier and a type of wood that you prefer.

A selection of different types of wood and sizes of plywood for use with wood lithography.

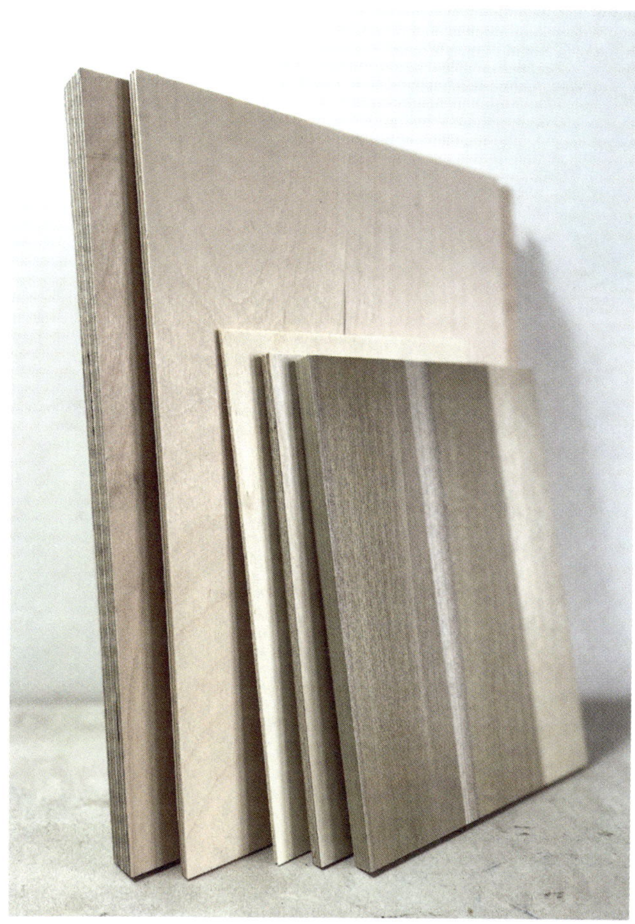

Preparing the plate

Choose a side of the plywood with the woodgrain that has the most appeal to you. A more pronounced woodgrain can be incorporated into your image.

Once you have finished sanding down the plate, wipe off the excess dust with a clean paintbrush or lint-free cloth and try to avoid touching the plate as much as you can, as you don't want to transfer any grease from your hands onto the plate. You won't transfer a fingerprint as with foil lithography, but a build-up of grease will darken that area much faster.

MATERIALS

- Plywood
- Sandpaper/wire wool
- Gum arabic
- French chalk
- Foam roller/traditional roller
- Cellulose sponge
- Water bowls for dampening water
- Printing ink
- Paper
- Water mister/spray bottle
- Lithographic tusche
- Photocopies and acetone
- Soap
- Conté crayons
- Carving tools

The materials needed for the wood lithography process.

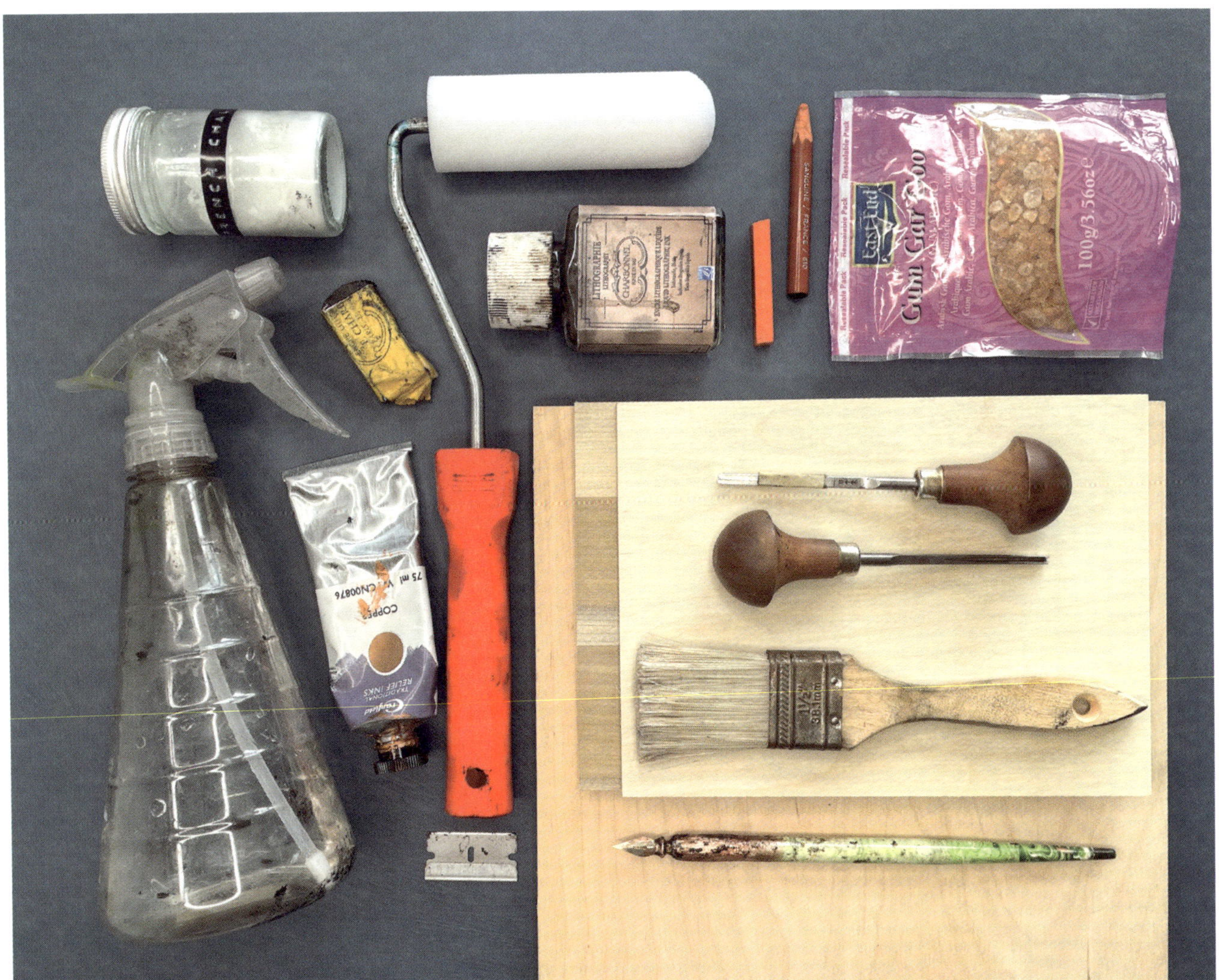

Preparing the plate

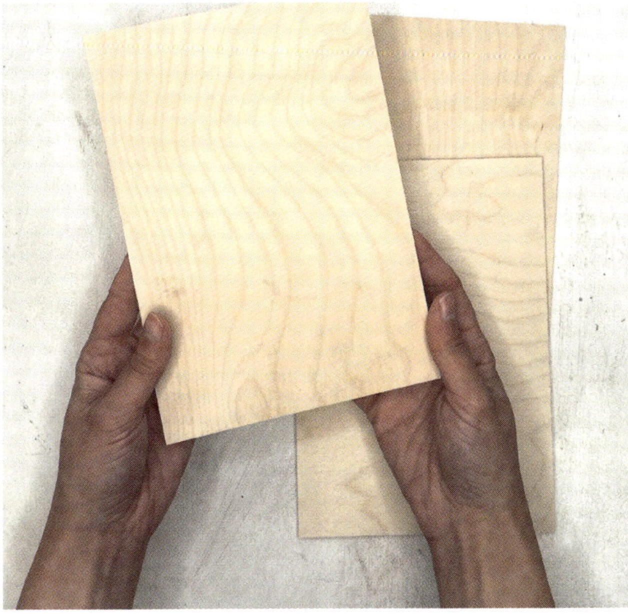

1. Select your piece of wood with consideration of its woodgrain. The woodgrain will become an aspect of the print's aesthetic so you can work it into your design.

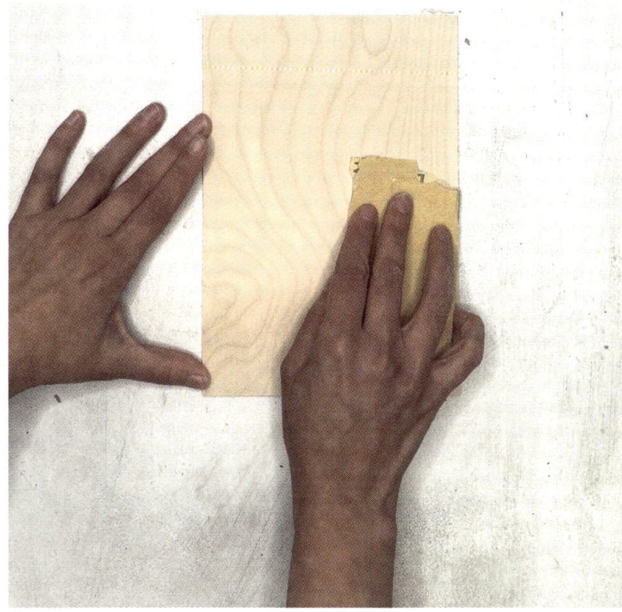

2. Sand the wood with medium sandpaper, sanding along the grain. You can use an electric sander to speed this up if you are working on a large scale.

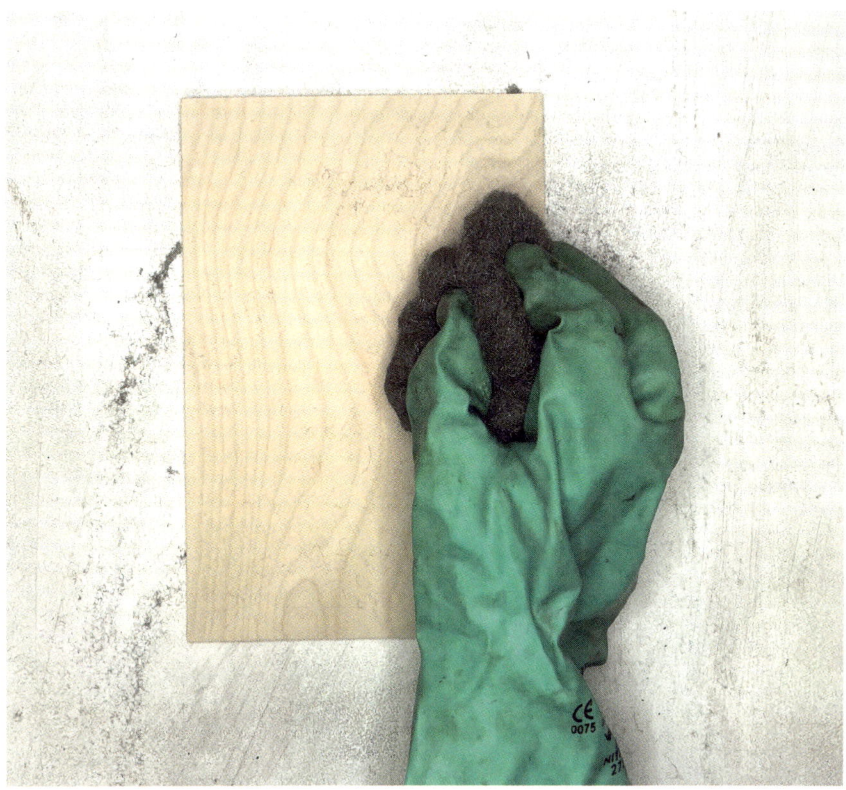

3. Polish the plate with fine sandpaper or wire wool for a smoother surface. A smooth surface will be easier to draw on but will show less woodgrain through initially.

Creating your image

I always recommend producing a test plate before you move on to create a more detailed image. Use this plate to test all the drawing materials you have and see what range of marks you can achieve. You should be considering this first plate as a learning experience rather than seeking to achieve a success, or risking a failure from it by placing too much importance on the resulting image.

Experiment with different tools to create a variety of mark-making. If you are using crayons or oil pastels, they will need to be quite heavily applied, or they won't fix to the plate. It helps when using crayons and oil pastels to warm the plate with a hot hairdryer or place it on a radiator to fix the crayon to the wood after drawing. You will find that the crayon marks will print well at first but will detach from the plate quickly, and so won't be reproduced in later prints in the edition.

Areas of the plate left without any drawing material will pick up a light amount of ink along the grain of the wood. It's important to allow space for the woodgrain to show through. You may feel compelled to fill in all the available space on the plate with drawing material but prints which allow space for the woodgrain to be seen are the most successful. The wood grain is a feature of this process, so you need to give it the space to shine through.

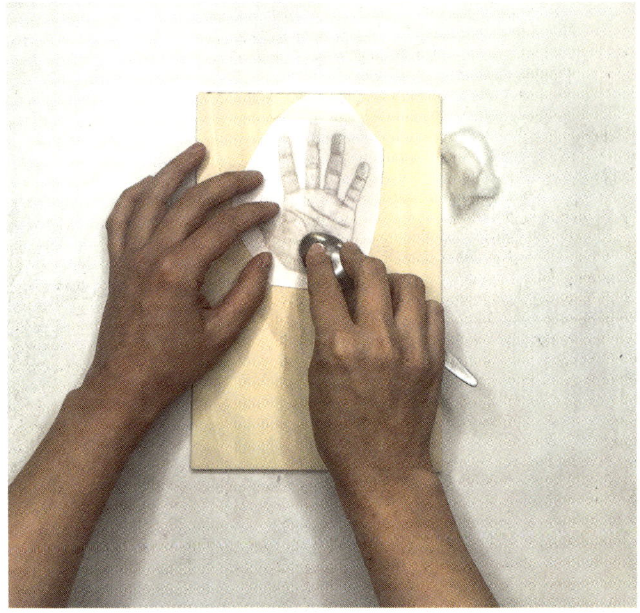

1. Use fresh photocopies or laser prints to transfer photographic imagery onto the plate. Tape the photocopy to the plate and use cotton wool to apply acetone to the back of the photocopy.

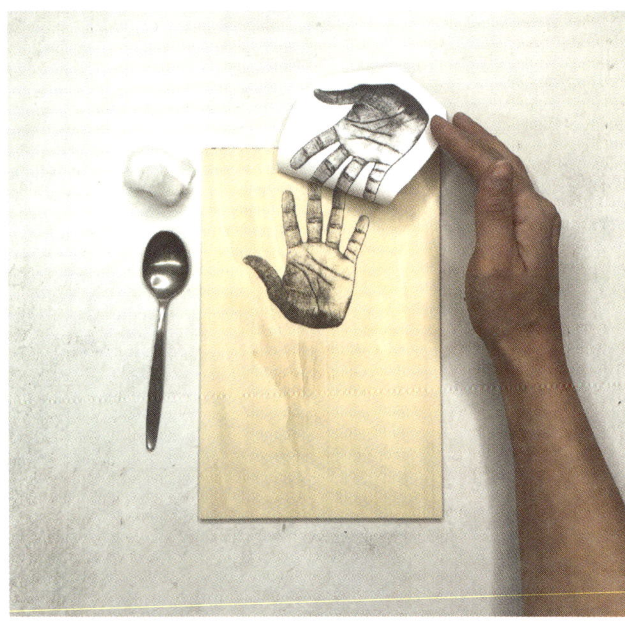

2. Working quickly, use firm pressure with a metal spoon to burnish the back of the photocopy to transfer the toner to the plate. You can also run this through a press with a sheet of plastic on top.

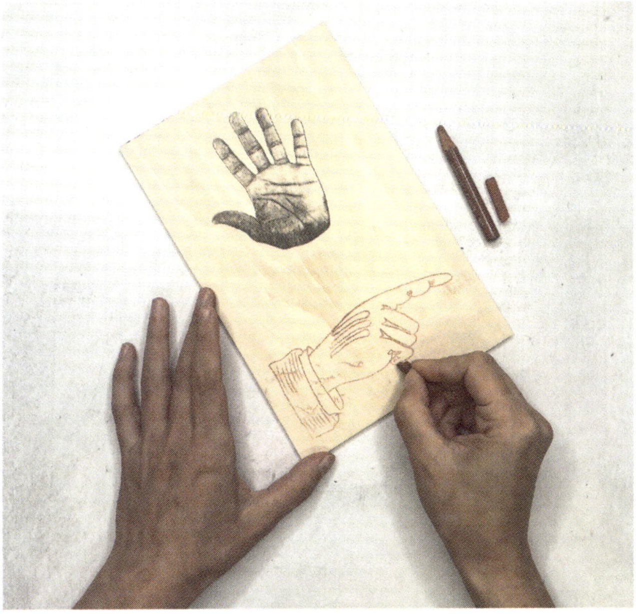

3. To make an initial sketch without leaving a greasy mark, draw a guide onto the plate with conté crayon, or chalk-based crayons. These drawing materials don't contain grease so won't print.

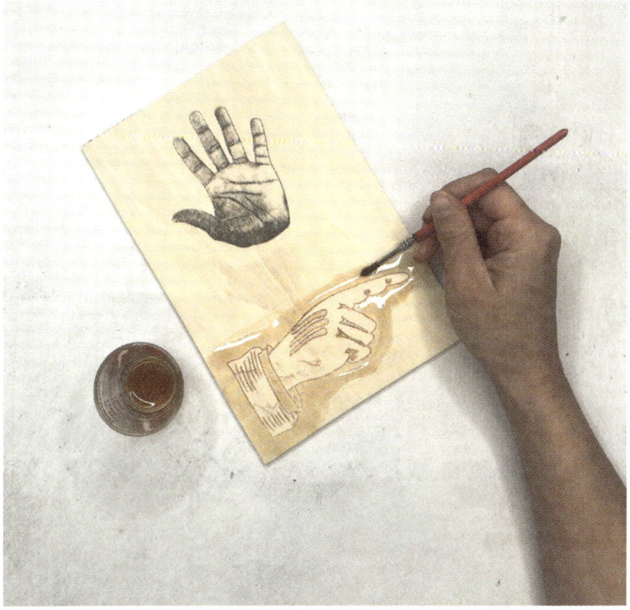

4. Gum arabic can be used as a resist to protect areas of the plate from the drawing material. Apply a generous layer of gum to form a barrier on the plate as it will absorb into the woodgrain.

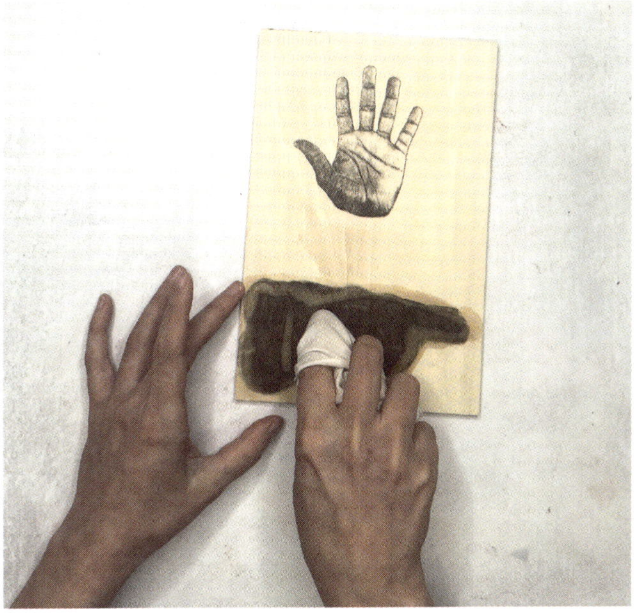

5. To create solid dark tones, rub diluted printing ink into the area you want to darken. To retain some detail of the woodgrain, buff the printing ink to a thin layer with a cloth.

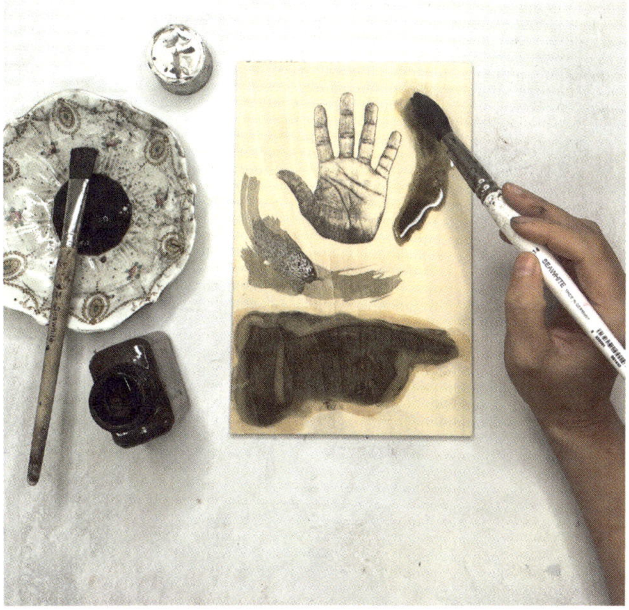

6. Apply undiluted tusche direct to the block with a brush for solid marks or try different dilutions for varying tones. Pool water onto the plate and drop tusche into the water to create reticulated marks.

Creating your image *(continued)*

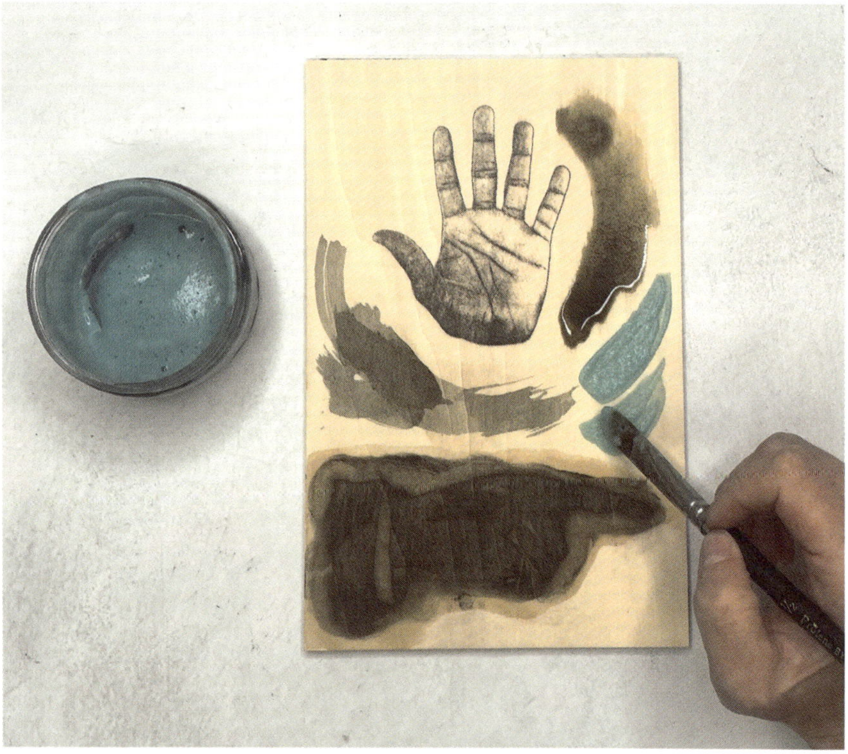

7. Soap marks vary depending on the soap you are using, as the amount of grease/oil in the soap is not dependable like a specialist drawing material. You may get faint marks or strong marks, so test what you have.

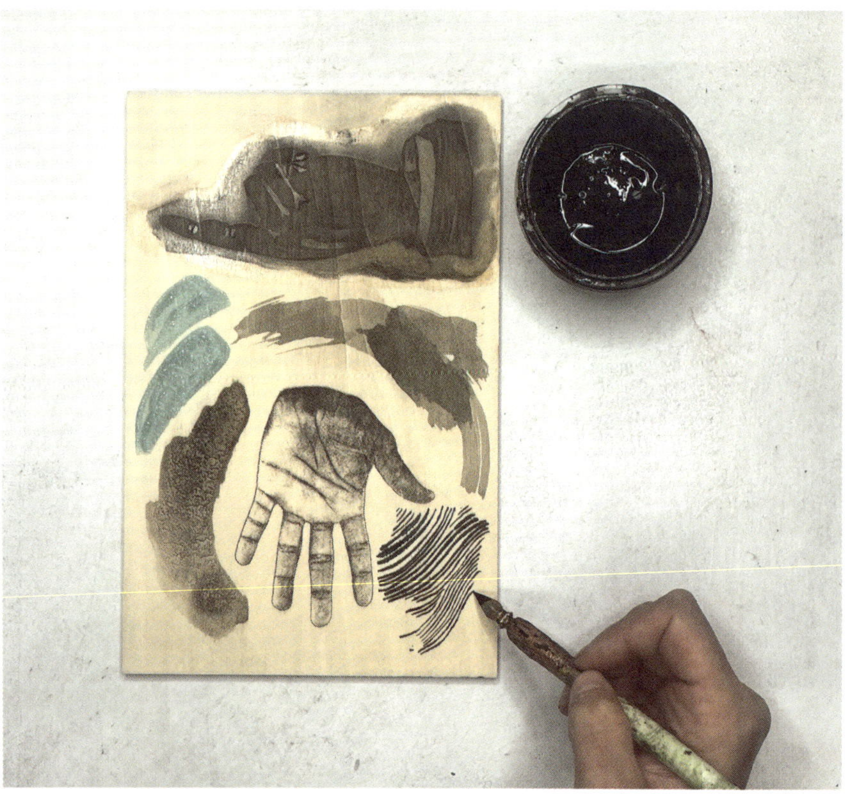

8. Tusche, diluted printing ink or stopping out varnish can be used with a dip pen. Don't dilute your drawing material too much as it will bleed into the woodgrain and lose definition.

Gumming the plate and adding carved marks

When your drawing material is dry and you're happy with the image, you will need to seal the non-image areas with gum. The gum will soak into the wood and create a hydrophilic film that will attract water and repel the printing ink.

While the plate is curing with the gum on it you can carve into it. Anywhere you carve will create a non-image area that will stay clean and crisp and won't show the woodgrain through. As the wood lithography plate darkens you will have areas of dark tone from the inked image, areas of mid-tone from the wood grain and areas of light where you have carved away, so try to think in these three tones when carving into your image.

As when you were drawing on your plate, consider the marks you are making while you carve. Vary the marks: change the size, the shape, the distribution and the direction of your carving. You will find that carving along the grain is easier than carving against it so make sure your tools are sharp and that you take care not to apply excessive pressure when carving in case you slip and accidentally cut areas of the plate, or worse, cut yourself.

You don't need to carve very deeply into the block; if you are experienced with woodcut then you will be used to this, but be aware that if you will be inking up with a soft foam roller the ink can be squashed into the carved recesses and be held there – so very fine or shallow lines can fill in with ink.

As always, it's best to test out the range of marks you can achieve on your test plate before moving on to a developed design. We wait until after the plate has been coated in gum and allowed to dry before carving the block because it is a very demonstrative process to carve, and it would be near impossible to carve the block without touching it. If we carved the block before gumming it we would transfer grease to the block with our hands or smudge the drawing material.

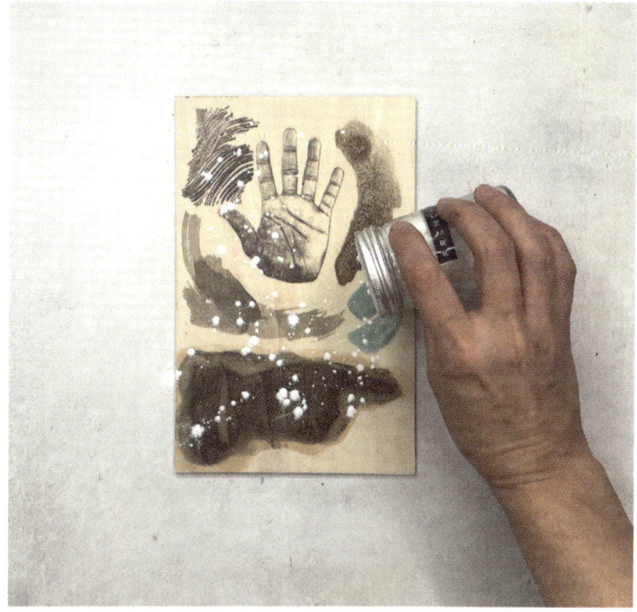

1. Sprinkle French chalk or talc over the plate to break the surface tension and help draw the gum close to the greasy drawing material.

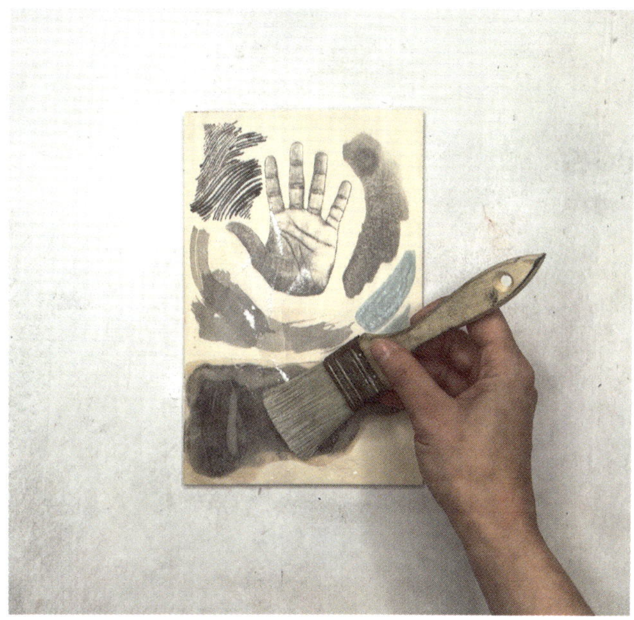

2. Use a soft brush to spread the French chalk over the plate and into the woodgrain. Avoid using a cloth or cotton wool, as it will get caught in the woodgrain.

Gumming the plate *(continued)*

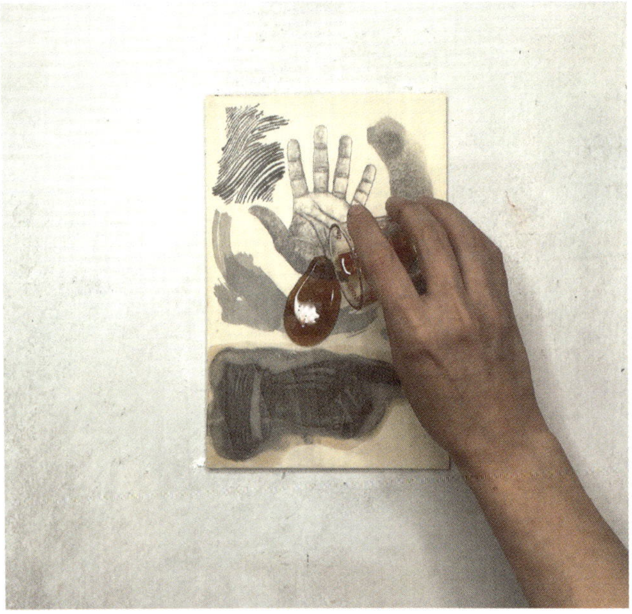

3. Apply liquid gum arabic generously to the plate, allowing it to soak into the wood. The drawing material on top of gum resists will come away now, so wipe it off with a cloth.

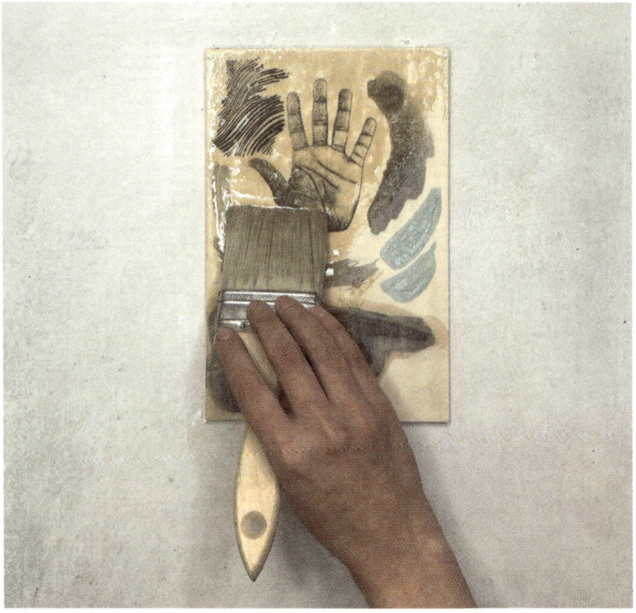

4. After 5 minutes, once the wood has soaked in most of the gum, apply a second layer of gum, but avoid letting the gum pool on top of greasy drawing areas.

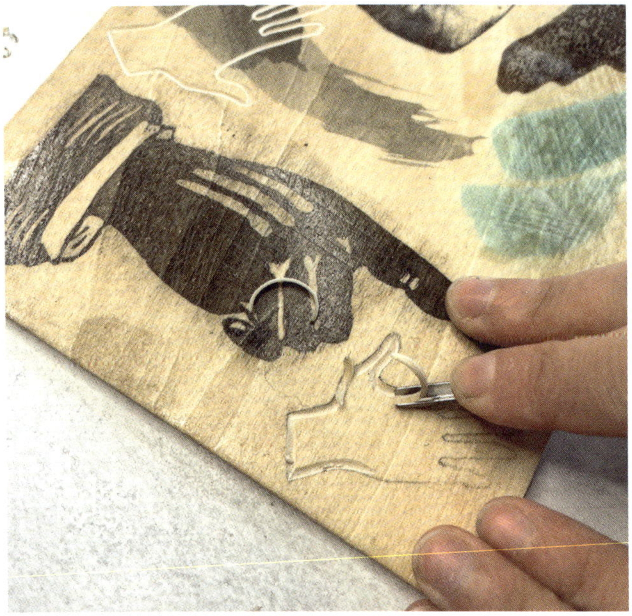

5. Once the gum is dry, use your carving tools as you would drawing tools, varying your mark-making, creating white lines. You don't need to carve too deeply.

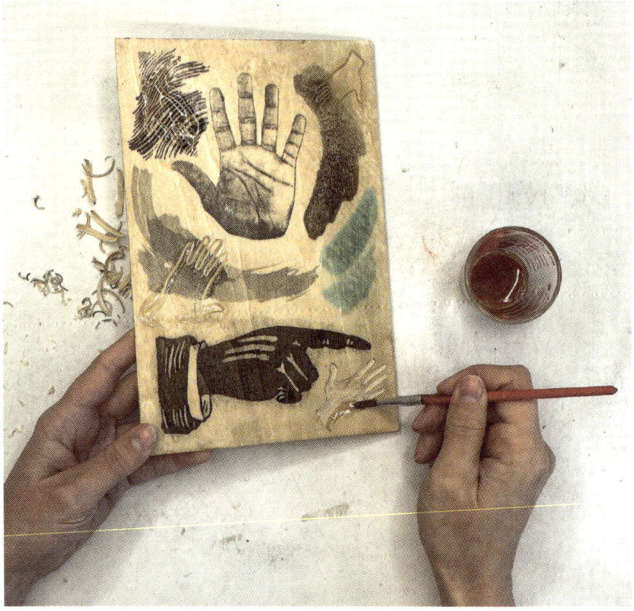

6. Apply fresh gum arabic to the carved areas. Leave the gummed plate in sunlight and warmth for at least 24 hours but a few days is best.

Printing a wood lithograph

Once you start printing you must finish. You cannot close the plate and continue printing later, so plan your time well.

Your ink will need to be modified slightly for wood lithography to make it a little looser, especially when using a foam roller. Add a little oil to your ink so that it flows easily off your push knife. It's easy to add too much oil so start with a couple of drops of oil to a teaspoon of ink and add more later if you find the ink isn't transferring very well.

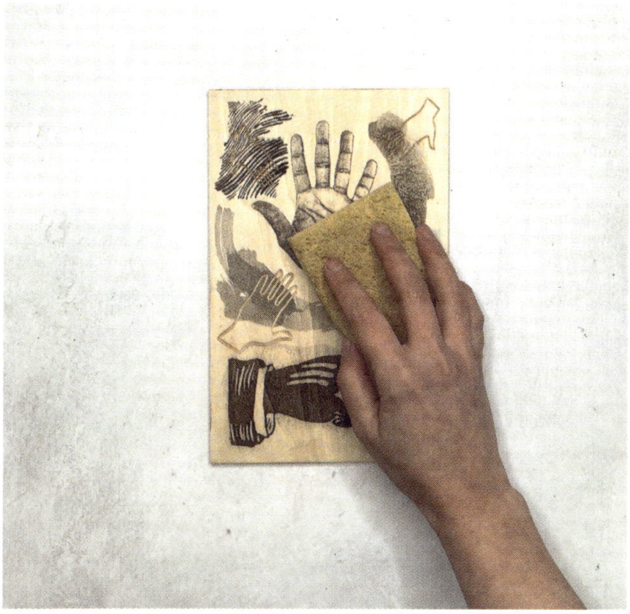

1. Under a tap, remove the excess dried gum from the plate. You will feel the gum as a slimy layer; gently massage it under the water until it's washed away. Use your sponge to blot excess water from the plate.

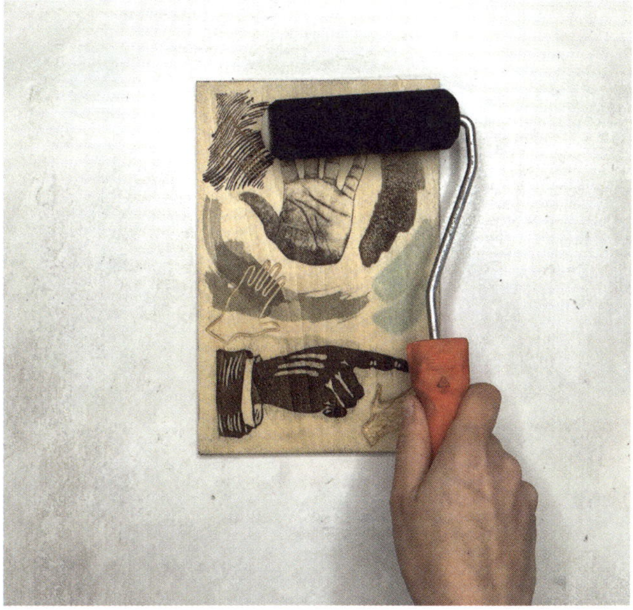

2. Using a sponge roller, roll quickly back and forth over the plate straight on top of the drawing materials, using light pressure. Try to roll over the entire plate from edge to edge to avoid leaving inky roller marks in the centre.

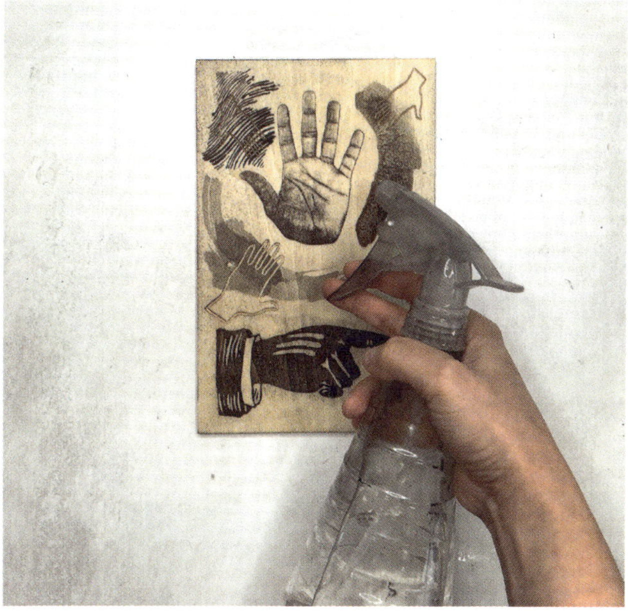

3. Keep your plate damp using a water spray bottle. If possible, avoid using a sponge to dampen the plate as this can push ink residue into the grain of the plate and make it darken faster.

Printing wood lithography *(continued)*

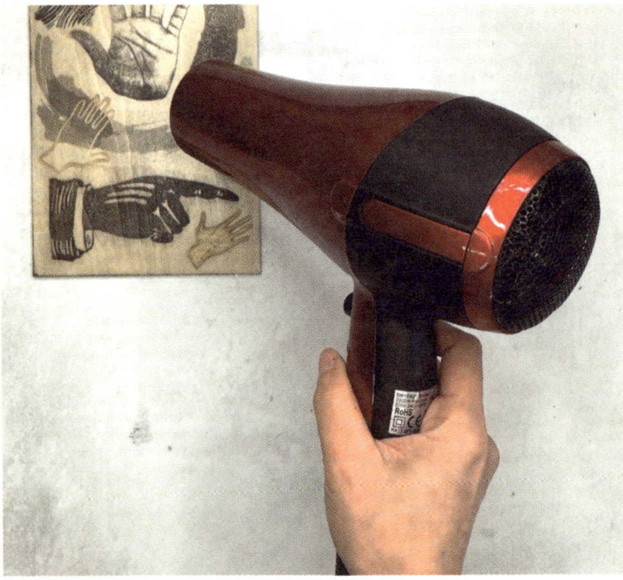

4. When your drawn images have started to darken to the colour of your ink, dry the surface of your plate with a fan or cold hairdryer. We need to build up the ink slowly so don't worry if some parts don't look dark enough yet.

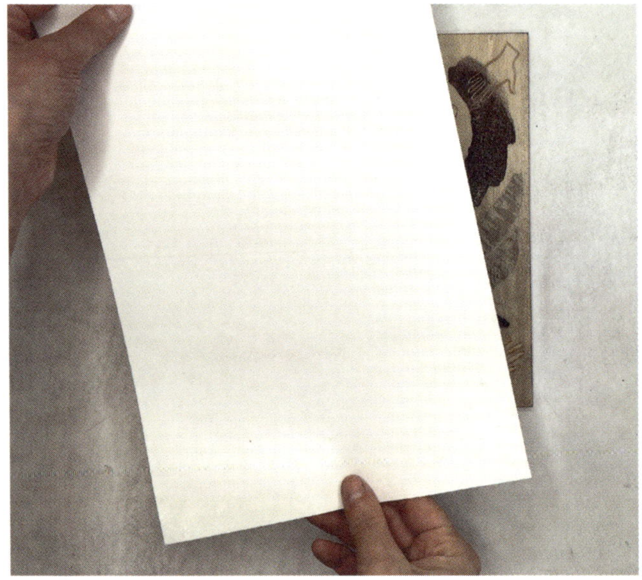

5. Place your printing paper on top. If you are using heavyweight paper then you will get the best results with dampened paper. For the first couple of prints you will only want to use scrap paper or newsprint.

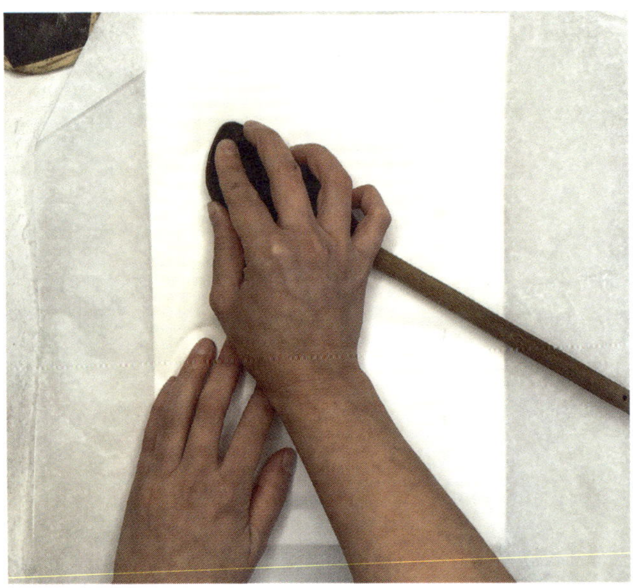

6. Hand burnish your entire plate. I like to use a baren first to pick up the woodgrain all over and then a wooden spoon for the details. You may need to add a couple of layers of thin paper as cushioning to avoid creating burnishing lines.

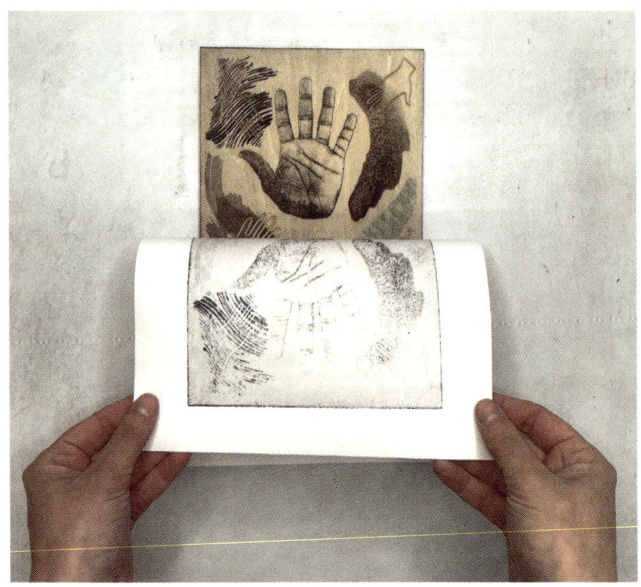

7. As expected, your first print will be light as the ink needs to build up on the plate slowly. Dampen your plate again and ink up for a second time. Some drawing materials will be quicker to hold ink so you will need to ink those areas selectively.

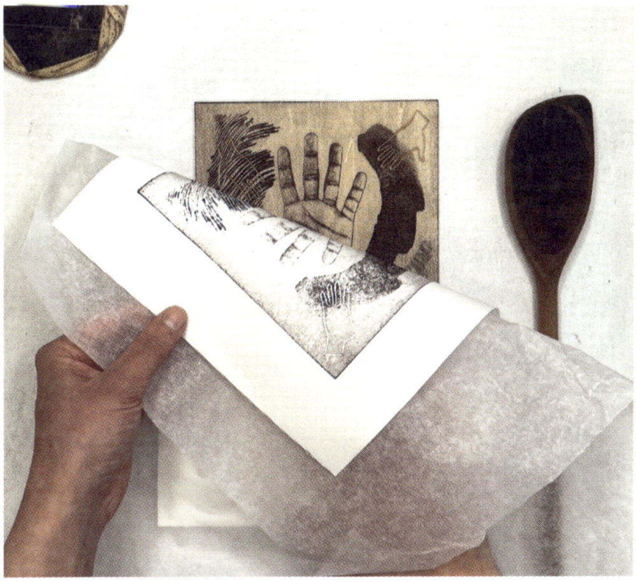

8. Dry and burnish your print again. While hand burnishing you can carefully peek to see how the ink is picking up. Keep one hand on the plate to stop the paper from moving while you're checking.

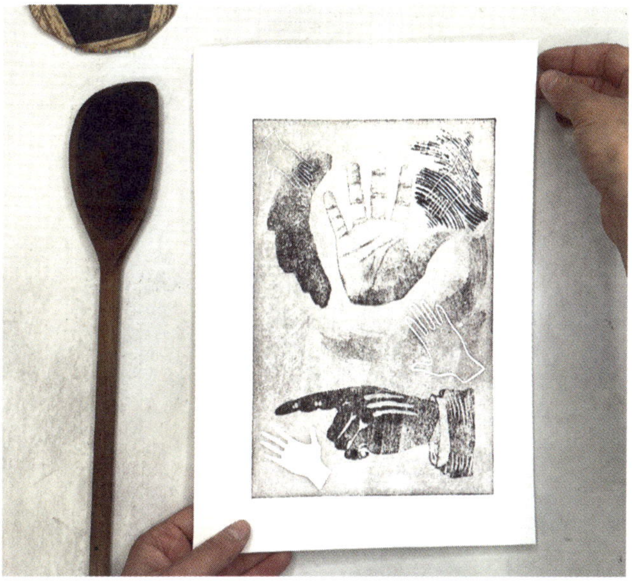

9. This next print is much darker, and the ink is building up well on the plate. Some mid-tone areas are looking good but the dark tone areas will require more focused inking next time.

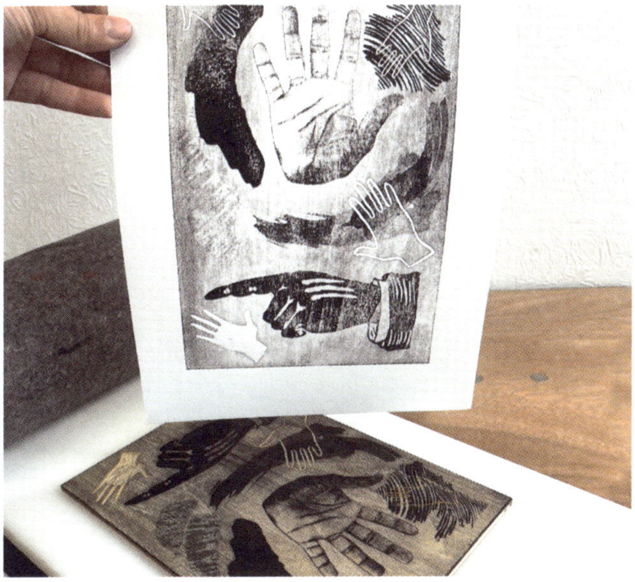

10. Wood lithographs printed using a press will print darker and with more clarity due to the additional pressure. You may still need to hand burnish some areas of the plate if it has an uneven surface or the plate has warped.

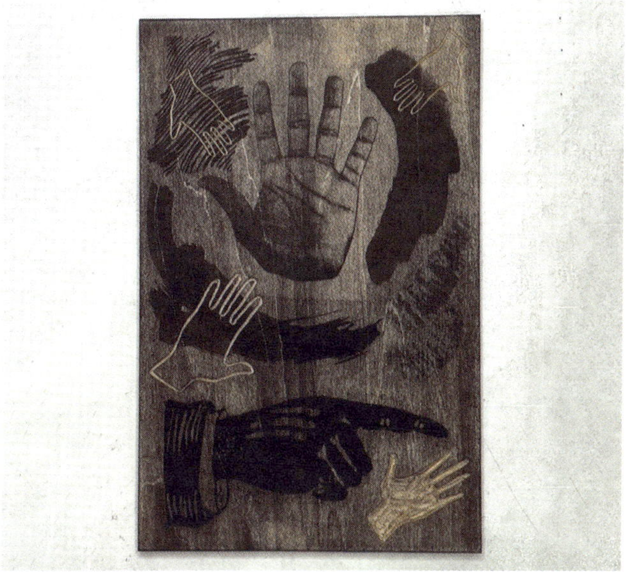

11. The wood lithography plate will darken significantly over time as it picks up more ink. The plate is deceptive though, as it looks much darker than the print. To lengthen the edition and retain clarity, switch to printing onto dry paper.

Printing wood lithography *(continued)*

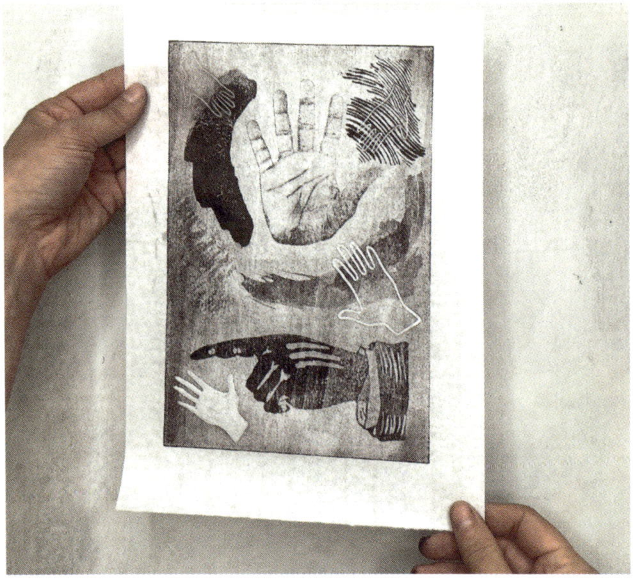

12. Wood lithographs print with most clarity onto smooth papers, either heavyweight or lightweight. As the block darkens printing onto more textured papers will transfer less ink and form a lighter print.

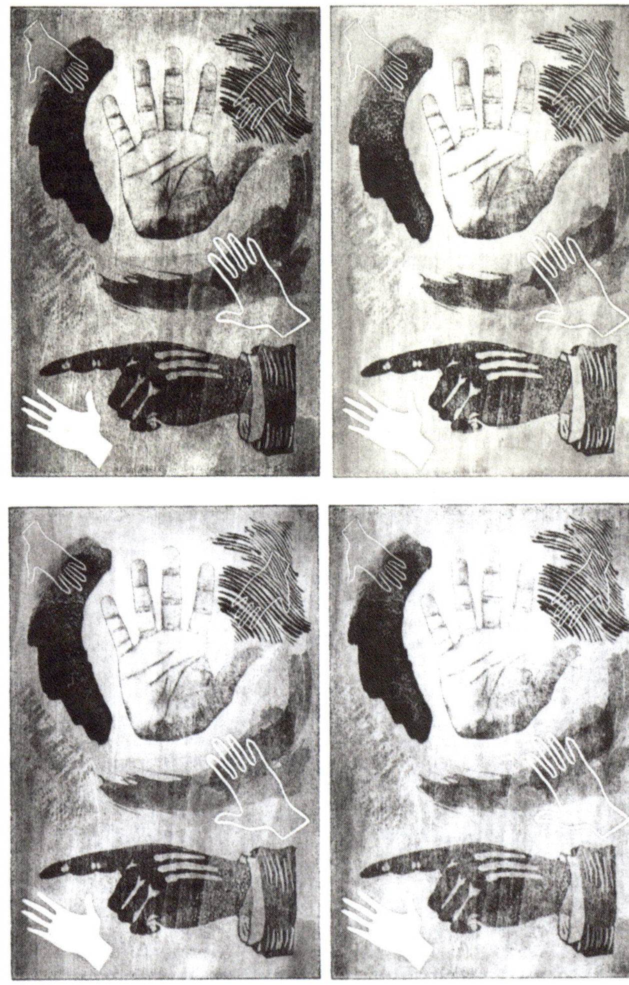

Print comparison (clockwise from top left): textured lightweight paper; smooth lightweight paper; dampened heavyweight paper; dry heavyweight paper. All prints were printed using a press.

MODIFICATIONS FOR PRINTING BY HAND

You will see a difference between prints that have been hand burnished and those that have been put through a press. Hand burnished prints tend to be a little lighter and can pick up slightly less detail, especially of the wood grain. When hand burnishing, remember to use a sheet of greaseproof paper/baking paper to protect the back of the printing paper from damage. Lightweight papers are easier to print by hand and require less pressure. You can use a baren but in order to apply enough pressure to pick up all the lithographic details you will need to use a wooden spoon, or something with a smaller area of concentrated pressure. To avoid creating marks which trace the path of your burnishing you may want to burnish through a few sheets of newspaper to cushion the pressure. Consider the size of the plate: even if your image is on just a small part of the plate, you may still want to burnish the entire surface to pick up the wood grain details. Or thinking of this in the opposite way, you may choose to only hand burnish a selected area so that you transfer only that image area onto the print.

Drawing with soap

Soap can be a contrary drawing material. Due to the variations of the ingredients in different soaps, results are not consistent across different bars of soap; you will find that one bar of soap will work differently to another. However, when it works well, a soap wash can create a painterly mid-tone mark on the print. Soap washes can be difficult to see when applied to the wood, so it can be useful to add a little drawing ink to a soap-and-water mixture to make it more visible.

RE-USING THE PLATE

If your plywood plate is thick enough it can be used on the same side for a second time. There will need to be enough wood to sand down to a level past the absorbed gum and drawing material. As these materials can sometimes soak in quite far, it is often easier to use the reverse side of the plywood instead.

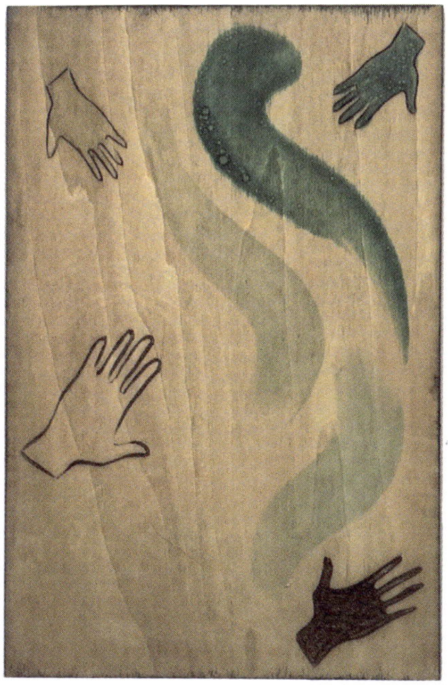

Soap has been used as a crayon on the left, painted on with a little water and a brush in the centre, and painted on generously after lathering in a bowl, on the right. Notice also, the softened, shallow, carved lines from the first use of the plate.

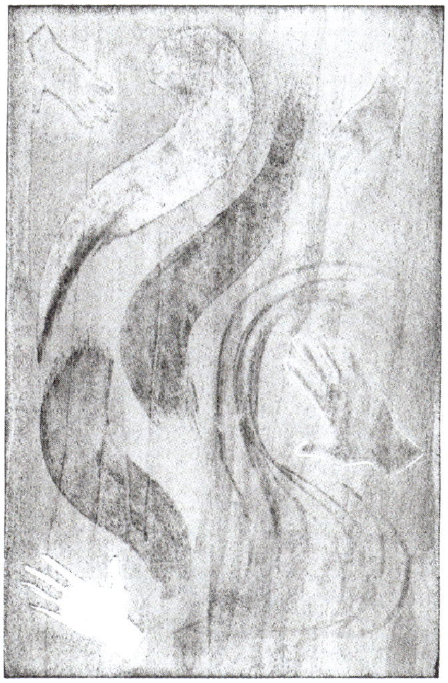

The soap has worked characteristically unpredictably. The drawn lines have transferred successfully and are stable on the plate, unlike normal litho crayon. The generous application of soap has formed a reverse mark, rejecting the water.

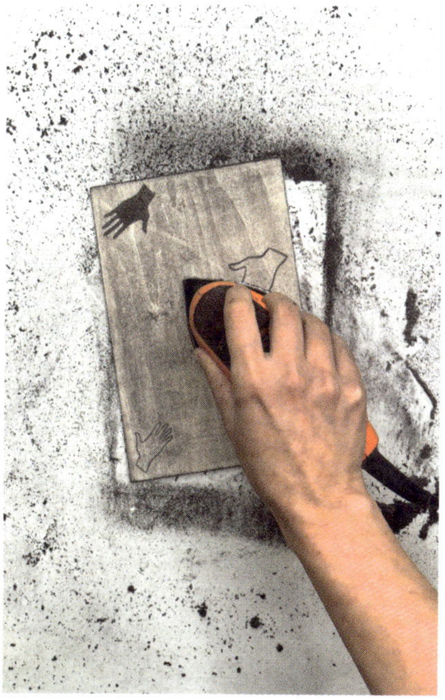

If your plate is thick enough, then you can sand it down and use it for a second lithograph. Wait until the plate has fully dried and sand it until no trace of the previous ink remains. Using an electric sander speeds up this process.

Multi-layered and reduction prints

Once you've made your test plate and you are comfortable with the process you can start to become more adventurous with your image-making and work closer to the way you normally draw, to see how the process translates your marks and affects your normal drawing habits. Drawing straight onto the wood can be daunting, and it is sometimes difficult to translate an idea that will inevitably be reversed. You can instead use Conté crayons or iron oxide powder to create a grease-free image on the block that won't print but will act as a guideline. You can paint iron oxide powder mixed with a little methylated spirits onto a sheet of paper to use in the same way you would use carbon paper. Or you can apply Conté chalks to the back of a drawing and draw over the top of it, transferring the chalk to the block as you would with tracing paper. Remember to reverse the image before you transfer it to the block.

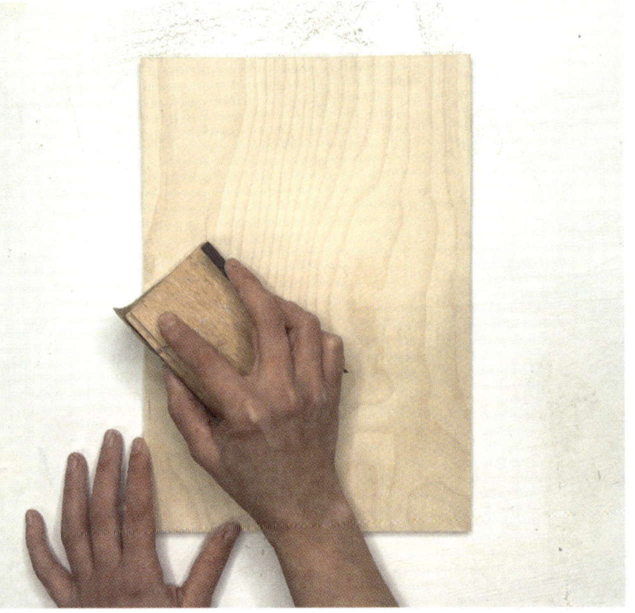

1. Select a plate with a woodgrain that is appealing and can be incorporated into the design. A prominent and curling woodgrain can be an attractive feature for wood lithography but can be difficult to carve into. Sand the plate until smooth.

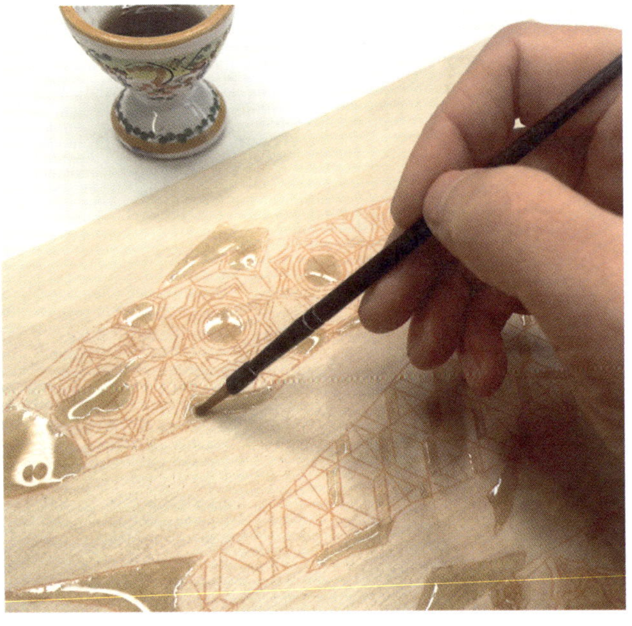

2. Protect any areas that you want to avoid picking up colour on this layer, but don't want to carve away, by applying a generous layer of gum. They may still pick up a little ink but far less than normal.

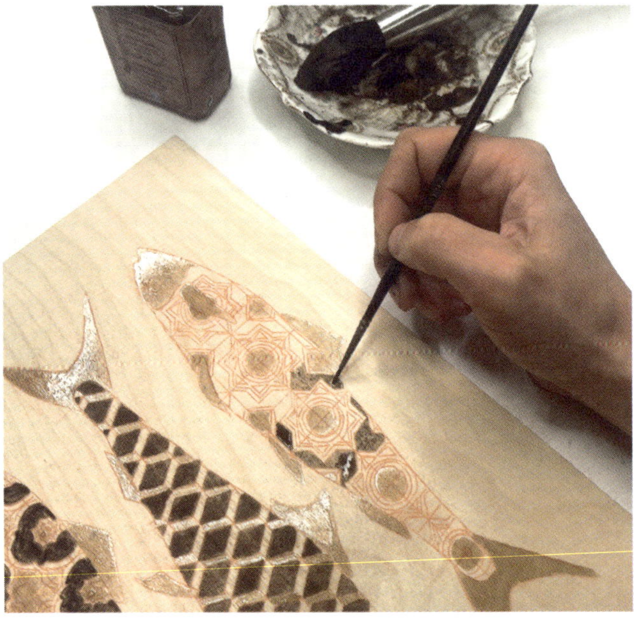

3. Paint on undiluted tusche straight from the bottle, or concentrated hand-mixed tusche, for areas of solid colour. If the tusche is diluted it will show more of the woodgrain through.

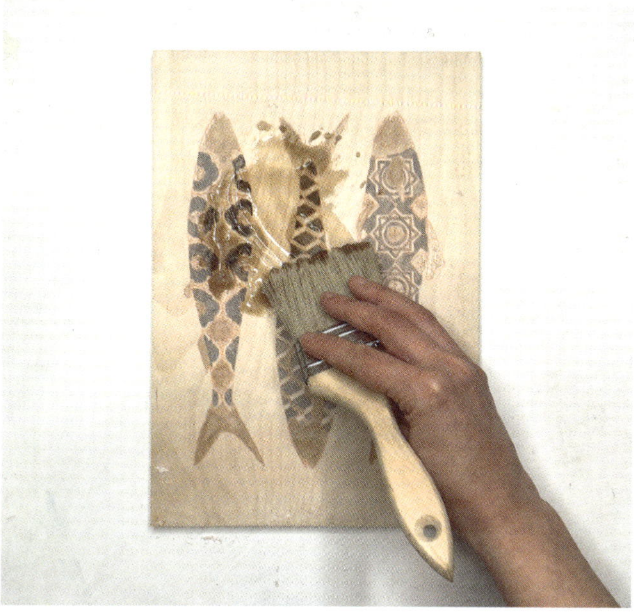

4. When the tusche is dry, process the plate as normal. Apply French chalk to the entire plate with a soft brush and apply two layers of gum arabic, allowing the gum to absorb between layers.

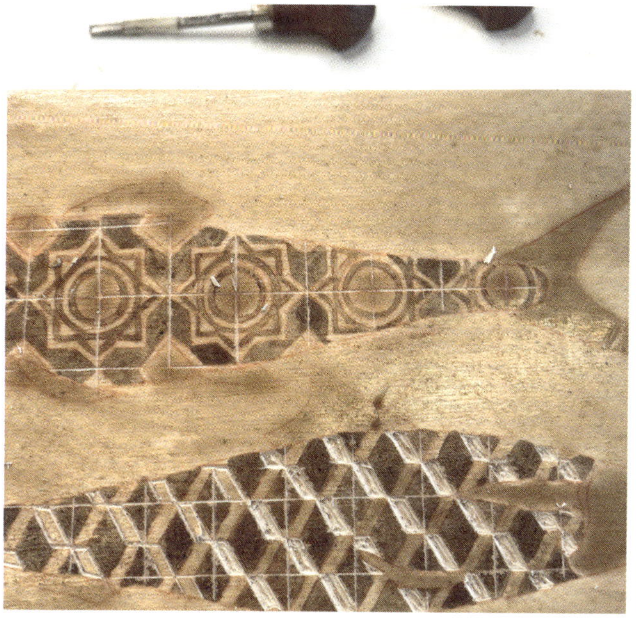

5. Carved areas of the block will become important marker points for the next layers. They are the only parts of the design that will stay white on both layers even as the plate degrades and collects more ink.

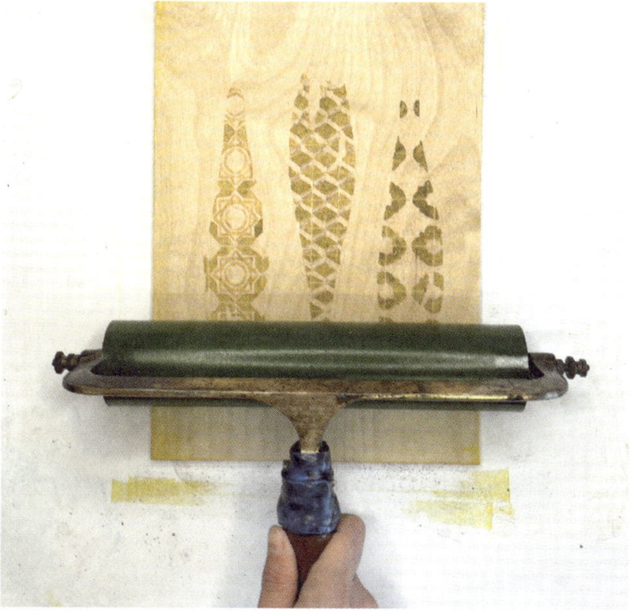

6. As I want the design to print in solid colour, with no tonal detail, I am inking using a normal roller rather than foam. To avoid roller lines from the firm edges of this roller I'm using a large roller to cover the whole block.

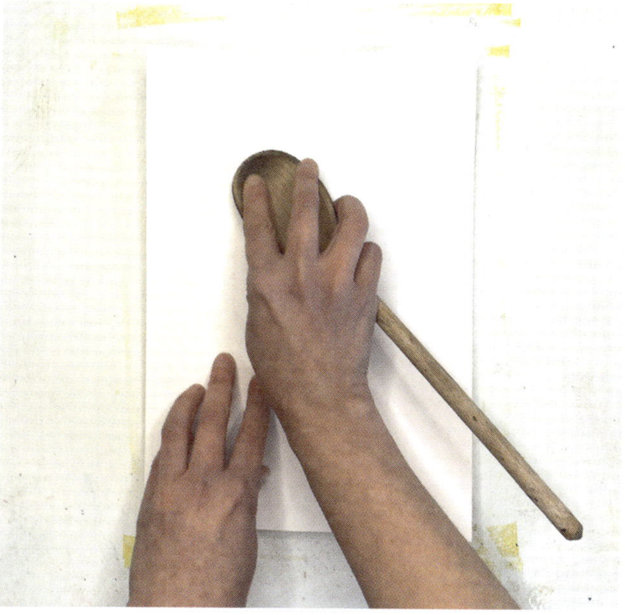

7. I don't want too much of the yellow colour to come through in the background, so I am hand burnishing only in the central area of the design. I could also use a paper mask.

Colour printing *(continued)*

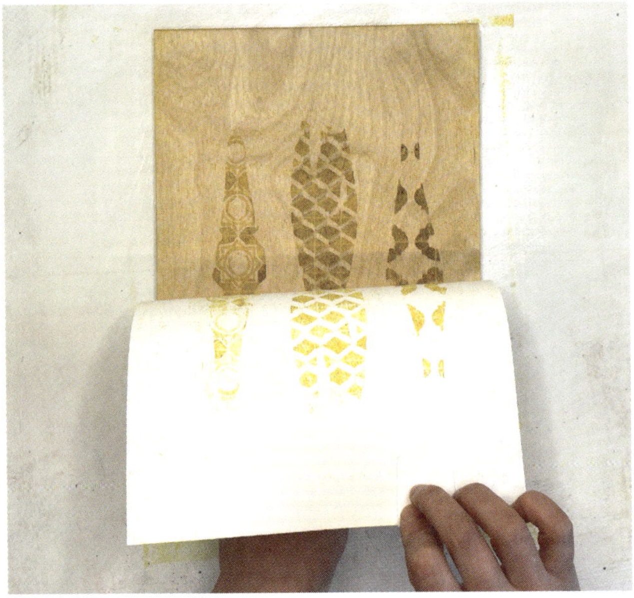

8. When printing with a press, to avoid too much background colour picking up, I am printing onto dry paper and making sure the surface of the plate itself is dry before printing it.

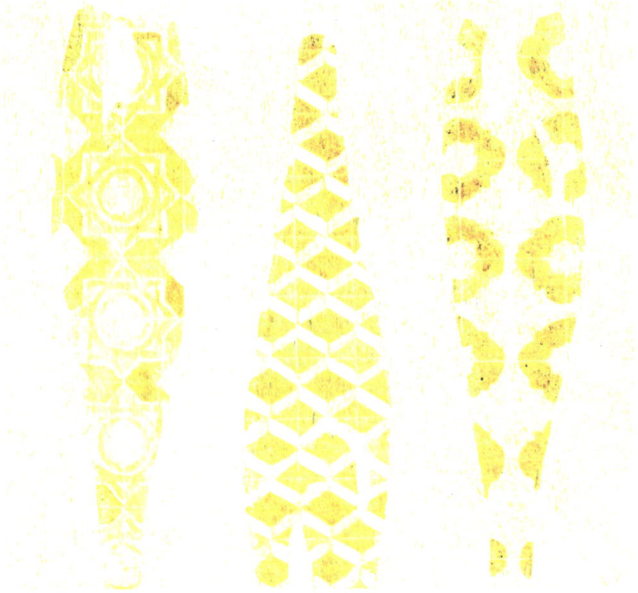

9. When using a light colour, the first prints can transfer some of the drawing materials and muddy the colour. This isn't noticeable when using darker colours. This will stop after the first few prints.

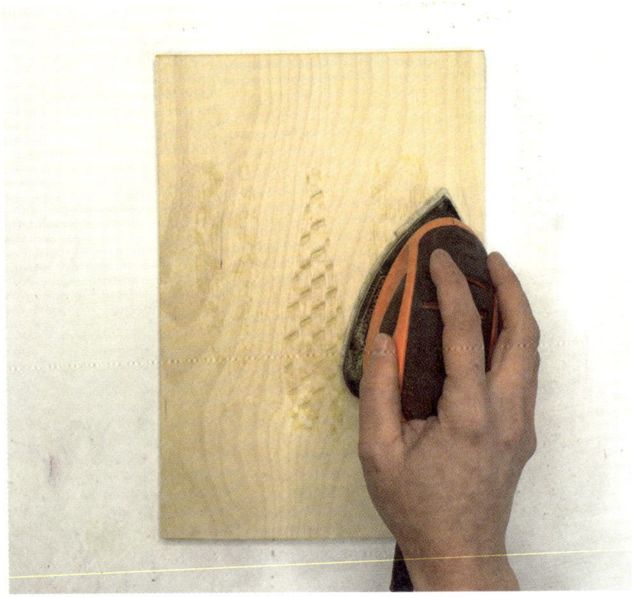

10. Once the plate is completely dry, sand down the wood until the ink traces have disappeared, ready for the next layer. This can only be done a limited number of times and only with thicker blocks of wood.

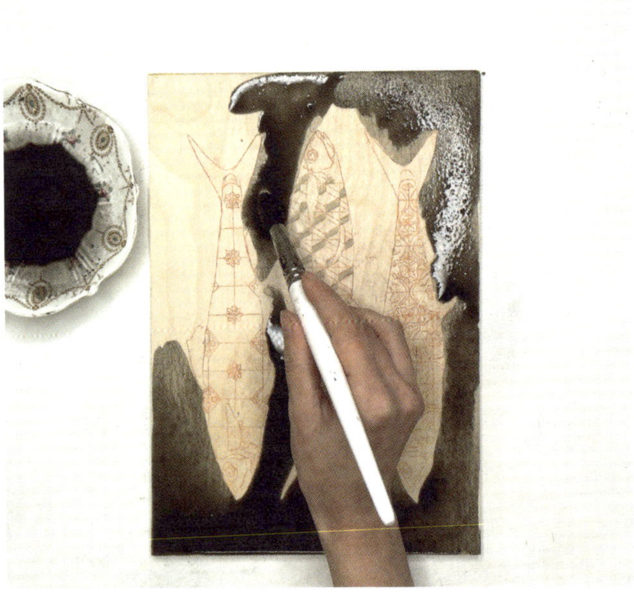

11. In order for the woodgrain to print clearly in the background of this layer, apply a generous amount of tusche in the background and allow it to soak in.

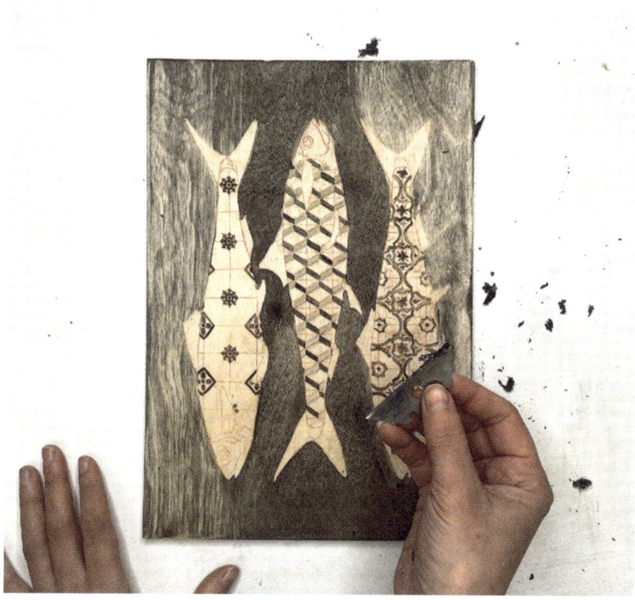

12. When the tusche has dried, use a flat blade to remove the excess tusche sitting on top of the plate that has not soaked into the woodgrain. Process with French chalk and gum as normal.

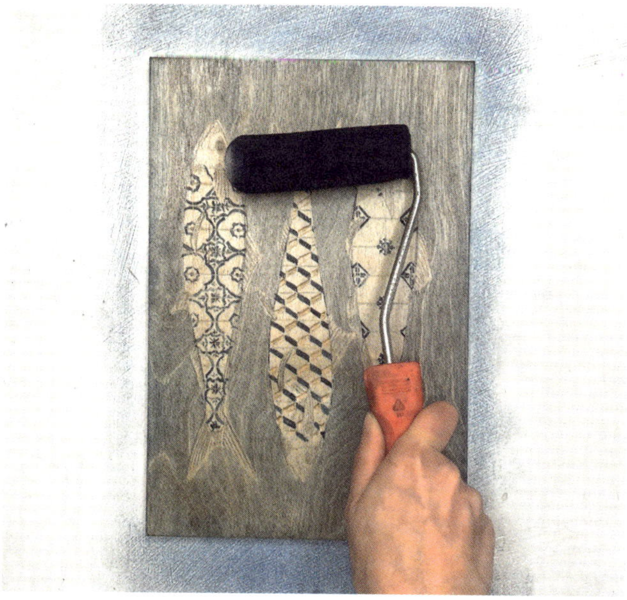

13. When inking up in the next colour, the background woodgrain will start to transfer to the print straightaway and will darken over time, eventually filling in.

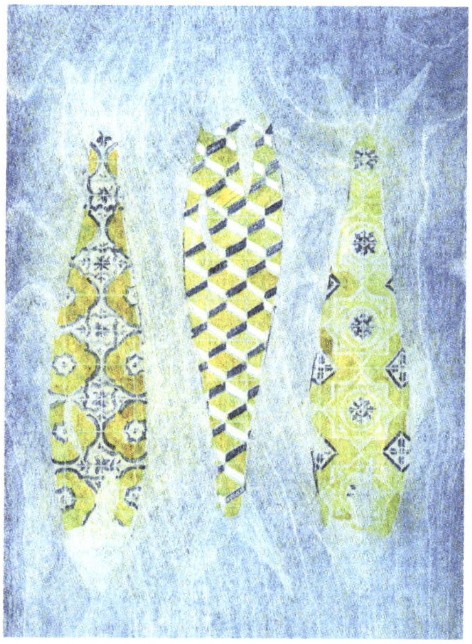

14. Notice how the heads and tails of the fish, which didn't receive any additional gum, have begun to darken, but remain lighter than the background. Some areas of yellow have started to look slightly green where traces of blue ink have collected.

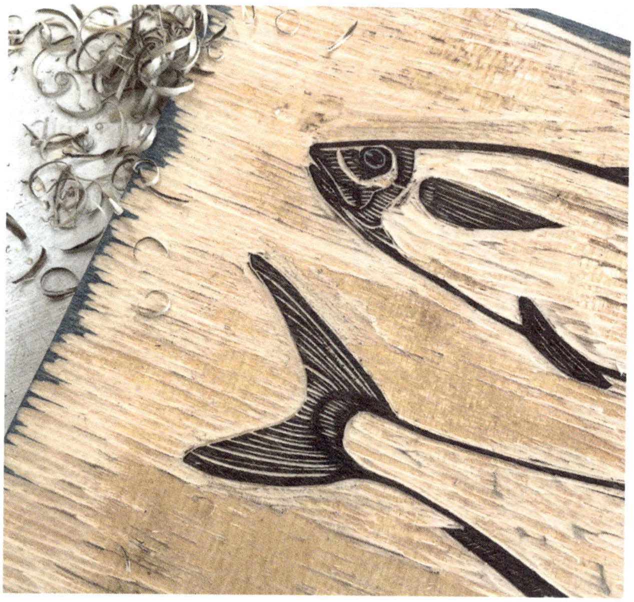

15. When the plate is dry you can use the lithographic image on the plate as reference points when carving a design to print in relief. Remember, you can also use the back side of the plate for another relief layer.

Colour printing *(continued)*

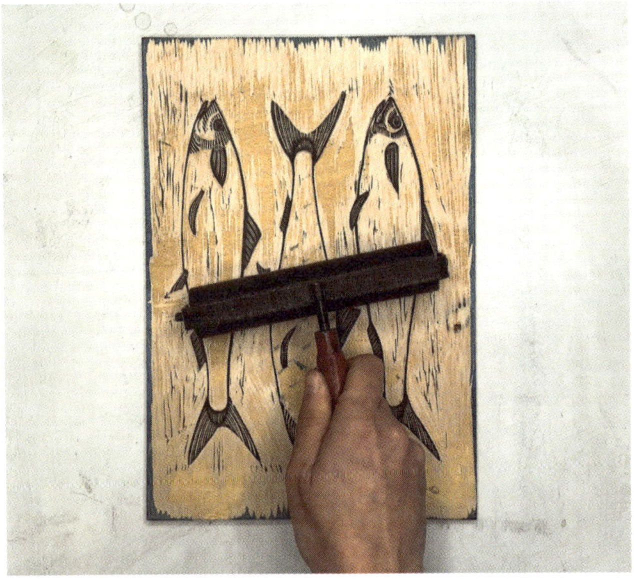

16. When inking up in relief your ink may need to be stiffer than the ink used for the lithographic layers. You will also need to return to a traditional roller so that the recesses of the plate don't collect ink.

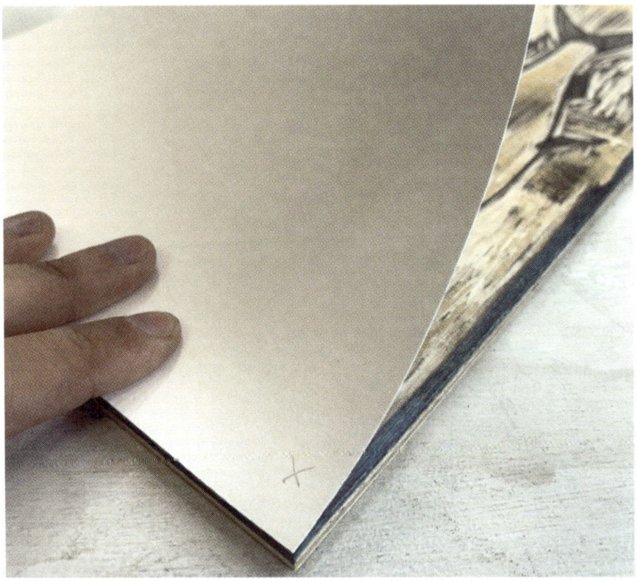

17. The registration for this bleed print, on a consistently sized plate, has been easy. One side of the paper has been aligned to a corresponding side of the plate, with the same corner in registration.

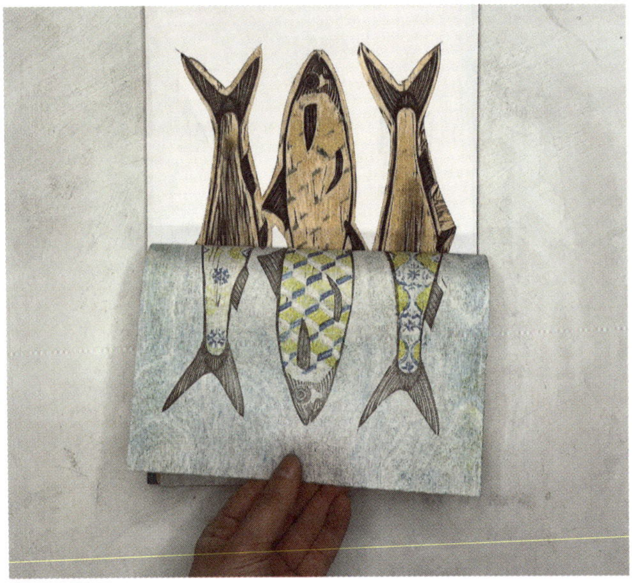

18. Use a paper mask to protect the background of this print from collecting ink from unwanted areas of the relief layer. Ink the plate as normal and align the mask before printing; remove it again when re-inking for the next print.

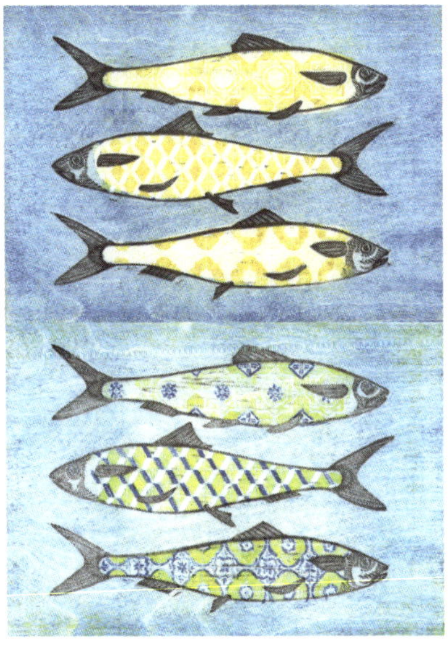

19. Top print: yellow layer printed dry, blue layer printed with the paper dampened and a paper mask over the central sections of the fish. Bottom print: printed onto lightweight paper, showing the hints of green through from the blends of colour.

TROUBLESHOOTING

Pale prints

Remember your first prints will be pale so you are expecting this. You may need to apply more pressure when you're burnishing; there will be shiny ink left on the plate that could have been collected if this is the case. Or you may need to apply more ink to your roller (foam rollers soak up a lot of ink, so you'll need to roll out more ink than normal). If you're printing onto heavyweight or textured paper, you will need to lightly dampen it to produce a darker print.

Overly dark prints

If your print has come out unexpectedly dark or blurry then it is probably because your plate was too damp when you printed it. If you added too much oil to your ink, you will find that the ink on the plate becomes blurry and spreads out over the plate. It will also come away much more easily onto your sponge and darken much faster. Roll off the ink from your foam roller onto some scrap paper as much as you can and ink up again with ink that has not been mixed with oil. Alternatively, you can throw away that foam roller and replace it.

Blurred prints

If you have blurred lines or double printing, then the plate or paper could have moved when you were burnishing. Try to keep a downward pressure when you burnish and hold your other hand on top to keep the paper in place. If this happens when using a press, then place some non-slip mat under your plate or a couple of sheets of scrap paper on top of your printing paper to stop the plate or paper from slipping. Adjust the pressure of your press accordingly if you add these.

Burnishing lines

Unexpected lines on your prints are probably marks from burnishing by hand using a wooden spoon or similar tool. You will recognise them because they will mimic the marks of your burnishing and appear as spirals or zigzag lines. To stop this happening again, you will need to put some sheets of scrap paper on top of your printing paper to cushion your burnishing tool while you are burnishing.

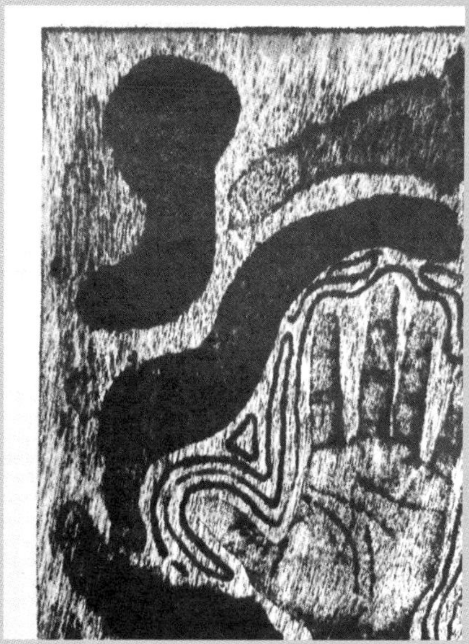

Overly dark, blurry and shiny print due to too much oil in the printing ink.

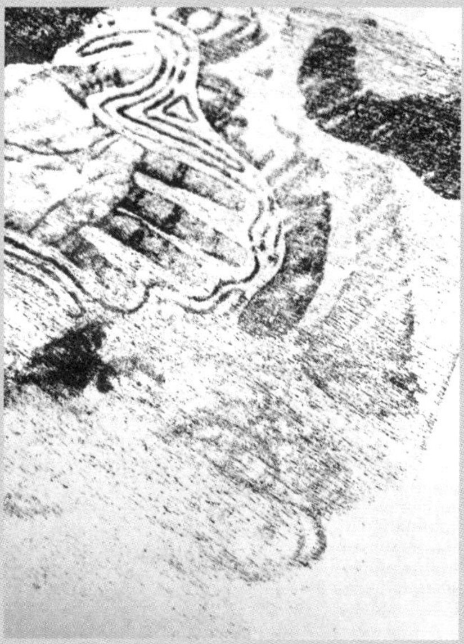

Burnishing lines showing through on the print from uneven/lazy burnishing.

Kathryn Desforges (UK)

kathryndesforges.co.uk

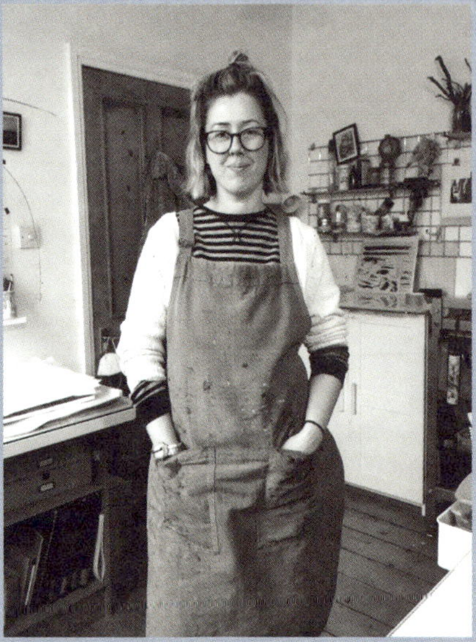

Kathryn Desforges is a Yorkshire-based artist printmaker and educator who has been exploring wood lithography in her work for over 10 years. She exhibits and teaches printmaking courses across the UK.

I make process-driven, contemporary artworks which explore my fascination with unseen and in-between places, presenting fragmented glimpses of half-real, half-imagined worlds, transforming ordinary scenes into extraordinary narratives and igniting a sense of curiosity and wonder in the viewer. My work spans multiple disciplines including painting and drawing, but has its strongest roots in printmaking.

I first heard about wood lithography through conversations with other printmakers while I was doing a year of stone lithography training at Leicester print workshop back in 2013. I fell in love with stone lithography and all its wonderful intricacies; however, I was also acutely aware that after the training ended, I would be unable to continue to travel to Leicester to access their wonderful facilities. I wanted to find a way that I could continue to practise lithography without having access to the specialist equipment needed.

Material experimentation and the physical act of making are key elements of my practice. I distil and refine through manipulation – carving, scratching, sanding back, painting over. In recent work, I have been using wood lithography in combination with other processes such as etching and woodcut, to create hybrid works which exploit the nature of the materials used. The hard, clean lines of hard-ground etching on steel are juxtaposed with the softer wood-carved and painterly marks which wood lithography enables, to highlight the push and pull of disparate elements within the work.

I also teach a lot of workshops in wood lithography. I think printmakers are really interested in it as a means of making images, especially since the pandemic, as it's something that can be done in a home studio, without harsh chemicals or solvents. Teaching it is a whole other ball-game – students really test the boundaries of a process. I've found new, more robust drawing materials which don't pull off and enable more consistent editions, and have trialled different gum mixtures to keep the block from filling-in for as long as possible. It's fantastic to see students from the courses I've run taking the process and running with it. I always get questions about whether this or that drawing material would work, and I always answer – try it! I've also been paying more attention recently to where the wood I'm using comes from – trying to source FSC and PEFC certified wood, and using re-claimed wood.

Kate Desforges, *A Way Through*, 2020. Etching, wood lithograph and woodcut. Varied edition of eight, 21 x 28cm.

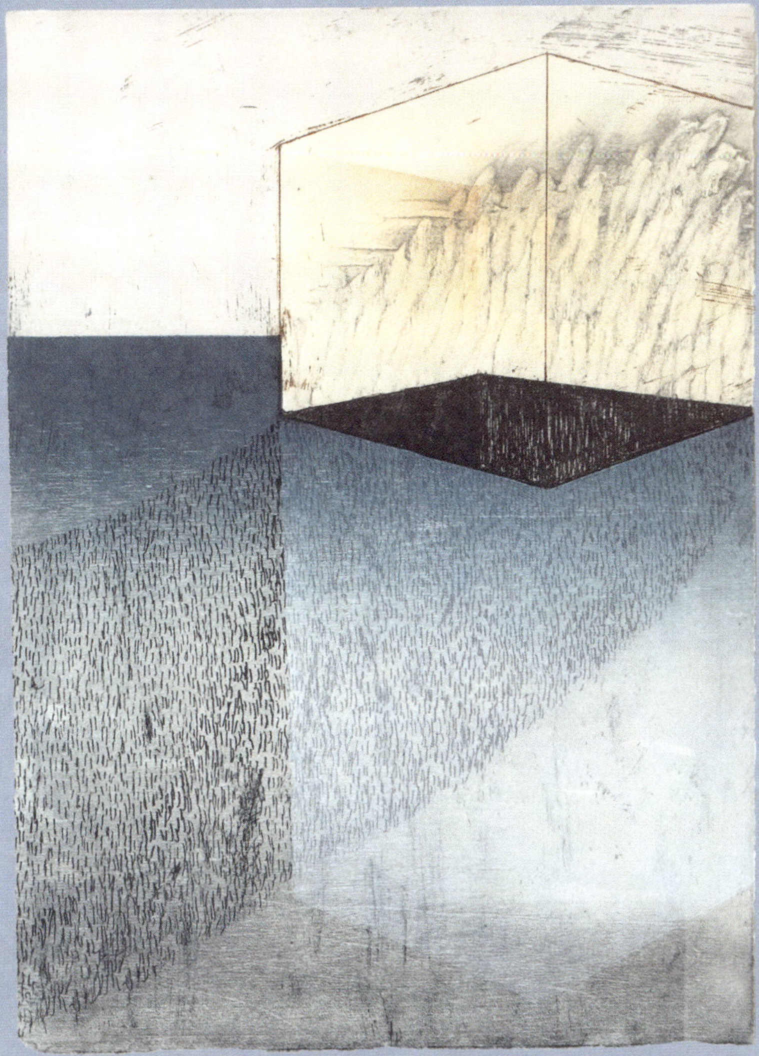

Kate Desforges, *Relics*, triptych, 2022. Wood lithograph on Somerset paper. Composite print made up of 18 panels. Varied edition of three. Approx 1.4 x 3.6m.

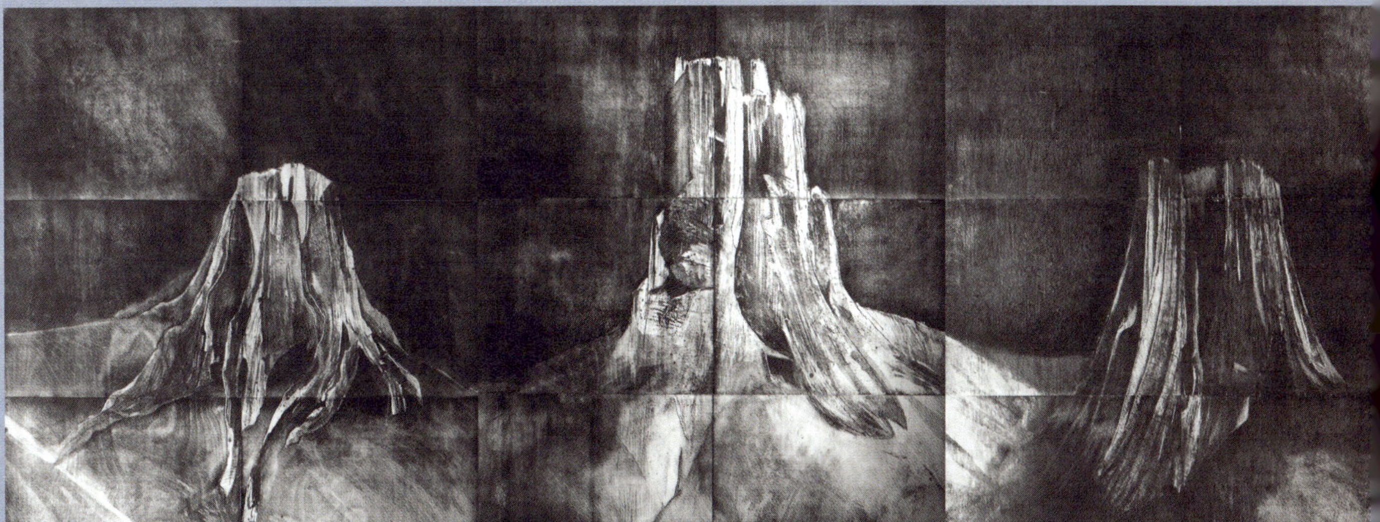

CHAPTER 6

Lino lithography

At first glance lino lithography appears to be essentially the same process as for wood lithography, but with traditional hessian-backed lino replacing the plywood. It is also *so* much more than that, with endless potential for combining multiple processes within one plate, and without the rigid drawbacks of wood lithography.

The main attractions of lino lithography are ease and flexibility; you are not inhibited by the surface quality as you are with wood lithography. Lino is easier to draw onto and easier to carve, it's easy to change the surface quality from smooth to rough, depending on your desires, and you can continue to work with the same piece of lino, sanding it down for multiple additional lithographic layers. More details are retained in the lino lithograph print compared with a plywood lithograph, impressively so. Reticulated tusche washes transfer faithfully in the prints, as do crayon marks and delicate speckled inks. As lino is our matrix, we can also employ all the normal relief techniques we would usually use with lino too.

Artist Mary Dalton has been developing the lino lithography process for the past few years under the name 'lithino', with a level of success that almost makes you want to abandon all other printmaking processes in favour of lino lithography. Her drive is to be as environmentally conscious as possible and lino

FACING PAGE
Carving into the lino after it has been printed as a lithograph. The traces of the lithographic image are still visible on the plate and can be used as a guide for carving.

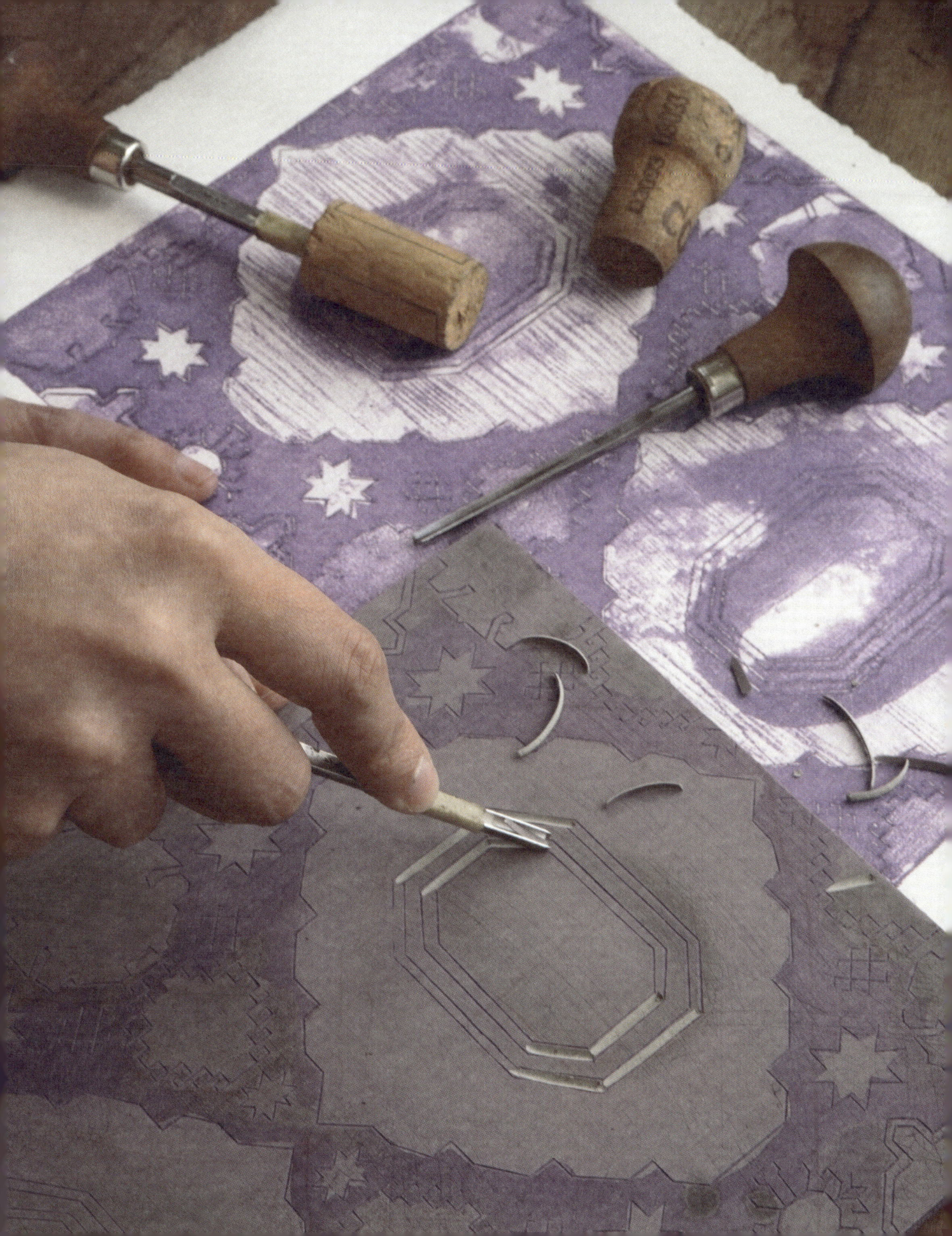

lithography is proving to be the perfect process. Lino is made up of a mixture of linseed oil, pine resin, ground cork dust and sawdust. It's fully biodegradable so when you've finished with it you can cut it up and put it in your compost bin.

FACING PAGE
Lino lithography test prints from Scarlett Rebecca's technical file. Testing tusche washes, crayon, re-sanding, gum transfer, and a relief layer.

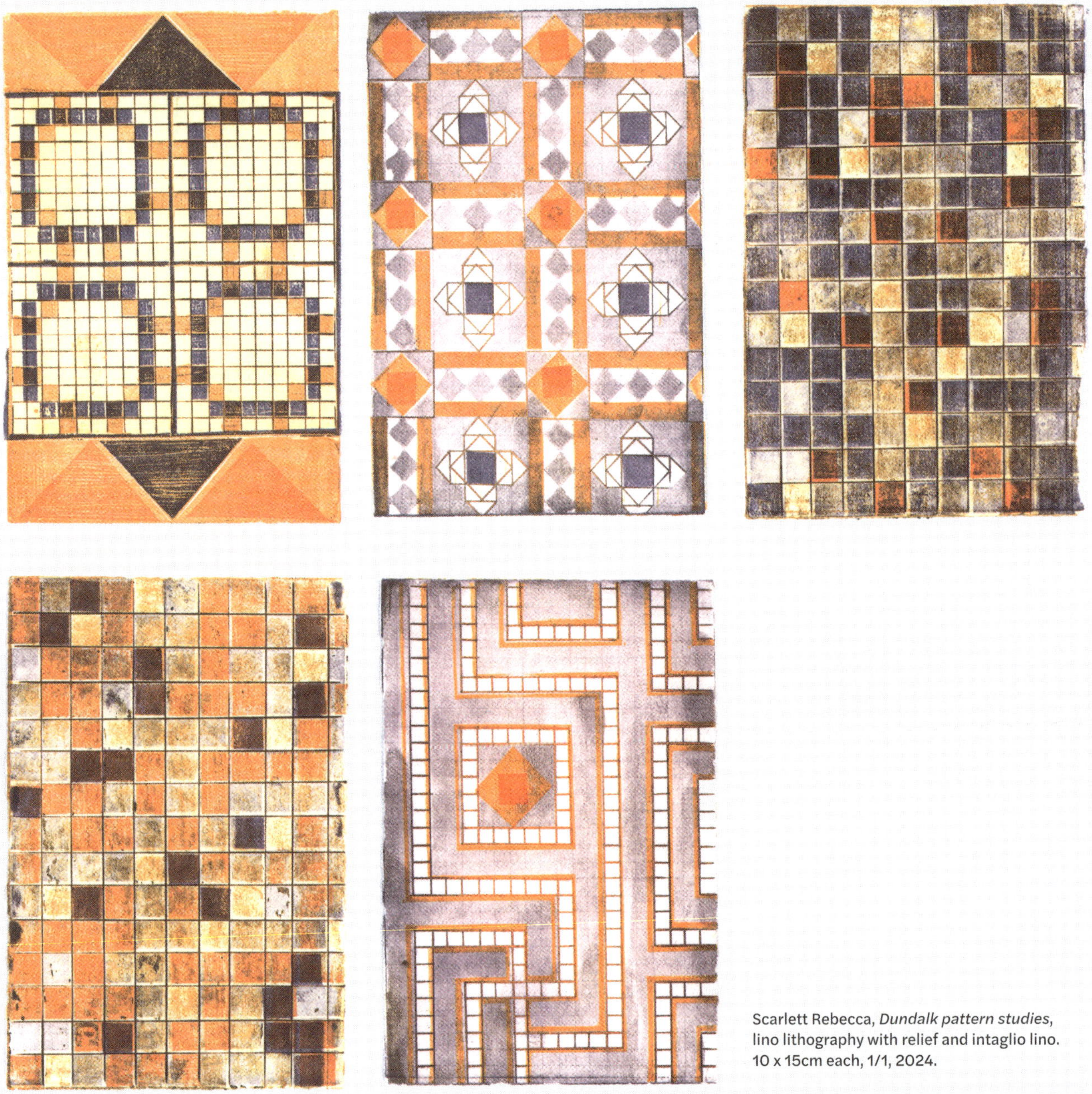

Scarlett Rebecca, *Dundalk pattern studies*, lino lithography with relief and intaglio lino. 10 x 15cm each, 1/1, 2024.

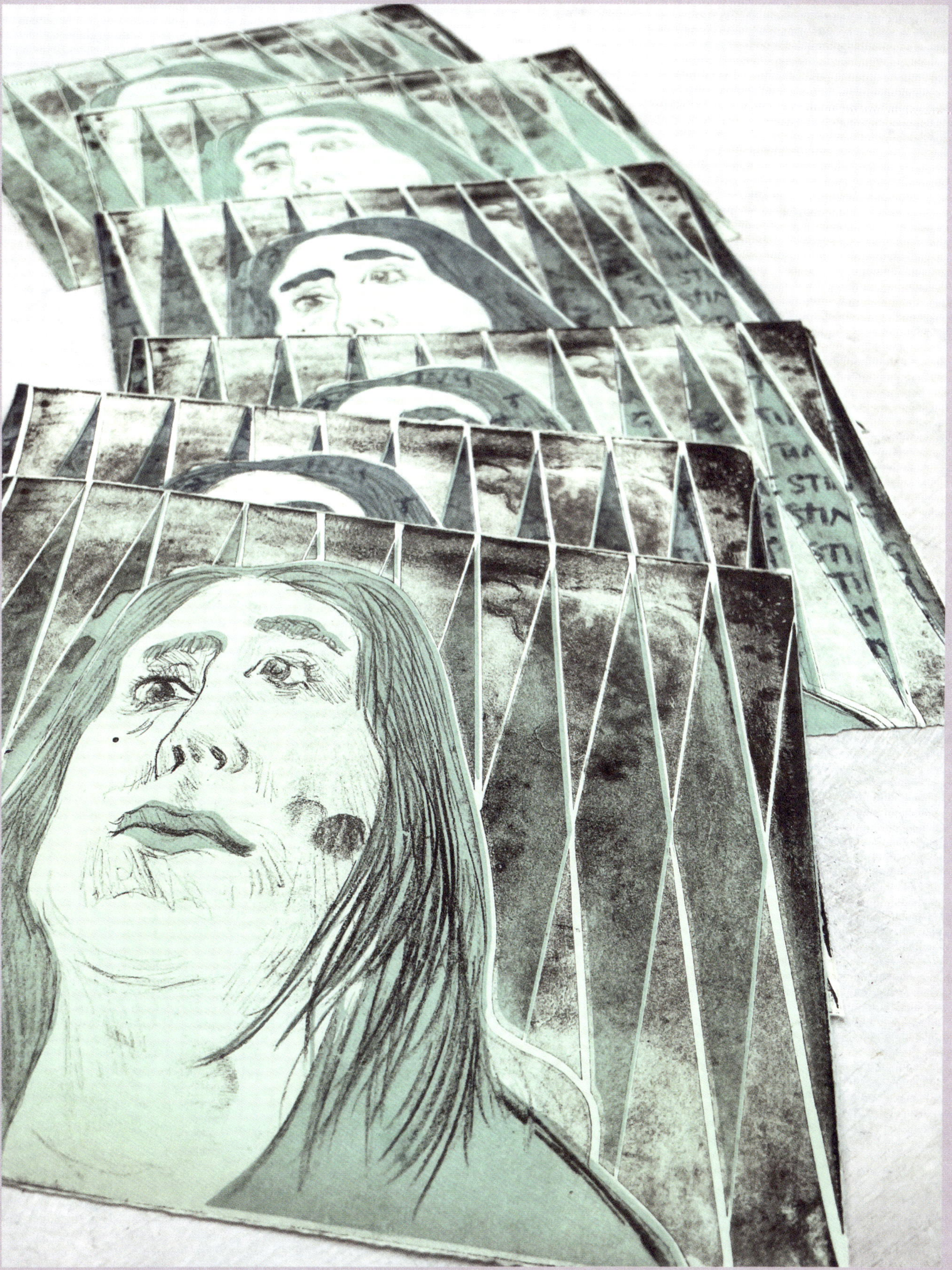

Preparing the plate

The key to making a successful lino lithograph is in the preparation. It takes much more care and attention than plywood lithography but stick with it and you will reap the rewards. Sanding down the lino will remove any unevenness and impurity on the surface; it will also remove the waterproof top coating to the lino which will inhibit the lithographic process. As the lino is quite soft it is not recommended to use an electric sander as the lino can become easily marked or dented. The lino particles will also catch and build up on the sandpaper, and if not removed, they will transfer back onto the lino, making your job twice as hard.

As a popular flooring material, lino is inherently water resistant, and it is this that we are fighting against throughout the printing process. It means that the printed edition will begin to darken as the lithographic surface degrades. However, with good preparation and careful printing, respectable edition sizes can be achieved.

MATERIALS

- Lino
- Sandpaper/wire wool
- Gum arabic
- French chalk
- Foam roller/traditional roller
- Cellulose sponge
- Water bowls for dampening water
- Printing ink
- Paper
- Lithographic tusche
- Lithographic crayons
- Oil pastels
- Carving tools

The materials needed for the lino lithography process.

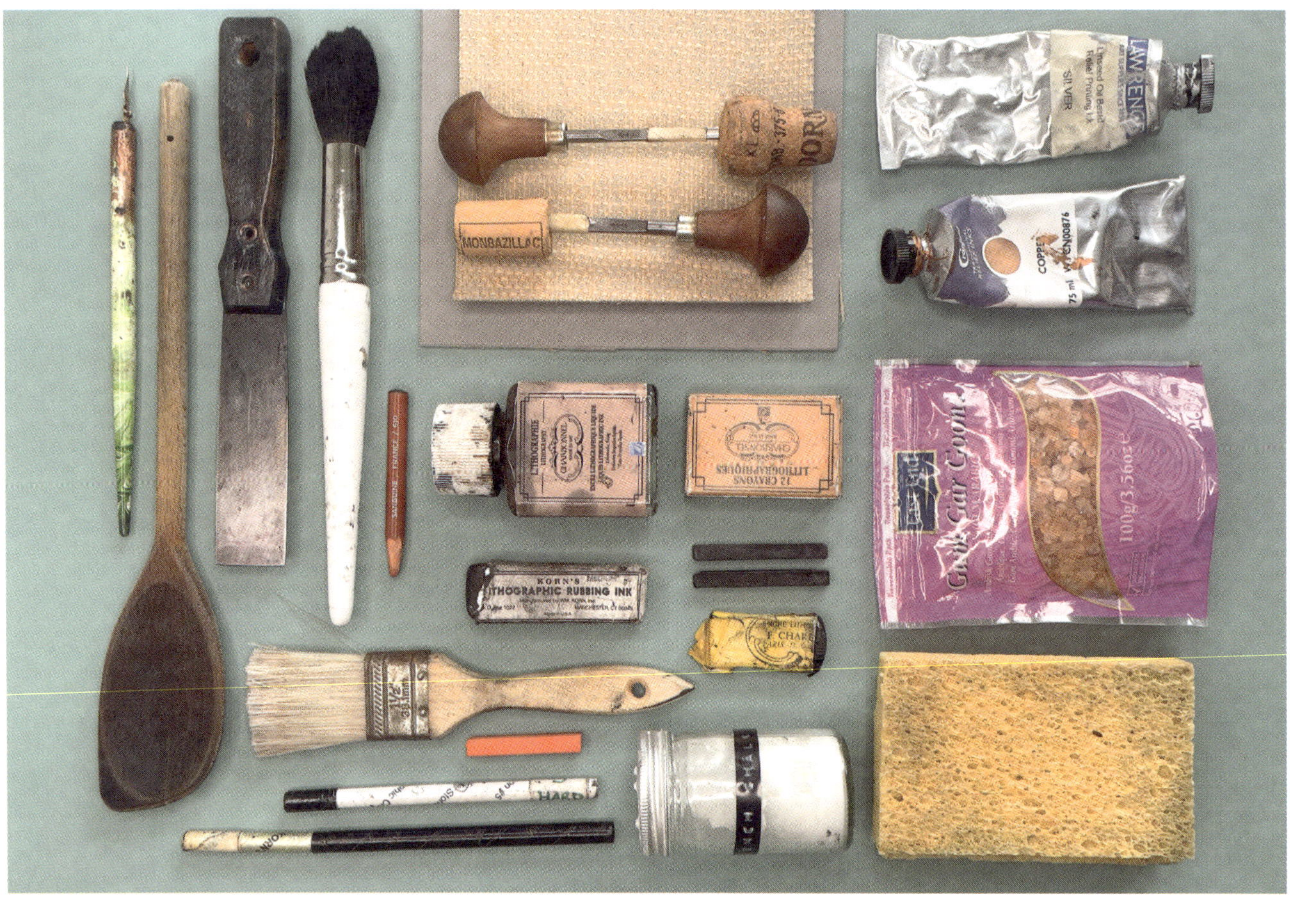

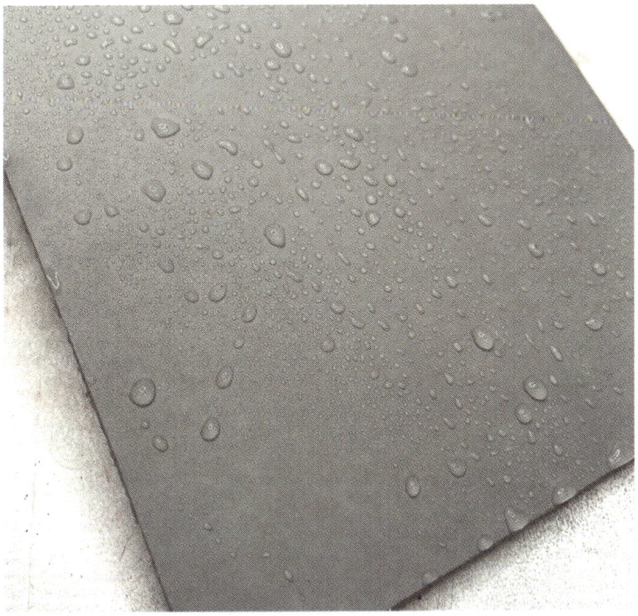

1. Test the lino surface with water before use. Notice the water droplets sitting on the water-resistant surface of the unprepared lino.

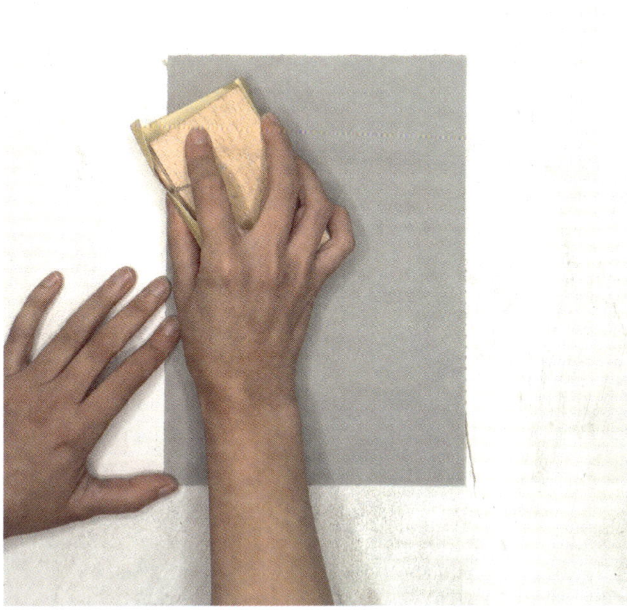

2. To prepare the lino methodically sand the lino, top to bottom, then left to right, multiple times using medium grade sandpaper.

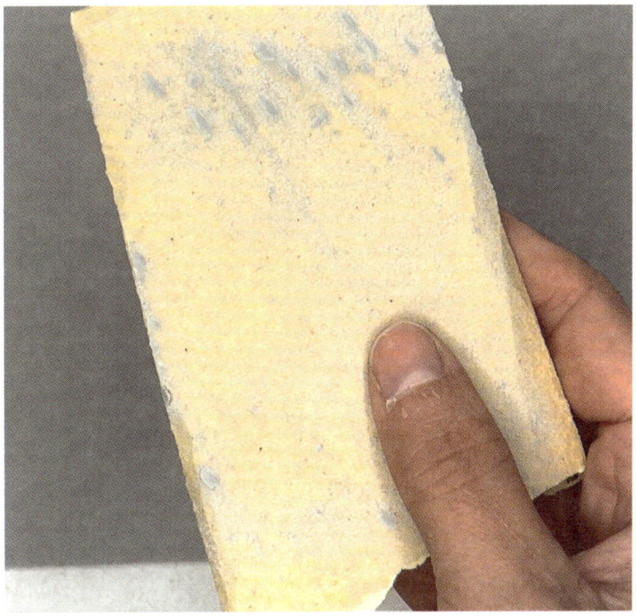

3. While sanding, little pieces of lino will frequently gather on the sandpaper and will need to be removed. Wire wool can be used instead, to avoid this.

4. After sanding, test the lino again with water. The water should sit evenly over the surface with no signs of resistance.

Creating your image on the lino

As always, I encourage you to make a test plate first to experiment with the drawing materials you have and to test the process in full, enabling you to become comfortable with it in a low-stakes way.

The surface of the lino is a surprisingly enjoyable surface to work on and more akin to stone lithography than all the other alternative processes in this book. It is also very receptive to corrections; you can use wire wool and scalpel blades to remove areas of drawing material to make alterations while you're working.

Lino is prone to warping and twisting, especially if it has become wet on the hessian backing. Keep your lino upside down under heavy boards for a while to flatten it out before using water-based materials. Otherwise, the tusche washes will run off and pool at the edges of the lino.

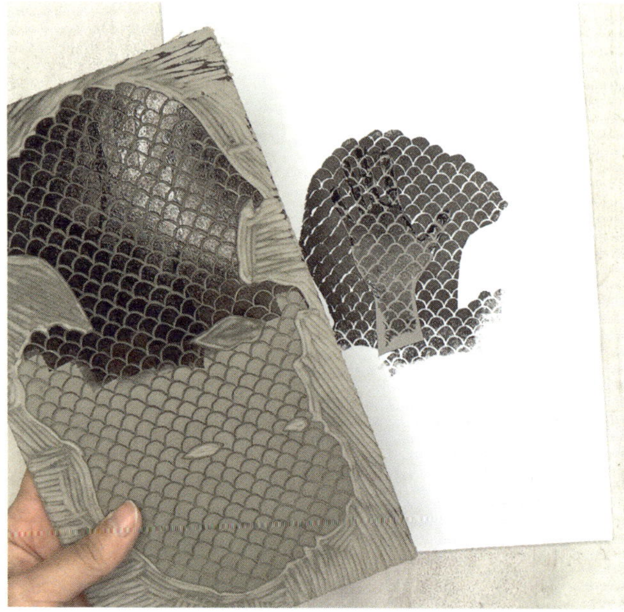

1. It feels odd, but printing a linocut onto the lino lithography plate, using an oil-based ink, works very well. You can use paper masks to protect the plate from unwanted ink, or to create a silhouetted design.

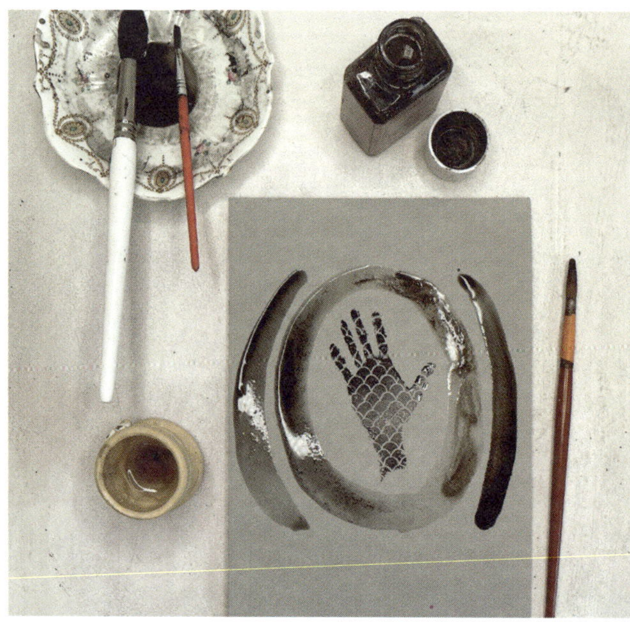

2. Paint tusche onto the lino surface straight from the bottle for solid tones, or drop neat tusche into pools of water on the lino and allow to dry slowly for reticulated wash effects. Explore varying dilutions of tusche for varying tones.

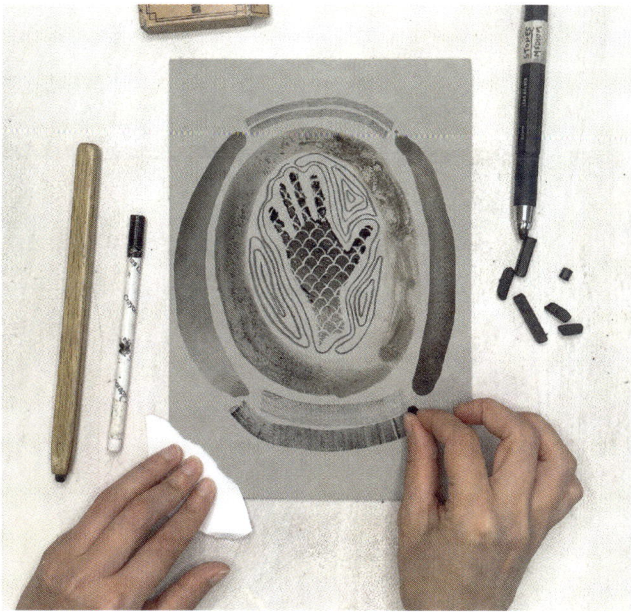

3. Oil pastels and lithographic crayons of different grease levels can be used on the tip like a pencil, or on the side for larger areas of tone. The surface quality (rough or smooth sanding) of the lino will show through in the use of crayons.

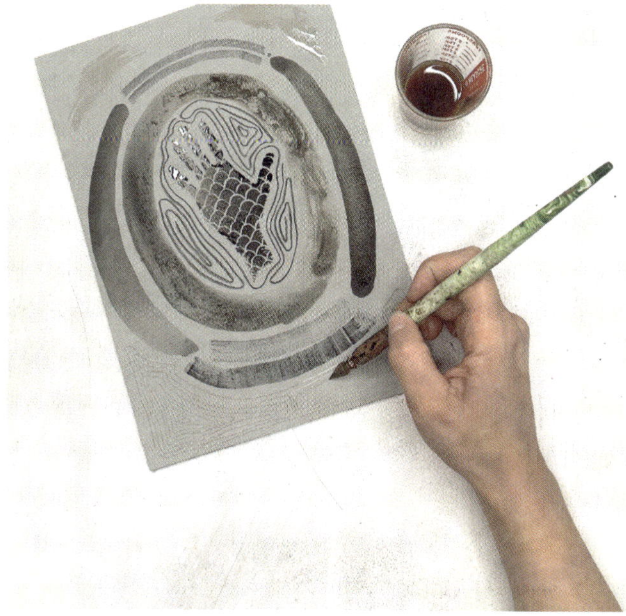

4. Like with wood lithography, gum can be used as a resist for dry or solvent-/oil-based drawing materials. It can be painted with a brush, stippled, or applied using a clean dip pen.

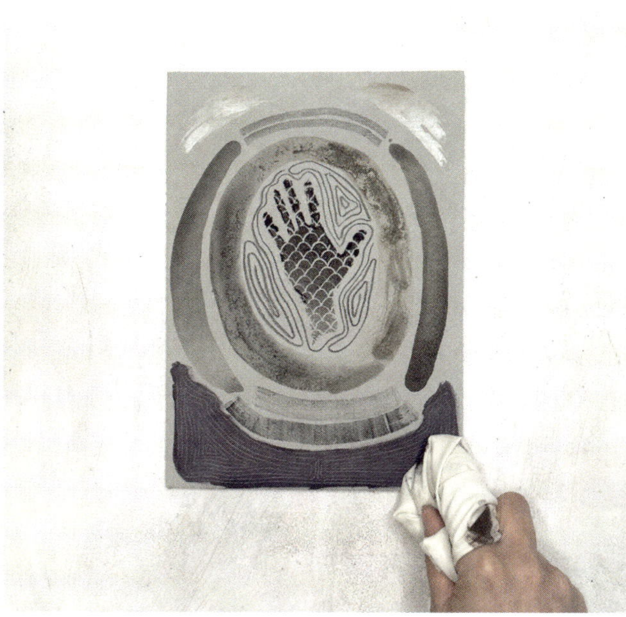

5. For a solid area of dark tone, buff a little printing ink onto the plate using a rag or cotton bud. The rag or cotton bud can be used as a drawing tool in this way and the previously applied gum will act as a resist to the buffed-in printing ink.

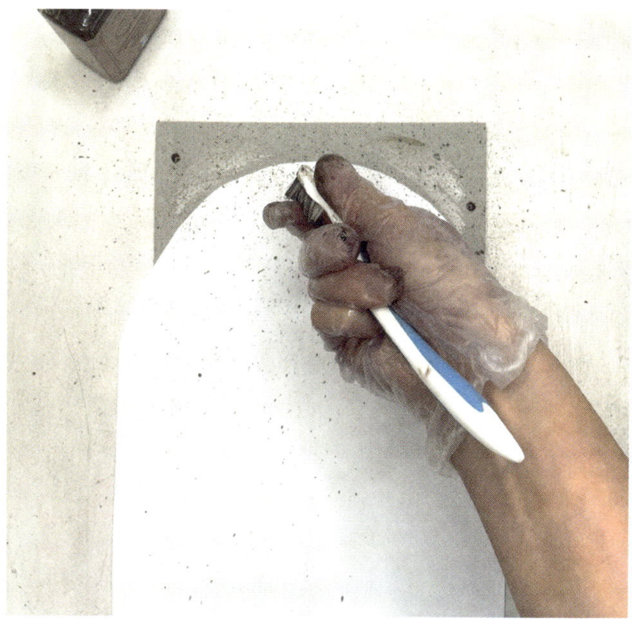

6. Splatter on liquid drawing materials (tusche, diluted printing ink, diluted stopping-out varnish) with an old toothbrush or stiff bristled paintbrush. Use a piece of scrap paper to protect areas from unwanted ink splatter.

Processing the plate

Once the lino has had a coating of gum arabic it should be left at least overnight, but ideally for longer, and it won't harm the plate to be left for weeks. There is no rush when it comes to lino lithography.

When too thick a layer of gum has been applied to the surface of the lino, or if it has dried too quickly, a crackled effect will appear on the gum layer. If left it can create a very delicate crackled marking across the print. It won't pick up at first but as the plate darkens it will become more apparent. I've not included this as a troubleshooting problem, as I don't see it as a problem but instead as a beautiful side effect which can be embraced.

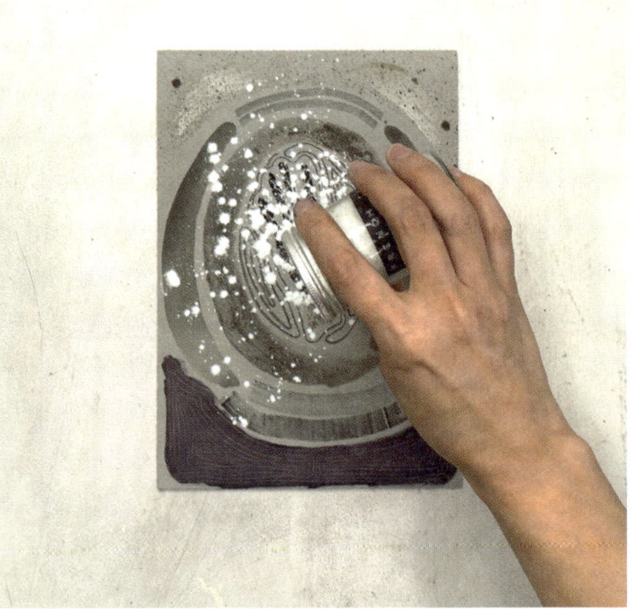

1. Ensure all the drawing material on the plate is completely dry before processing. Spread French chalk all over the plate using a soft paintbrush or cotton wool.

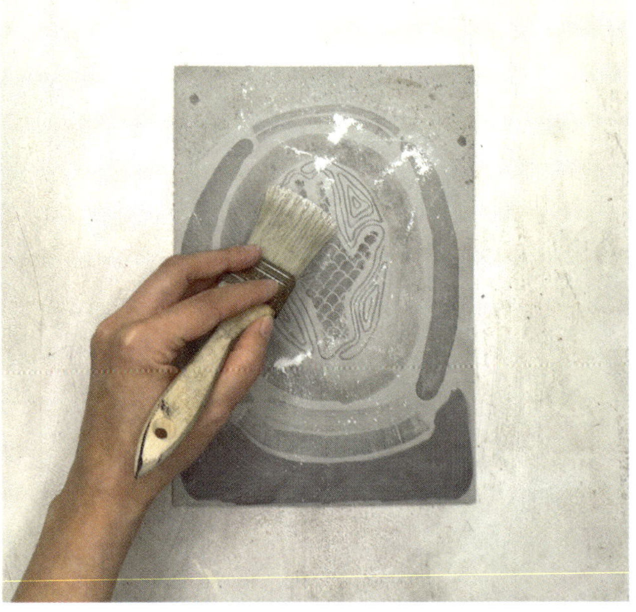

2. The French chalk will allow the gum arabic to sit evenly on the lino surface and gather close to the greasy drawing material.

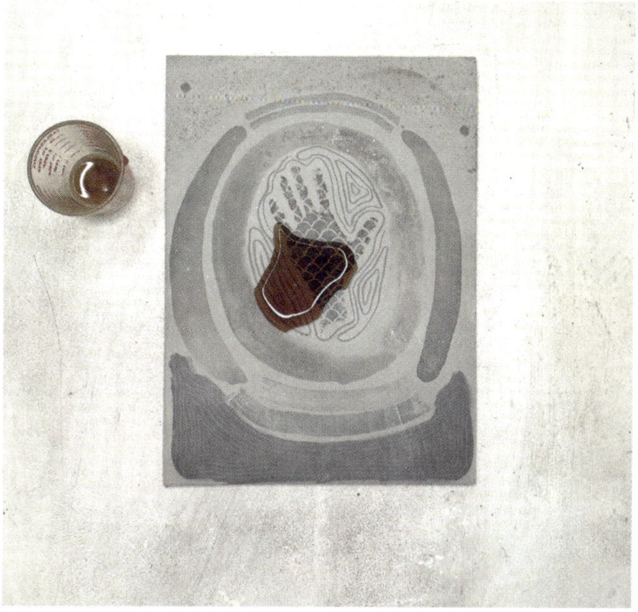

3. Spread a small amount of gum arabic over the surface of the lino using a soft brush, trying to avoid disturbing the drawing material. The gum will create a water-attracting layer on the non-image area of the lino.

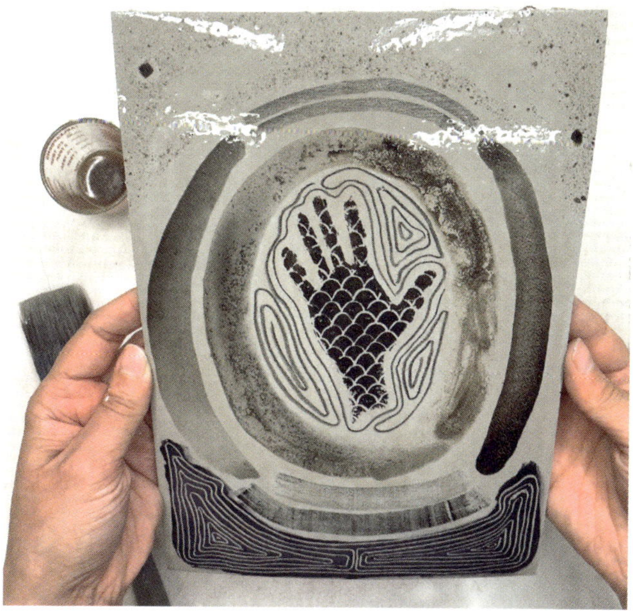

4. Once an even coating of gum has been applied to the lino, allow it to dry in warmth and sunshine. Leave it for at least 24 hours but ideally, for as long as possible.

Printing a lino lithograph

If you are using a foam roller it is recommended to modify your ink to make it a little looser, so add one or two drops of oil to a teaspoon of ink. However, if you are using a traditional roller, don't modify the ink as the tackiness will be of benefit when employing slightly more force with the flat roller.

As with wood lithography, we ink up straight on top of the drawing material on the lino. If you are using a light coloured ink, your first prints may be slightly muddied by the pigment in the drawing material transferring, but it will pass after a print or two.

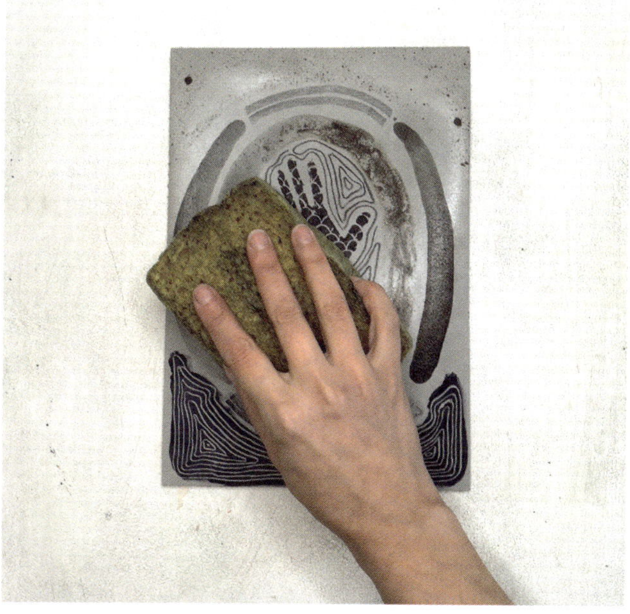

1. Under a tap, remove the excess gum with water. The excess gum will feel slimy on the surface; use a damp sponge to gently remove the last of the excess gum. Try to keep the back of the lino dry or it will curl.

Printing a lino lithograph *(continued)*

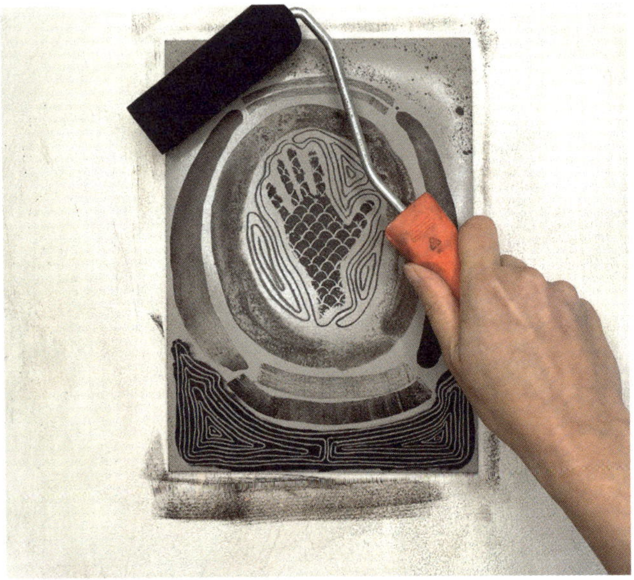

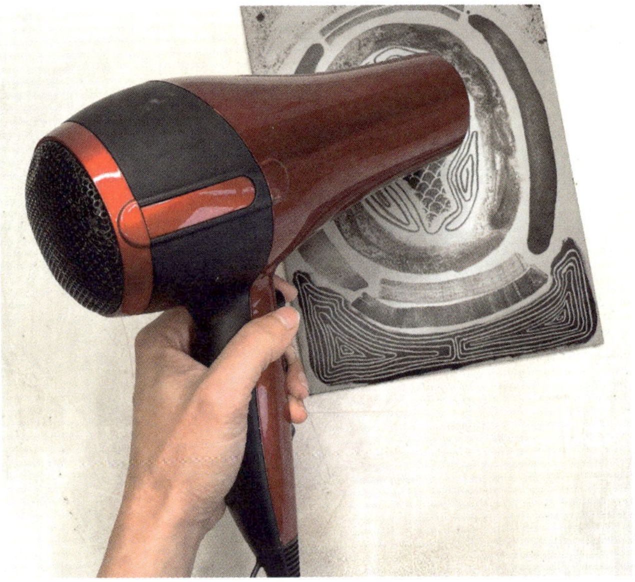

2. Keeping the plate damp with your sponge, and using a foam roller (or traditional roller) with light pressure, roll over with ink quite quickly and in multiple directions, until your image is evenly coated in ink.

3. Dry your plate with a fan or cold hairdryer. As lino is naturally water-resistant it won't hold water like a wood lithography plate and will dry quite quickly.

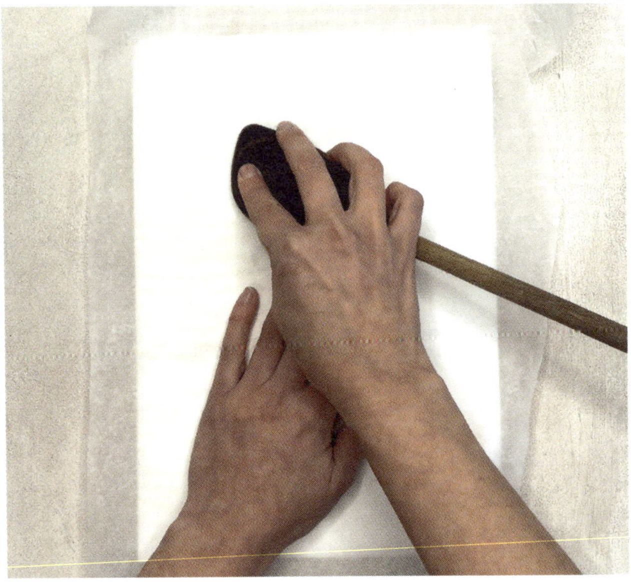

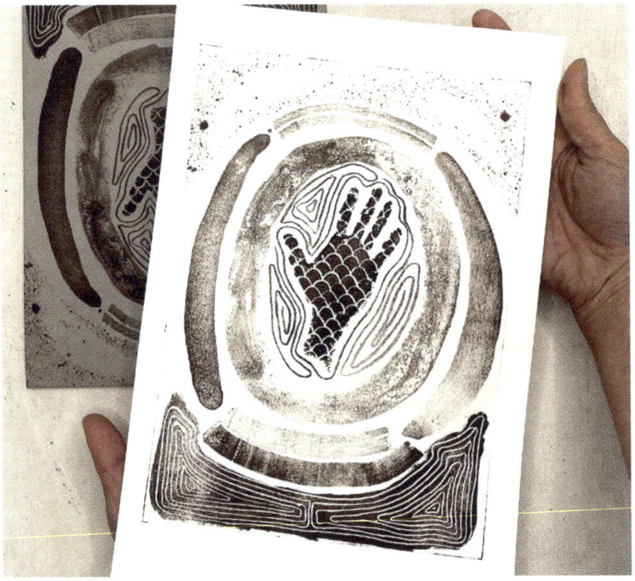

4. Place your dampened paper on top and then a protective sheet of greaseproof paper. Hand burnish with strong pressure all over the plate, using a wooden spoon or similar tool.

5. The first print has picked up the detail well, especially within the central tusche wash areas. There are areas at the bottom and on the outer tusche washes that are still a little light and require further inking.

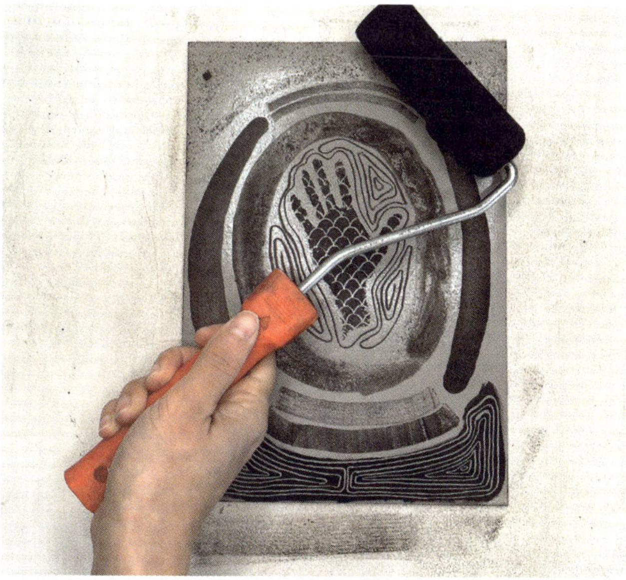

6. Using your sponge, dampen the plate again. Try not to allow the plate to remain dry for too long after printing. Ink up the plate again, noticing where it is darkening quickly and where needs more focused inking.

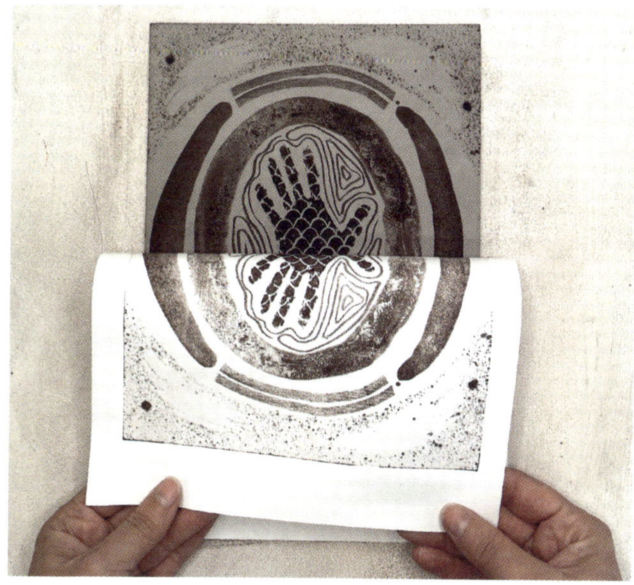

7. The plate will start to print darker; with careful inking it will even out, and subsequent prints will repeatedly print at a similar level. Try to repeat your inking pattern for repeated prints in an edition.

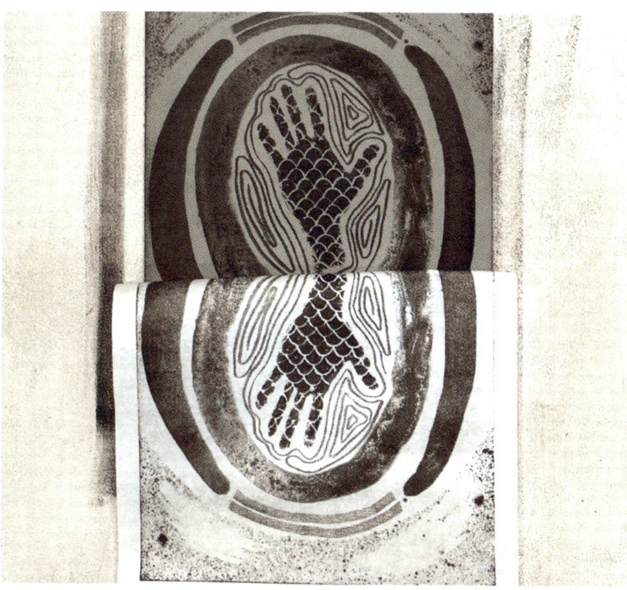

8. Smooth, lightweight papers will pick up the detail of the print very faithfully and don't require dampening. Lightweight papers also require less pressure when hand burnishing.

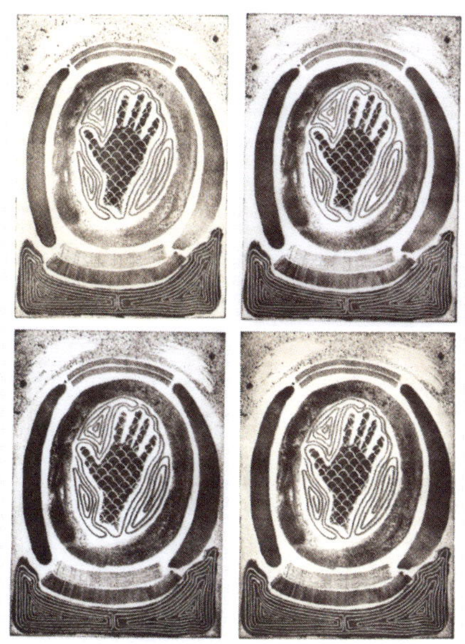

9. Between these – the 2nd, 4th, 9th and 10th prints in the edition – there is not a huge amount of variation. Only some darkening and scumming around the edges can be seen to be developing.

Reusing the lino

Due to its resistant surface, the drawing materials, gum and ink sit on top of the lino and will not be deeply absorbed into it. This means that you only need to sand away a thin layer of lino to reuse it, and the same piece of lino can be sanded back many times. When you have removed the ink of the previous layer, allow the lino to fully dry before sanding it again. Damp lino will be softer than normal, and it is far easier to scratch it while it is in this weakened state. The same piece of lino can be used multiple times, which of course makes registration much easier, as you only need to register the one piece of lino. The same piece of lino was used for all the examples in this entire chapter.

TOP
Thoroughly remove all traces of the printing ink from the lino using a rag and some vegetable oil or solvent and allow it to fully dry.

BOTTOM
Sand down the block again, removing all traces of the stained ink to create a fresh working surface. Test how water sits on the lino before starting to draw again.

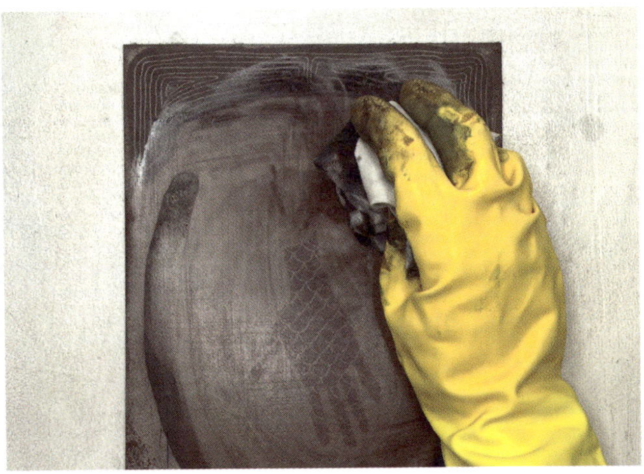

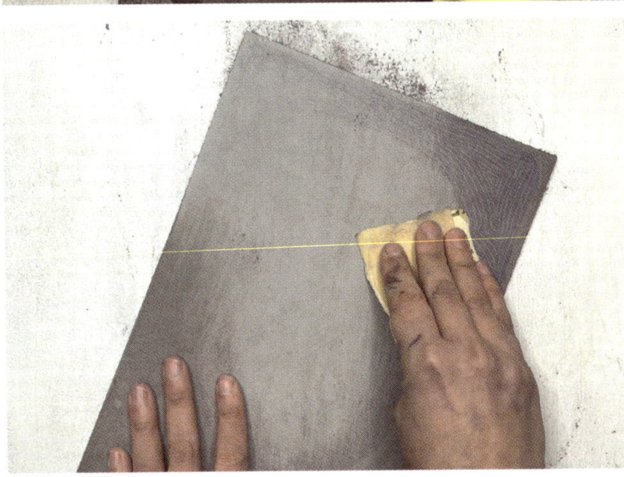

Making transfer paper

Transfer papers are incredibly easy to make, using only gum arabic and water. You can draw your image onto the transfer paper in any location as it's easily transportable, and without worrying about transferring grease with your fingers. You can use the transfer paper to take rubbings, trace images onto it using a lightbox, or collage pieces of transfer paper. One of the biggest benefits of using the transfer paper method is the fact that your drawing will print the same way around as you drew it; you don't need to worry about reflecting the image, so you can draw onto the transfer paper without any inhibition.

You need to use lightweight and smooth paper for transfers, which won't disintegrate or buckle when wetted. I use 120gsm smooth Canaletto paper. This process is easier to use with a press, but it is possible with hand burnishing; it is labour-intensive if you are hand burnishing, and you must take care not to smudge the image.

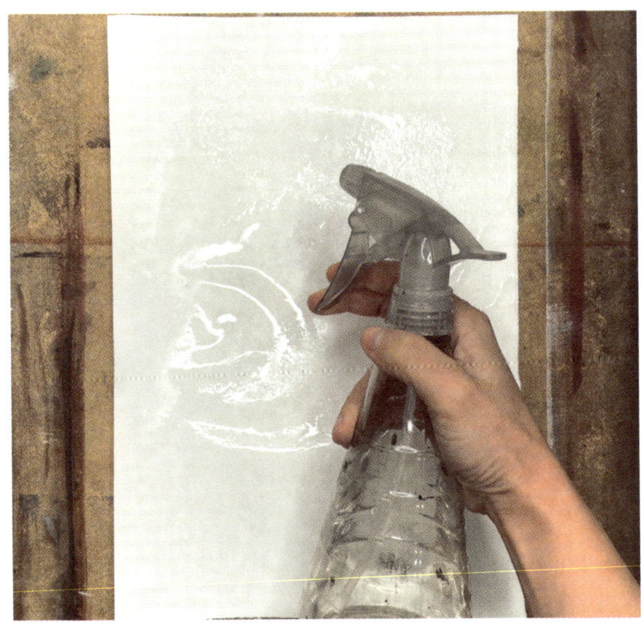

1. Soak paper ready for stretching, in a tray or by using a spray bottle. Remove the paper from the soaking tray and allow it to rest for a few minutes before blotting off any excess water from the surface.

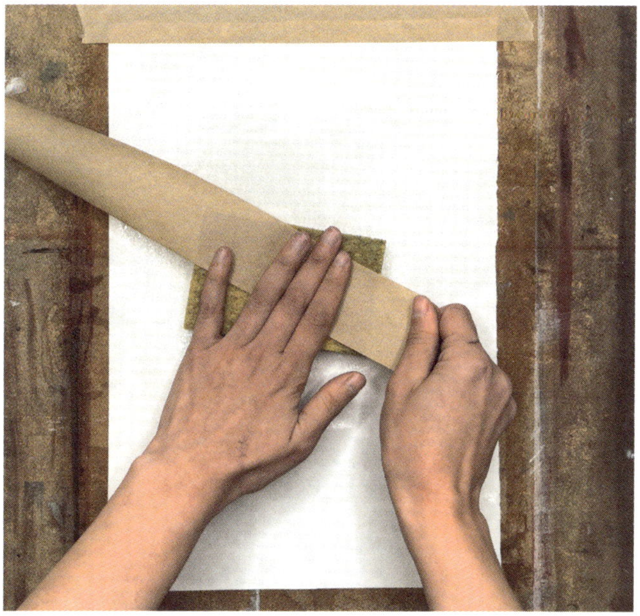

2. On a prepared flat board, dampen strips of gum tape using a sponge. Tape the paper to the board around the edges of the paper and allow it to dry completely. It will stretch and flatten as it dries.

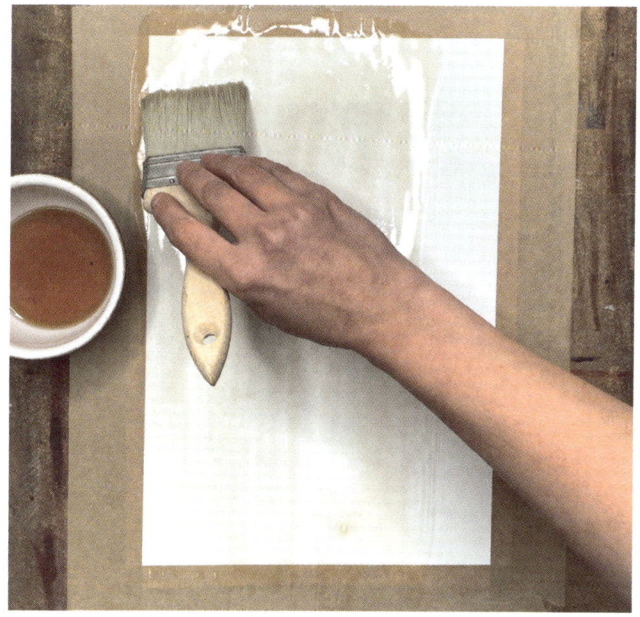

3. Mix a 50:50 solution of gum arabic and water and coat the paper using a wide brush. Allow this coat to dry and apply another one or two coats. Once dried, remove the gum tape using a damp sponge to soften the tape on the board.

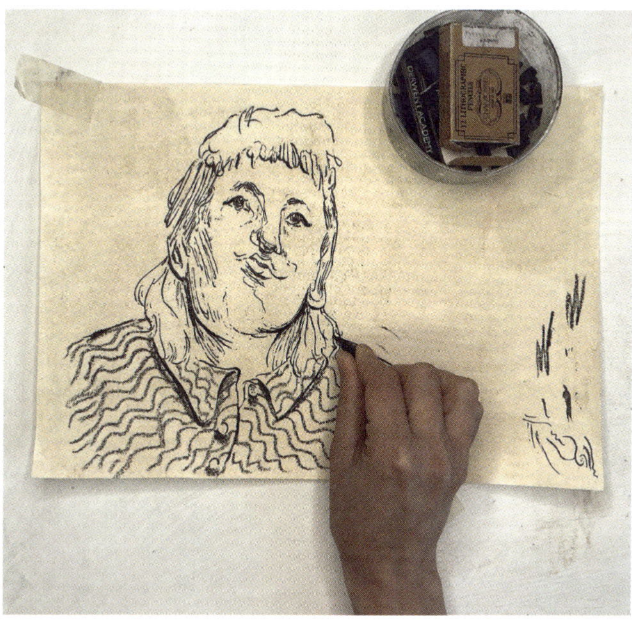

4. Draw onto the transfer paper using dry materials like crayons, or oil-based materials like stopping out varnish or diluted printing ink. Don't use water-based materials as they will damage the water-based gum arabic coating.

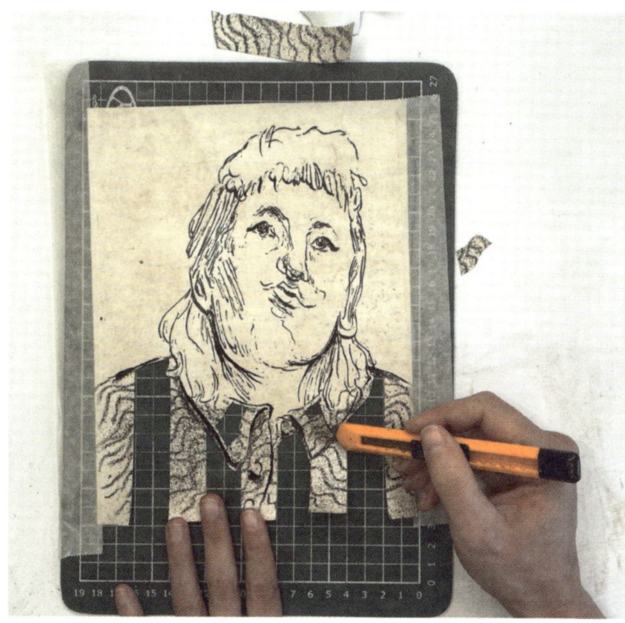

5. Cut down your transfer paper to the size of your drawing. Cut away areas of unused paper as this will transfer gum to lino surface and create a gum resist, so you won't be able to add more drawing in that area.

Transfer paper *(continued)*

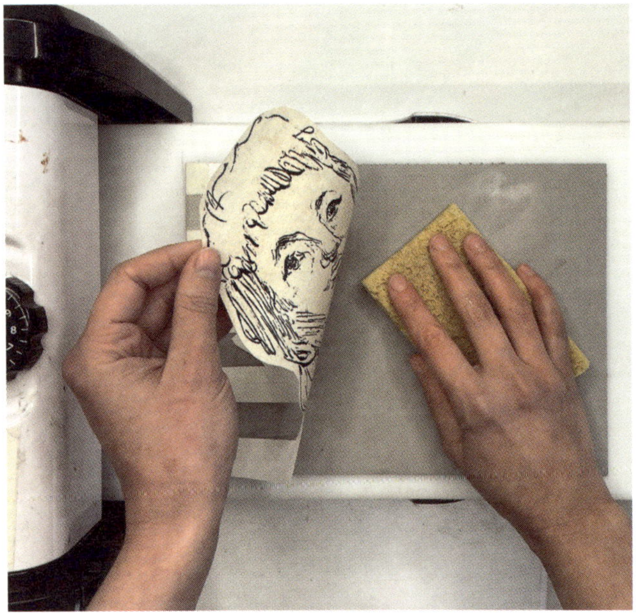

6. Tape the transfer paper to the lino so that it won't move in the press. Lightly dampen the lino and place the transfer paper face down onto the dampened surface of the lino.

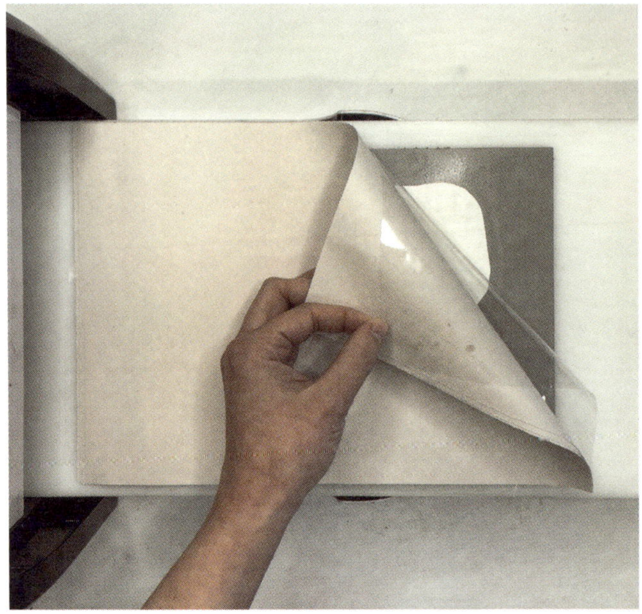

7. Place a thin sheet of plastic on top to trap the moisture in this layer, and then a sheet of newsprint too for cushioning in the press. Run this through the press on medium pressure.

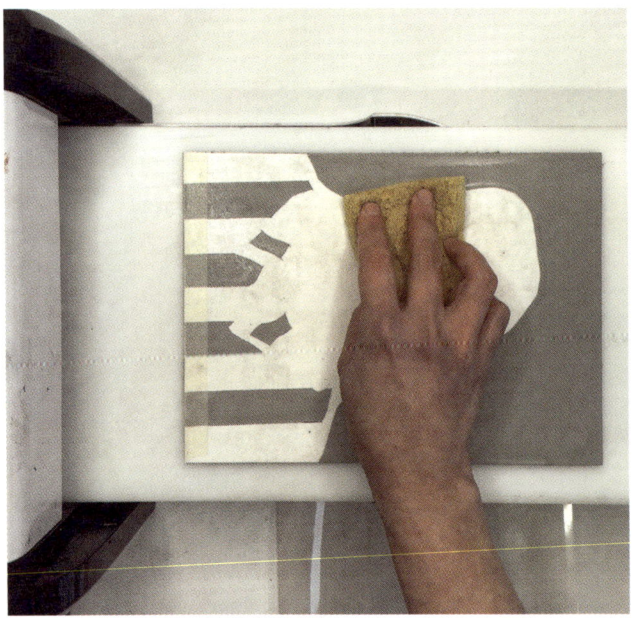

8. Run the lino through the press a few times; each time remove the plastic and lightly dampen the back of the transfer paper, then replace the plastic and newsprint. Increase the pressure on the press if necessary.

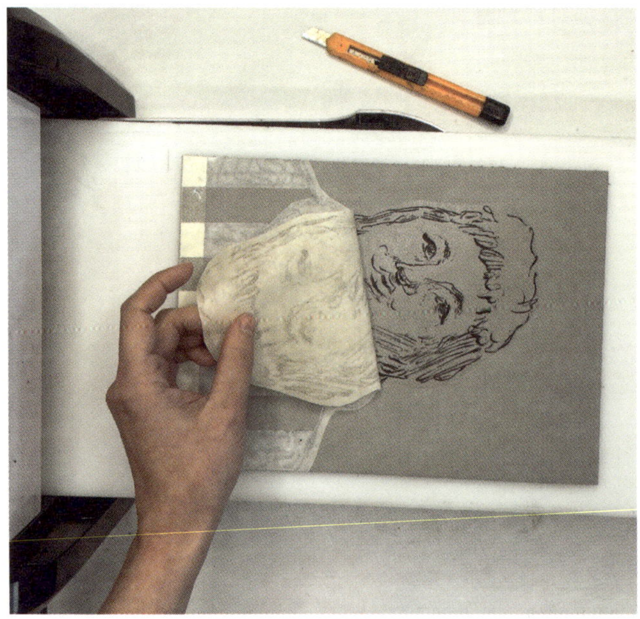

9. When the transfer paper becomes semi-transparent and you can see the image through it, it's time to carefully remove the transfer paper. Dampen the paper once more and slowly peel back the paper.

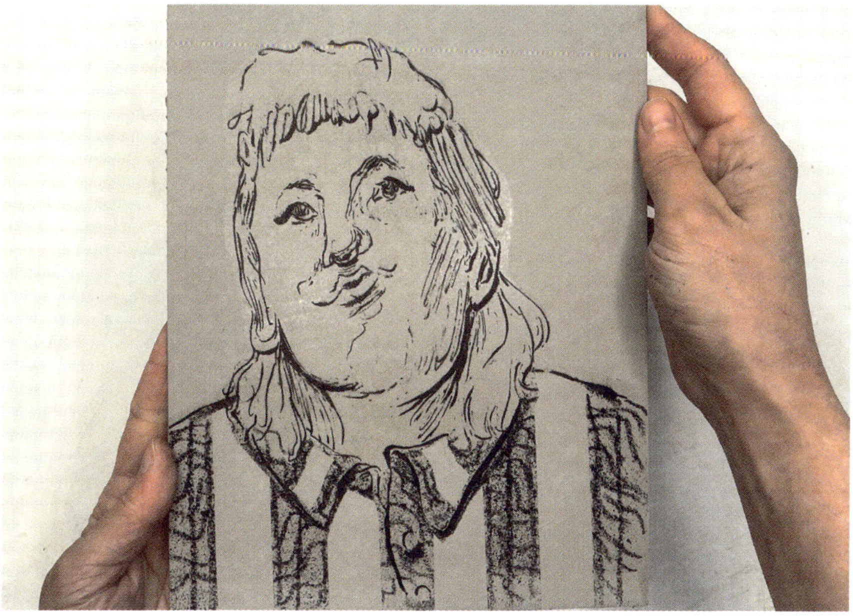

10. Allow the transfer to fully dry on the lino before continuing to develop your image. No further imagery can be added to any areas where gum has been transferred onto the plate.

Lo-shu washes

Lo-shu washes, also known as gum washes, create a delicate white line wash with an inked background. A tiny amount of gum arabic is mixed with water (3–5 drops in 30ml water) and pooled on the surface of the plate. As the solution dries the gum forms a delicate resist in tide lines on the plate. Forced drying of the wash with a hairdryer compared to allowing it to dry naturally will create different markings. The washes can be overlaid to create intricately detailed washes, but avoid using too many layers as the build-up of gum will just form a silhouette of resist.

As the deposit of gum is very fine and delicate it will darken quickly on the lino as it will be in constant battle with the water-resistant nature of the surface. Each print will be different from the next as the wash darkens. So, it is best to embrace each print in its individuality and to forget about aiming for an edition.

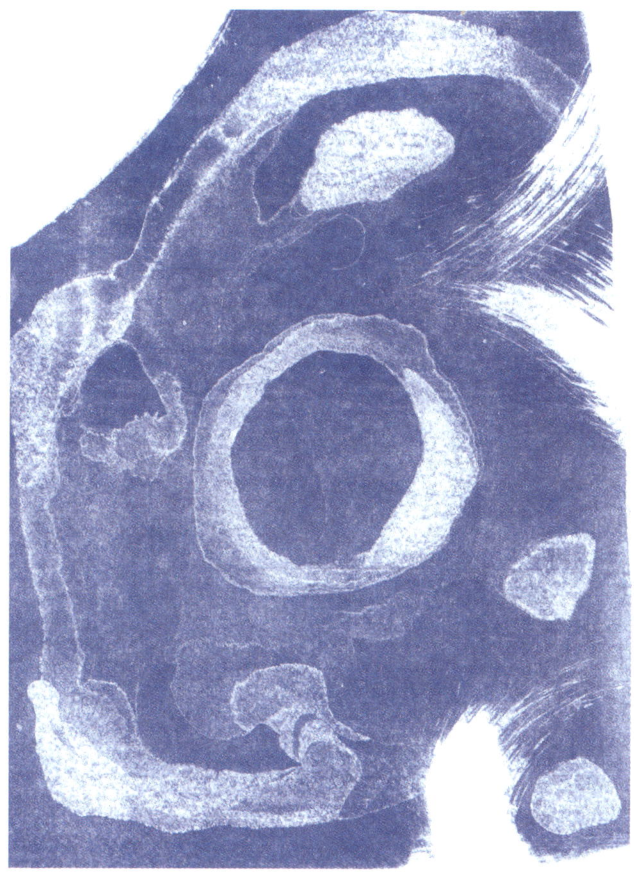

Lo-shu test print with gum resist brush marks. 21 x 30cm, 1/1.

Lo-shu and print

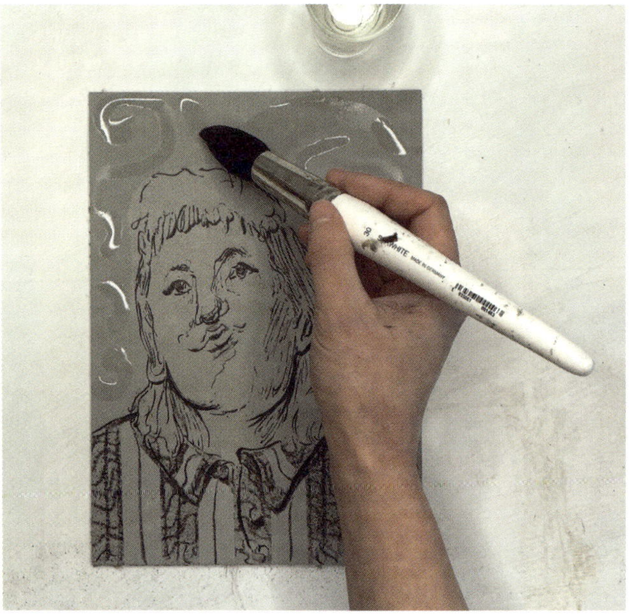

1. Mix 3–5 drops of gum in 30ml of water. Using a clean brush that can hold plenty of water, paint on the gum water generously and allow it to pool.

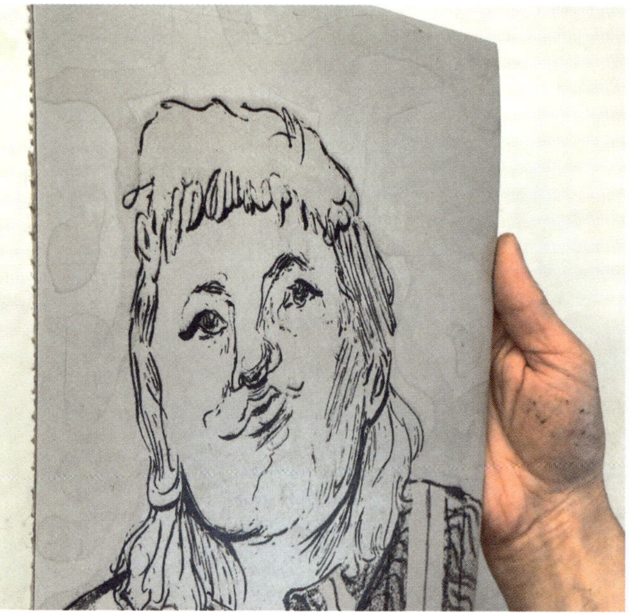

2. The gum water can dry naturally or be force dried with a hairdryer. When it's dry you can see the faint tide lines of gum that will act as a resist.

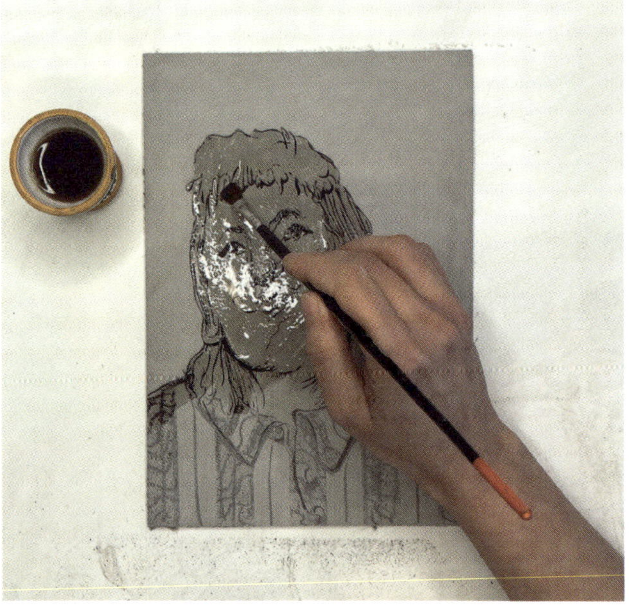

3. Apply French chalk to the plate and apply gum to the drawn elements of the plate – don't apply gum to the lo-shu area, just leave it bare. Leave the block for as long as possible before printing.

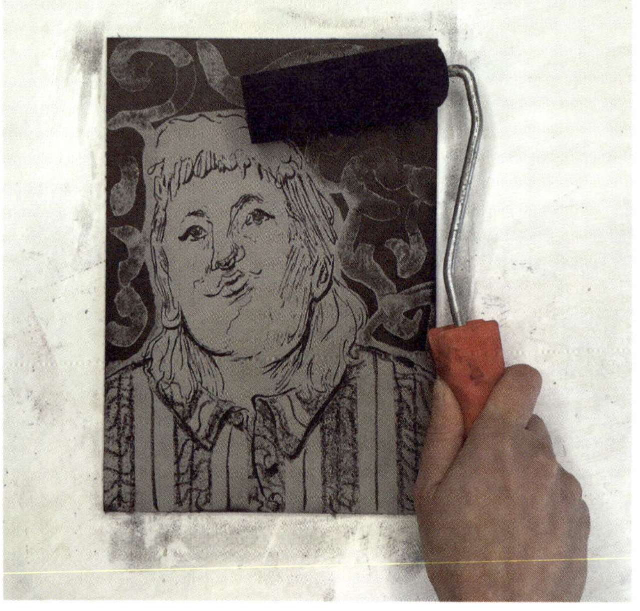

4. Dampen and ink up the plate as normal, being careful not to overly ink the lo-shu area. A foam roller is recommended for inking up a plate with lo-shu.

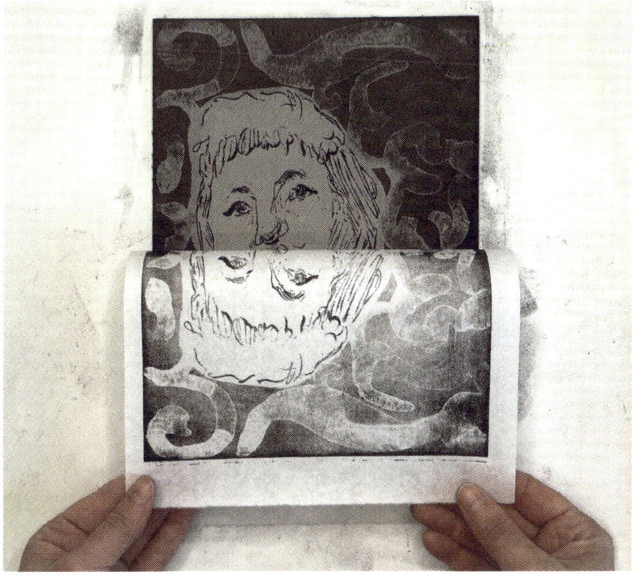

5. It can be difficult to find the balance between fully inking the solid areas of the background between the lo-shu washes, and not filling in the delicate lo-shu areas. This first print is too light.

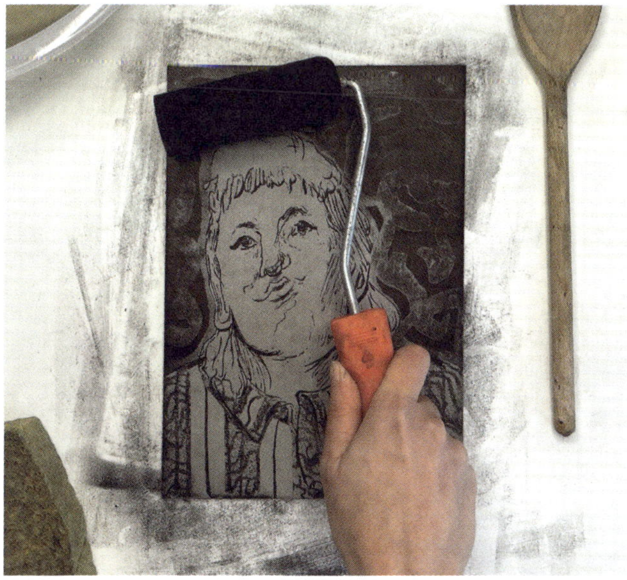

6. The lo-shu areas of the plate will darken quickly compared to the rest of the plate. It's important to make sure you are keeping the plate damp when inking it, but it is unavoidable that it will darken.

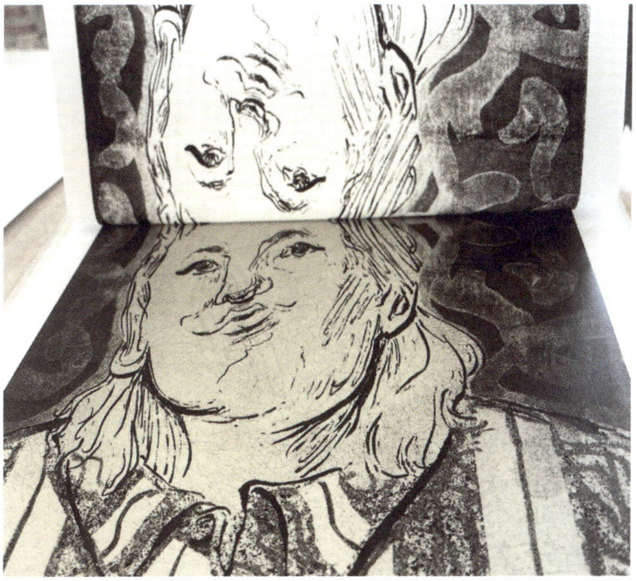

7. As the lo-shu area is darkening it creates interesting marks on the print and each print will be uniquely different from the others in the edition. The other drawn elements are staying crisp.

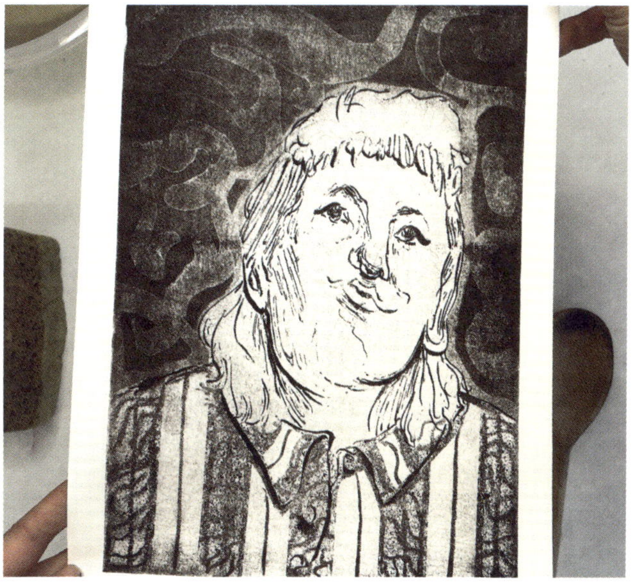

8. As the block starts to darken you can change from printing on dampened paper to printing onto dry paper; this will print slightly lighter with more clarity. Or stick with damp paper and embrace the deterioration!

Multiple layers and incorporating relief print

When working in relief on a reductive linocut, the area to be printed becomes smaller with each layer, as the same piece of lino is being used throughout, being carved ever smaller. This produces a build-up of ink in subsequent layers on the print. When using the lino lithography method, when the lino has been sanded down between layers, the entire surface area of the lino is back in action, ready to be used again. So, we have more scope for the interplay of colours with overlaid layers.

When changing the colour of the ink part way through printing a lino lithograph, you have to roll the new ink straight onto the plate, on top of the previous ink. This means that there will be a cross-over of colours in your print edition, where the traces of the first colour on the lino will mingle with the new colour. The new ink will become dominant after a couple of prints, after the traces of the previous ink have faded.

There are no rules for when to print a relief layer and when to print a lithographic layer. Lino which has been carved can then be sanded down to accept a lithographic drawing. Take note that the edges of the carved areas will be softened by the sanding and will not print as graphically as before.

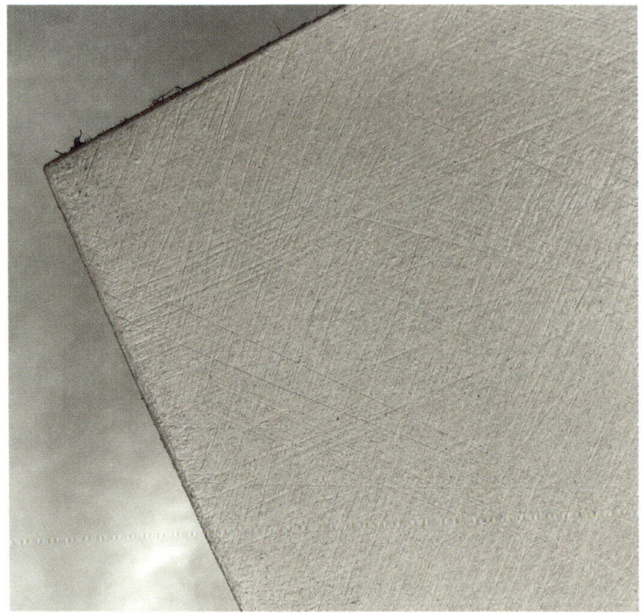

1. Remove the ink and sand down the lino ready for the next layer. Coarse sandpaper can be used for a textural effect for the crayons and washes.

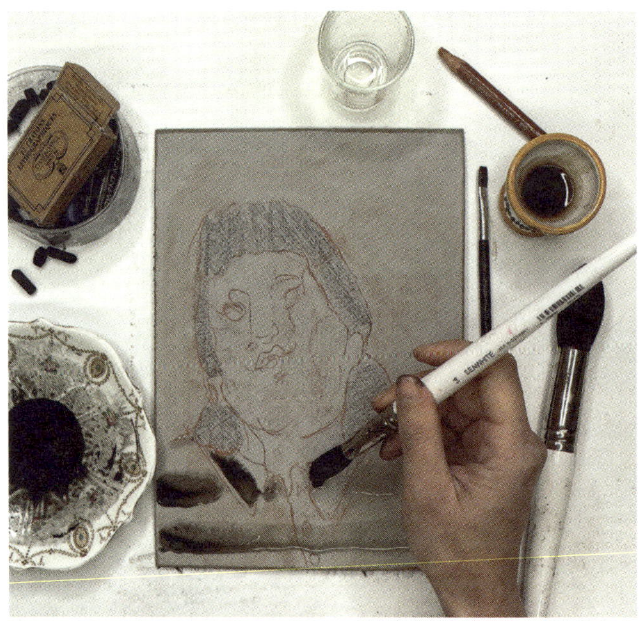

2. The crayon will pick up the texture of the coarse sandpaper on the lino beautifully, and the tusche wash will dry differently, compared to a wash on a smooth surface.

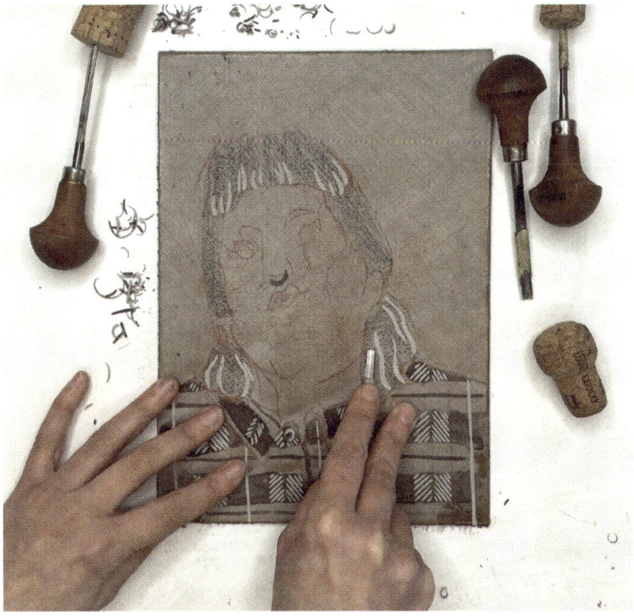

3. After French chalking and gumming the lino you can carve into the plate. As this is the second layer, wherever you carve away will show the previous layer through.

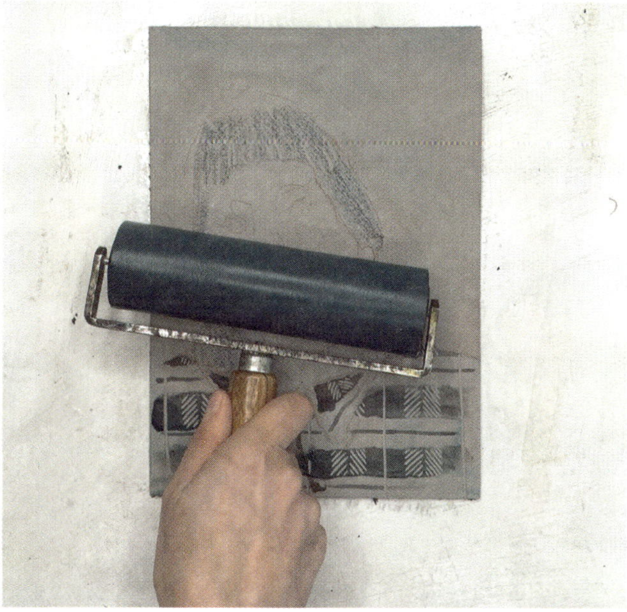

4. Remove the excess gum under the tap, keep the plate damp and ink up as normal. Use slightly less ink when inking the plate with a traditional roller and watch out for roller lines if your roller is smaller than the plate.

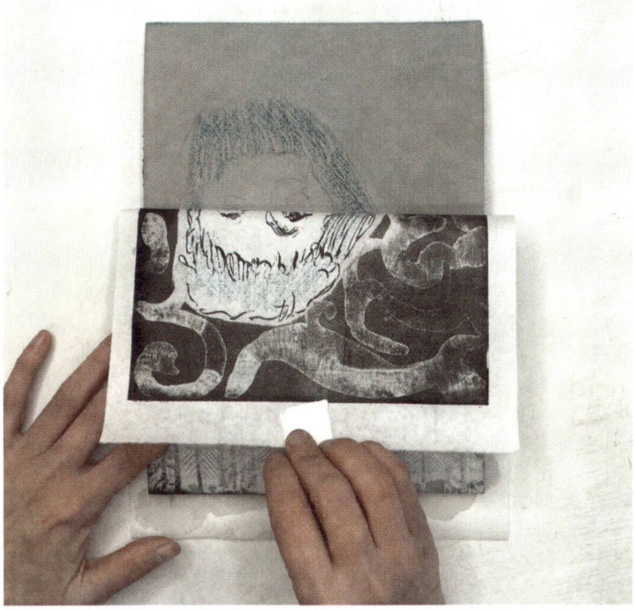

5. Dry the plate and hand burnish or print using a press. Assuming that you have been using a registration guide, this second layer will print in perfect position on the first layer.

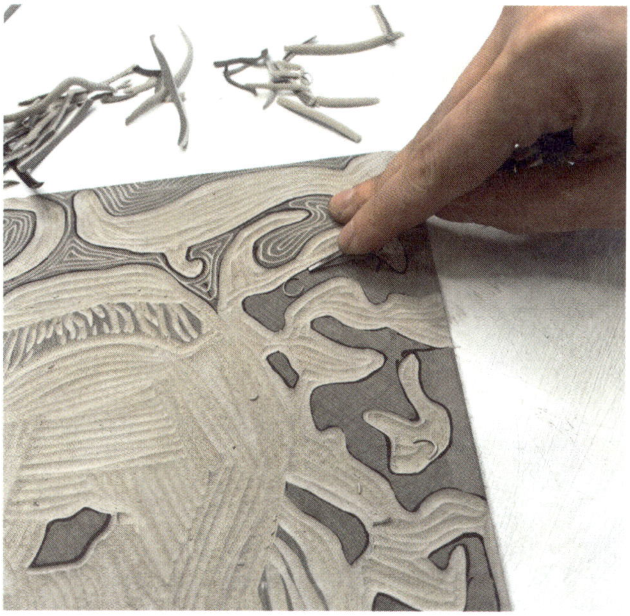

6. Using the lithographic marks on the plate as a guide, carve away the lino like a normal relief print. Use different-sized tools and varying your carved marks for interesting effects.

Adding layers and relief *(continued)*

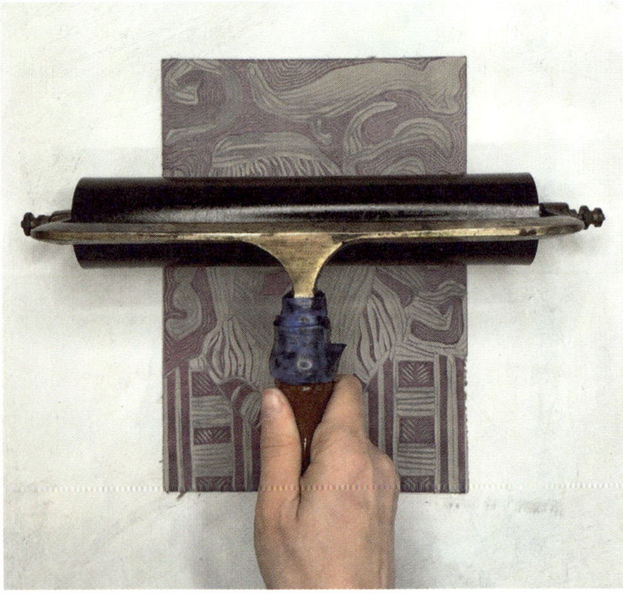

7. Mix a generous amount of extender into your ink for this layer to increase the transparency. More ink is transferred with relief prints compared to lithography so it can be easy to dominate a print with an opaque relief layer.

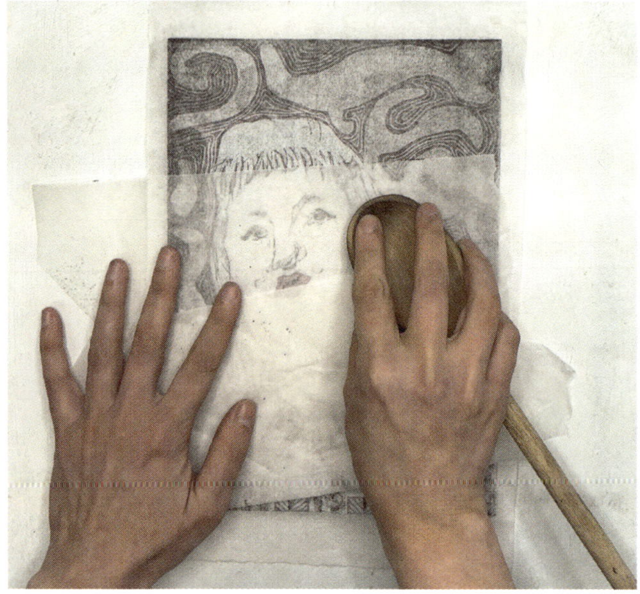

8. When hand burnishing this relief layer you can use less pressure than when burnishing a litho layer. Be careful when using a press as it can emboss and distort your registration. You may want to avoid using a blanket for this reason.

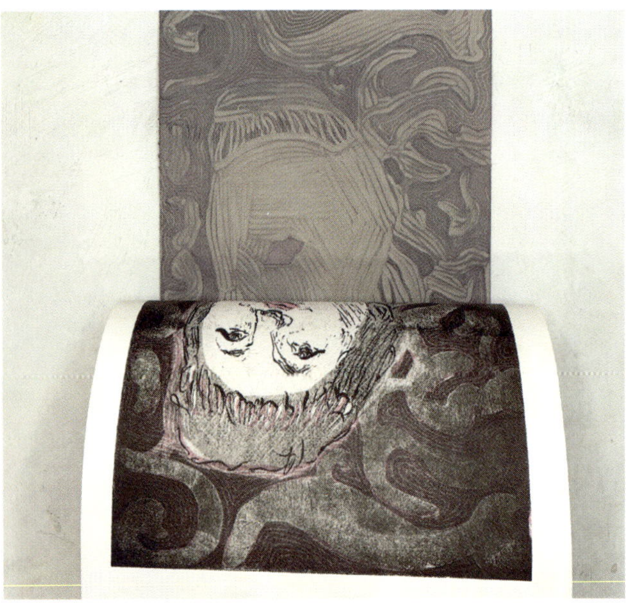

9. The transparent ink layer will sit on top of the previous layer, affecting the colour but still showing the details of the previous layer through without dominating it.

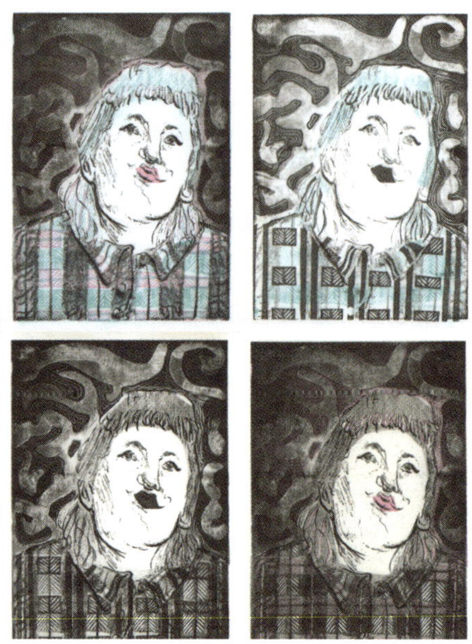

10. To change ink colour while printing a lino lithograph you have to apply the new ink straight on top of the old ink. With a relief layer you can remove the ink from the lino and replace with a new colour. These examples show a combination of colour tests.

TROUBLESHOOTING

Plate darkening very quickly

If your plate is starting to darken too quickly, counteract this by stripping back the ink. Print your plate onto scrap paper a couple of times, without re-inking, to take off some of the ink from the plate. Your ink may be too oily, or you may have too much ink on your roller. Adjust your ink and roll up with less ink on your roller. If you haven't sanded down your lino well enough, then this darkening will be unavoidable. Make sure next time to prepare the lino more thoroughly and test how water sits on the lino before starting to draw.

Scumming

Scumming is where ink starts to collect in unwanted areas on your plate, especially around your image area. This may occur because your ink is too loose or has had too much oil added to it. Or it could be because your plate was drying while you were inking up. Once the scumming is established it will get worse. To remove areas of built-up ink from the plate before printing, use a damp rag with a little oil to remove the ink, and then wipe off any oil residue with a clean damp rag.

Bleeding ink

This will occur if too much oil has been added to your printing ink. Scrape up your ink and clean off your roller, replace with unmodified ink. If you are using a foam roller, squeeze the ink from the roller into a rag and roll up in unmodified ink.

Roller lines

The inflexible edges of traditional rollers will sometimes leave lines of ink over the plate, including in the non-image areas. If you can, use a roller that is bigger than the plate, or use less ink or less pressure when inking up. This is less likely to occur with a foam roller.

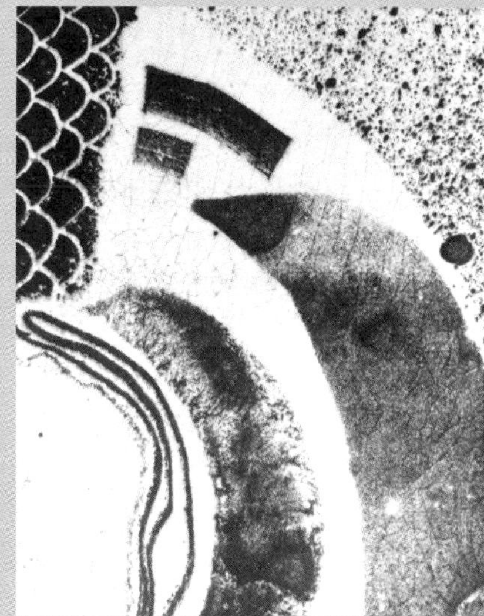

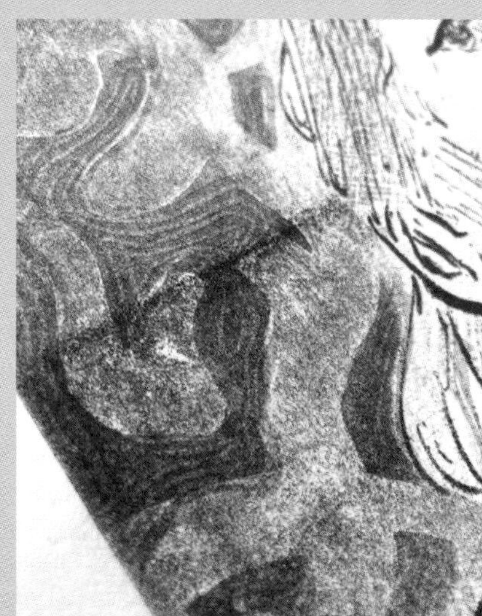

TOP
Crackle-effect lines can appear on a lino lithograph if the gum has been applied too thickly. It is not necessarily a problem as the effect is quite visually pleasing and can be created intentionally.

MIDDLE
Traditional rollers can leave lines on the lino at the edges of the roller. Using a roller larger than the plate can help avoid this but, once established, these lines can be difficult to stop darkening.

BOTTOM
Roller lines can appear when using a sponge roller if too much force has been used when first applying the roller to the plate. These lines can be evened out with swift rolling or stripped back when printed.

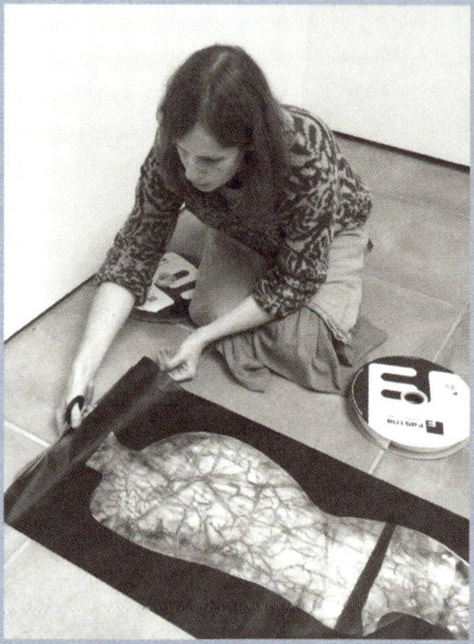

Mary Dalton (UK)

marydalton.co.uk

Mary Dalton is an artist working across multiple disciplines, from installation to toy making. She trained at the RCA as a traditional etcher and lithographer but has since developed a printing practice that is unique to her methodologies and her workplace.

I currently work from home with the family and children supporting every step. My current workspace has no press set up and is the top of my plan chest. I have developed methods of working that enable me to process and make within this space or other facilities at locations I can cycle to. The work very much responds to the space I make it in and the facilities it has.

I use printing presses at different studios in the South East, which are predominately reached by pedal bike, attaching my work and materials onto the pannier rack. The size of the lino which I use must be able to be rolled and fit on a bike. Working on large-scale textile printed pieces has been a revelation over the last few years because they fold down small, are lightweight to carry and allow beautiful sculptural manipulation. I keep my printing practices as non-toxic and ecological as I possibly can. I work from home and I cannot risk any toxic substances being introduced.

My training for years as a traditional etcher using nitric acid had to be overturned when I started working from home, and further when I researched into the ecological credentials of the process. The nature of my workplace and my emphasis upon human and planet health meant many of these processes were weaned out from my practice. Yet the love of the intaglio mark or the expressive lithographic wash was still intrinsic in my print-based thinking and so I began to develop techniques that enabled me to pursue these expressions but without the harmful risks.

Lithography on lino, or lithino as I named it, was born out of these explorations. It allowed me to develop expressive marks freely upon the surface of traditional biodegradable lino whilst keeping the integrity of the graphic lino cut.

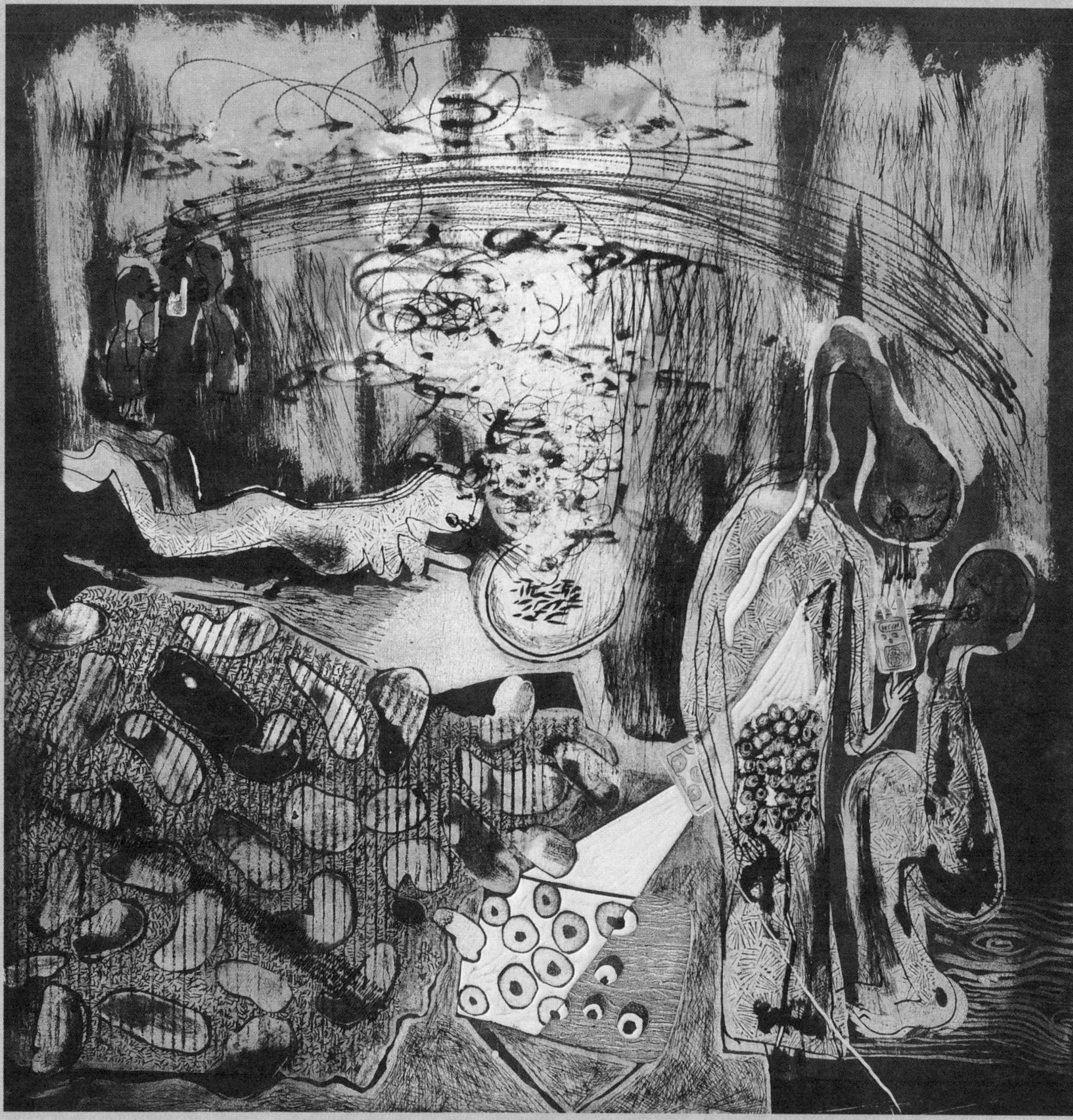

Mary Dalton, *Winter Solstice II*, lino lithography with additional processes, 2024. Unique print, 45 x 45cm.

CHAPTER 7

Paper plate lithography

Paper plate lithography is incredibly cheap and fast. You're able to create multiple layers easily and transfer photographic images onto different surfaces: wood, metal and three-dimensional surfaces, not just onto printmaking paper. There is a wonderful sense of freedom in the image making for paper plate lithography, and you're not inhibited by worrying about transferring unintentional grease to the image. There are no restrictions to the drawing materials and ways of image making as the design will be photocopied, scanned or photographed. So, you don't need to worry about finding specialist equipment, or sourcing costly lithographic materials. It is also easy to incorporate photographic imagery, use found materials, and use collage to create exciting compositions.

Paper plate lithography is also known as gum arabic transfer or toner lithography. It uses photocopies or laser prints as the printing matrix, as the toner in the laser copies is receptive to the greasy ink. Paper plate lithography can be a difficult process to master, as it relies on careful inking and handling of the plates, but once you get the hang of it, you'll be unstoppable. You're only held back in scale by the size of printer or photocopier you can use to make your plates, but with clever tiling of the plates, as seen in Mina Rakidžić's work at the end of the chapter, even that won't stop you.

FACING PAGE
Rolling out the ink ready to print.

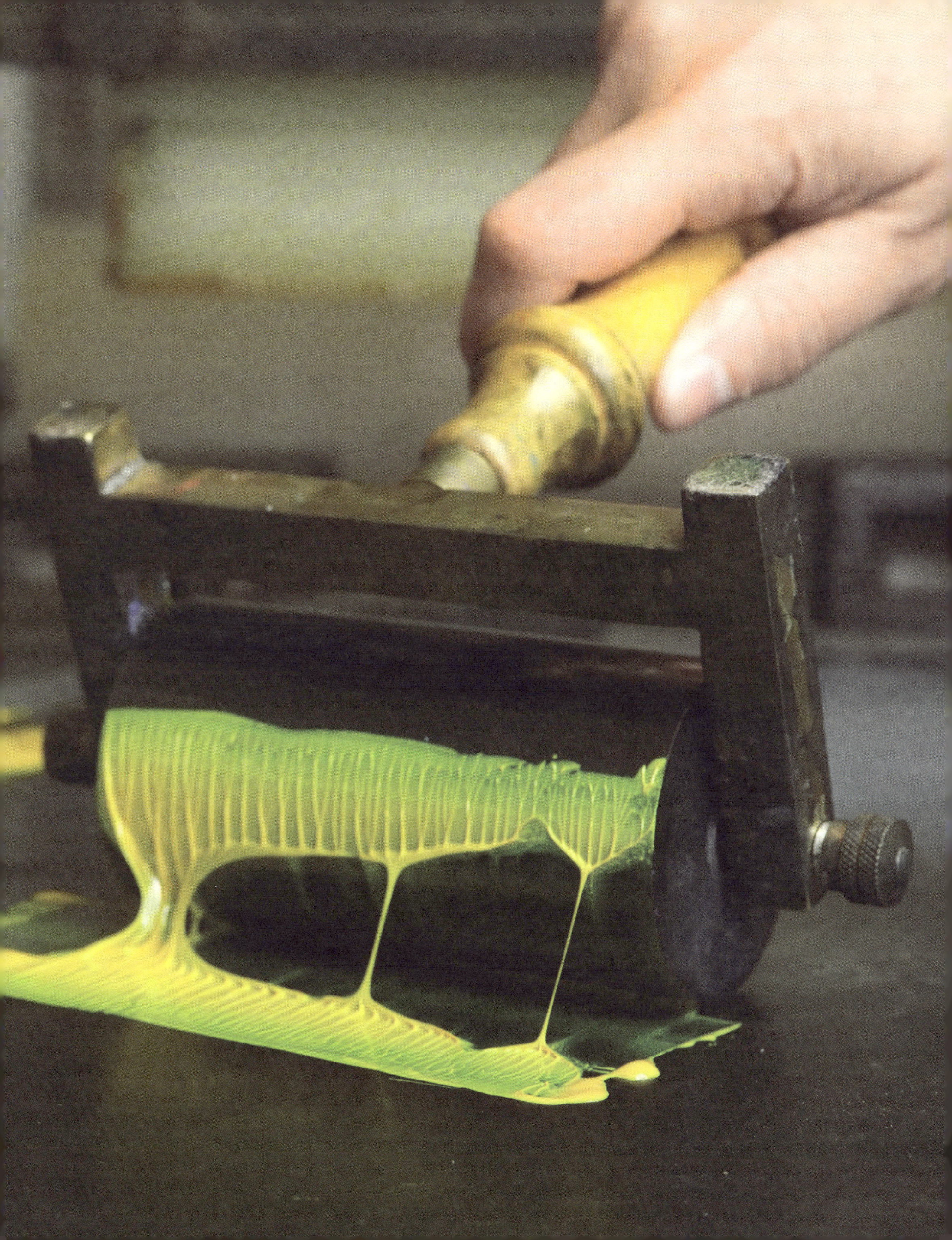

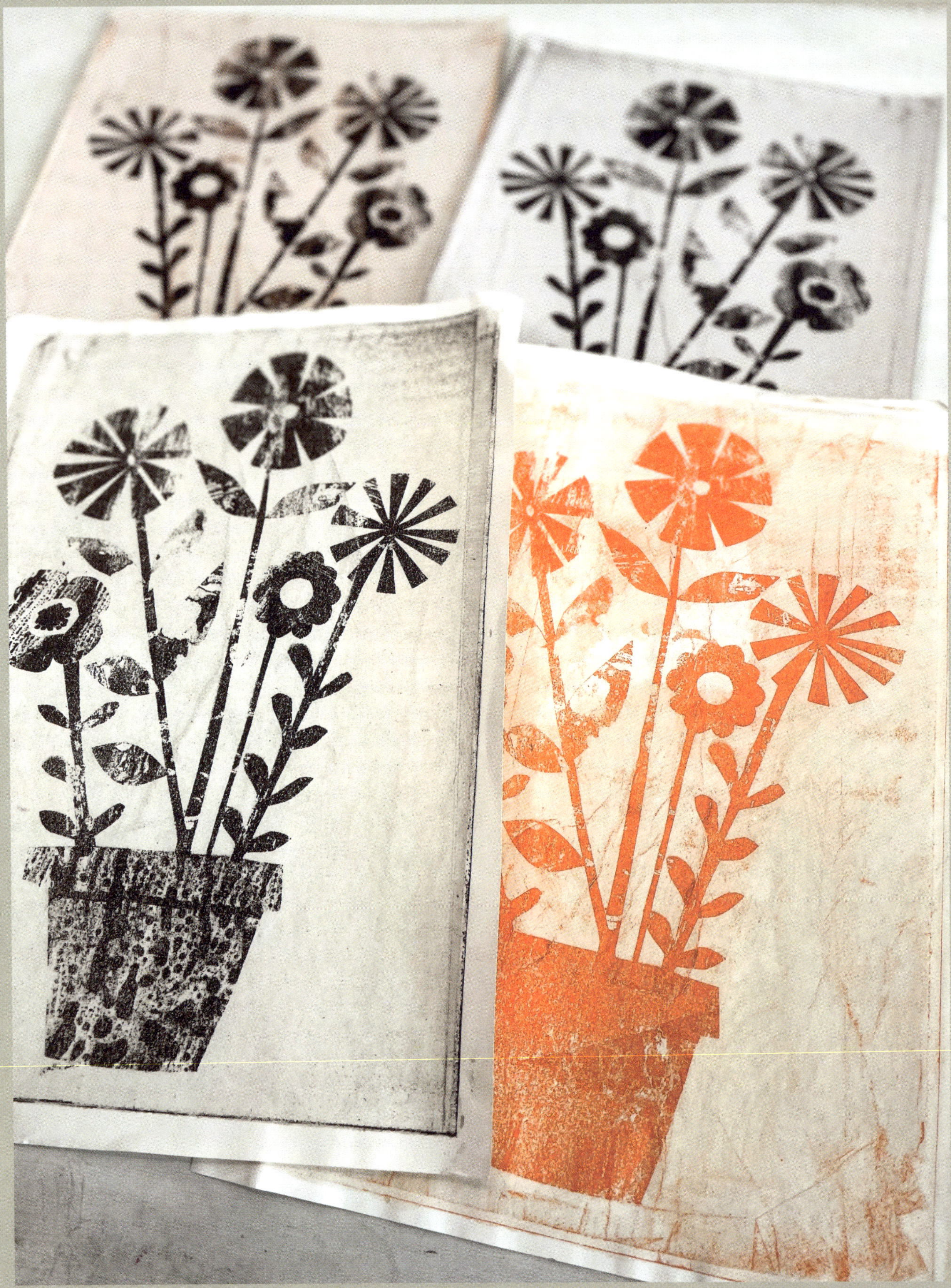

Making a collage plate

When you produce your imagery for a paper lithograph, you need to create a highly contrasted image, working in black and white, with few, or no grey areas. All areas of toner on the paper lithograph will pick up ink indiscriminately. So, a light grey area will pick up just as much ink as a black area.

You have complete freedom while you're making the imagery for your plate. You can use any drawing materials and incorporate collage methods and photographic imagery. The process of creating your imagery is also not as inhibiting as other lithographic processes as there is a separation between the image-making and the plate. You can relax and rest your hand on the surface while you're drawing, because the grease-receptive quality of the plate comes from the printer/photocopier toner, not from greasy drawing materials.

As always, I recommend making a test plate to trial the process without the pressure of making a piece of artwork. You will also need to get to grips with how dark and light to make your imagery and test these boundaries with all the drawing materials you have. This is your opportunity to explore new and innovative ways of mark-making.

Do not use an inkjet printer as these printers use water-based inks, not toner, so the image won't accept grease and the image will just bleed when it becomes wet. Once you've printed your paper plates you will need to leave them for a day or two to cure. If they are used too soon the photocopy toner will still be delicate on the plate and will be easily removed by the printing ink.

MATERIALS

- Photocopies/laser prints
- Gum arabic
- Traditional roller
- Cellulose sponge
- Water bowls for dampening water
- Printing ink
- Black acrylic paint
- Marker pens
- Charcoal
- Glue stick

FACING PAGE
Paper plate lithography test prints with plates behind.

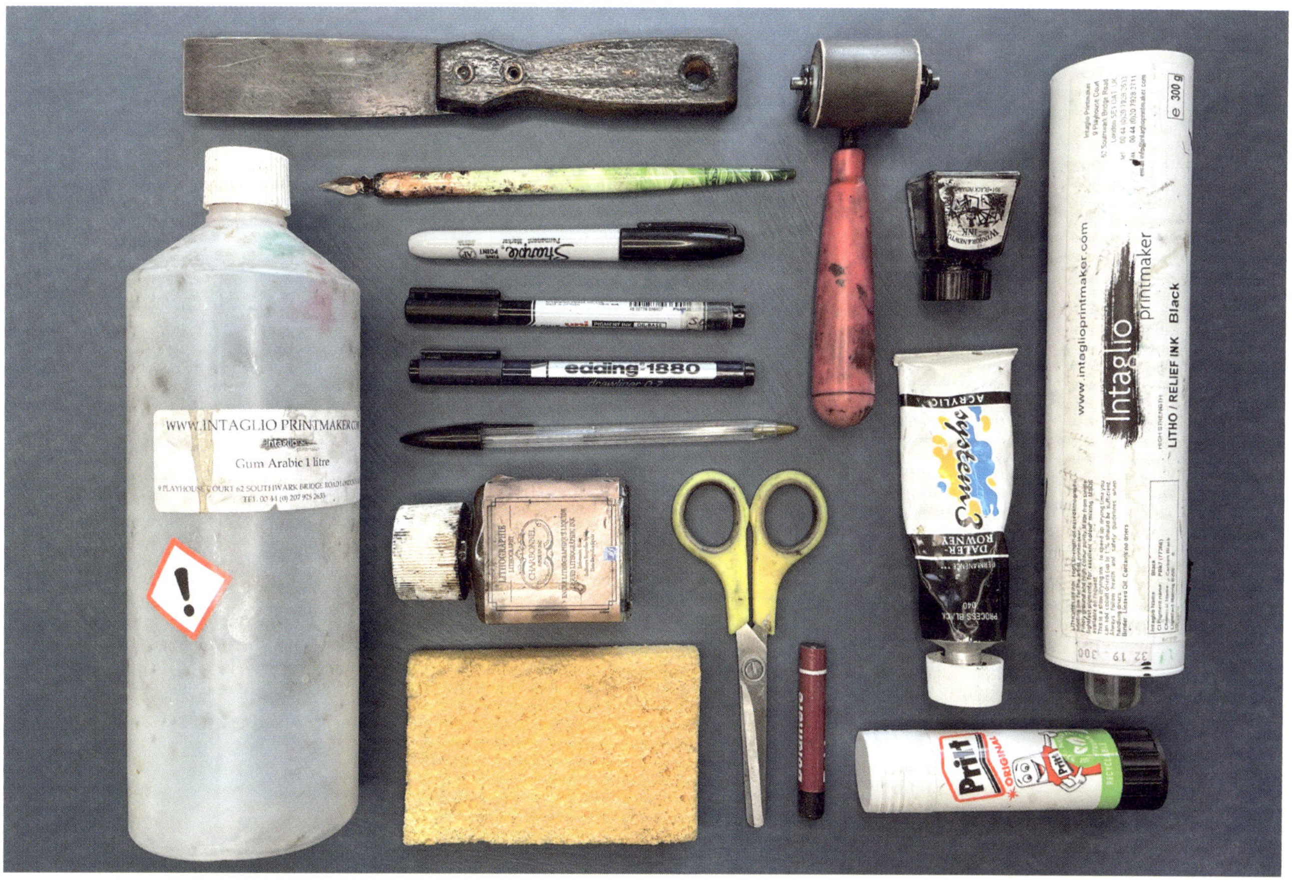

The materials needed for the paper plate lithography process.

Making a collage plate

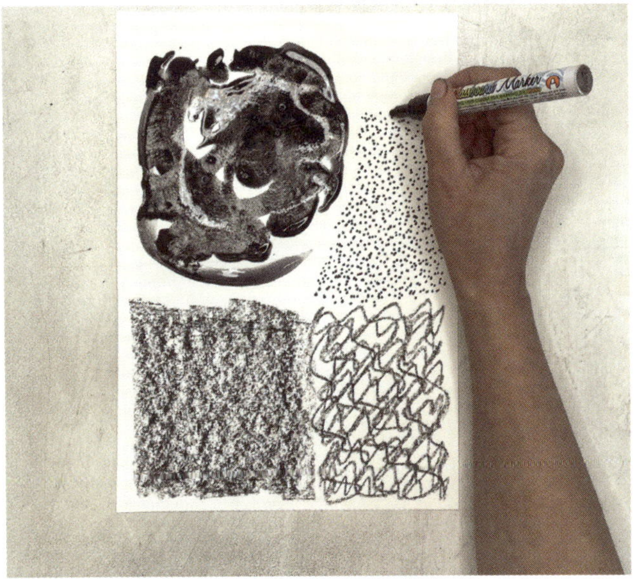

1. Playful mark-making, pattern, texture and line are all things to be explored for the first tests of making a paper plate lithograph. Toner washes can make gorgeous patterns but will require ironing to fix them to the paper.

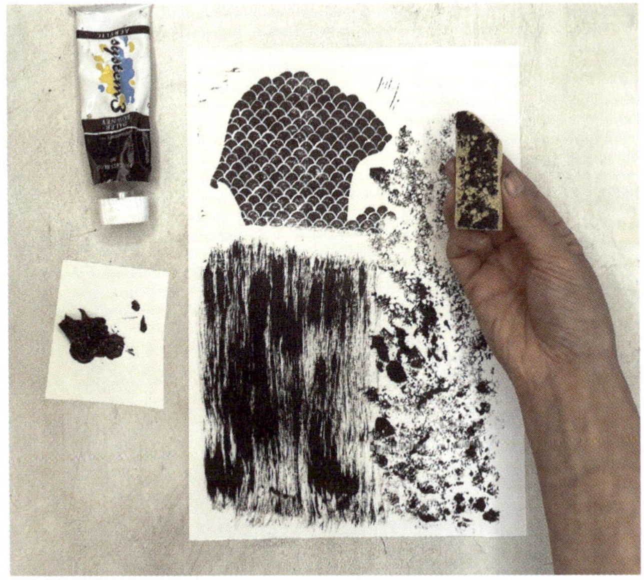

2. Look for objects with interesting textures to transfer onto the paper with acrylic paint. Or print an existing linocut onto the paper in black ink. Dry brushes can make gorgeous marks with acrylic paint or Indian ink.

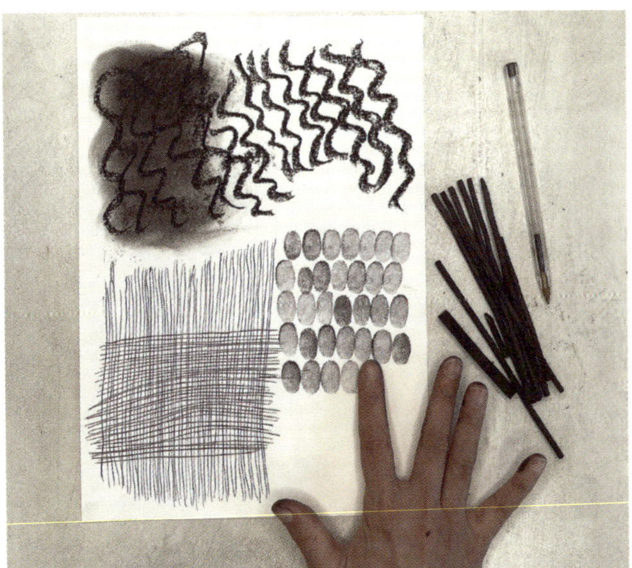

3. Also think about fine lines. The paper plate process can cope with quite small marks so biro lines and fingerprints can be successful. Blended charcoal could lose definition if not contrasted enough, but will create subtle marks.

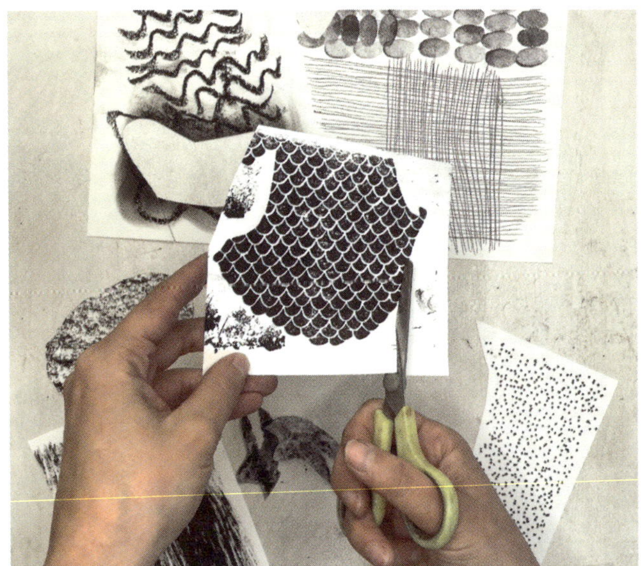

4. The image-making element of this process is not as restrictive as other lithographic processes. You can collage and draw your plate with relative creative freedom.

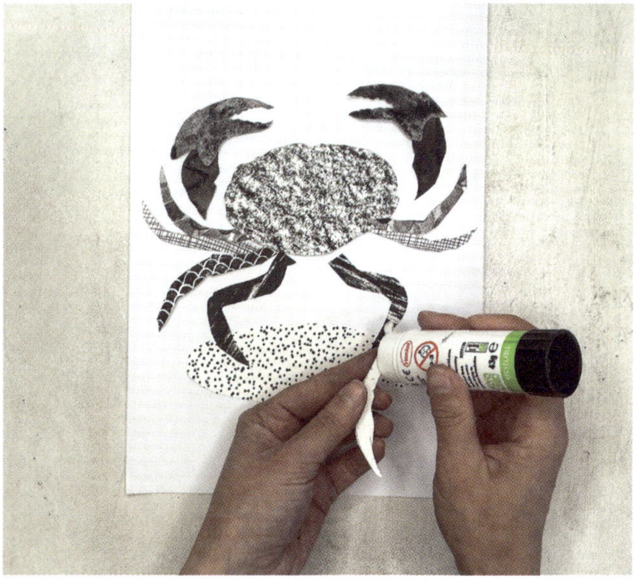

5. Assemble your test plate selecting a range of different mark making examples and tonal examples so you will be able to see their varying results.

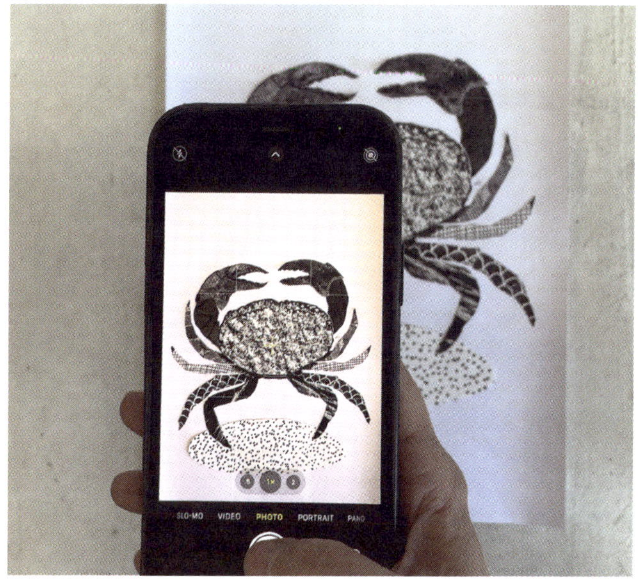

6. Scan or photograph your collage under even lighting. Adjust the contrast of your image on photo editing software on your computer or in the image edits on your phone. Convert to black and white or add a black and white filter to remove grey areas and increase the brightness.

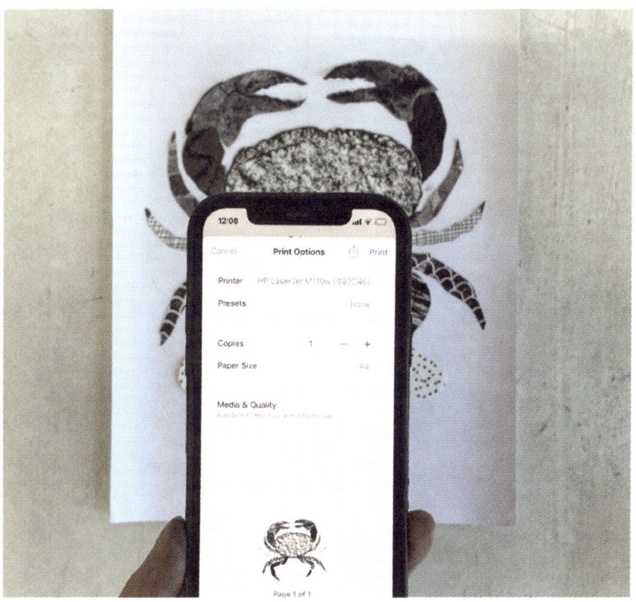

7. Print out your images using a laser printer or photocopier. We want a printer which uses toner, not an inkjet print. Use a smooth paper and a heavyweight paper if possible.

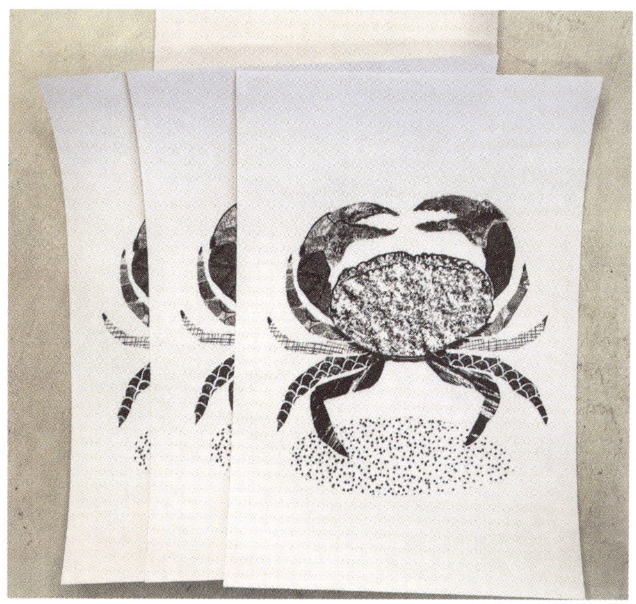

8. Print multiple copies so that you have spares to make mistakes and try out different colours. You will need to leave the photocopies for a couple of days before printing so it's best to be well prepared with multiples.

Printing a paper plate

There's a lot of discussion over what is the best method of printing a paper plate lithograph, but there are two main methods which I'll demonstrate. Both methods are suited to certain types of imagery and paper quality and can also be combined.

You will need to reduce the tackiness of your inks slightly for paper plate lithography so that the ink doesn't stick too tenaciously to the paper plate. If it is too tacky then the plate will scum very easily, and fine areas of toner will be pulled off the plate by the sticky ink.

Rather than preparing a second plate for a different colour test, you can change the colour of the ink you're working with and roll straight over the previous ink on the plates. The plate will still hold some ink from the previous colour so it will print with a mixture of these colours until the new colour becomes dominant. As the paper plates deteriorate, they will start to hold a tint of the ink colour in the non-image area and transfer this to the print. This is a trait of the process which I absolutely adore but which can be avoided by using the paper plates fewer times and by allowing them to dry more before printing them.

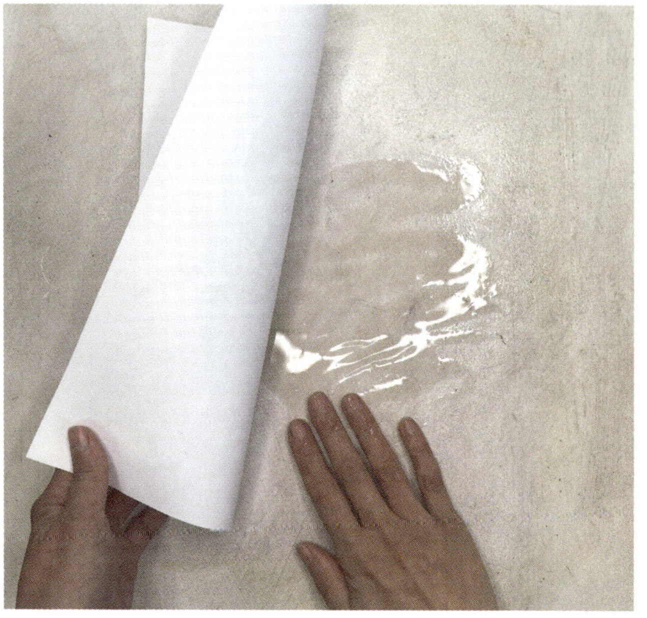

1. Apply a layer of gum arabic to the surface of your inking area to hold the paper plate to the surface. Your inking area should be smooth and easily cleaned.

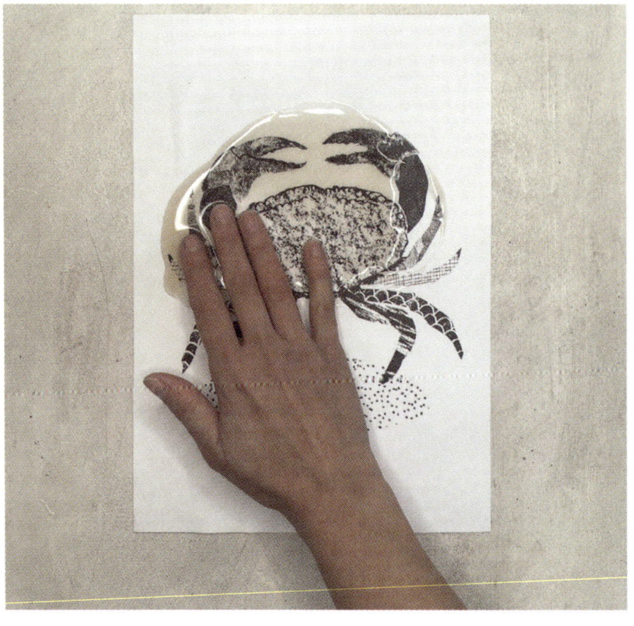

2. Apply a layer of gum arabic over the paper plate and gently massage it into the plate with your hands for a few seconds.

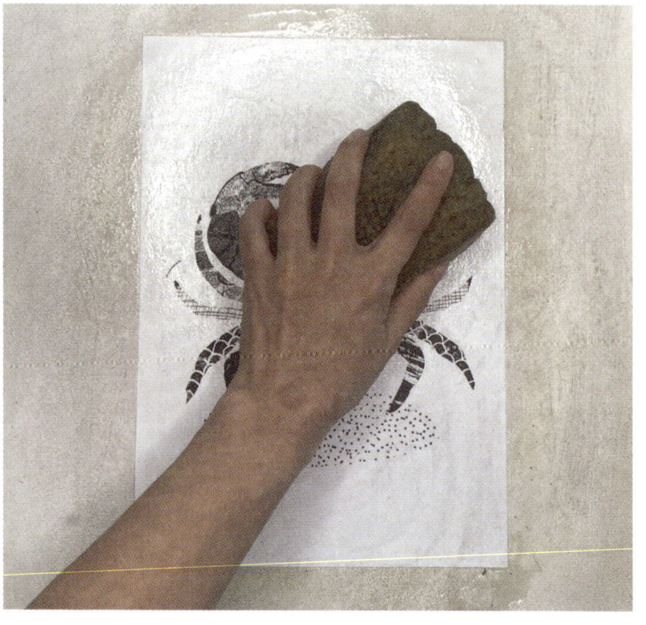

3. Use a sponge and a 50:50 water and gum dampening water solution. Sponge over the plate to carefully flatten down any creases in the paper and remove any excess pools of gum.

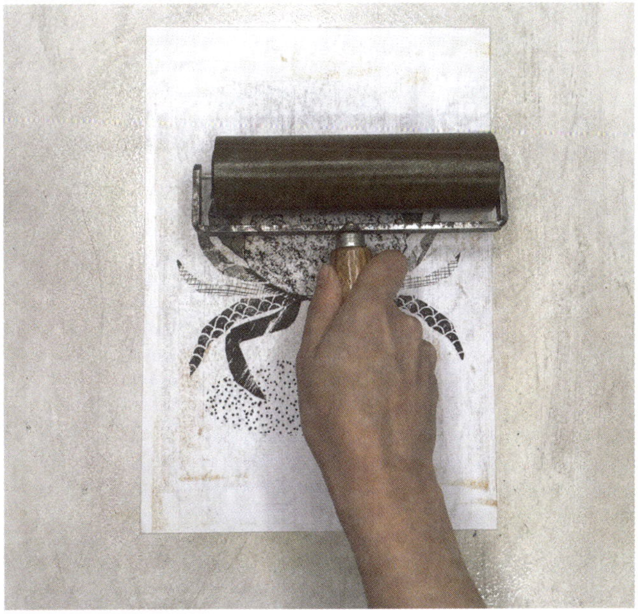

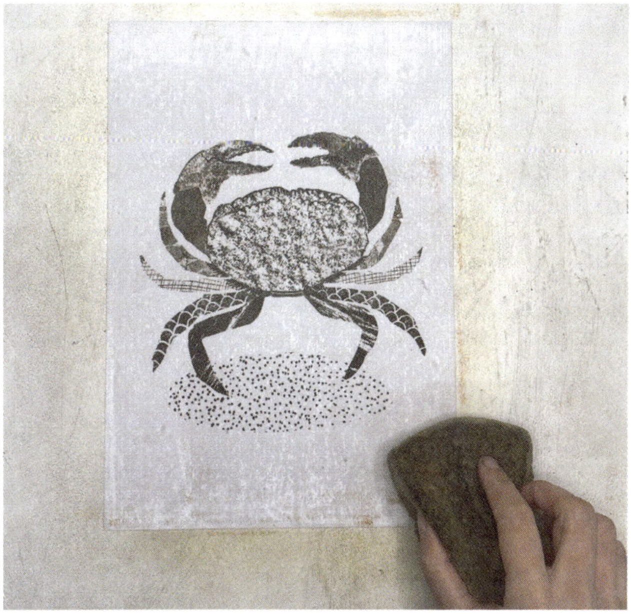

4. Ink up your plate in one direction. Do not disturb the paper fibres too much by inking back and forth. The plate is very delicate when it's wet and can be easily damaged by excessive wear.

5. Keep inking until you can see a sheen of ink on the image area. Carefully remove any unwanted ink with your sponge and squeeze out your sponge into your dirty dampening water bowl.

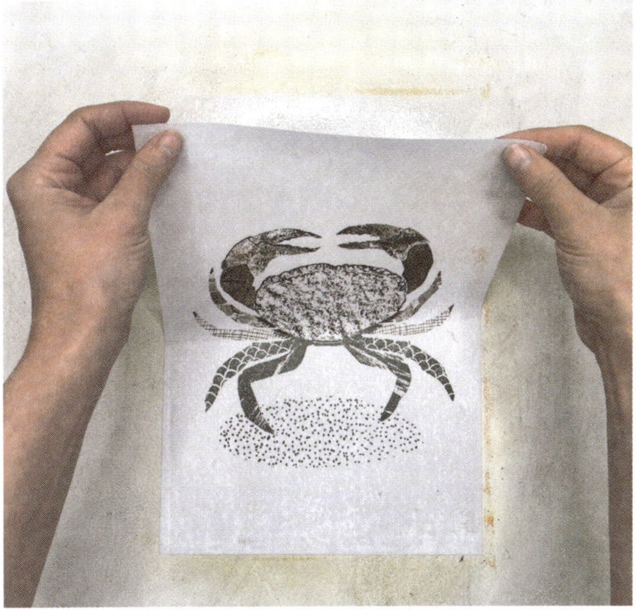

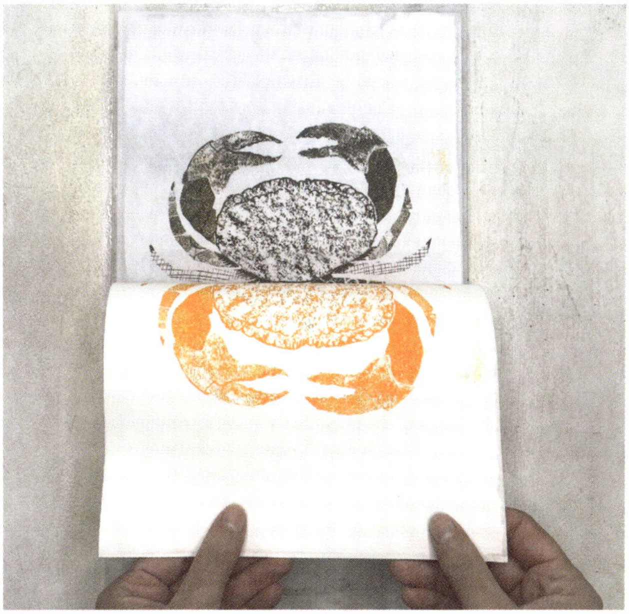

6. Blot off any excess dampening water using a clean sponge. If you are printing on a press carefully pick up and move the paper plate to the press bed to print. Or clean your inking area if you are hand burnishing there.

7. Run your print through the press on medium pressure. As the paper plate itself is damp you don't need to print onto dampened paper, the moisture of the plate will transfer to the printing paper during printing.

Printing a paper plate *(continued)*

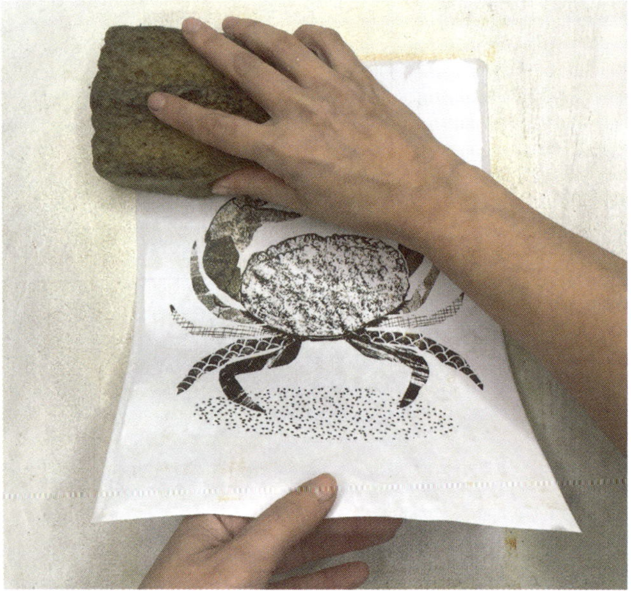

8. Carefully pick up your paper plate and place it back down on the inking area, using a damp sponge to flatten it out onto the inking surface. Dampen the plate with your gum dampening solution and ink it up a second time.

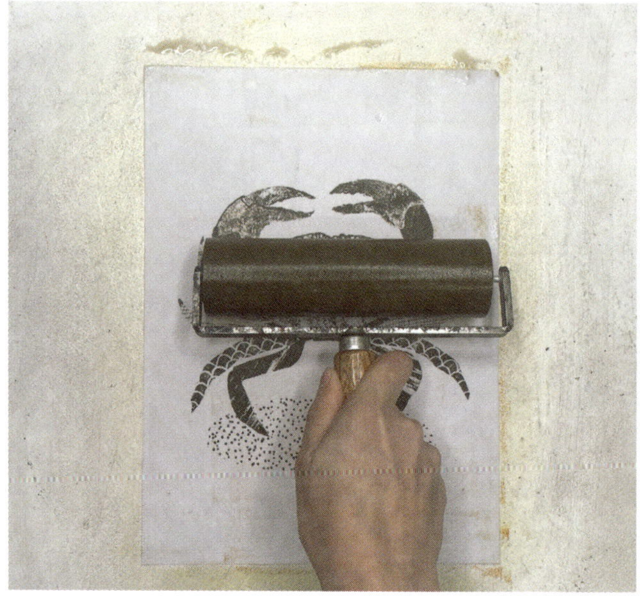

9. For the second inking you will need to be more careful, as the plate is fragile and the toner will be much more delicate. Some of the toner may come away and stick to the roller this time.

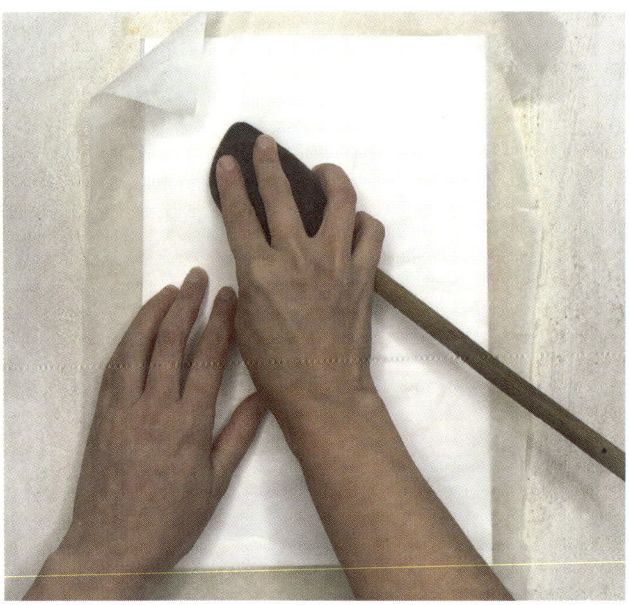

10. Either carefully move your plate to a printing area or clean your inking area ready to hand burnish. With a sheet of protective greaseproof paper covering the printing paper, use a spoon to apply firm pressure in small circles all over the plate.

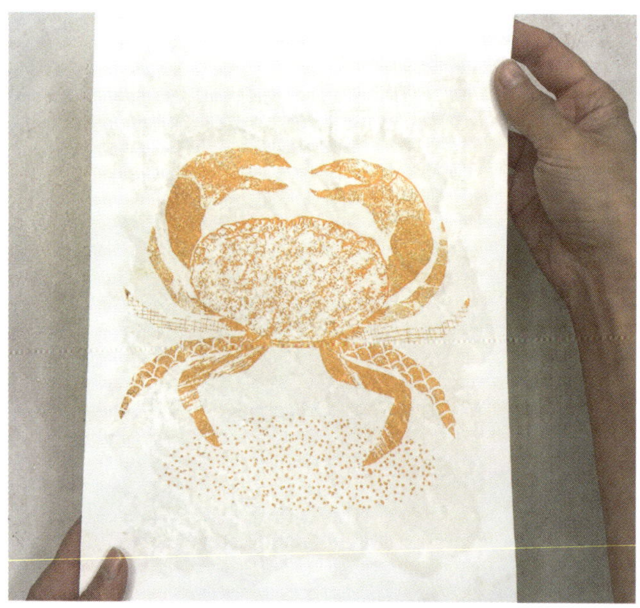

11. In this second print the details are still printing very well, although some very small areas of toner have started to come away. You can also see that the plate has started to muddy from ink and gum, and this has stained the paper.

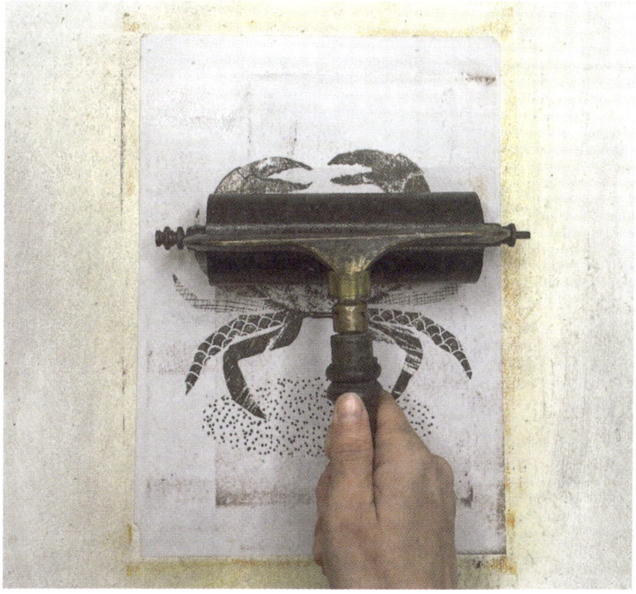

12. To change your ink colour mid-way through using a plate, apply the new ink straight on top of the old ink on the plate. The two colours can blend at first so keep this in mind when choosing your next colour.

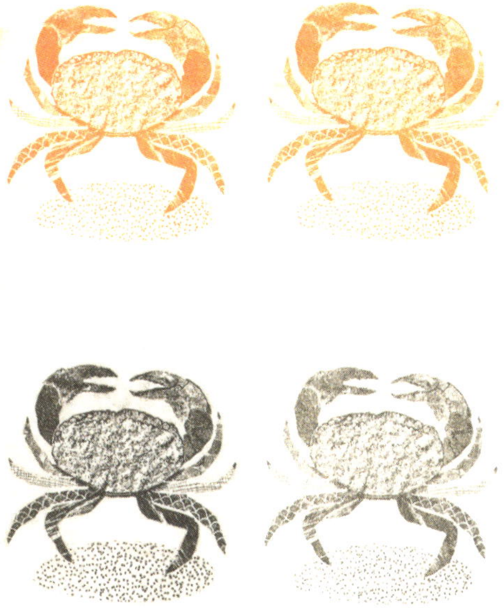

13. Four prints from the same paper plate. You can see the gradual degrading of the image on the plate as the prints get lighter and lose detail. The bottom left print also shows bleeding from ink that was mixed too oily.

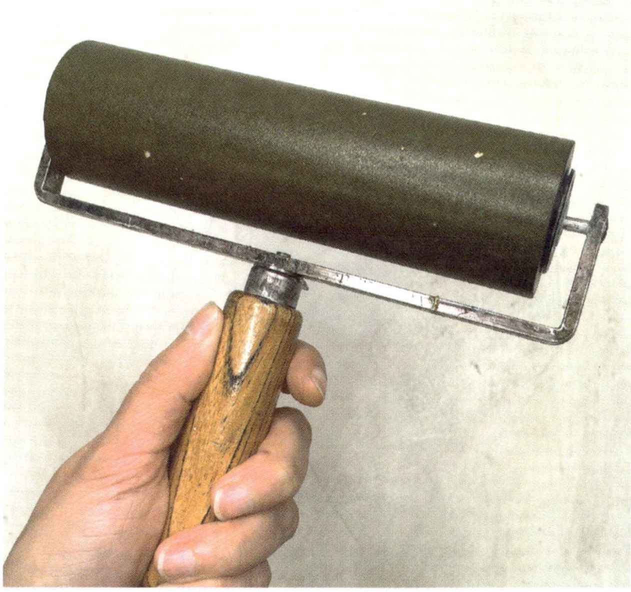

14. While you're inking up your paper plates the gum may form a film on your roller which inhibits it from picking up ink when you recharge the roller. Paper patches can also tear off and stick to your roller.

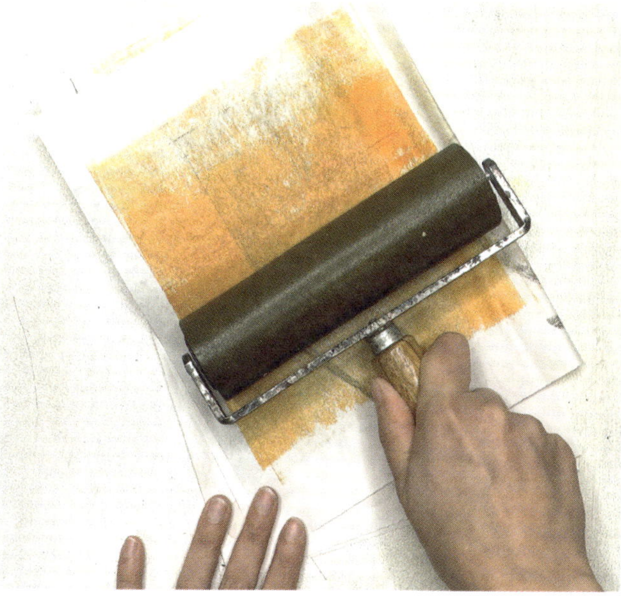

15. While you're inking your plate, after every few rolls, roll your roller onto scrap paper to remove some of the mucky ink and gum, to try to keep the roller clean. Listen out for the shushing sound of the ink on the roller.

Alternative printing method

The second method for printing a paper plate lithograph is good if you have used lightweight or delicate printer paper and if your image has fine details. There is less friction and agitation to the surface of the plate when it's wet and in its most vulnerable state. This means delicate areas of toner will be less likely to detach and stick to the roller, and the plate is less likely to scum. Using this method the plates can only be used once, reliably, so you will need to prepare many photocopies if you want multiple prints.

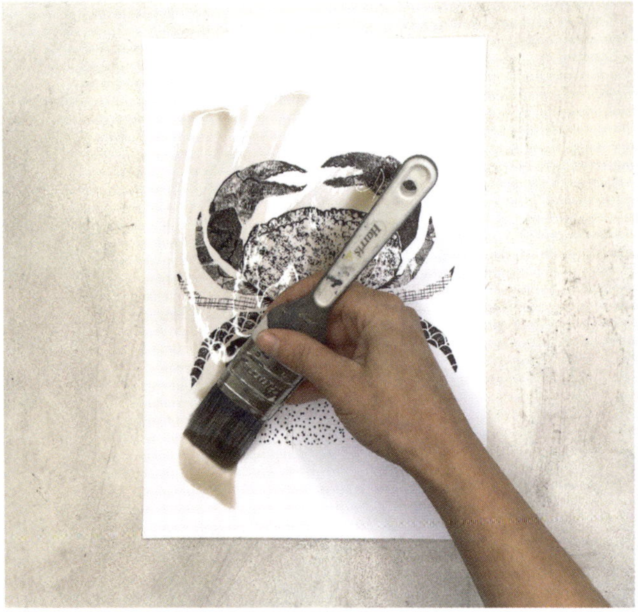

1. Using a clean brush, paint a layer of undiluted gum arabic over your dry paper plate. You may want to coat a few copies at once to save time later.

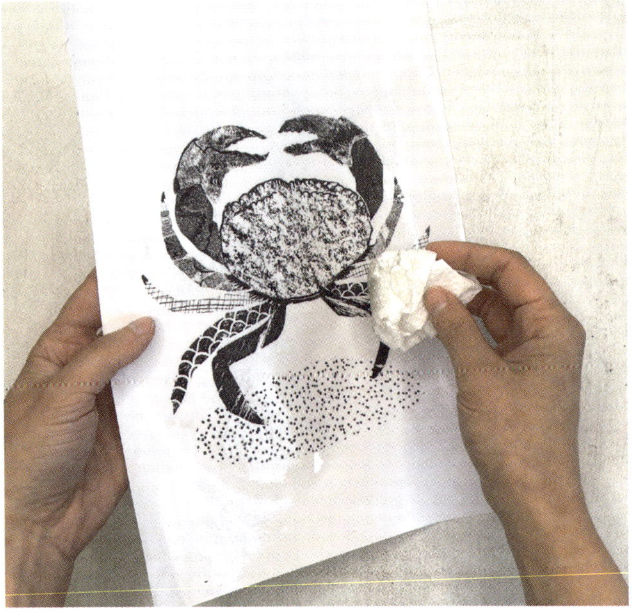

2. Carefully blot off any excess gum where it is sat on top of large areas of toner. If there is too much gum sat on top of your toner image it will act as a barrier to the ink.

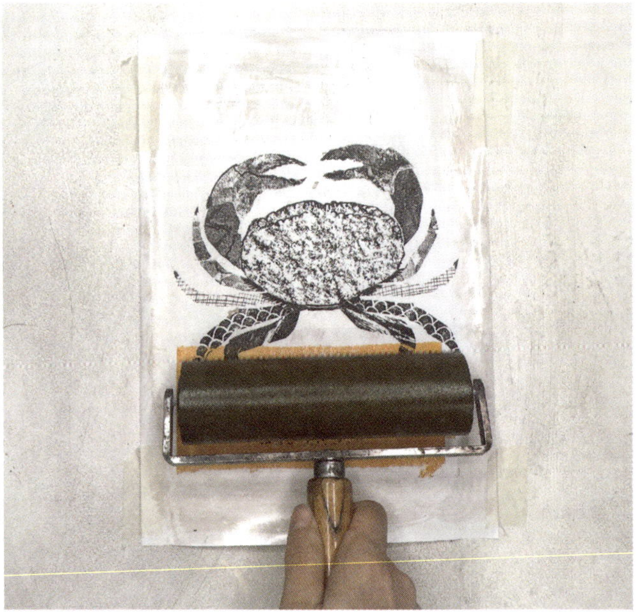

3. When your paper plates are dry, ink up the plates on top of the gum. Still use ink which has been modified with a little bit of tack reducer or oil. Avoid inking the non-image areas.

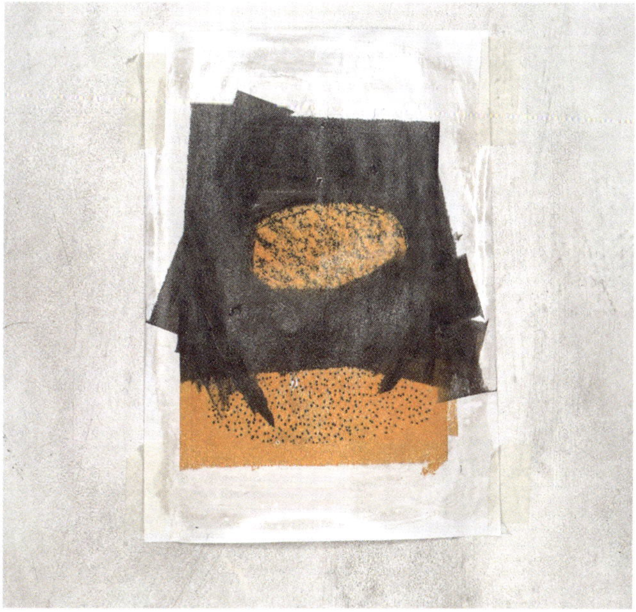

4. If you have a selection of small sized rollers, you can cleverly ink up sections of the same paper plate in different colours of ink.

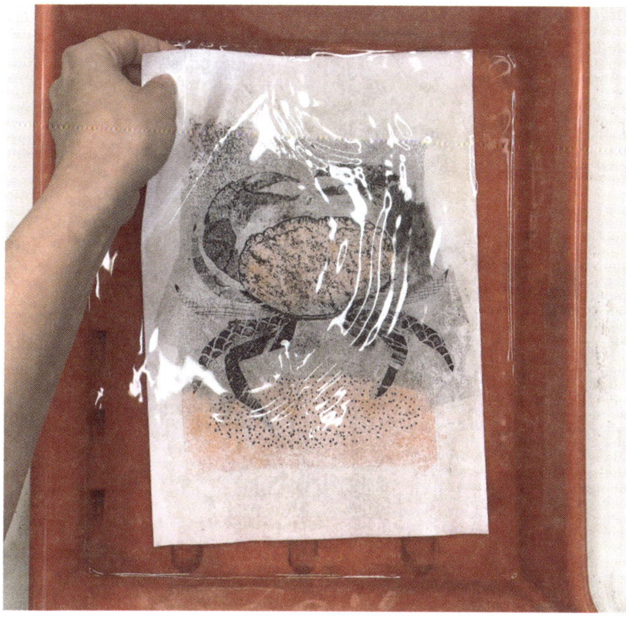

5. Submerge your entire paper plate in a tray of cold water for a few minutes, to allow the gum layer to soften and dissolve. You will see a difference straight away.

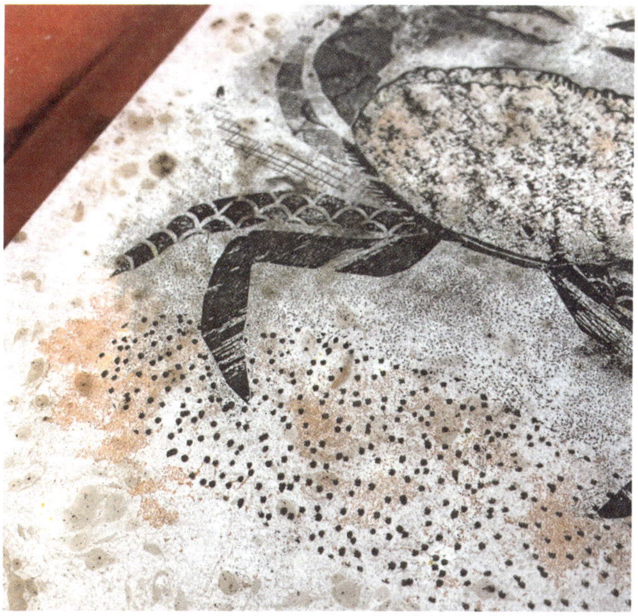

6. Very gently agitate the plate underwater. You will see the ink that was on top of the gum layer come away and sit on the surface of the water.

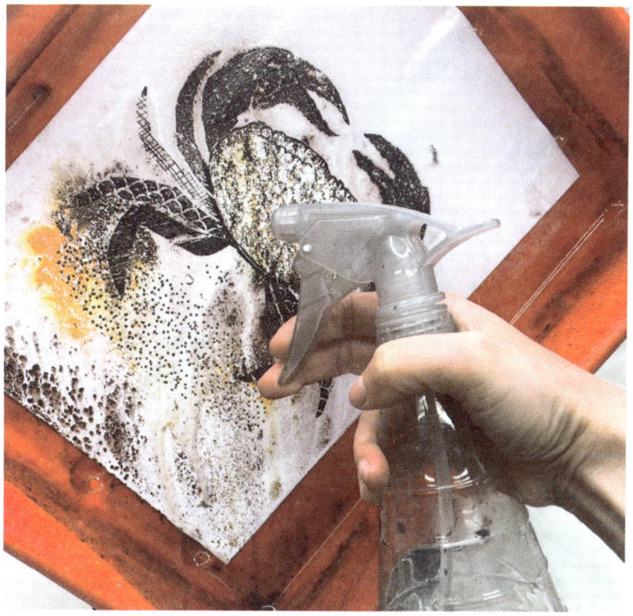

7. Sit the paper plate in a tray over a bucket, and spray with water, using the smallest nozzle with a concentrated stream of water. Be careful not to pierce a hole through the paper.

Alternative printing method *(continued)*

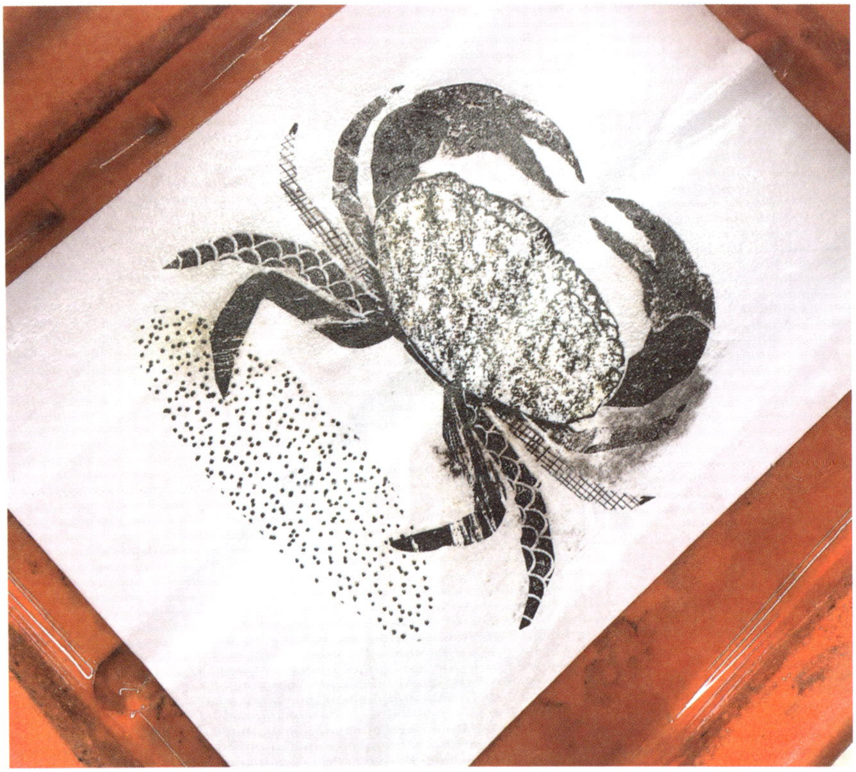

8. Keep spraying the paper plate with water until the plate looks clear of excess ink in the non-image areas. The ink can be tenacious so it can take a little while.

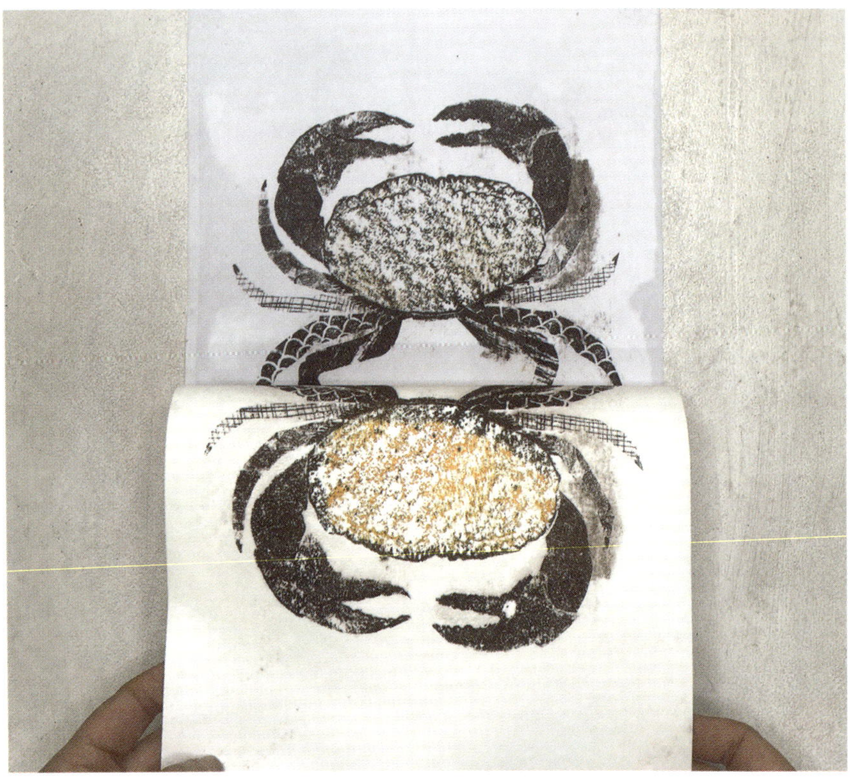

9. The paper plate will be soaking wet at this point so very carefully transfer it to your printing area and blot off the excess water with a clean sponge. Print the plate as normal.

Multi-layered prints and jigsaw printing

If you can, give your photographic image a halftone. This will convert your greyscale image into a discrete pattern of tiny black dots; the distribution and size of the dot will trick the eye into thinking there are grey areas. Alternatively, digitally increase the contrast of your image so that there are black and white areas only.

The delicate nature of the paper plate can be exploited to create interesting effects. The paper will warp and shrink and warp again when it is coated in gum, dried and wetted again. So, tight registration, especially that of a CMYK separation, is not advisable. However, if you are not concerned with tight registration, you can still use the CMYK method effectively to create visually striking prints.

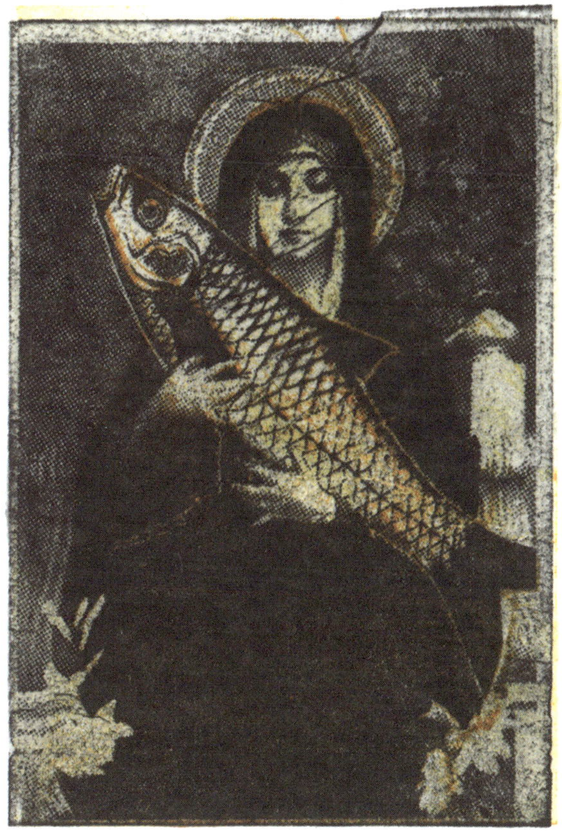

The impact of colour layering can be seen beautifully in this two-layer print. The orange on top of the blue-black creates a rich dense black, separating the figure from the background.

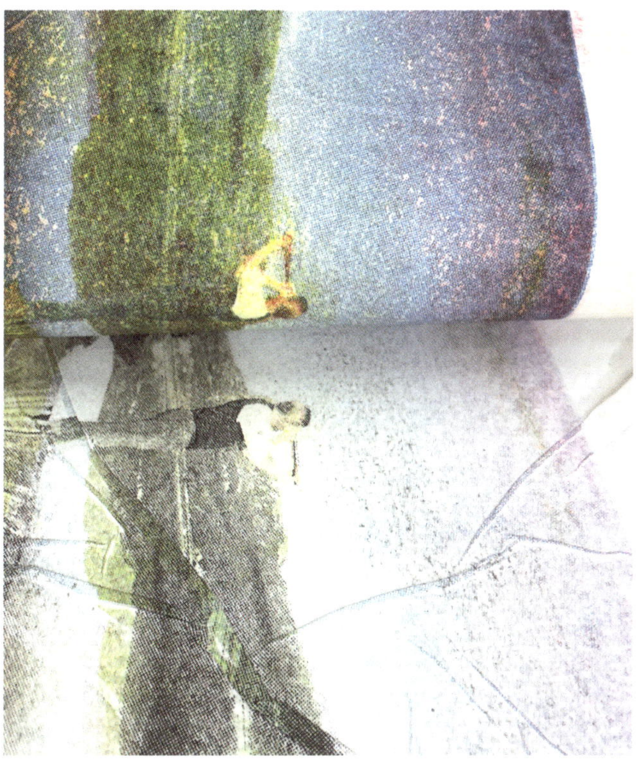

The paper plates themselves are soft and easily manipulated. Creased and scrunched paper plates can be put through the press with no damage to the press.

As the layer of ink used with lithography is so thin, it allows for base-layers to affect overlaid layers, without the use of extender in the ink. This does mean that light colours printed on top of dark colours will not be as dominant but will instead have an effect on the darker colour. This means, when planning the order of your layers, you will need to consider which layers will affect subsequent layers. The norm is to print your 'key-plate', the layer which holds the vital information or the design which pulls the image together, last, and in black or another dark colour. If you were to instead print the key-plate first and allow the subsequent lighter layers to sit on top, the colour overlaying will have a different visual effect on the whole image.

Jigsaw printing – cutting your plate up into sections – enables you to be flexible with the positioning of your layers, which can be useful for registering paper plates as the plates themselves can shift position. It also allows you to ink separate sections of the plate in different colours and print them simultaneously.

Jigsaw printing

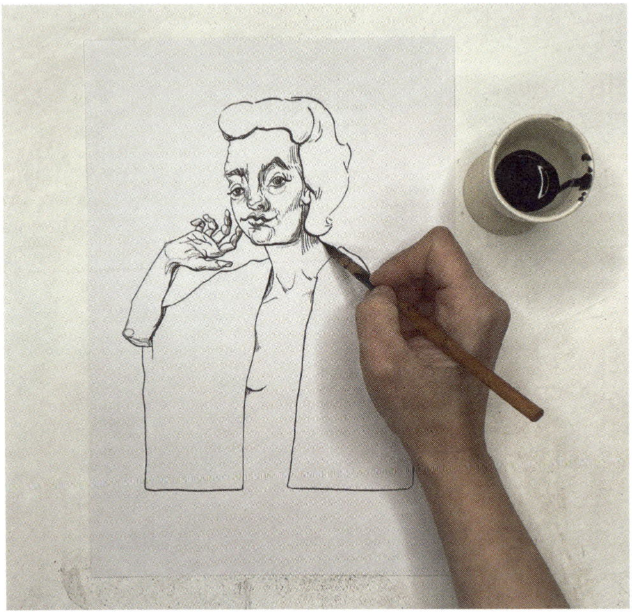

1. Using a dip pen and Indian ink will create an opaque strong black line which will photocopy well and create a solid area on the paper plate.

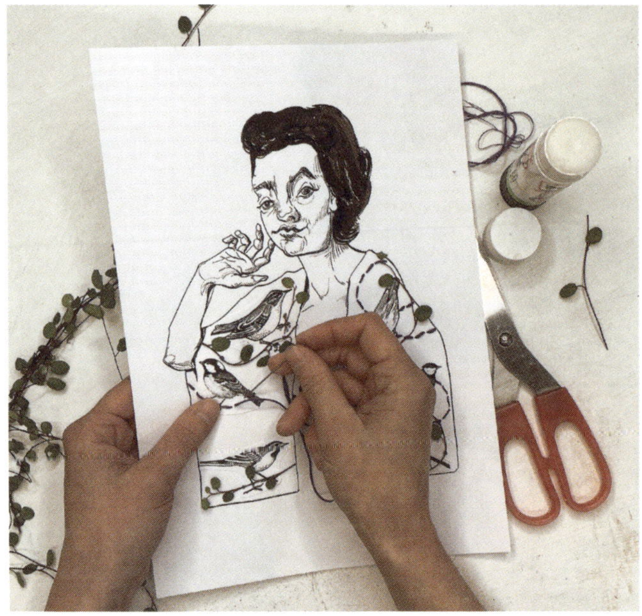

2. Alongside traditional drawing techniques, strongly contrasted photographic imagery can be used. As the plate is created from a photocopy, unconventional techniques and found objects can be included in the collage.

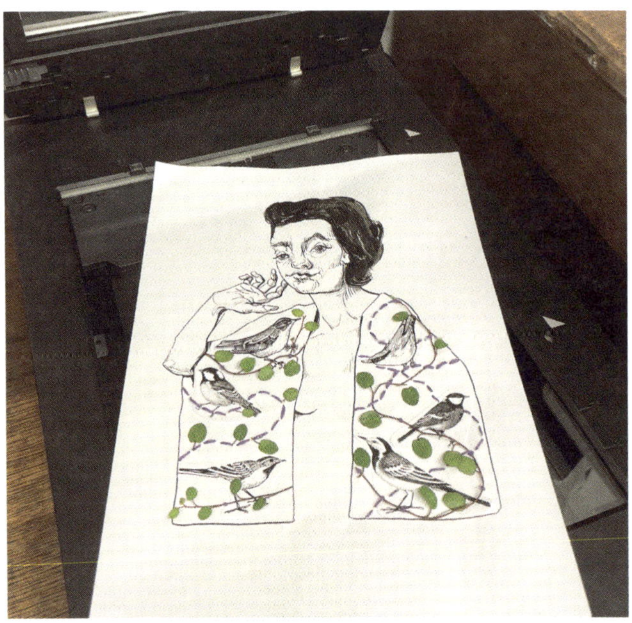

3. Scan, photograph or photocopy the collaged drawing to create the plate. When 3D objects are used you must consider whether to flatten them in the scanner or include a slight shadow in a photograph.

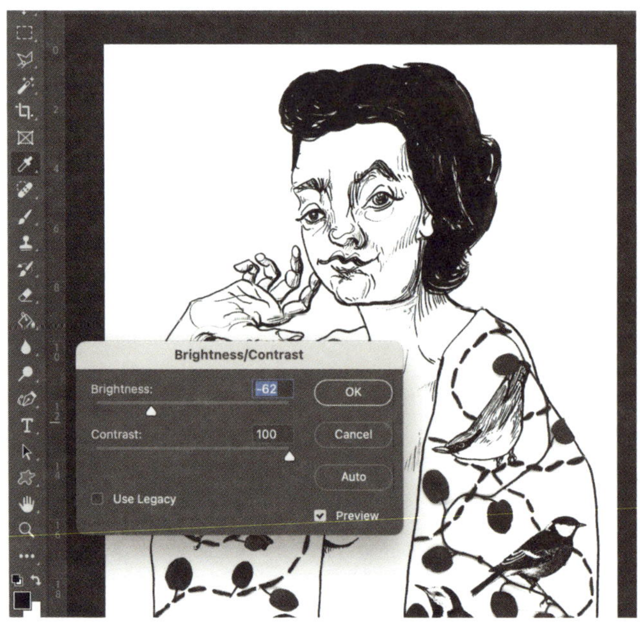

4. Using photo editing software, for example Adobe Photoshop, convert your image to black and white and adjust the brightness/contrast to brighten any light greys to white and darken any dark greys to black.

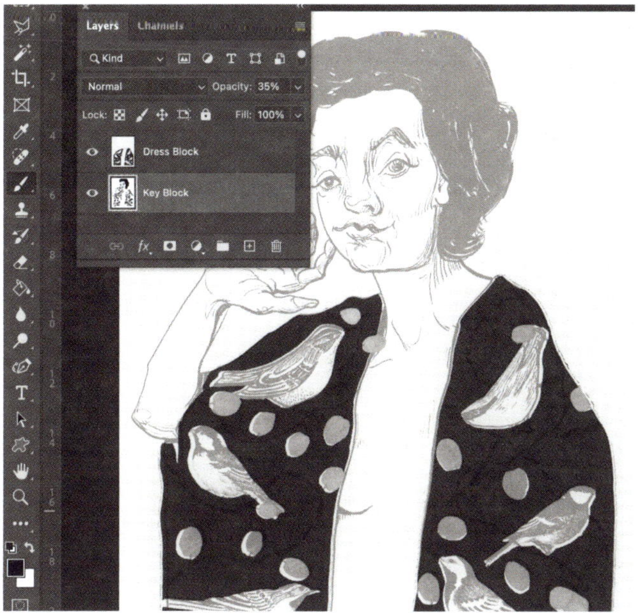

5. Using the layers function in Photoshop you can create multiple layers which will align to the original drawing. Adjust the opacity of the layer to decide where the crossover of the colours will occur.

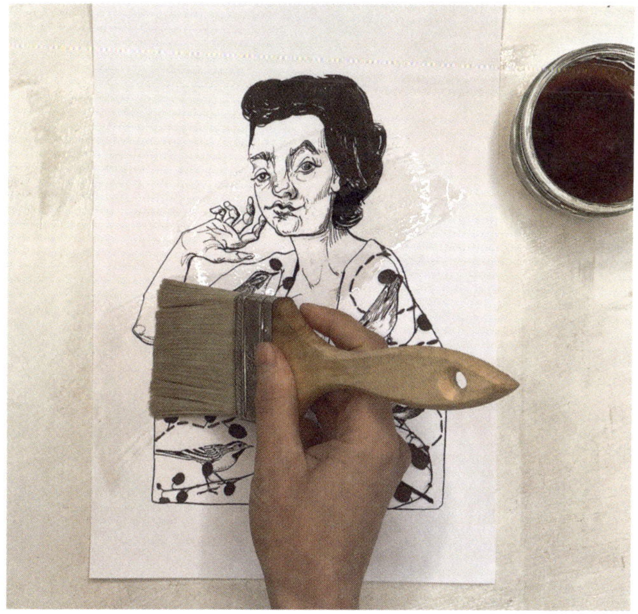

6. Paint on a layer of undiluted gum over the paper plates. Blot off any large areas of gum sitting on the toner using a cloth and allow the plate to fully dry.

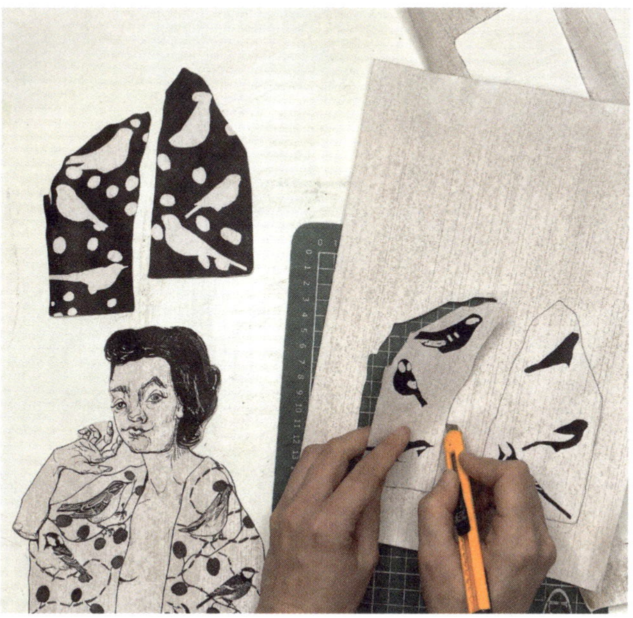

7. As these plates will be printed using the jigsaw method, cut around the images with a scalpel. The shape of the plates will have slightly warped due to the gum, so we will be registering them loosely on a registration guide.

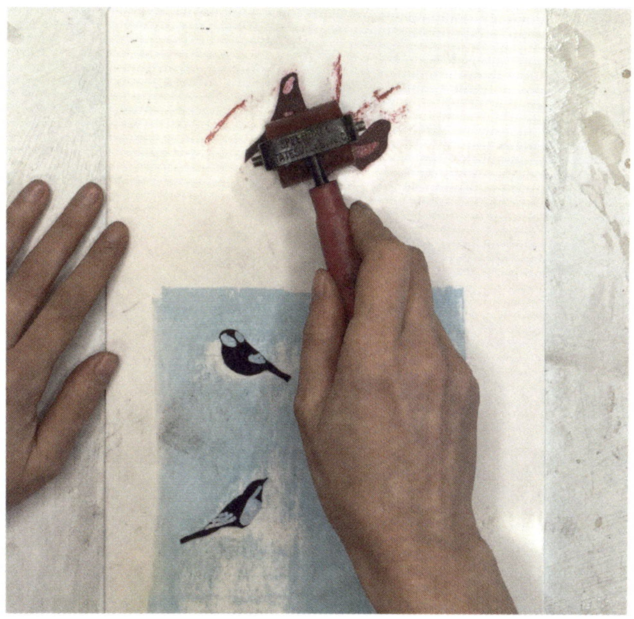

8. When inking up tiny pieces, take care as they will stick to the roller and can tear. They will need to be handled delicately, especially when they become wet.

Jigsaw printing *(continued)*

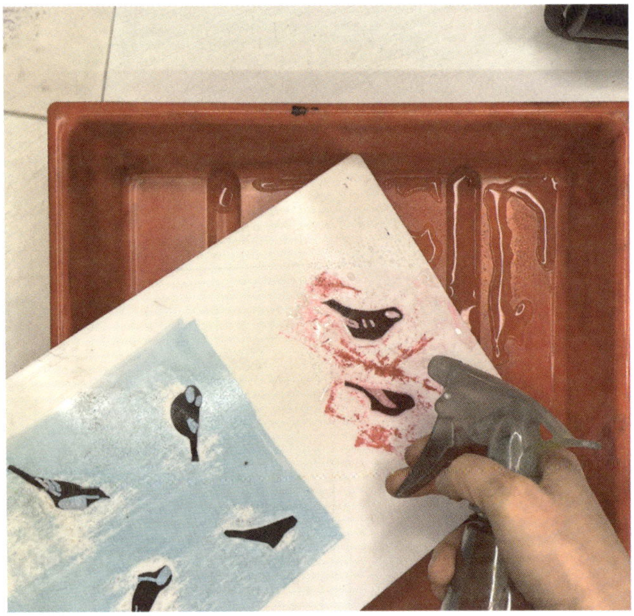

9. Submerge the pieces in water to dissolve the gum and very carefully use a water spray bottle to remove any excess ink. Blot off the excess water with a clean sponge before printing.

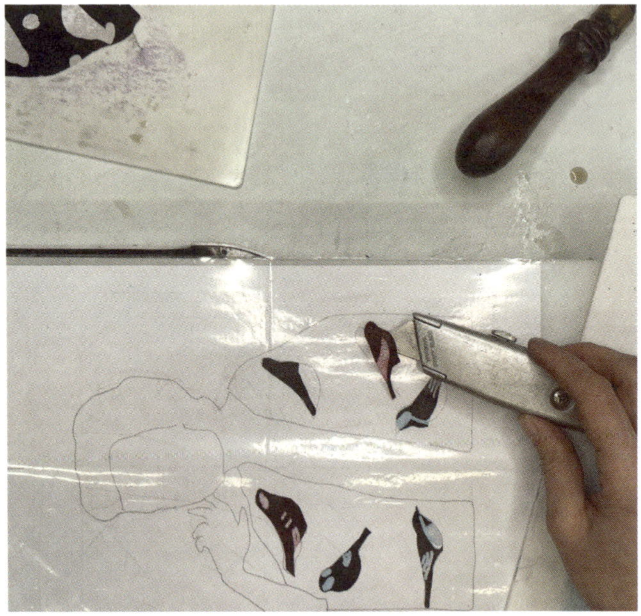

10. Carefully align the small pieces on a registration guide. This registration guide has been made using a tracing of the original image. As the paper plates will have warped slightly there is an expectation of offset layering.

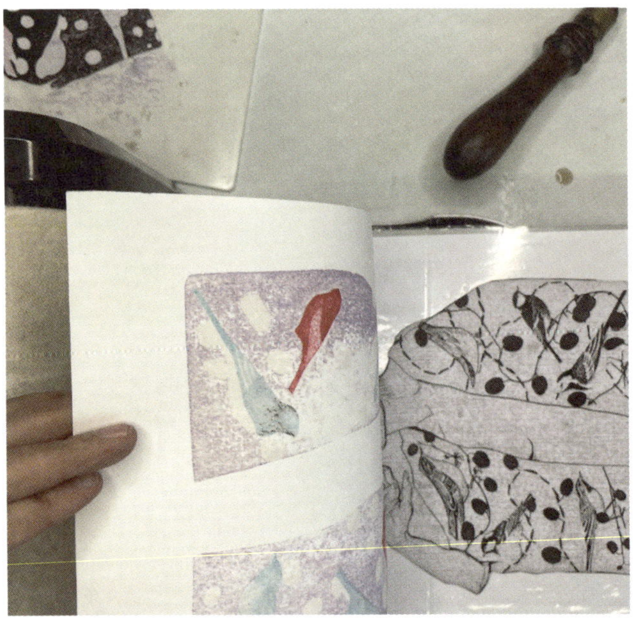

11. Prepare all your layers to print at the same time, one layer after another, so that there will be no further change in the registration. If the printing paper dries and needs to be re-dampened it will warp further.

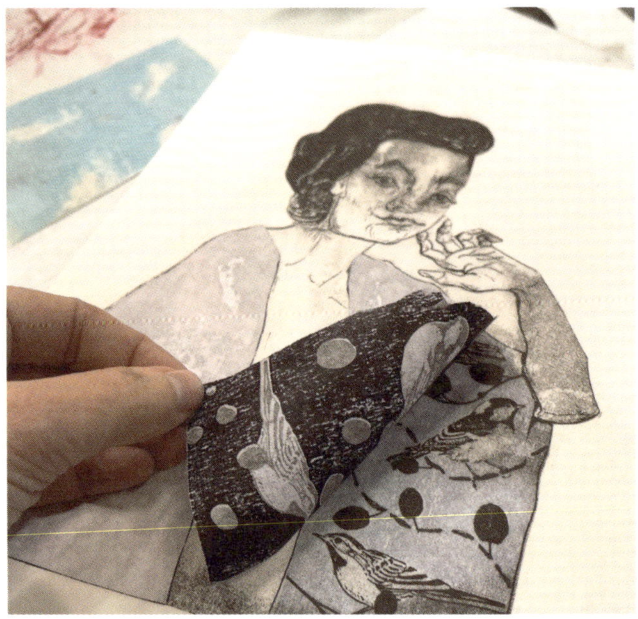

12. You may find it easier to print the keyplate first and register the small jigsaw pieces *on top* of the printing paper. As the plates are so thin, you can put them through the press, or hand burnish them either way around.

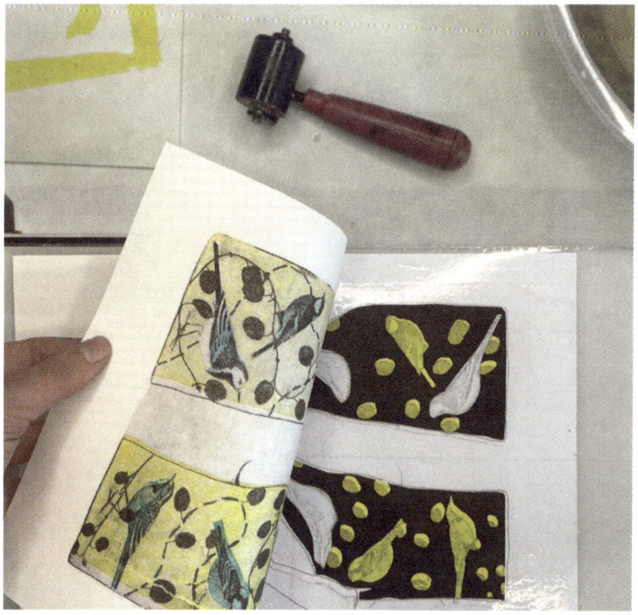

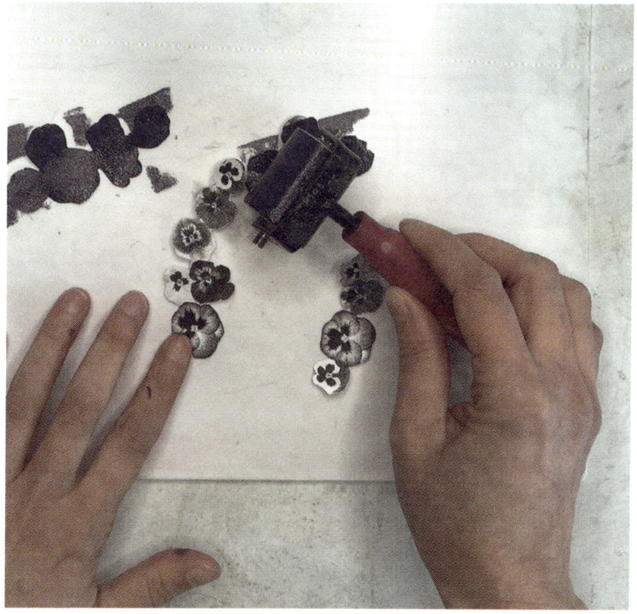

13. If you want to print solid shapes of colour without any lithographic details, you can ink up pieces of paper and print them as monotype jigsaw pieces, without dampening them. They will only be usable for a single print.

14. It is difficult to retain very fine details with very small pieces of paper plate lithography but the images can still be effective. These photographs have had a fine half tone added to them in Photoshop to keep the details.

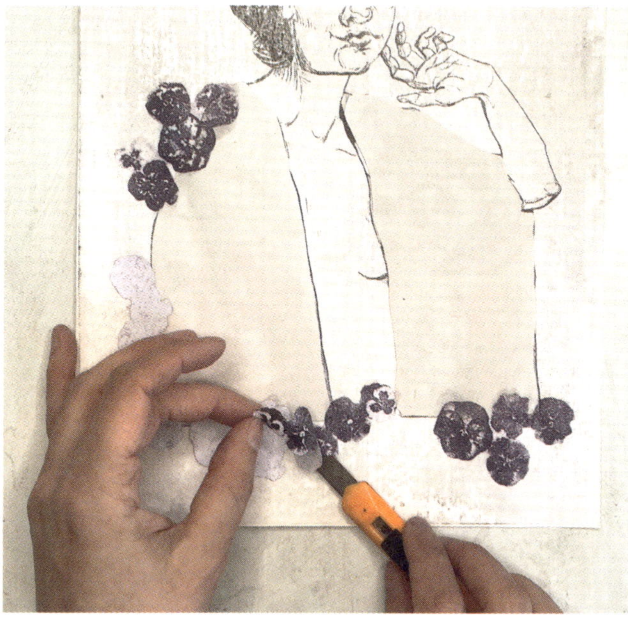

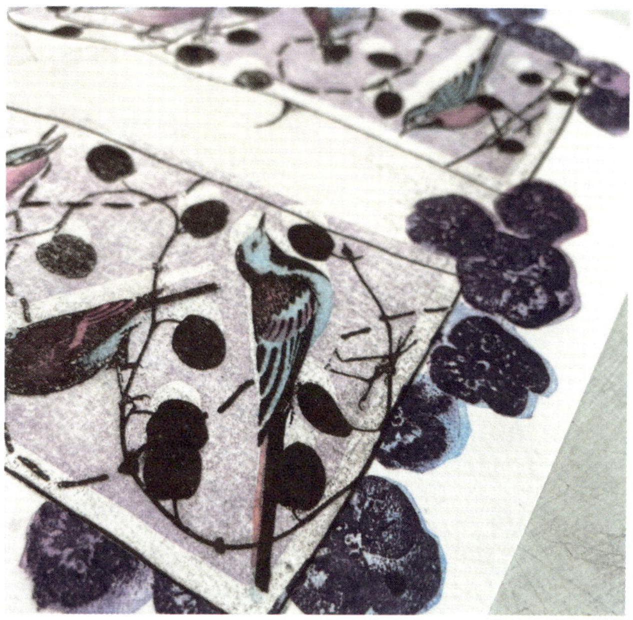

15. If you want to be selective of where the jigsaw pieces print you can cut a mask out of scrap paper and place it onto the print in the areas you'd like to protect from ink. Then place the jigsaw pieces on top and print this way up.

16. Paper masks have been used to protect areas of this print from the added flower layers. A second layer of blended colour has been printed on top of the flowers using a piece of paper as a monotype plate.

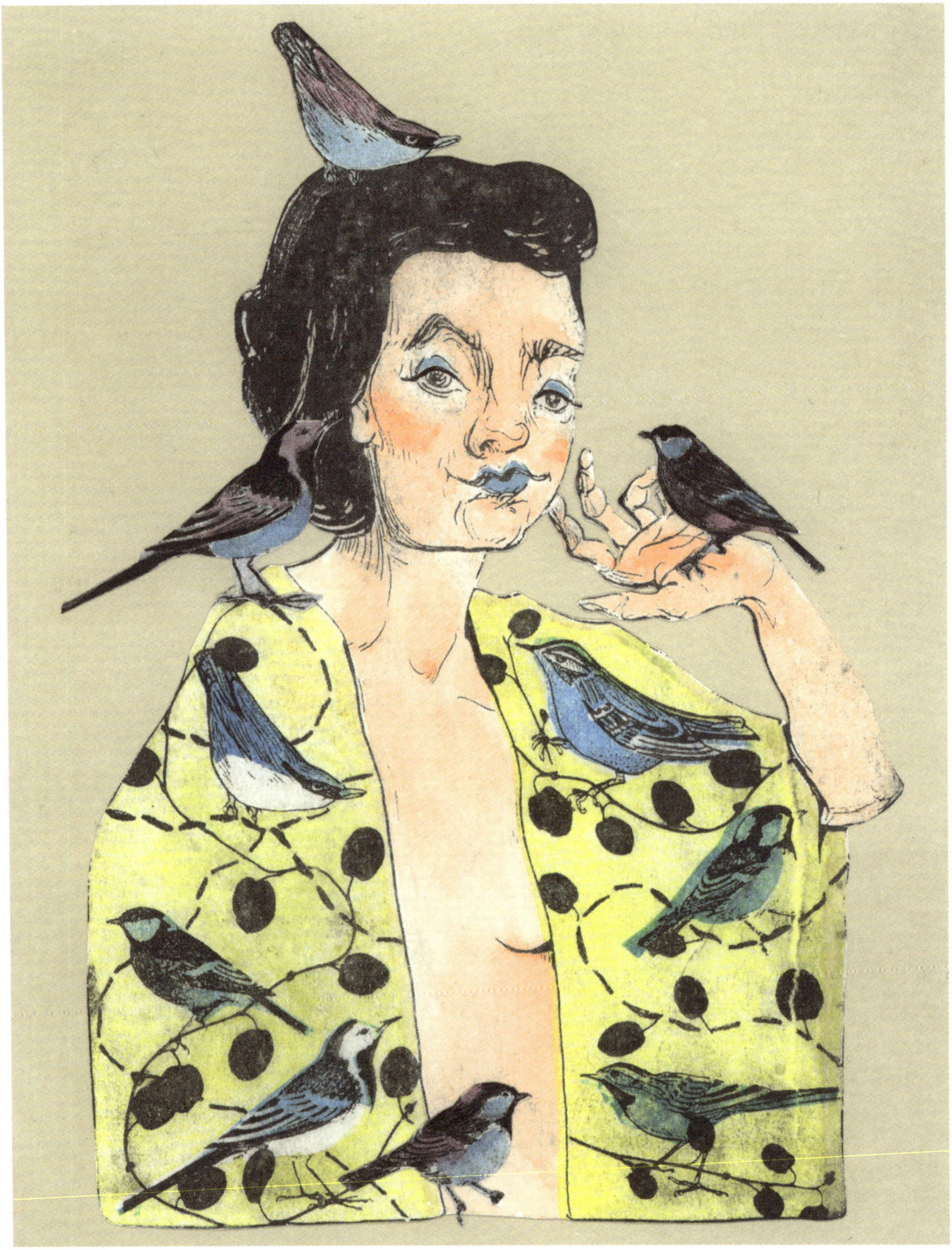

17. You can see in this print how some of the blue birds are a subtly different shade of blue thanks to the yellow layer underneath. This print also uses chine collé and hand tinting, which is explained later in the book.

TROUBLESHOOTING

Ink not picking up on the image

If no ink is picking up or the image on the paper plate looks to be bleeding, you are probably using an inkjet print. Some new photocopiers use more environmentally friendly or economical toner substitutes, which don't work with this process.

Paper plate sticking to paper

This usually occurs when using a press because of the additional pressure the press employs. Reduce the pressure on your press and reduce the tackiness of your ink so that the ink will be more inclined to detach from both plate and print. The paper plate may stick to the printing paper if the printing paper is dry; it can bond to the printing paper like a piece of chine collé and sometimes it will tear as you try to remove it. Try printing onto dampened paper.

Dark areas of the plate

If you haven't applied a thick enough layer of gum arabic to your plate, using the second printing method, it won't be a strong enough resist to the printing ink. Similarly, if you have blotted off the gum from an image area of the plate, before letting it dry, you may have taken off too much gum from the surrounding areas, weakening the protective layer.

Image completely filling in

If the image fills in completely, your image may have too fine details, or not have enough contrast between light and dark areas in the image. Alternatively, your ink could be too oily and it's spreading over your entire plate.

Toner coming away

Make sure you have left your print-out at least overnight so that the toner has had time to cure on the paper. Make sure you are not oversaturating your plate with water and not disturbing or touching the plate surface too much as this will weaken the toner. If your ink is too tacky it will also pull the toner off the paper.

Print too light

If your print is too light, it may be because your roller has been coated in gum which is acting as a barrier to the ink and not allowing it to transfer to the plate. Clean your roller and replace the ink on your ink slab more often. Listen out for the shushing sound of the ink when you ink up your roller. A light print could also be due to the plate needing more ink, or the print needing more pressure when it was burnished. If your laser printer or photocopier is low on toner then it may not have produced a solid enough deposit of toner on the paper lithograph for the oil-based printing ink to be attracted to. Replace your toner cartridge.

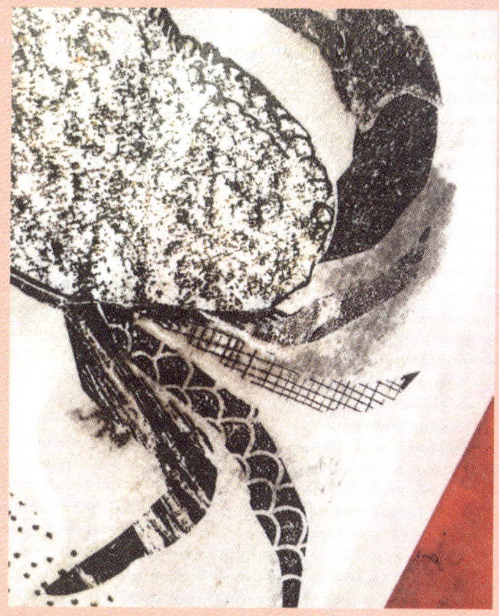

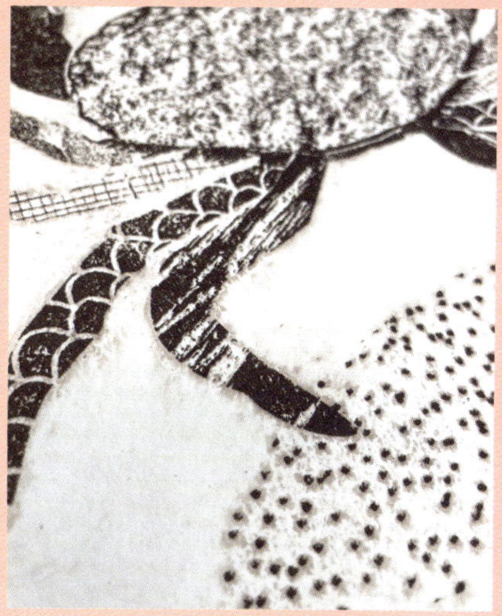

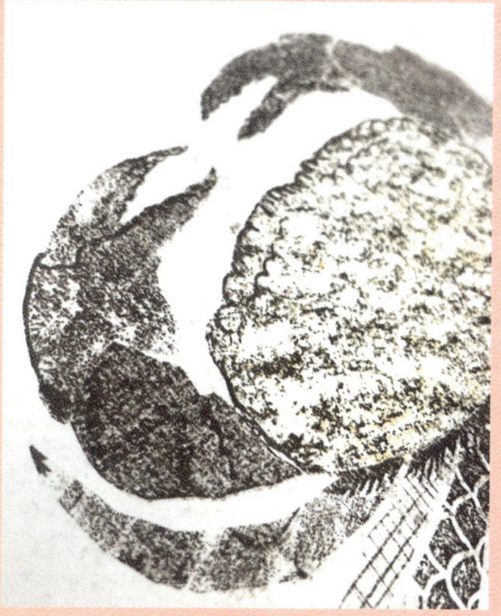

TOP
A clouding of ink where the protective layer of gum arabic wasn't a strong enough barrier to the ink.

MIDDLE
Blooms of ink around image area on the plate due to adding too much oil to the printing ink.

BOTTOM
Areas of the plate which should be solid and dense look patchy where the toner has come away.

Mina Rakidžić (Serbia)

behance.net/minarakidzic

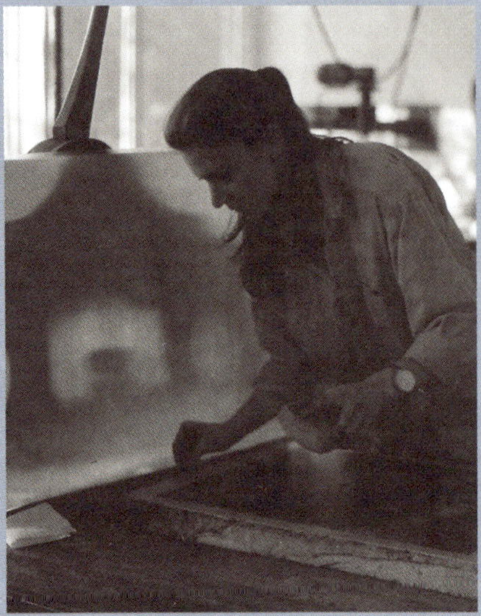

Mina Rakidžić is an artist and academic whose practice revolves around the concept of reprography, both in terms of the process of reproducing and copying documents and in its symbolic significance.

Through my projects, I aim to support the idea that 'high art' – especially in the context of graphic media – does not necessarily have to emerge under conditions of high production, in specialised studios and workshops, but can also manifest in improvised conditions, utilising do-it-yourself skills.

My interest in paper plate lithography commenced before it became the focus of my doctoral project. The discovery of this technique I owe to the one-month course named Printmaking Strategies led by Professor Elisabeth Schmirl in Summer 2015 at The Salzburg Summer Academy in Austria. Thanks to this experience, I started unearthing alternative methods to create artwork that not only carries the distinctive signature of the printmaking discipline but, when executed successfully, yields exceptional results in controlled conditions, leaving behind traces that are indiscernible.

As one of the biggest concerns of traditional printmaking is edition, it has to be mentioned that paper plate lithography although it doesn't revolve around it, can be reproduced multiple times. And unlike traditional printmaking media, it allows reproductions on various substrates. Therefore, the final identity of each copy has to be considered through the context of its presentation.

Graphic techniques can become so alluring that they become an end in themselves. The workshop principle in printmaking studies is prioritised at the highest level, sometimes leading to a shift of focus from the artwork itself to the discipline and choreography of the printmaking process. Openness to experimentation for expressing specific content places these methods in the service of pure artistic expression.

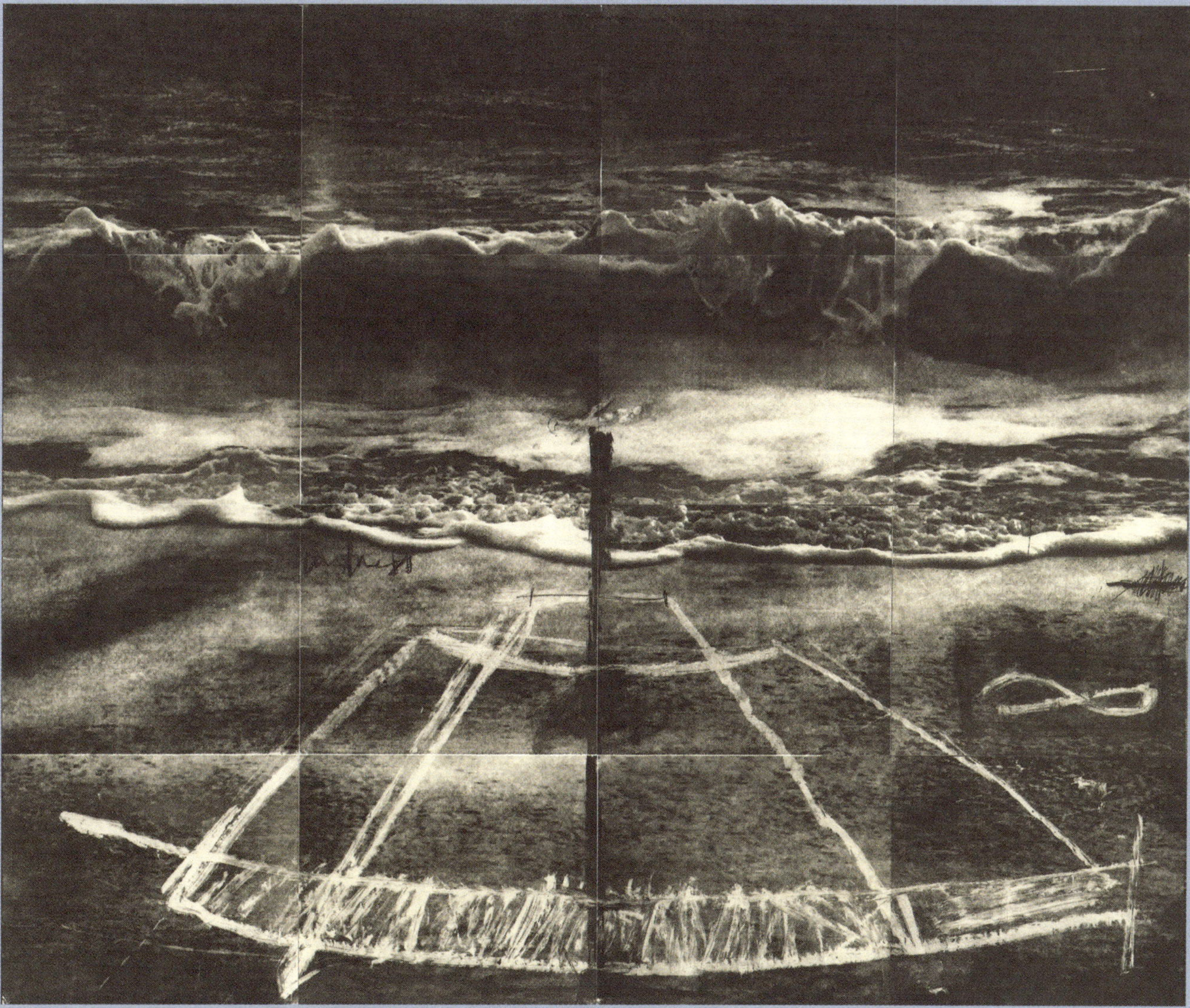

Mina Rakidžić, *Archetypal Settings – The Sea*.
Paper plate lithography, polyptych, 125 x 160cm,
2018.

CHAPTER 8

Polyester plate lithography

Polyester plates were designed to mimic metal plate lithography and are used in large-scale commercial lithographic printing. They were developed as a cheaper alternative for use with commercial offset lithography but can easily be adapted for printing by hand. Polyester plates are also known as 'pronto plates' among other brand names. The plastic of the plate has a rough surface with pores that hold the drawing material. They work beautifully with a range of drawing materials and can hold tusche washes and toner washes. Polyester plates are fantastic for photographic work as they can be put through a home laser printer or photocopier. They are receptive to both water and grease but are prone to scumming. They require the use of a fount solution (specialist dampening water) to mimic commercial printing conditions to keep them stable.

A downside of using these plates, aside from the fact that they are plastic and not environmentally considerate, is the cost. The plates are relatively expensive, which can be off-putting as a beginner, especially when anticipating the costs of learning through mistakes. They are robust, however, and can be stored and printed again multiple times.

FACING PAGE
Painting a lithographic tusche wash onto a polyester lithography plate. As the wash slowly dries the tusche will leave tide marks in beautiful reticulated patterns.

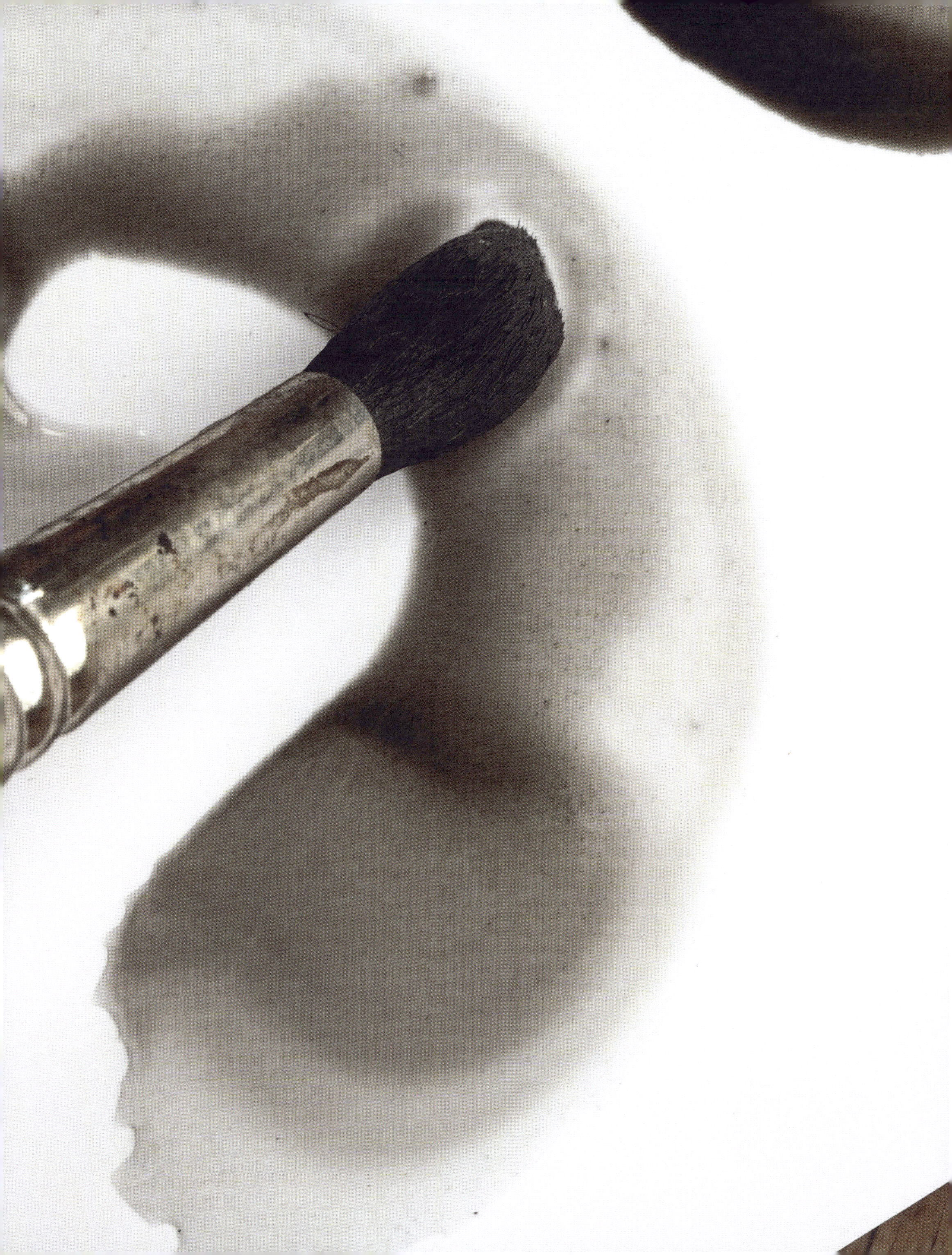

Drawing on the plate

It is worth noting that some polyester plates have a textured side and reverse/non-working side, and it is incredibly difficult to tell which is which. The working side will have a slight grain to it, used to catch and hold the drawing materials. Fingerprints will transfer to the polyester plate, as will hard pencil lines. You may not see them at first but as the plate starts to scum during printing, they can become more apparent. It's a good idea to apply a gum margin to the edges of the plate so it can be easily transported.

Ink will also collect on the edges of the plate while you're inking up and will print as a fine line. If you don't want this to print you can either leave a large margin of bare plate around the edge of your image, to avoid the roller needing to reach the edges. Or you can make your printing paper smaller than the plate. Hole punch/pin registration can be used to register these plates, and registration marks can even be drawn on the back of the plates. The plates are so thin that these registration marks can be seen through the plate.

Working on a polyester plate is not quite as enchanting as other lithographic surfaces such as wood or stone. But a useful characteristic of these plates that other lithographic processes don't have, is the fact that they can be used on a light box. This makes registering imagery over multiple plates and tracing key drawing elements very easy.

MATERIALS

- Polyester plates/pronto plates
- Gum arabic
- French chalk
- Muslin/cheesecloth
- Traditional roller/foam roller
- Cellulose sponge
- Bowls for dampening water
- Printing ink
- Toothpaste
- Citric acid
- Paper
- Lithographic crayons
- Lithographic tusche
- Toner
- Permanent markers
- Ballpoint pens

The materials needed for the polyester plate lithography process.

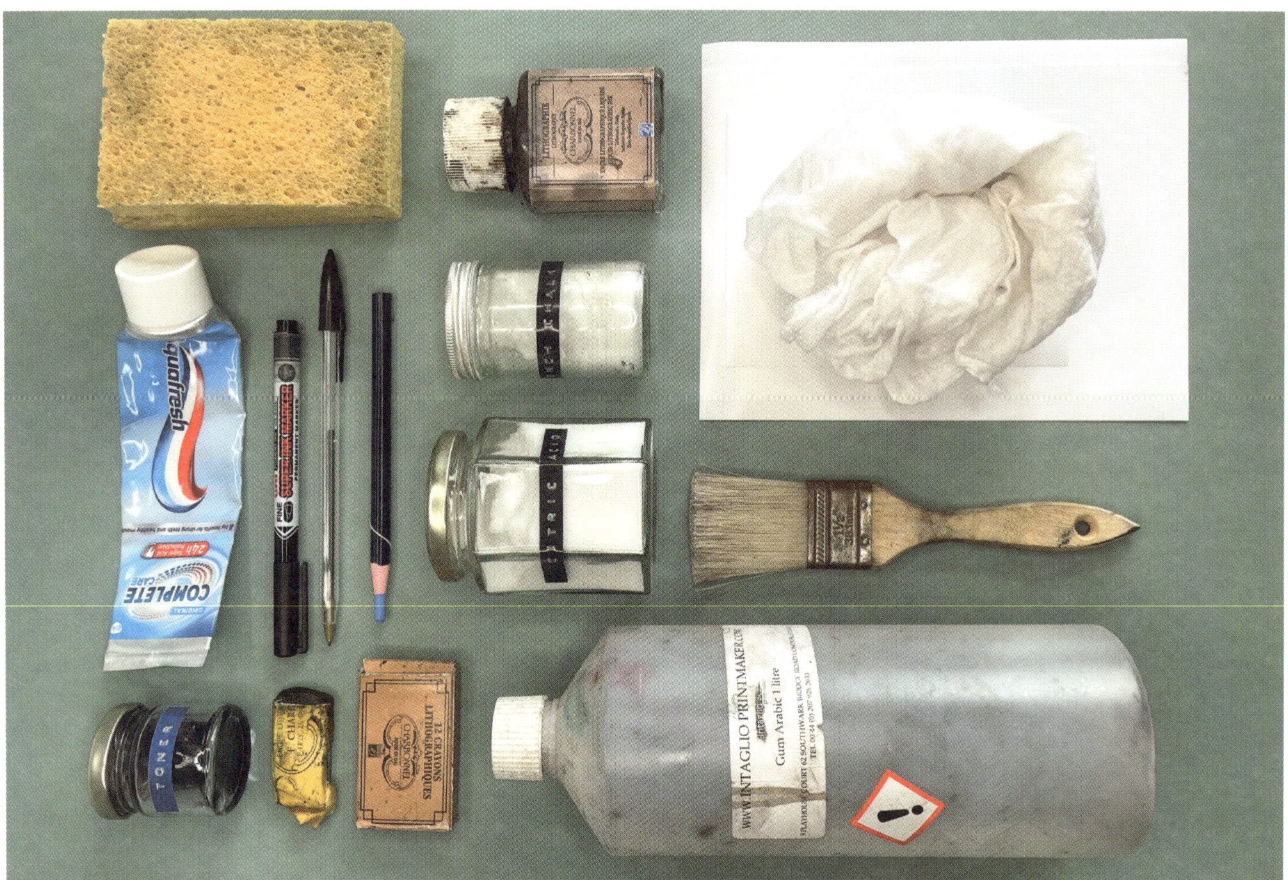

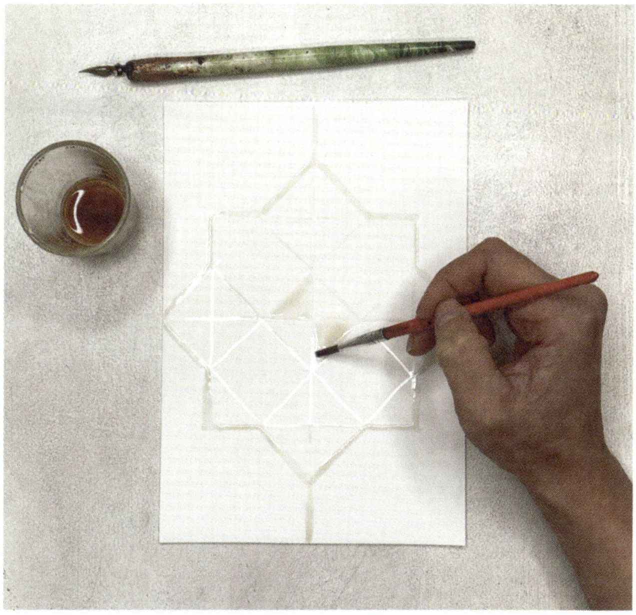

1. Make sure you are working on the correct side of the plate as some polyester plates have a working side. As with most lithographic processes, gum arabic can be used as a resist to protect the plate from accepting ink.

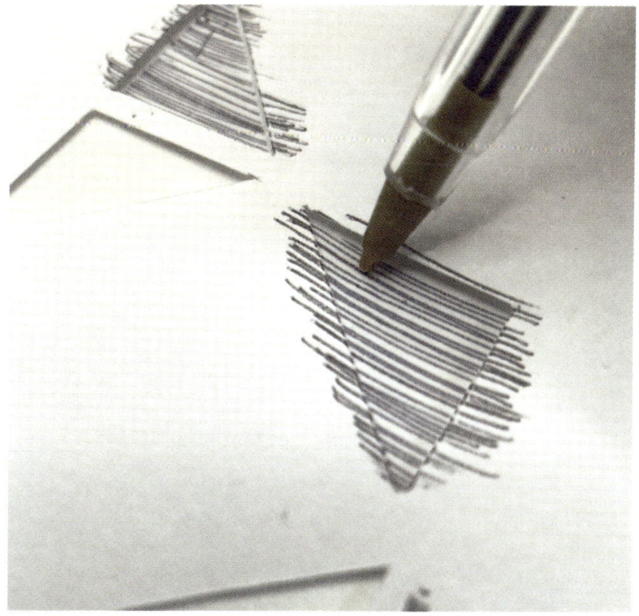

2. Ballpoint pens work brilliantly on a polyester plate and mean you can create very fine lines with ease. Using a paper mask will help to contain the drawn marks in an area or shape of your design.

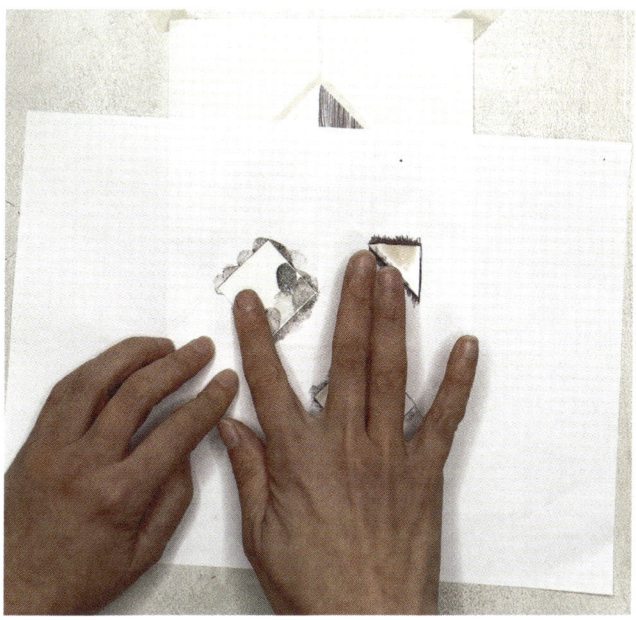

3. Thankfully, the polyester plates are not so sensitive that a fingerprint will leave a dominant mark (unless your hands are quite dirty/oily) but you can still incorporate fingerprint markings by dipping your finger in your oil-based printing ink first.

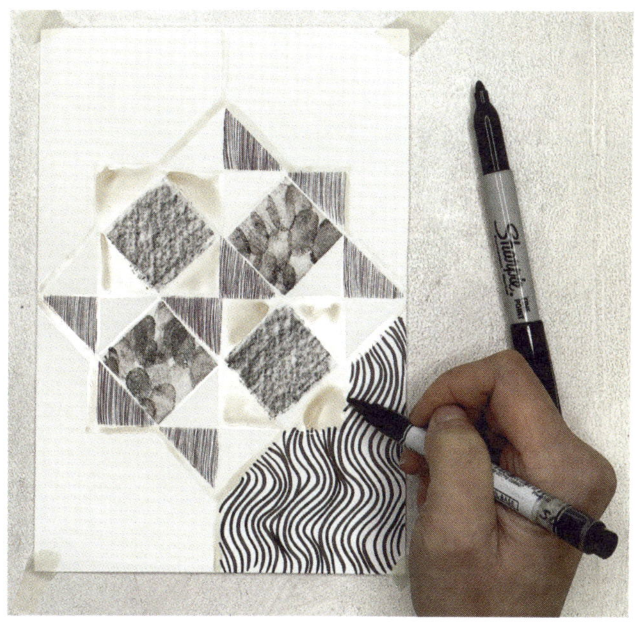

4. Permanent markers work very reliably on polyester plates and will create a dense mark. Use a variety of sizes and vary your line work to create areas of varied tone. They work well in combination with gum resists.

Test plate drawing *(continued)*

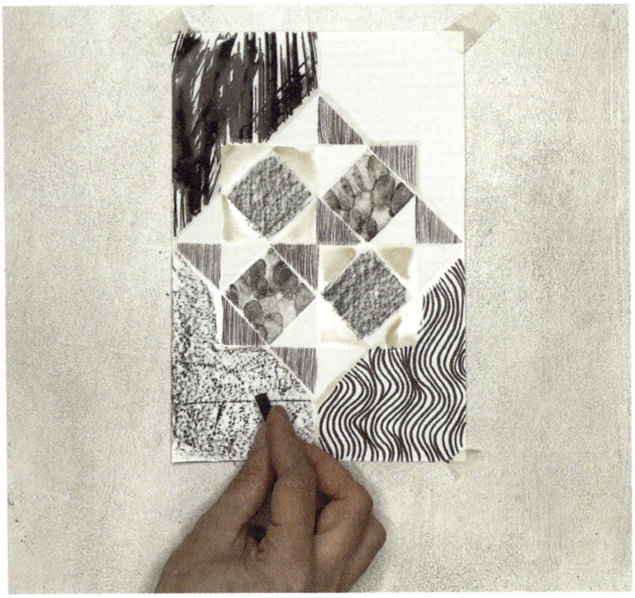

5. Interesting textures can be achieved using Indian ink and a dodgy old paintbrush, and oil pastel or litho crayon rubbings. The polyester plates are very thin so you can place textured materials under the plates and take rubbings of them.

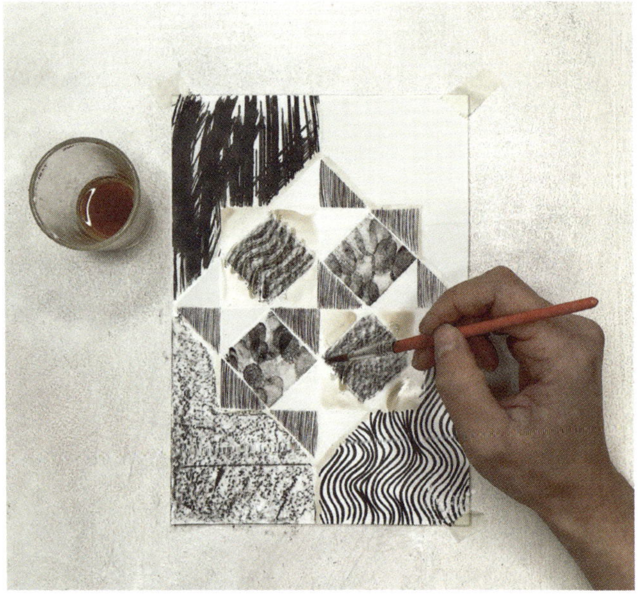

6. To create layers of markings you can use a gum resist again, but this time on top of the existing image. Apply French chalk to the plate first to break the surface tension to allow the gum to sit evenly on the greasy drawing material.

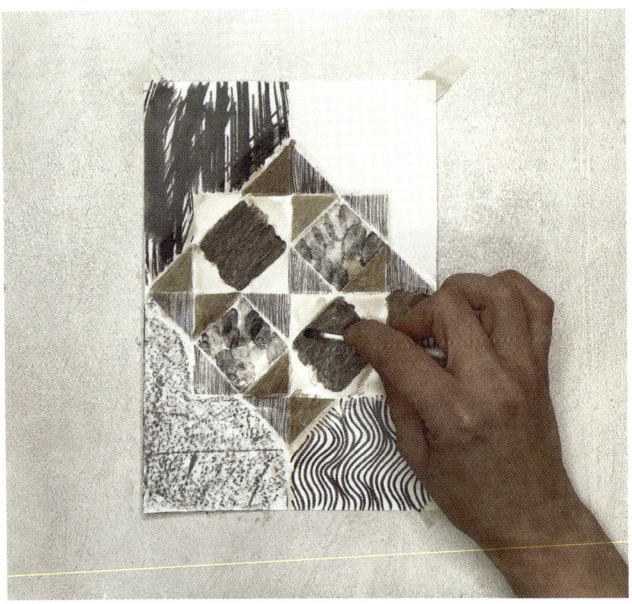

7. Use a second drawing material (which isn't water-based) on top of your gum resist. For solid shapes you can apply diluted printing ink using a paintbrush or cotton bud. The gum will protect the image underneath from this added layer.

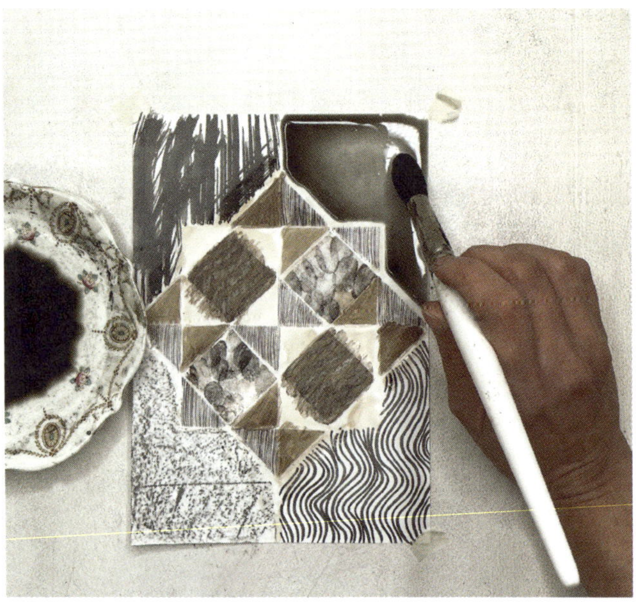

8. Pool tusche washes on the plate and allow them to dry naturally to form beautiful reticulated washes. Be careful when using tusche alongside gum resists as the tusche can penetrate the gum.

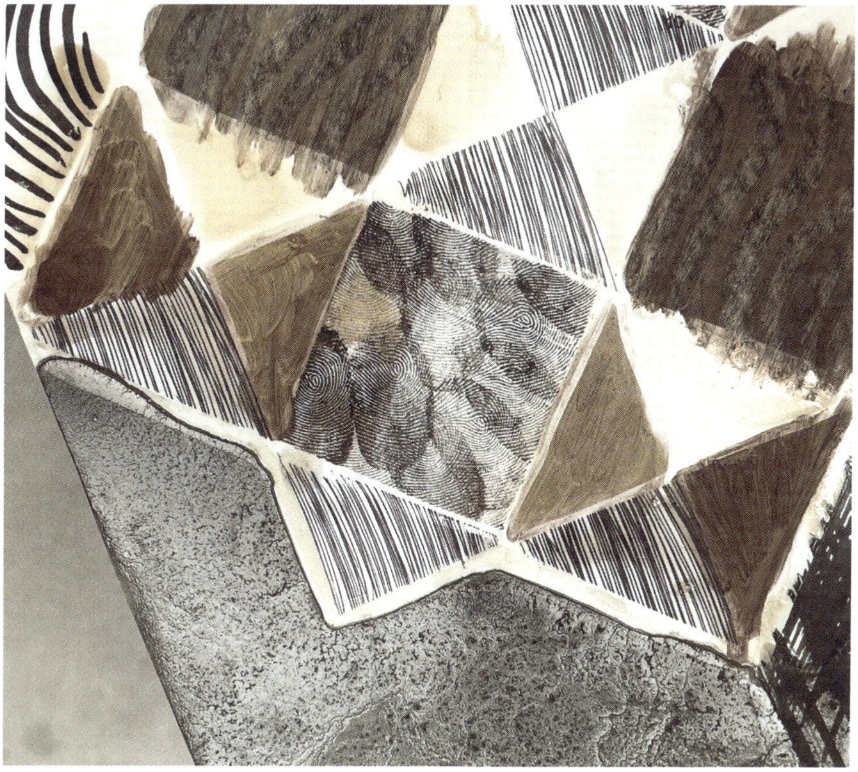

9. You can see the gorgeous tusche wash markings in this close up of the dry plate. Tusche is a wonderful drawing medium, I recommend exploring varying dilutions and methods of application of the tusche.

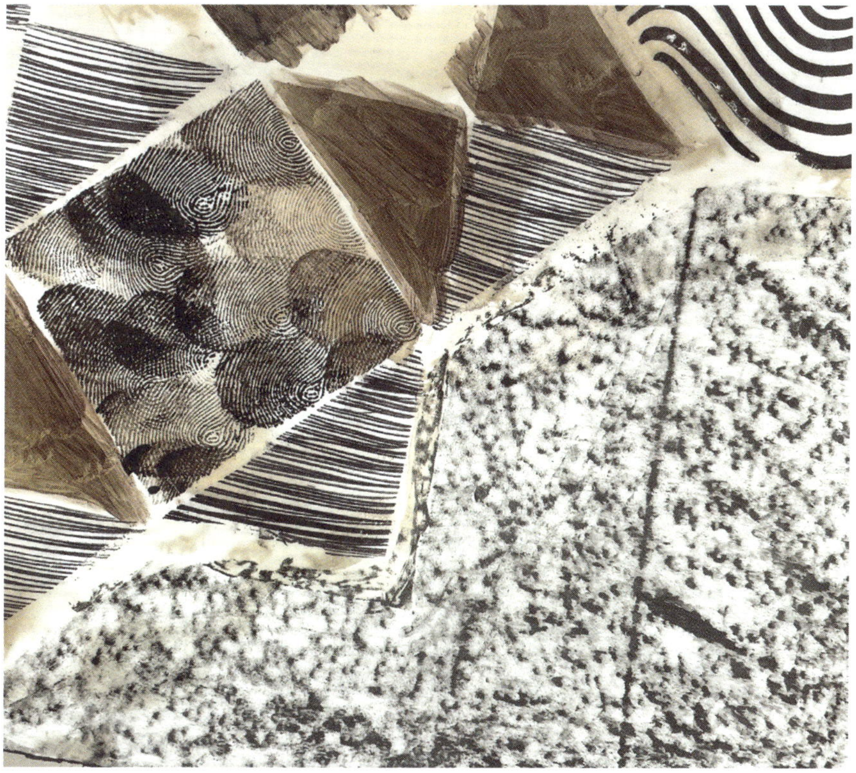

10. Note the fantastic details of the other drawing materials in this close-up and the layers of gum resist. Polyester plates will retain the fine details of these drawing materials and reproduce them faithfully in the print.

Processing the plate

Not all drawing materials will require heat fixing onto the plate. For example, it is necessary to heat the plate to secure toner and crayons but for permanent marker and ballpoint pen it is not necessary. Whether the plate is heated has an impact on some drawing materials more than others. When heating tusche washes it is easy for them to darken and lose detail, so it can be preferable to avoid heating them and instead use a softer ink and a foam roller when printing. The modified ink and foam roller will ink the plate more gently and will mean the un-fixed tusche will be less likely to come away from the plate.

To heat fix the plates, they will require 5 minutes in an oven at 180°C, or 30 minutes on a hot plate; alternatively you can use an iron with a protective sheet of greaseproof paper on top. If the plate is heated for too long it will become discoloured, the edges will curl, it will become brittle and it can burn.

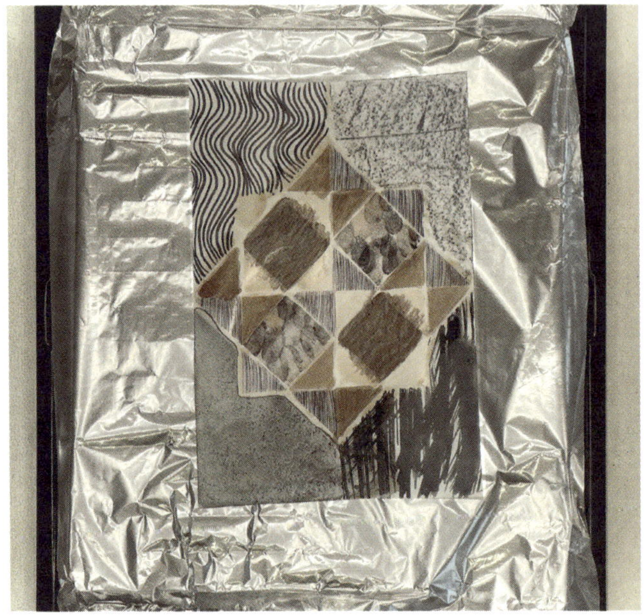

1. Fix the drawing material to the plate with heat. Protect the plate from the oven tray with foil or a baking sheet. Heat for five minutes at 180°C in the oven, or use a heat gun or hot plate.

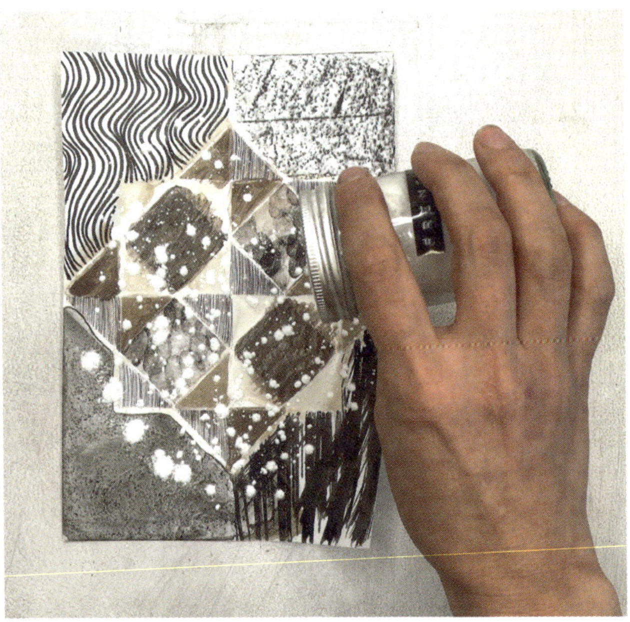

2. When the plate has cooled, dust the plate with French chalk and brush over with a soft brush or cotton wool. The French chalk will help the gum to cling close to the greasy drawing material.

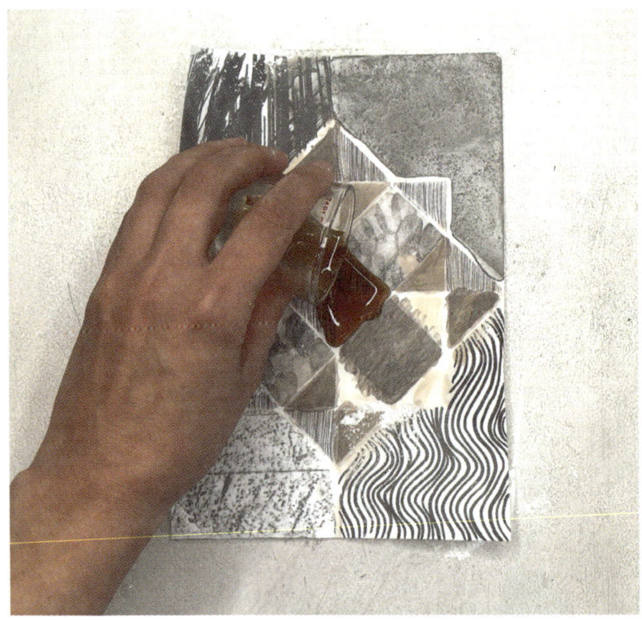

3. Apply gum arabic to the plate and spread it evenly over the surface with a sponge. The gum resists will dissolve at this point so gently massage them to loosen the excess drawing material.

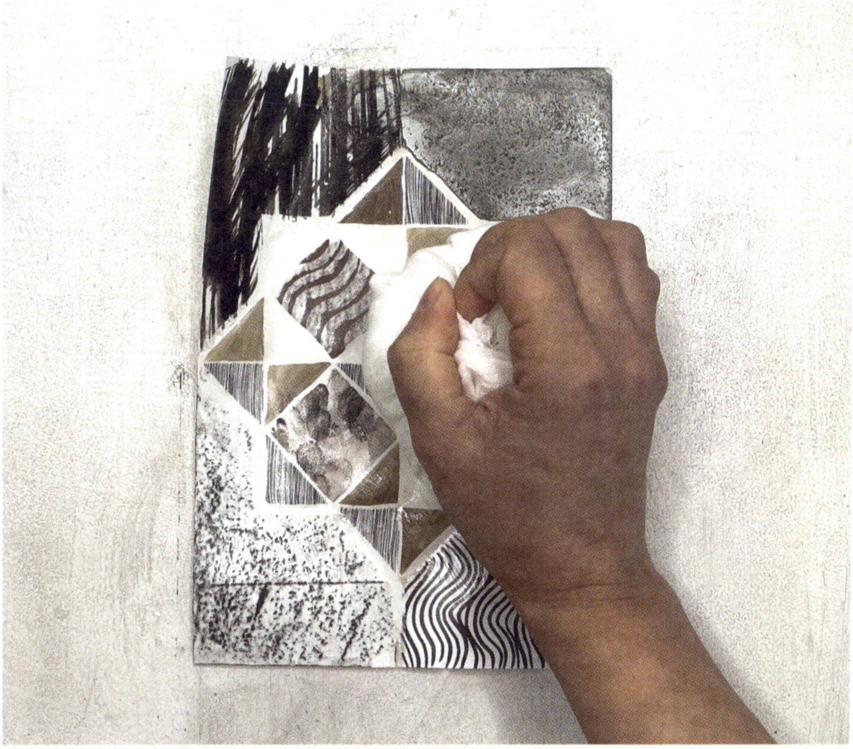

4. Using a ball of muslin, gently buff the layer of gum arabic down to a thin layer and allow to dry. For best results, the plate will now need to be left overnight.

Printing a polyester plate

Using a fount solution adds extra acidity to the dampening water, which helps to keep the plate clean and clear of scum. Polyester plates are prone to scumming so keeping an even level of water on the plate is important to prevent scumming.

For polyester plate printing, the ink needs to be relatively stiff to hold the details on the plate, but not too tacky. It's important here to note the difference between body and tackiness. Your printing inks may require tack reducer to make the ink less sticky, so that the ink will let go of the drawing material and not pull it off the plate. However, you do not want to change the body of the ink, to loosen it so that it will spread too easily on the plate and not remain held in the fine details. If the ink is too loose it will encourage scumming. If you don't have tack reducer and you're using oil instead, you will have to work a little harder when printing to avoid the plate scumming.

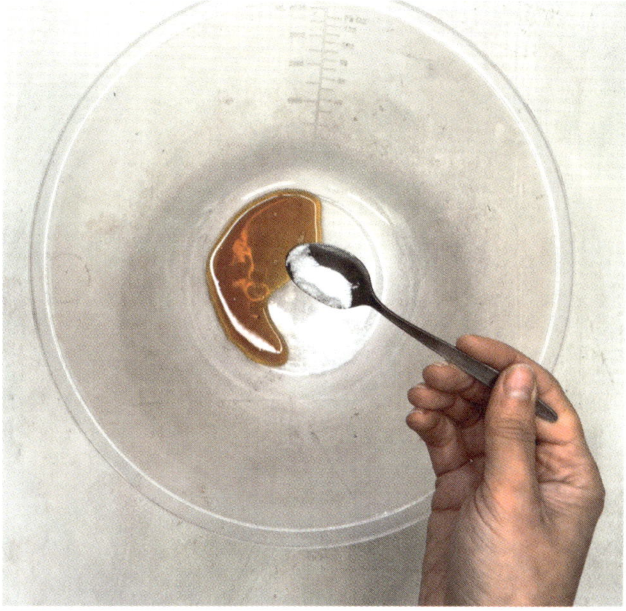

1. Mix your fount solution to use as your dampening water. This will help keep your plate clean and prevent scumming. Add 30ml of gum arabic and half a teaspoon of citric acid to 500ml of water.

Printing the test plate *(continued)*

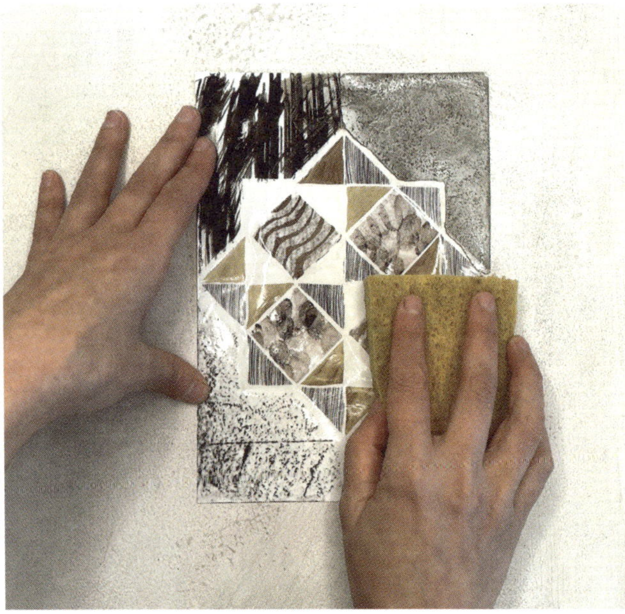

2. Remove the excess gum from the plate. Use a damp sponge to moisten the plate. The plate will feel slimy with the excess gum. Gently dampen and wipe the plate until the residue has been cleaned away.

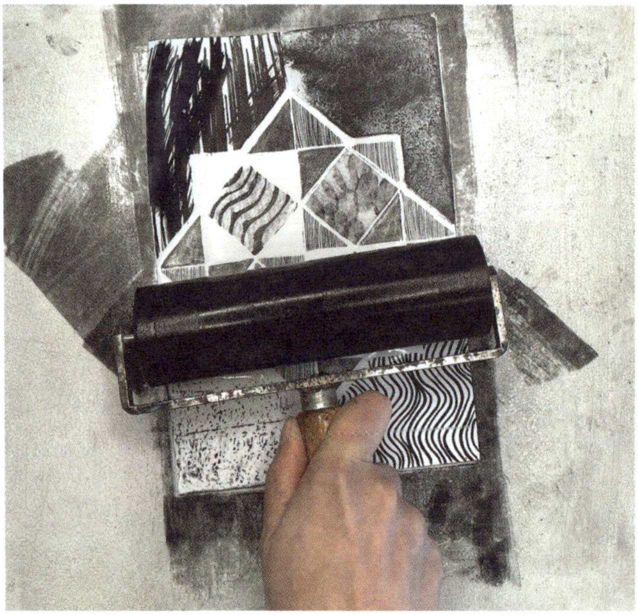

3. As the plates are so thin, you will need to work on a very smooth flat surface when inking up. Dampen under the plate to help it stick. Roll from the centre outwards to avoid the plate curling around the roller.

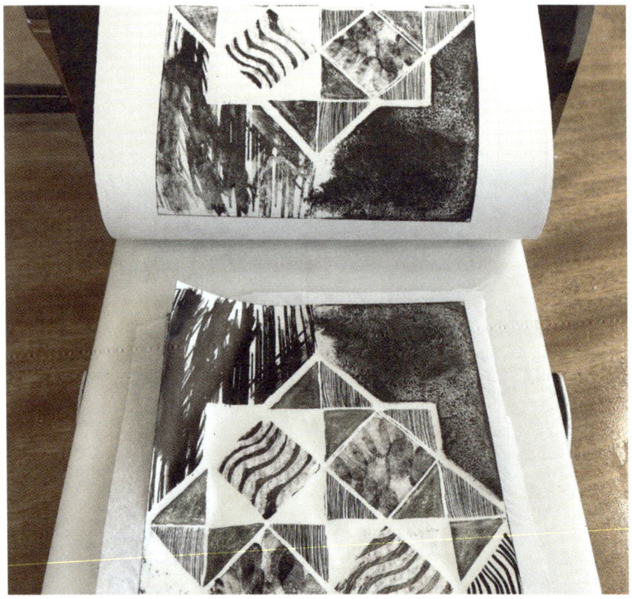

4. Ink up slowly; don't try to ink up the plate fully in the first inking. Take your first prints on newsprint or scrap paper as they will be light. This is the third print, on dampened printing paper, and it is still a little light.

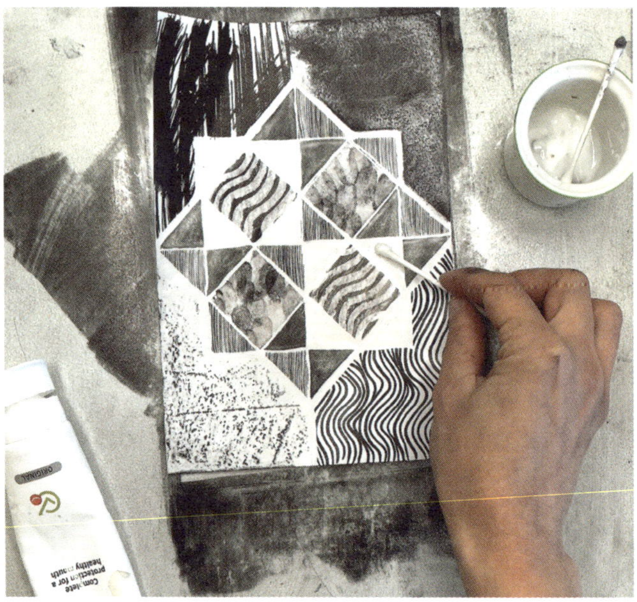

5. You can clean off unwanted areas of ink where the plate has scummed using toothpaste and a cotton bud. You can also use a scalpel or wire wool to permanently remove imagery but be careful not to damage the plate.

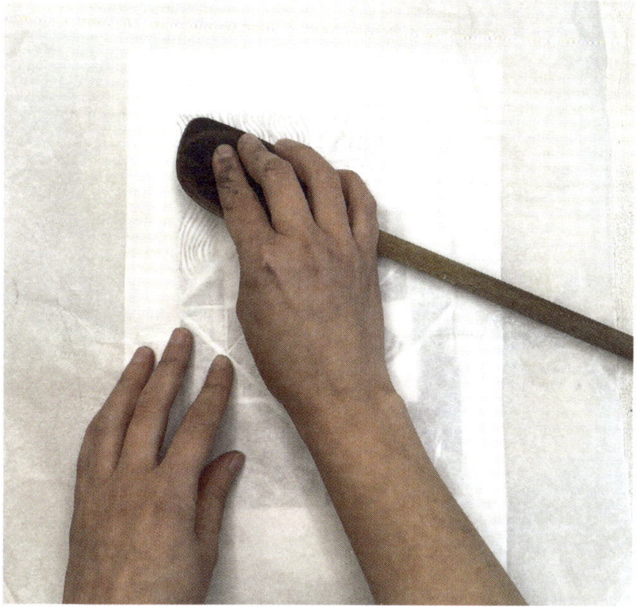

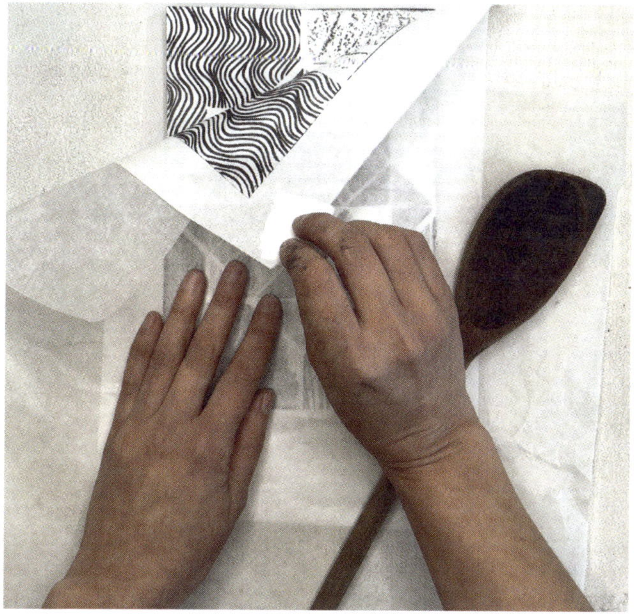

6. Ink your plate, dry the plate with a fan or cold hairdryer and place your printing paper on top. Use a sheet of greaseproof paper to protect the back of the print and use firm pressure with a wooden spoon to burnish the print.

7. There is a lot of fine detail to collect from a polyester litho plate. Keep one hand on your print to hold the paper in place while you peek at your print. Carefully place the paper back down and continue to burnish if necessary.

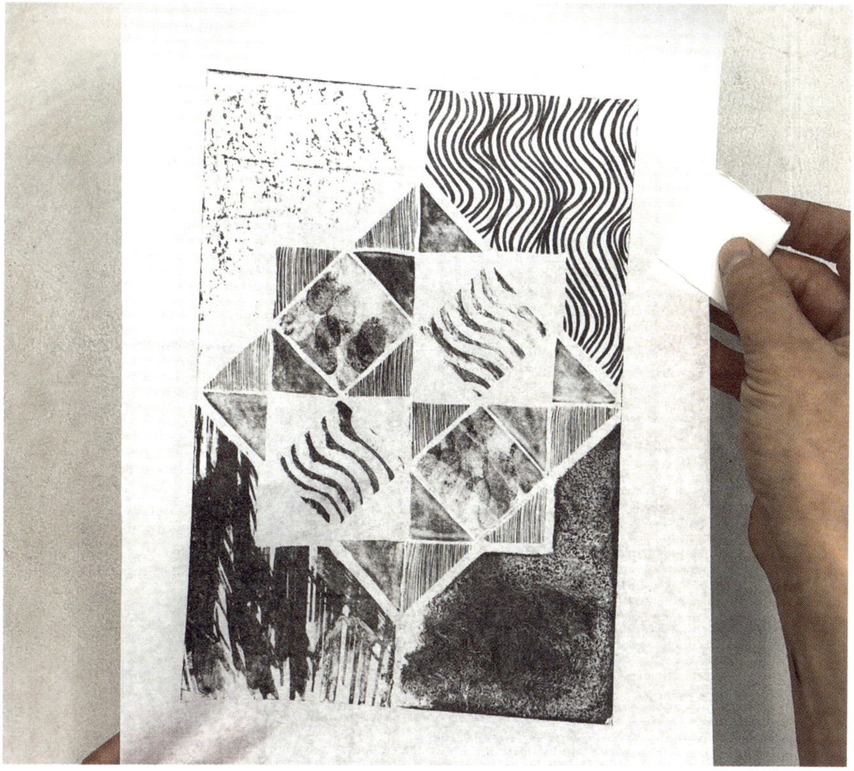

8. Hand-burnished prints or prints onto dry papers won't have quite as much density in the darkest areas of the print but will retain clarity in the details.

Cleaning and storing your plates

When a polyester plate is fully cleaned and protected with a layer of gum it can be stored for years. Toothpaste works well as an abrasive to clean off unwanted ink left on the plate, and washing up liquid can be used afterwards as a final degreaser if there are still traces of oils on the plate. Store the plates flat in a drawer. If taken care of they can be printed again multiple times.

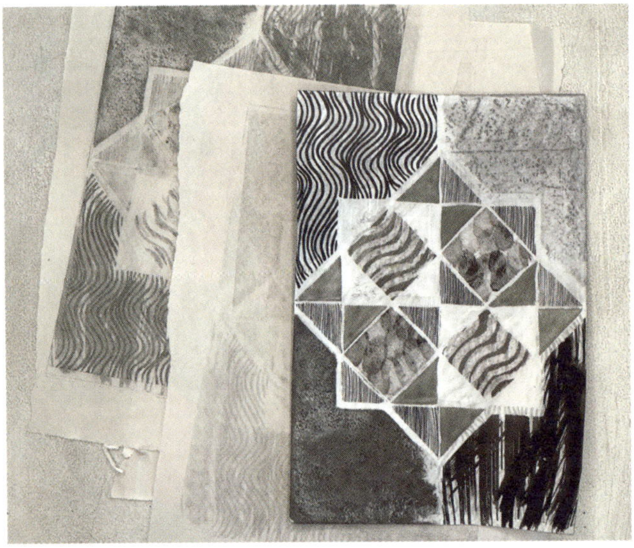

1. Without inking up, repeatedly take prints from the plate onto scrap paper to remove as much ink as possible.

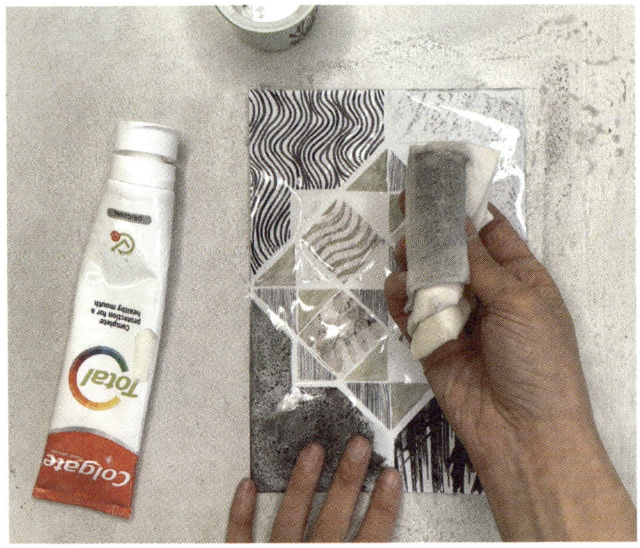

2. Use a little toothpaste mixed with water as a paste on a soft damp cloth to remove the remaining ink from the plate.

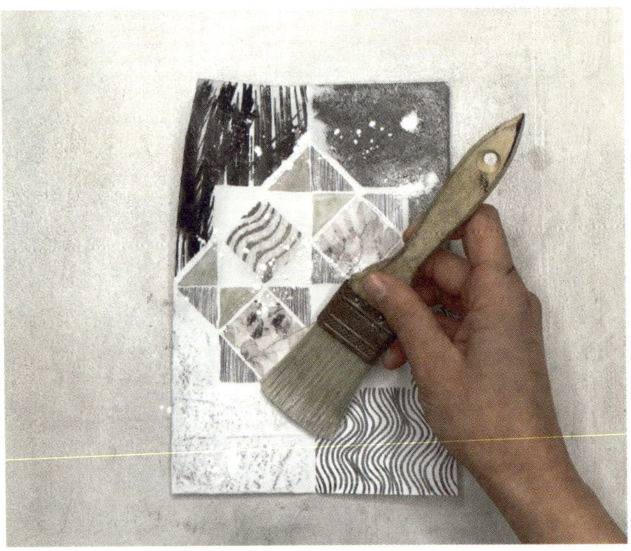

3. Dry the plate and sprinkle with French chalk. Dust the chalk all over the plate with a soft brush or cotton wool.

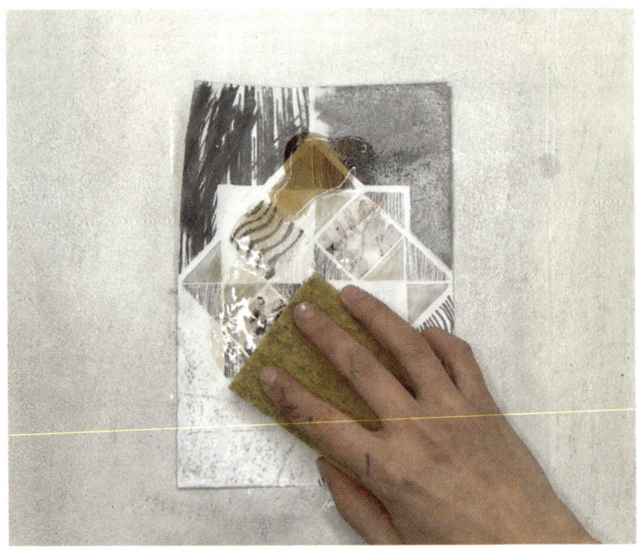

4. Apply a thin layer of gum to the plate and buff it down with a ball of muslin. You can now store the plate for use at a later date.

Printing a CMYK separation

In theory CMYK printing will reproduce the full spectrum of colours using the overlay of only four colour layers: cyan, magenta, yellow and black. K stands for 'key', the key layer which contains the most detail and is usually printed in black. Lithographic ink is printed thin enough that there is enough transparency for ink colours to overlay and produce another colour. Using a combination of these four colours and a halftone filter, a photorealistic image can be produced.

A halftone filter will translate a greyscale photographic image into a discrete pattern of solid black dots of varying size or distance to trick the eye into simulating a range of tones. The angle of the halftone will need to be irregular to trick the eye, a pattern at a 45° or 90° angle will be too easy to recognise and the effect will not be as successful. A CMYK separation of a full colour image will create a separate halftone layer for each of the 4 colours to be printed; cyan, magenta, yellow and black. When overlaid these layers will reproduce the image in full colour.

Registration is key for CMYK printing as misregistered prints can produce build-ups of colour unsuited to the original image or moiré patterns – conflicting angles of halftone pattern which show through as a distracting swirl pattern. You can use special software to create photographic CMYK separations or you can use the principle of CMYK overlays to create drawn/non-photographic layers by hand.

For single colour layers a 'diffusion dither' halftone will apply a random pattern of dots which can be more suitable for organic imagery or images with lots of greys, where a regular gridded pattern of dots would be too pronounced.

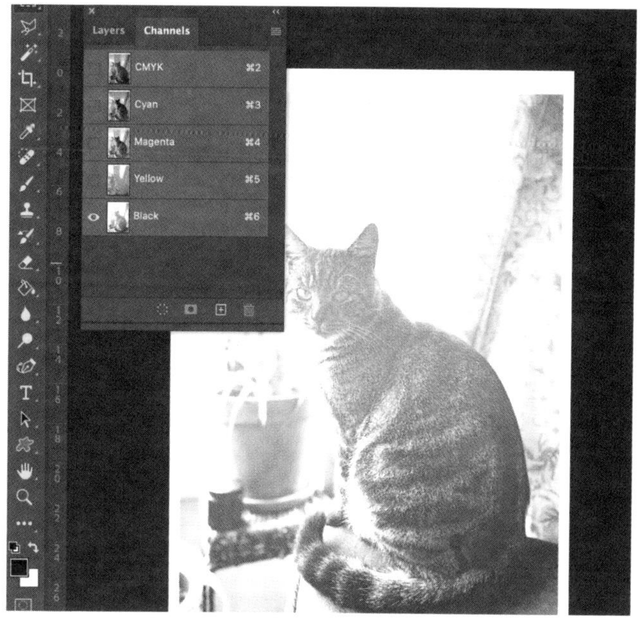

1. If using Photoshop, to create a CMYK separation first make sure you are in CMYK mode, rather than RGB. Head to the channels panel and isolate which colour channel to work with. Delete the rest.

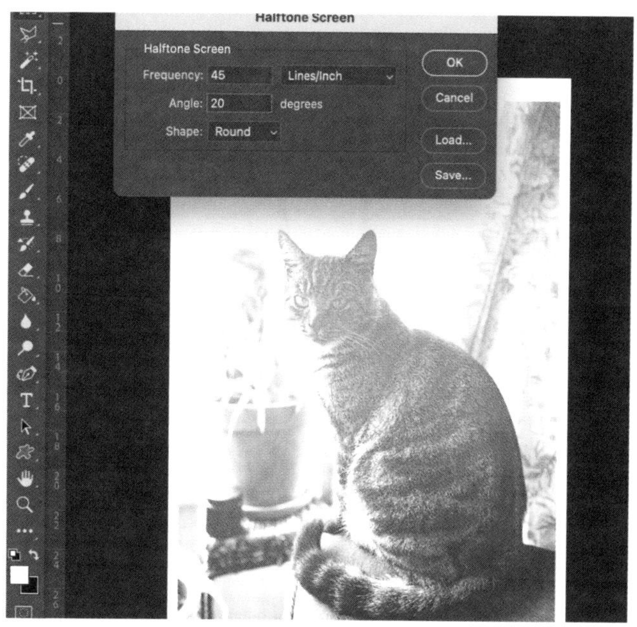

2. Convert to greyscale mode and then to Bitmap. Select Halftone Screen and choose a frequency (size of dot) no smaller than 45 lines/inch. Choose your angle of degrees (direction of dot) for your first layer.

CMYK separations *(continued)*

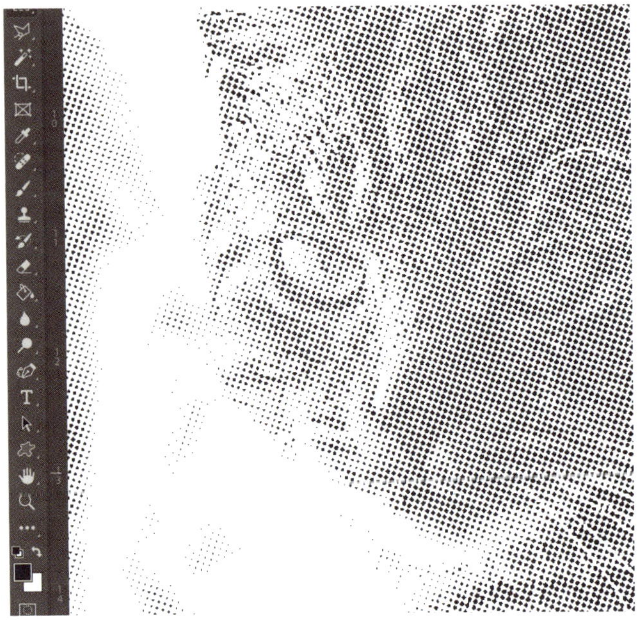

3. Repeat this process for your next three layers. You will need to change your angle by 30 degrees each time so that your layers don't overlap completely or conflict.

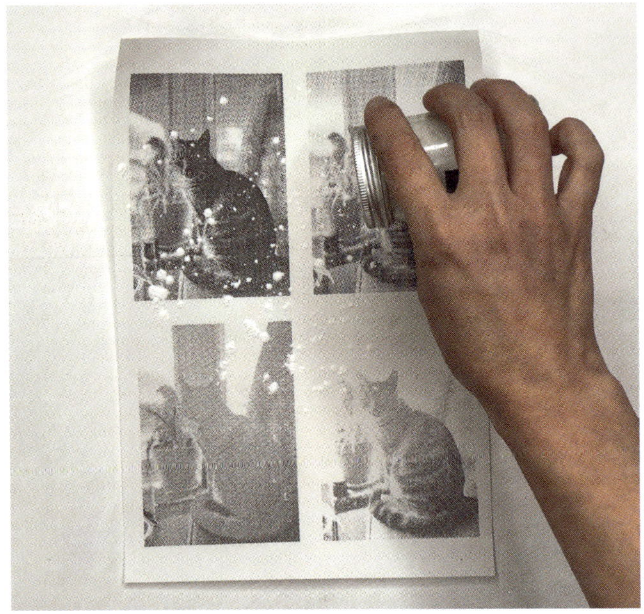

4. Print your imagery straight onto your polyester plate using a laser printer. Run the plate through the printer a few times (without printing on it) to heat set the plate. Dust with French chalk.

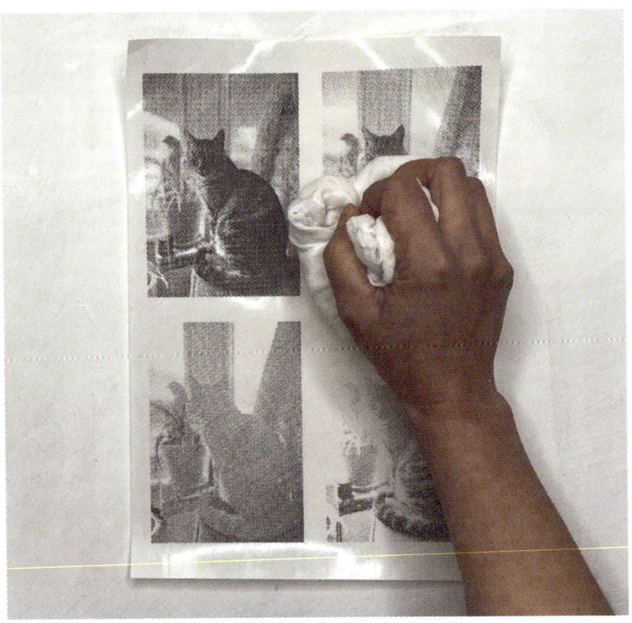

5. Apply a small amount of gum arabic with a sponge and buff it down to a thin layer using a ball of muslin. Allow the plate to dry and leave overnight for best results.

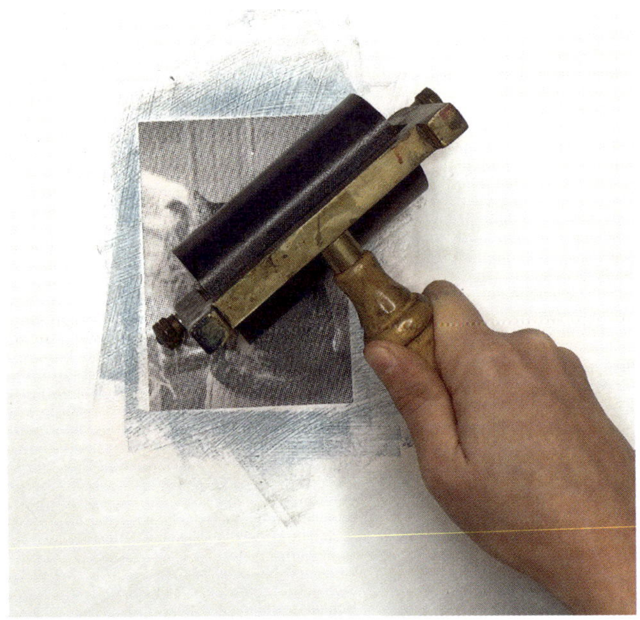

6. Dampen the plate and ink up very carefully using a traditional roller. Avoid leaving roller lines by using a roller larger than the plate, or use a foam roller. The plate will also be less likely to curl up around a foam roller.

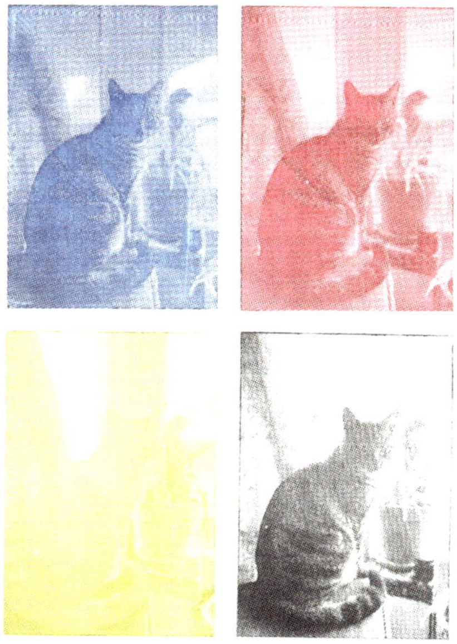

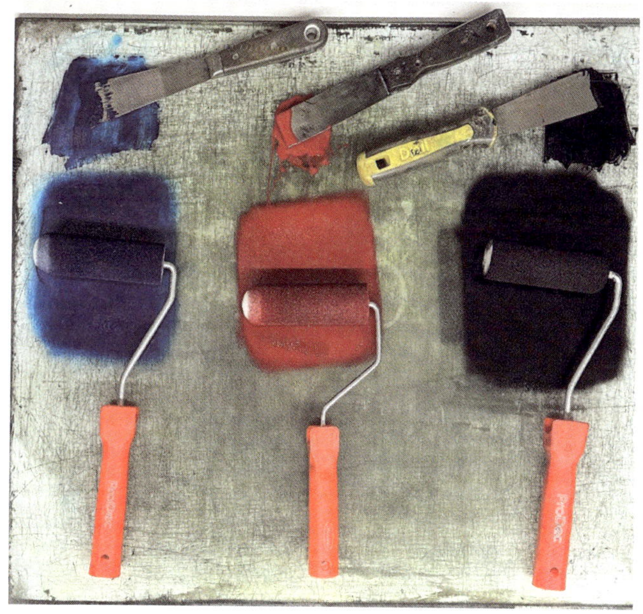

7. The CMYK separations of the photograph are quite aesthetically pleasing printed by themselves. Do note the edges of the plates will collect ink so you may want to print your separations in the centre of a larger plate.

8. Ink up all four of the plates at the same time so that they are ready to print consecutively in one sitting. This will remove the risk of misregistration when the printing paper dries and warps. Alternatively, print onto dry paper.

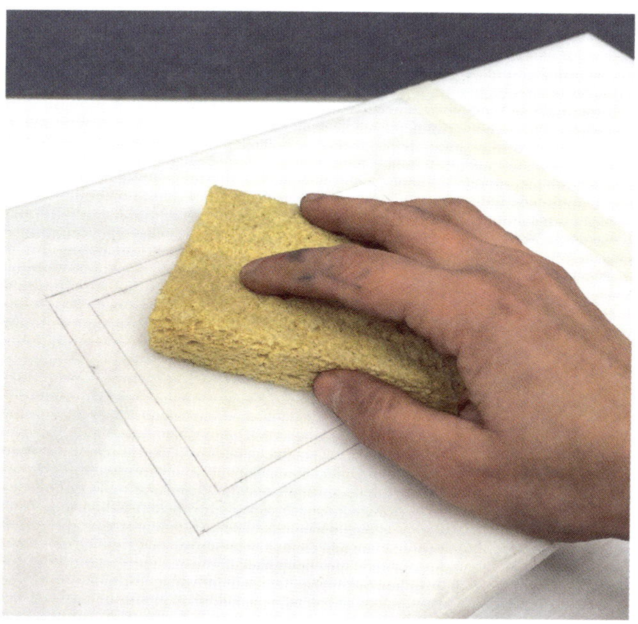

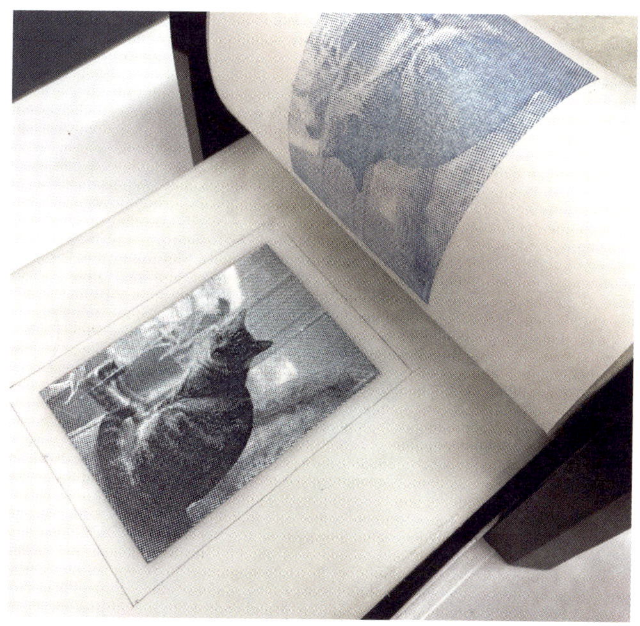

9. Good registration is key for CMYK printing so be discerning. Very lightly dampen the plastic registration guide so the plate will adhere to it in its correct position of registration.

10. After running the first layer through the press, keep the edge of the paper trapped in place under the roller (or with a weight if hand burnishing). This will ensure the paper won't change position.

CMYK separations *(continued)*

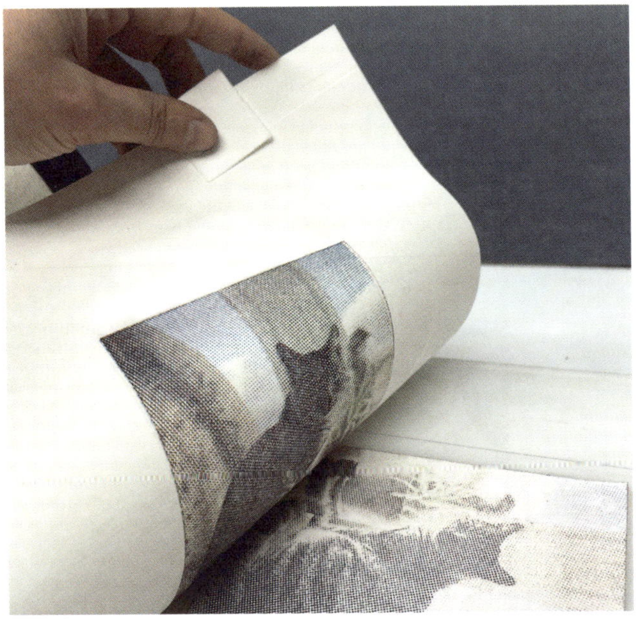

11. Print all four layers consecutively, cleaning the press bed in between layers. Work quickly so that the paper and ink don't begin to dry as this will affect the ink transfer and receptibility.

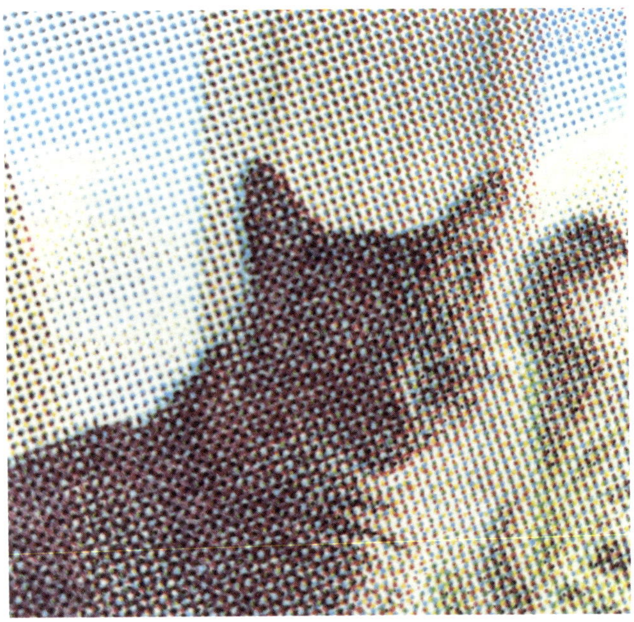

12. Printing a specialist mechanical process by hand is not easy and the CMYK registration may not be perfect when seen up close. But these traces of human interaction are one of the delights of hand printmaking.

Once you have your four CMYK layers you can play around with the sequence of the layers, remove layers, or swap the CMYK for other colours to completely change the overall feel of the image.

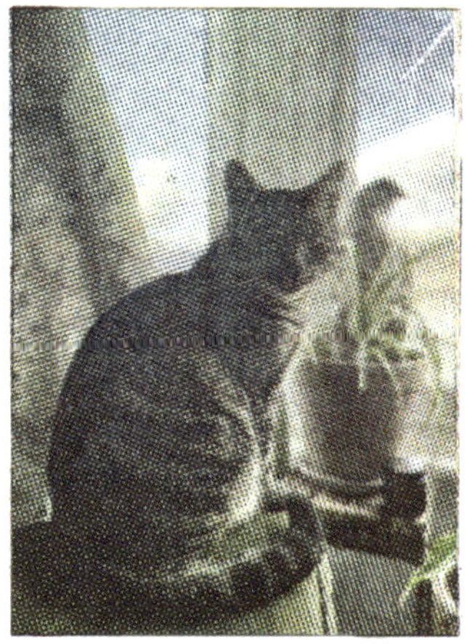

Plate 1: printed in cyan;
Plate 2: printed in magenta;
Plate 3: printed in yellow;
Plate 4: printed in black.

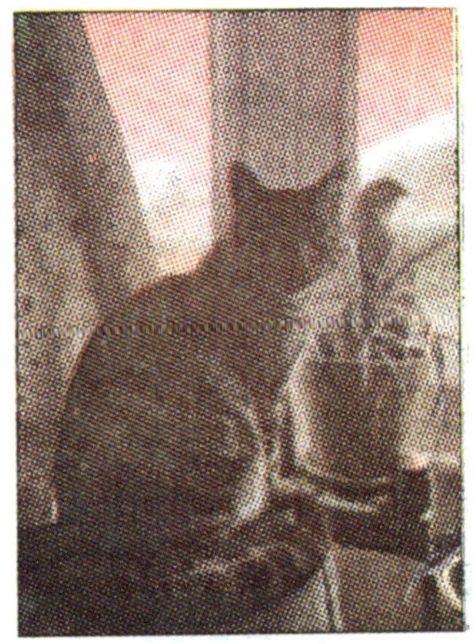

Plate 1: printed in magenta;
Plate 2: printed in yellow;
Plate 3: printed in black;
Plate 4: printed in cyan.

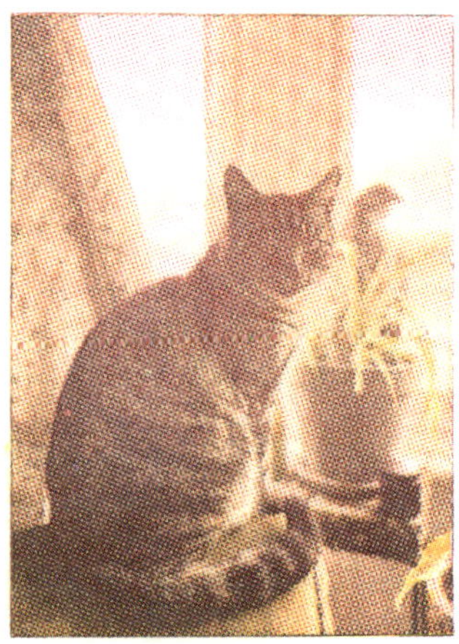

Plate 1: not printed;
Plate 2: printed in magenta;
Plate 3: printed in yellow;
Plate 4: printed in black.

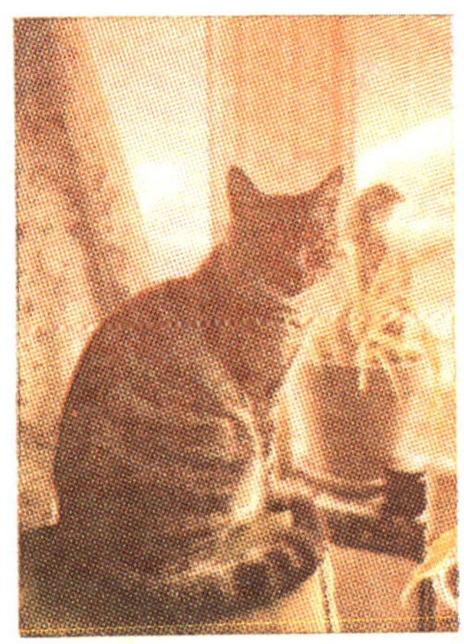

Plate 1: printed in orange;
Plate 2: printed in magenta;
Plate 3: printed in yellow;
Plate 4: printed in black.

Marbling

Once you have your 'Key' plate, the plate which holds the most information which is usually printed in black, you can play around with using it in combination with other layers. This is an opportunity to play with making patterned or textural marks to use with the key plate. All the important information of the image is held in the keyplate so these other plates can be unguided, free, and playful.

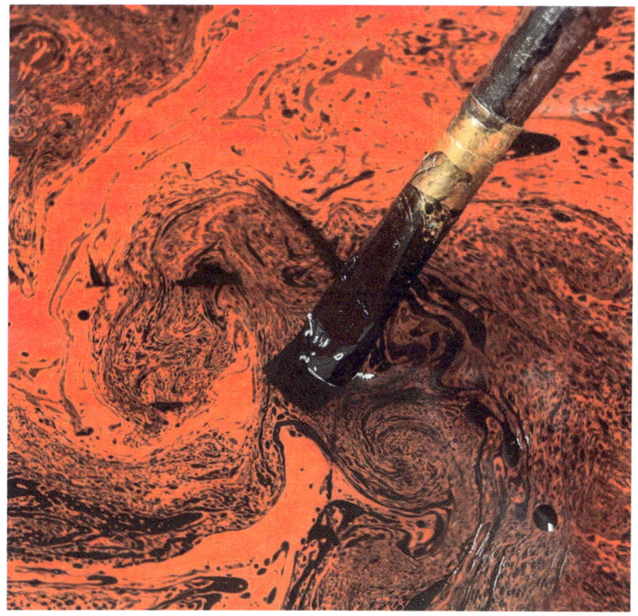

1. Printing ink is loosened with a little white spirit, and swirled on the surface of a tray of water.

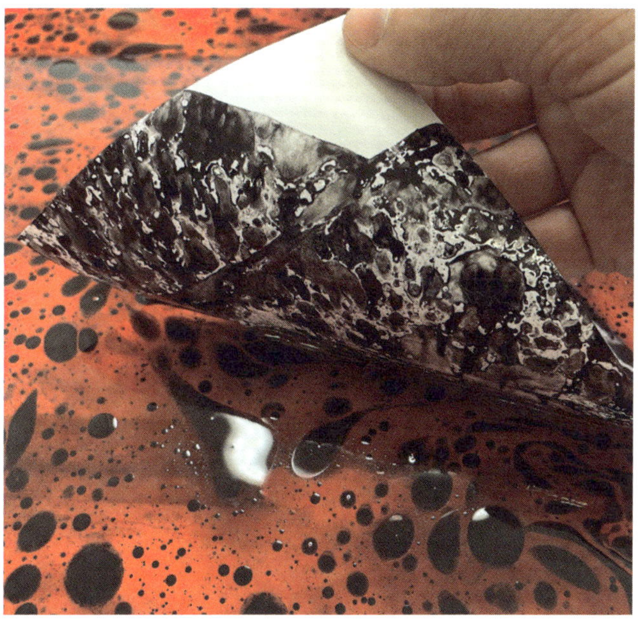

2. The polyester plate is carefully placed on the surface of the water and then pulled away.

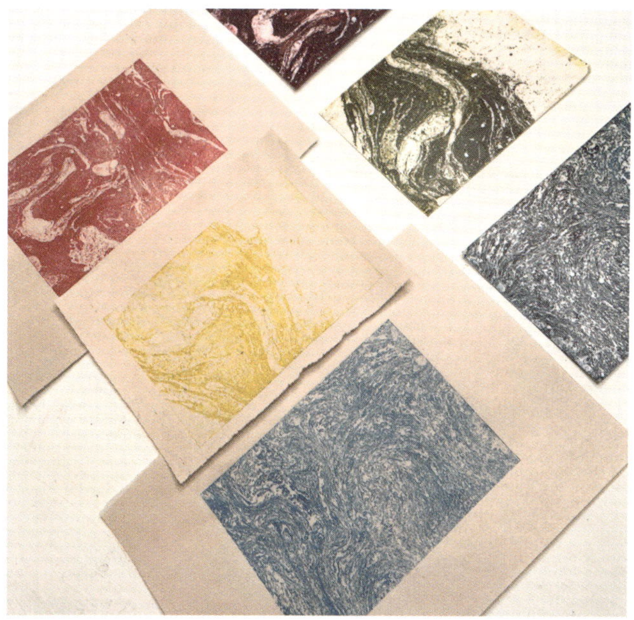

3. Varying marbled effects can be made by altering the amount of white spirit mixed with the ink.

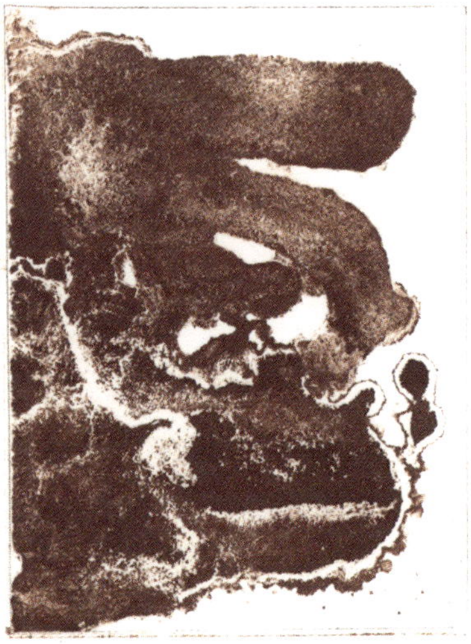

Tusche wash, fixed with heat. Fifth print.

Wash effects

Varying 'wash' effects can be made with a range of materials. Printing ink diluted with varying amount of solvent can be used to create marbled patterns when suspended on water. Adding salt crystals to a tusche wash will gather the tusche to the salt and create white spaces under the salt crystals, creating a gorgeous organic pattern. Toner can be used to create beautiful washes by either creating a solution or sprinkling it onto water painted on the plate.

Whether you decide to heat fix your tusche wash or not will affect the look of the wash. If a tusche wash has not been heat-fixed the heavier deposits of tusche will come away at first and then stabilise, retaining the very fine and delicate details.

When a tusche wash is heat fixed, the delicate particles of grease that we cannot see, that would normally wash away, will be fixed to the plate and all the grease in the tusche will spread out. This will create a much darker wash. The examples shown were painted using the same tusche mix.

To create a toner wash, mix toner particles in water with a little dish soap to break the surface tension and allow the wash to sit more fluidly on the plate. It is important to wear a mask when handling toner, so that you don't inhale the particles. Toner contains substances which can be harmful to health if inhaled in large quantities. Toner washes will need to be heat set on the plate.

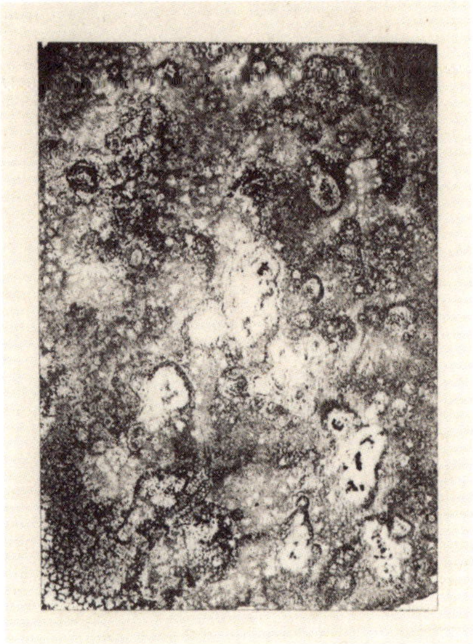

Tusche wash with added sea salt crystals, without fixing with heat. Second print.

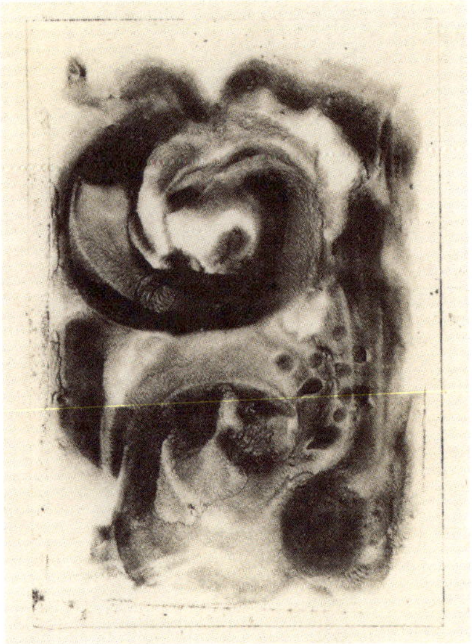

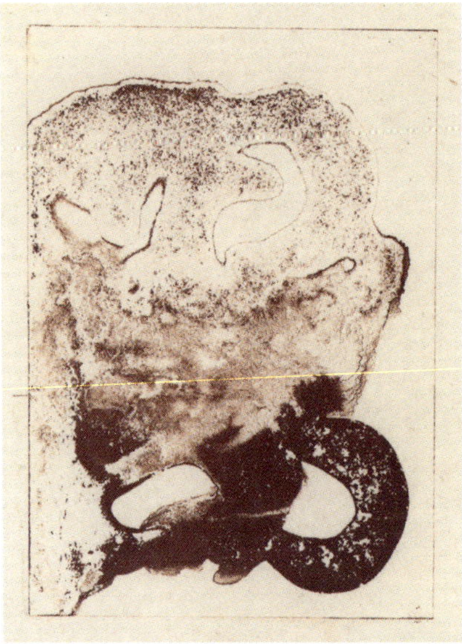

RIGHT
Tusche wash, without fixing with heat. Seventh print.

FAR LEFT
Toner wash, fixed with heat. Fifth print.

Masks

Using cut-out pieces of newsprint to mask off areas of each layer means you can play with a multitude of colour and layer combinations with countless potential. Polyester plates can also be easily cut with scissors instead of using a mask, and you could then print multiple plates at once in a jigsaw method, rather than having to cut out lots of paper masks.

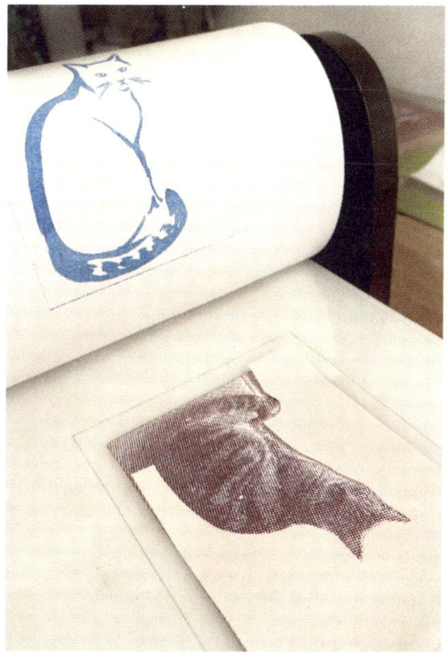

1. First layer: an Indian ink drawing, printed in cyan. Second layer: photographic image with halftone in magenta, with paper mask protecting the background.

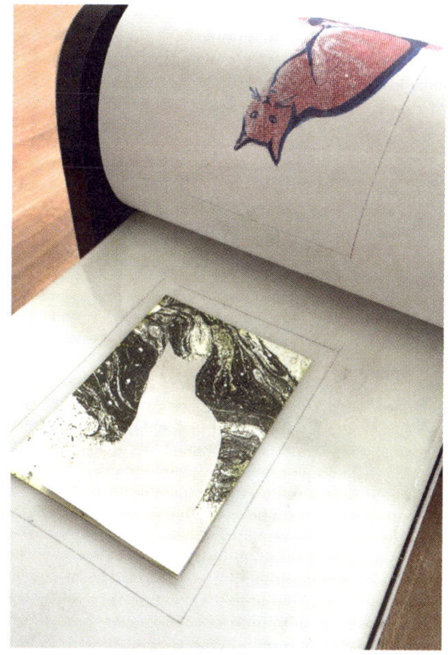

2. The other half of the paper mask used in the previous layer, used to protect the cat figure from the next layer; marbled pattern in yellow.

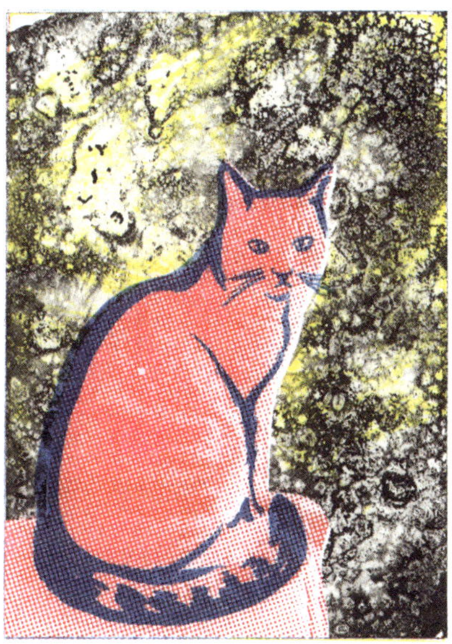

3. Final image with tusche wash and salt plate printed in background, using a paper mask again to protect the cat figure.

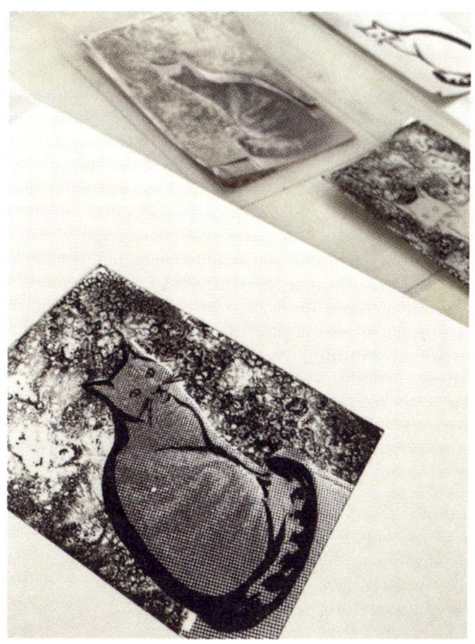

4. Halftone image, Indian ink drawing and tusche wash with salt, all printed using paper masks and only black ink.

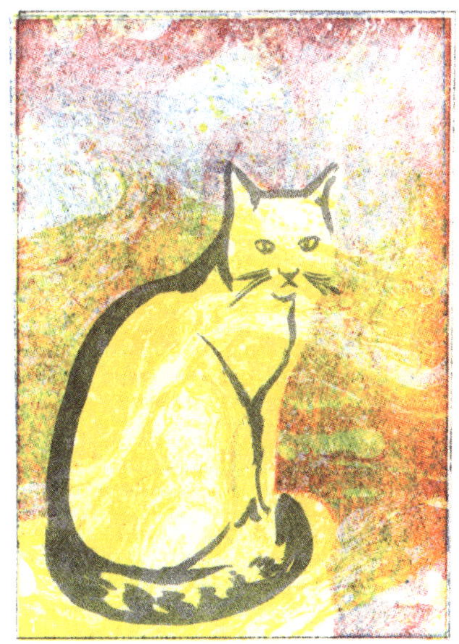

5. Ink drawing in black, cyan marbled plate and magenta marbled plate all printed from previously used plates without re-inking them. Yellow marbled plate on top.

Masks *(continued)*

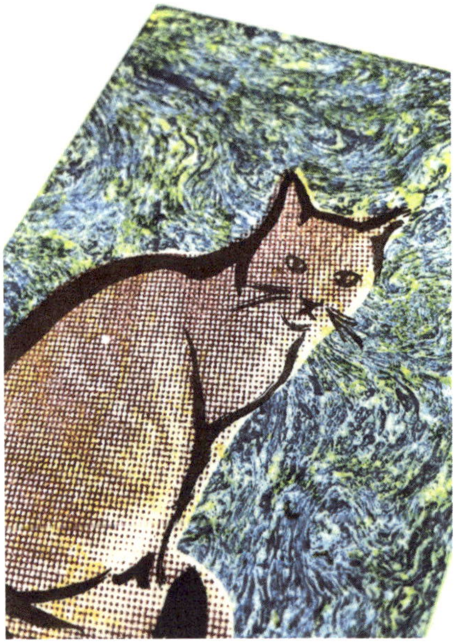

6. Yellow and cyan marbled plates in the background, no mask used with yellow plate. Magenta halftone plate, and black Indian ink drawing printed last.

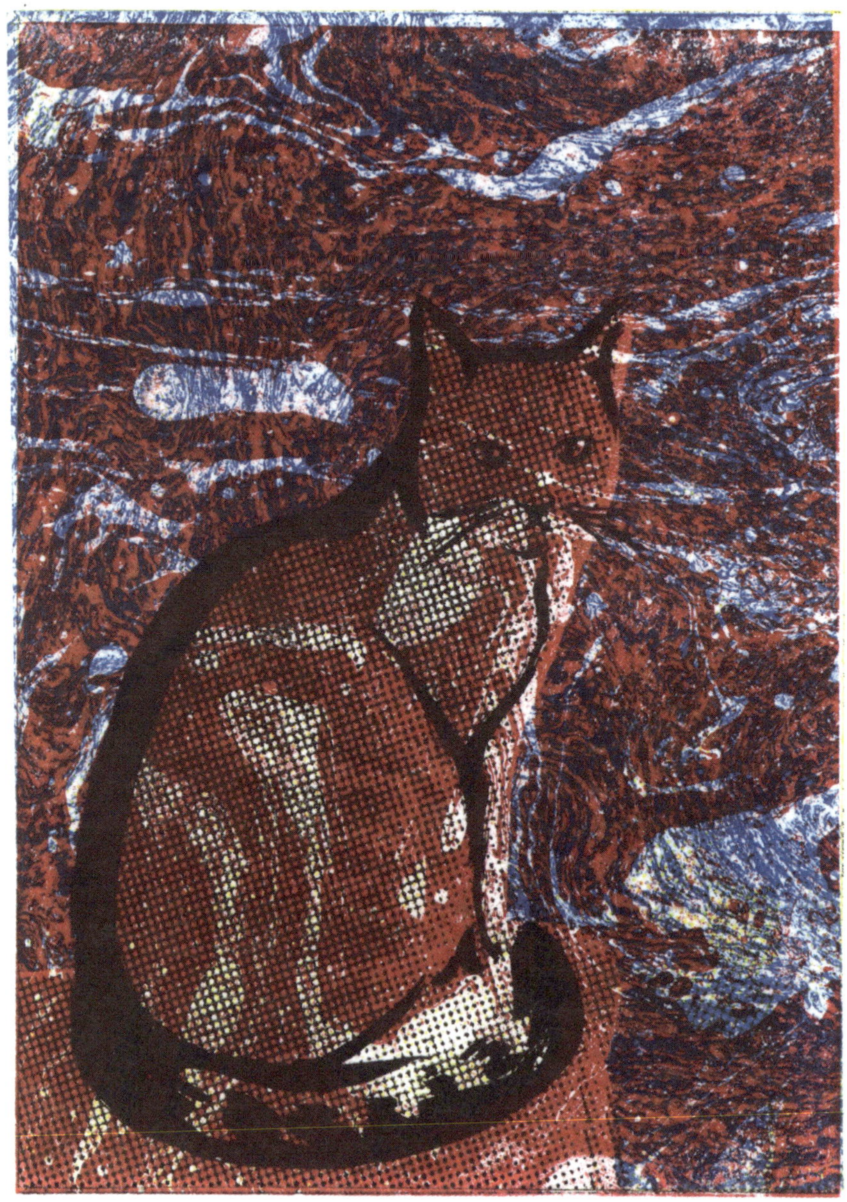

7. Cyan marbled plate with mask, black halftone plate with mask, magenta marbled plate without mask, and black Indian ink drawing plate.

TROUBLESHOOTING

Inking a dry plate

This is the most common mistake made with all lithographic printmaking, especially polyester plates as they require a fine level of dampening, and they dry very quickly. Without the protective layer of water, inking a dry plate will deposit ink everywhere. Do not try to collect the ink with your sponge as this will just smear the ink and contaminate your sponge. Instead, spray or splash water all over the plate and roll the roller quickly over the plate. The ink will detach from the plate and stick to your roller instead. This will ultimately over ink the plate for the next print, so strip the ink back by printing onto scrap paper a few times without inking in between prints.

Roller lines

Roller lines will appear on your image area, especially in solid areas of ink, if your roller is smaller than your image. Try to use a roller that is larger than your image area or vary your rolling pattern, so the roller lines don't become too pronounced. This problem is less likely to occur if you are using a foam roller.

Plate sticking to roller

This is the most annoying aspect of polyester plate printing. The plate can curl up around the roller, especially if there are areas on the plate which require lots of ink. Adhere the plate to the inking surface with a little water and try to ink from the middle outwards. You may need to tape the plate in position if the problem persists. This problem does not occur when using foam rollers.

Prints are too dark

This may occur because you have over-inked your plate or the ink you are using is too loose. Remove most of the ink from your inking slab and roll out using just the ink from your roller so that you are working with much less ink on your roller. You can also modify your ink to make it stiffer.

Prints are too light

Your ink may be too stiff and is not picking up on the plate. Your ink may be too tacky and has detached some drawing material from your plate. Either way, check your plate for signs of ink which haven't transferred to the print and then modify your ink if needed. You may also need to use less fount solution when dampening the plate. If you are printing on a press with a blanket, remove the blanket for a firmer pressure. You may also want to dampen your printing paper if you are not already.

Image not inking up at all

There may not be enough grease in your drawing material to attract the ink.

Image inking up too much

Your plate may have been heated for too long. Or the gum layer may have been too thin and not left long enough before printing.

Excessive scumming

Check the cleanliness of your sponge and fount solution. You may need to add more citric acid to your fount solution. Your ink may also be too loose and needs stiffening. You can remove areas of scumming with toothpaste and a damp cloth. If the scumming is happening all over the plate, is it best to remove all the ink and then ink it up fresh, after ensuring your fount solution and ink are suitable. You may also want to clean off all the ink and apply a fresh layer of gum to the plate. Buff the gum down to a thin layer and attempt printing again at a later time.

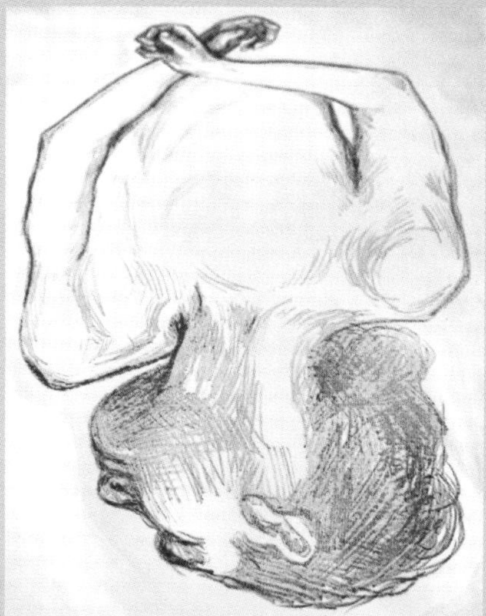

Pale trace of crayon drawing on polyester plate, not greasy enough to attract the printing ink.

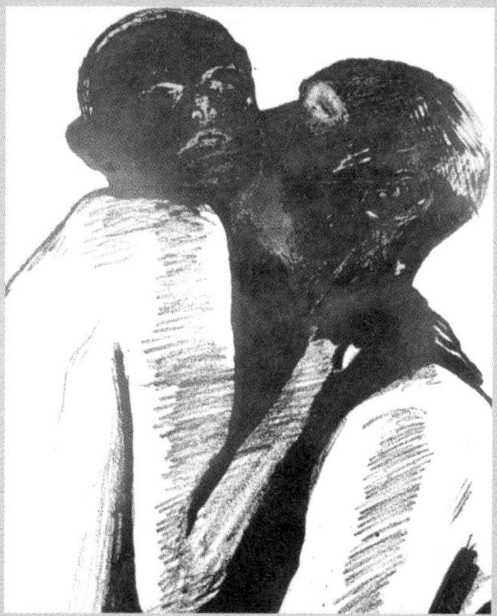

Loss of definition on polyester plate with complete filling in of ink, ruining the image.

Sue Jarman (UK)

suejarman.co.uk

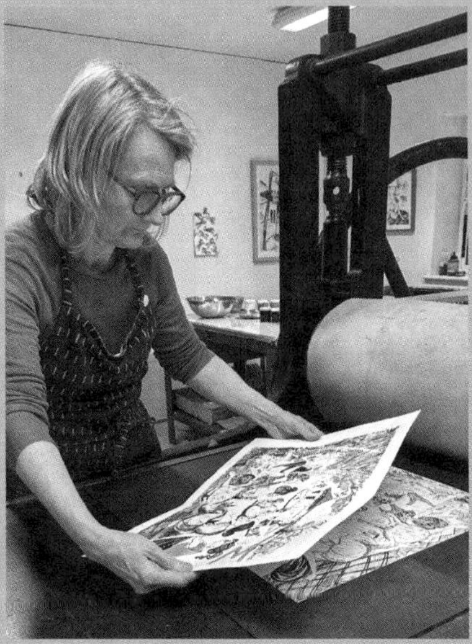

Sue is an image maker and printmaker with a spontaneous documentary style of working. Observational drawing is a fundamental part of her practice, a process she calls 'visual eavesdropping'.

Whether capturing figures to a soundtrack of conversations and unfolding narratives, or out in the landscape at the mercy of the elements, there is always a subconscious and emotional response and connection to time and place. This mix of observation, imagination, and memory is my visual stimulus and primary inspiration; and the foundation for resolving ideas through printmaking.

My choices of print processes echo my drawing, painting and mark-making. So, it is no surprise that lithography, drypoint, collagraph, monotype and etching are my current go-to choices for printmaking; they are particularly suited to combining the immediacy and sustained image-making within my practice.

My interest in lithography was sparked through a course on Mokulito. This discovery led me to polyester lithography with its thinner plates that can fit through the old, non-adjustable studio press I work with; and their potential for being more stable than wooden plates. Although the range of marks you can achieve is less extensive [than traditional stone lithography], there is still plenty of scope for variety; and you can combine traditional and more contemporary lithography media on the same plate. I have also had some interesting outcomes working onto clay with paper lithography too.

The *Parklife* print is a multi-plate print, inspired by drawing on location in Lincoln's Inn Fields in London. The three-colour lithographic print was a challenge, from getting all the different inks to handle in the desired way on each layer to avoiding the scumming. The best results were achieved using 110gsm Awagami Washi paper: smooth, strong and not needing to be dampened.

Combining other print processes, hand tinting and monotype is a plan for future work. Going forward, print is always there, always important, always evolving, whatever the surface and materials being used. And whatever the inspiration there is always a narrative, inspired, constructed or implied.

Sue Jarman, separations for *Parklife*, polyester plate lithograph.

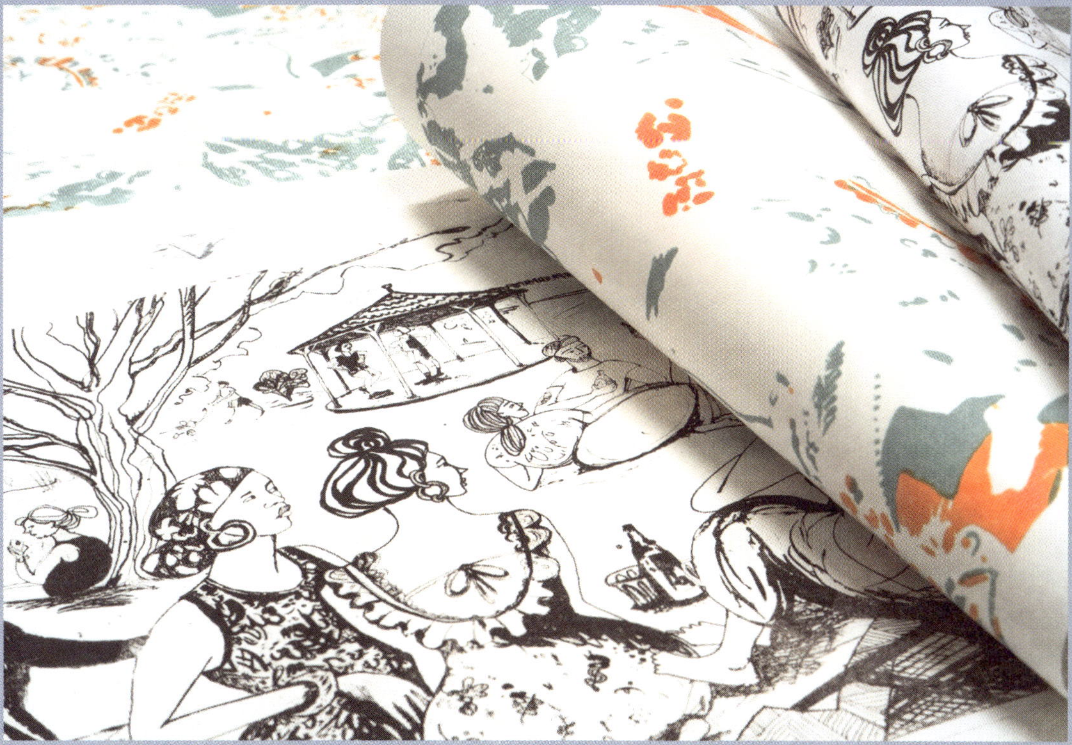

Sue Jarman, *Parklife*, three-colour polyester plate lithograph.

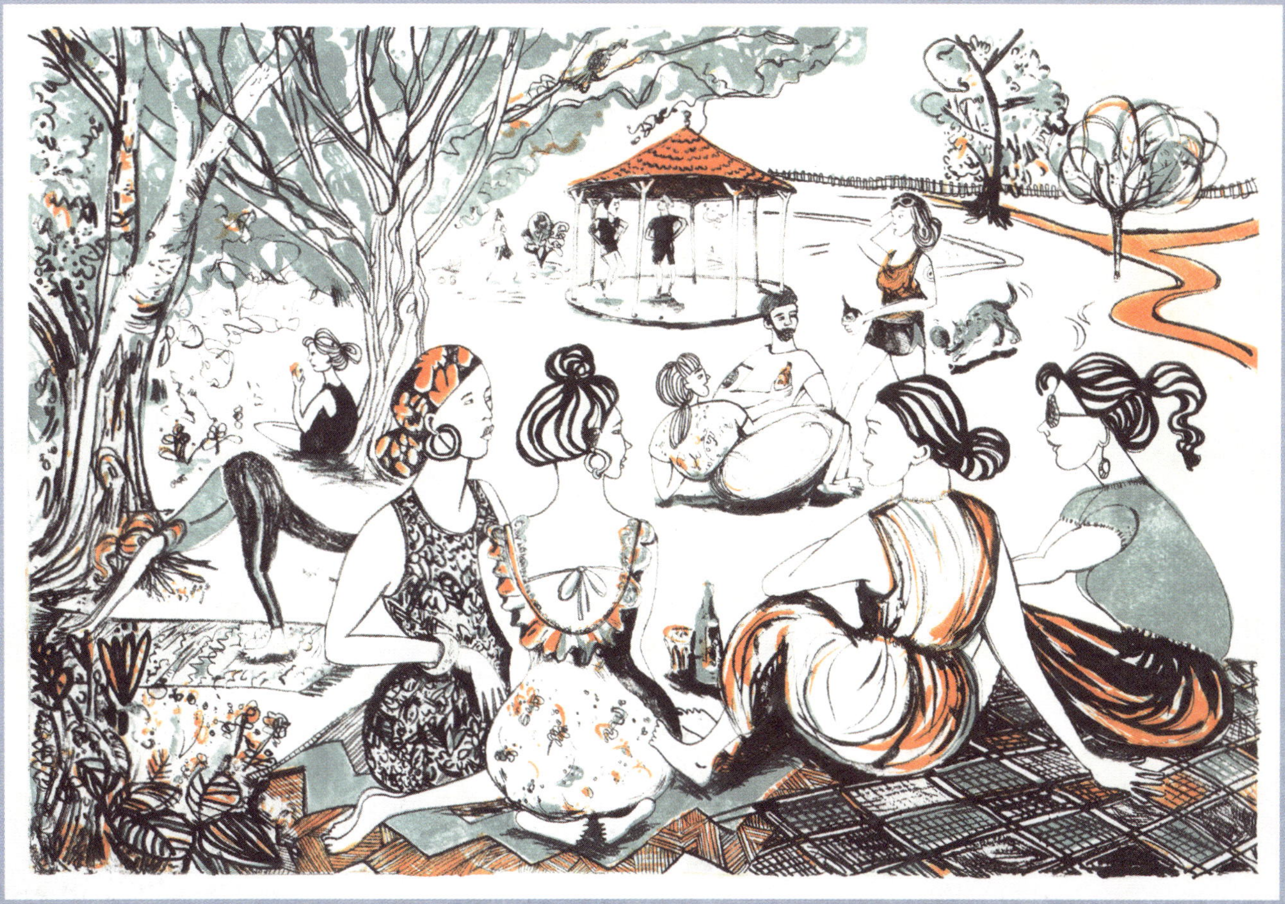

CHAPTER 9

Developing your prints

The methods of developing your prints are innumerable. Once you have got to grips with a process your first steps will be to work with multiple layers, multiple colours and then combining multiple processes. After that you are limited only by your imagination. You could apply your printmaking to innovative surfaces and explore using lithography with a glaze on ceramics as John Kindness did with his public sculpture *Big Fish*, pictured. You could consider how to translate your prints in 3D and construct objects or explore folded paper sculpture. You may want to research bookbinding techniques and collate your works in an artist's book, and pair it with text. Or you could consider extending your lithographic skills even further and work with one of the advanced techniques mentioned in this book. I always remind my students that there are no 'Printmaking Police', no one is going to check up on you and tell you what you're doing isn't allowed, or that it's 'not printmaking'. So, if you want to paint all over your prints, or print with something unconventional, or do something weird and wild, go for it!

FACING PAGE
Looking at colour samples and drawdown tests. Selecting colours from a homemade book of ink samples.

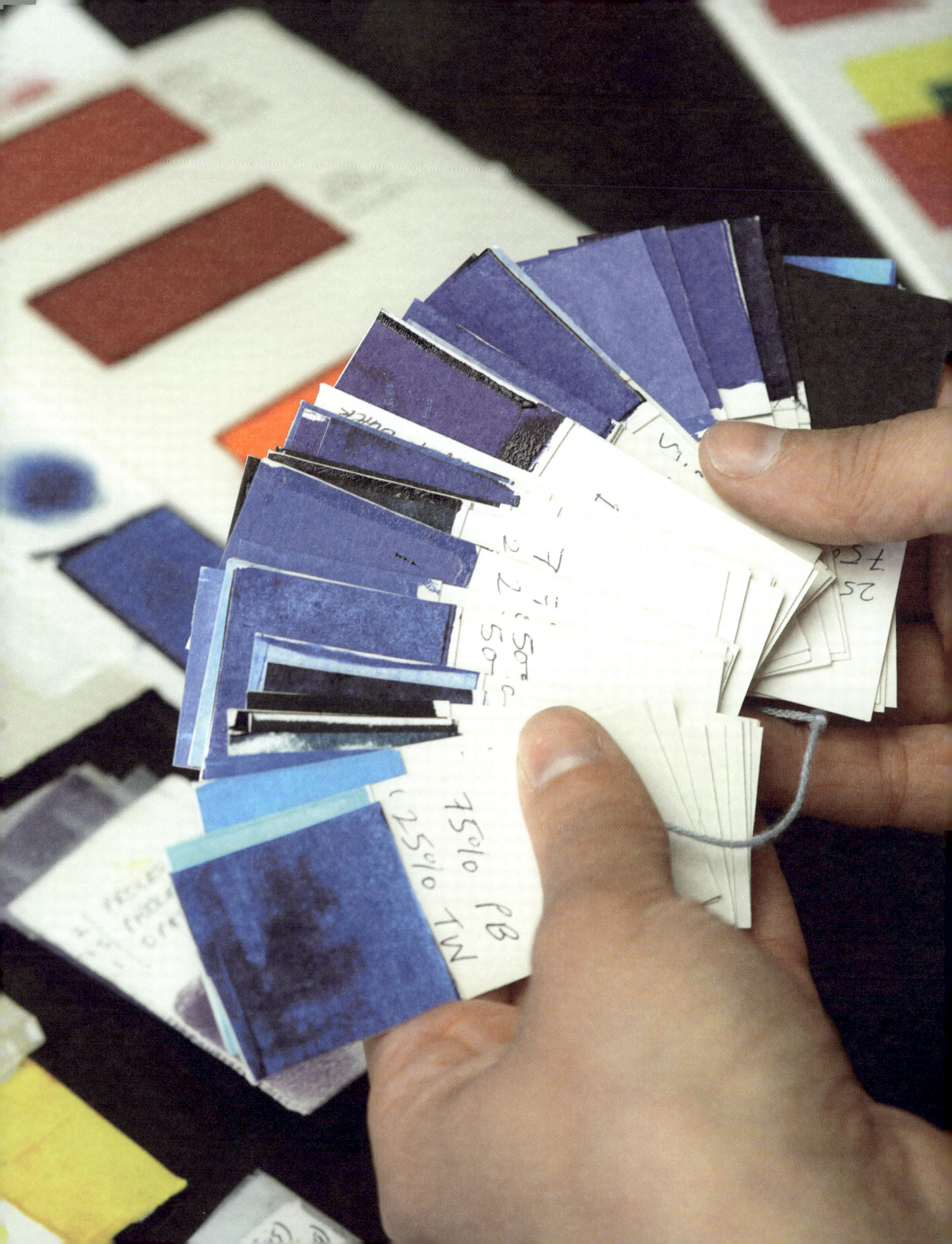
75% PB
25% TW

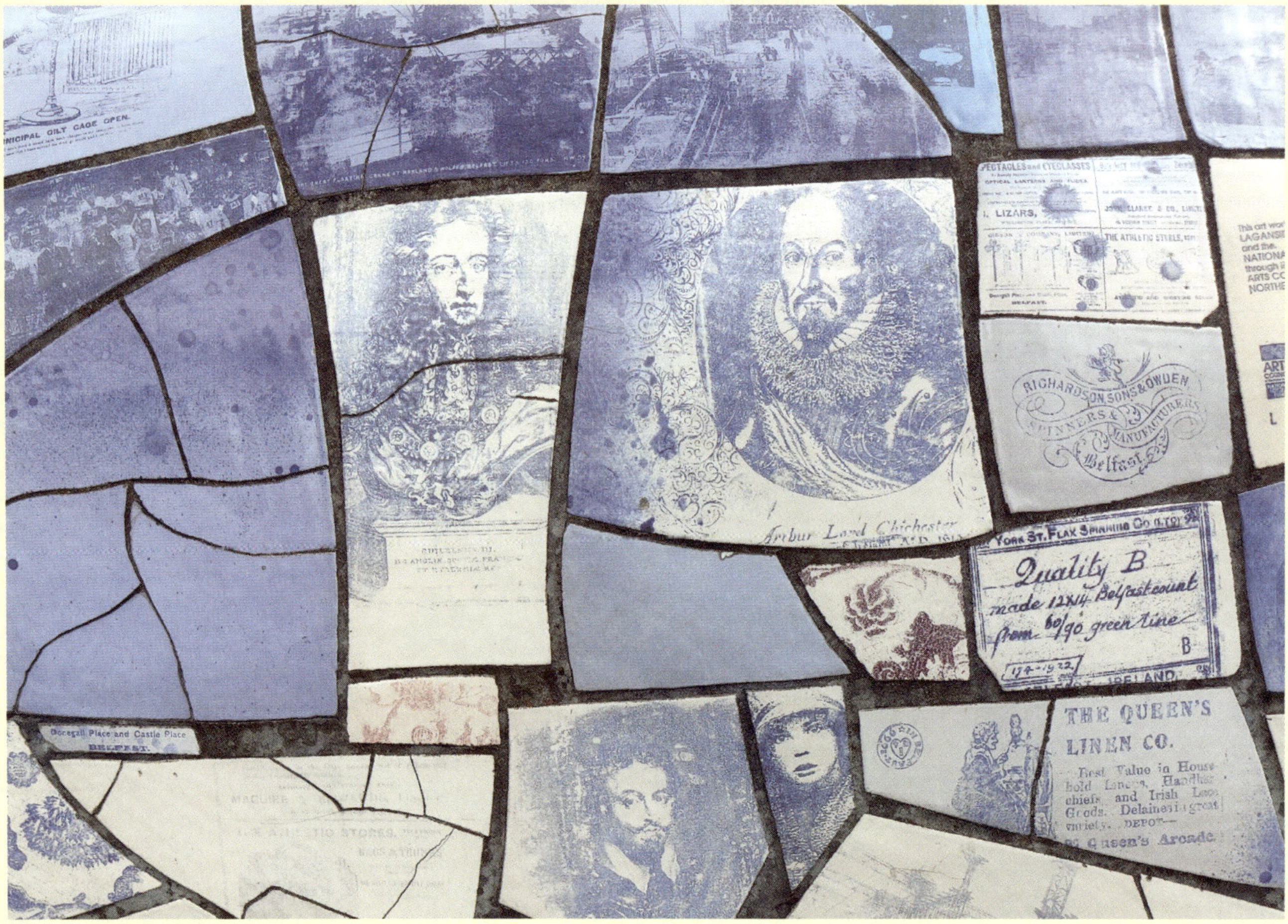

Close up of *Big Fish*. John Kindness used lithography extender mixed with ceramic stains and photocopies in a process similar to paper plate lithography, to transfer the image to ceramic. (Photo: Brandon Andrews)

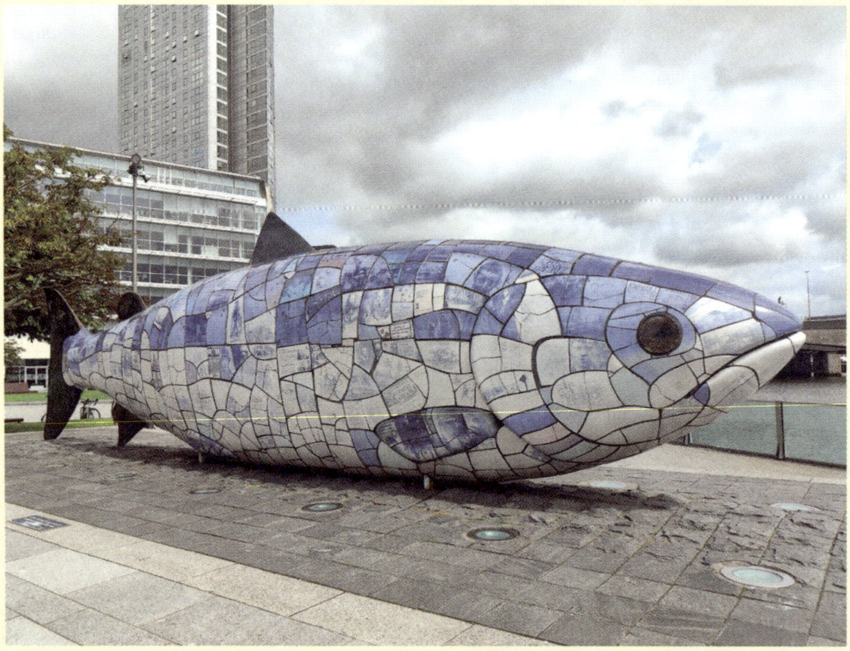

Big Fish, John Kindness, Donegall Quay, Belfast. Ceramic with underglaze lithographic prints. (Photo: Brandon Andrews)

Considering colour

This is not a chapter on colour theory; the complexity of colour theory can't be captured in a single chapter. There are many books dedicated to understanding colour and so I recommend carrying out some research to inform your own understanding, alongside your studio tests. In this section I will share with you a few practical things to consider about colour when working with lithography.

Many print publishers use a Pantone colour chart to exactly colour match the colours they need and follow the recipes the chart contains. This is a great resource if you can afford to buy the base set of inks required for this, but you may not need to reproduce all the colours possible. Also, when you're working with overlaid layers you will still need to consider what happens when colour layers overlap and produce another colour.

Printmaking inks can be expensive and so buying an extensive range of colours can be costly. I recommend considering which colours you are most likely to be working with and stick with a few base colours that you can mix to produce a broader variety. The basic set of cyan, magenta, yellow and black will set you up well as a beginner, and I recommend buying any specific colours that are harder to mix, or that you work with a lot. I always buy orange and violet as they are difficult to mix, and I am very precious about a certain tin of unlabelled blue ink that I inherited when a print shop near me shut down. You will build up a bank of inks over time and start to recognise what colours and brands you favour.

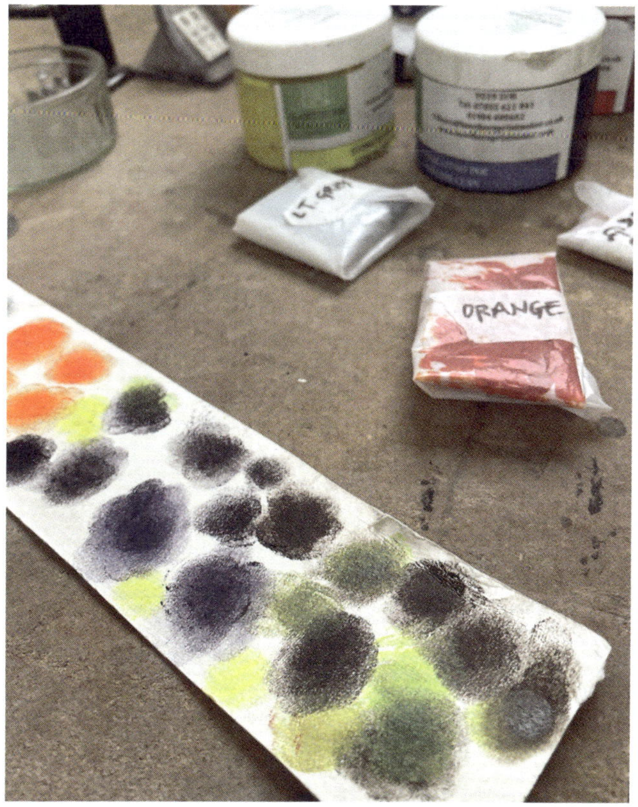

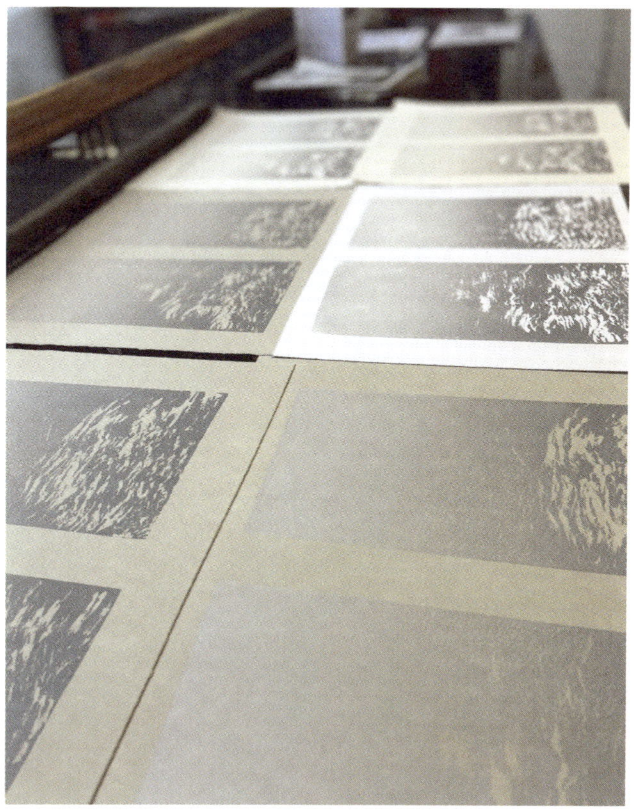

TOP
Ink packets and colour tests for a stone lithograph by Simon Burder at Oaks Editions.

BOTTOM
The same ink blend, printed onto four different colour papers, appearing to look like four individual ink blends.

Different ink brands have different levels of opacity and vibrancy, and every printmaker has their preferred brand. Two of the most important inks to have in your kit are transparent white/extender and opaque white. Lithographic inks are highly pigmented which means that when combined with varying ratios of extender or opaque white an enormous range of colour can be produced from just two inks. Transparent white/extender will disperse the pigment of the ink in a clear printing base, brightening the colour and allowing colour blending when overlaid on top of another colour. Opaque white ink will increase the opacity of an ink, allowing it to be less affected by base layers, and it will also lighten a colour.

When considering the order of colours when overlaying, the dominant colour will be on top. Simply put, when printing blue on top of yellow, the result will be a blue-green, but when printing yellow on top of blue the result will be more of a yellow-green. The order of your layers will determine how much transparency you want to mix into your overlaid ink.

There is an assumption with colour mixing with transparent inks that you will be printing onto white paper. The colour of the paper will show through when using transparent inks and affect the resulting aesthetic of the print. Printmaking papers also vary in their colours and one type of paper described as 'white' can be dramatically different from another. Similarly, opaque white inks will differ: some brands appear slightly blue while some appear slightly yellow. This will have a dramatic effect on both the colour of your mixed ink and how that colour will appear on different coloured papers. See the featured example for an illustration of this. As with all things printmaking related, you need to make tests. Before producing an edition of prints, you will need to do some colour swatches to check your ink colours and test them against the background paper.

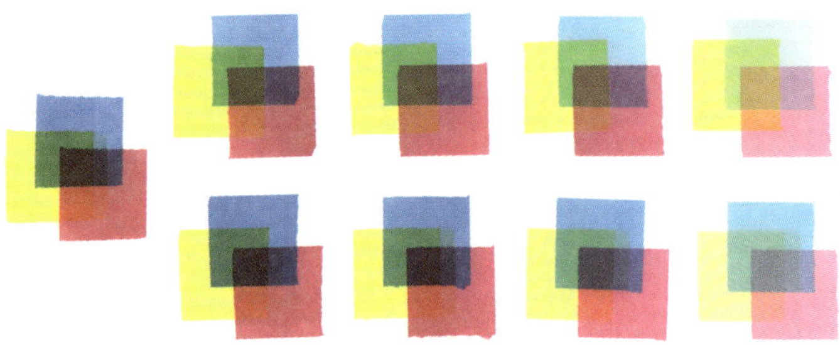

Left centre: full strength yellow on magenta on cyan. Top line: mixed with 25%, 50%, 75% & 95% opaque white. Bottom line: mixed with 25%, 50%, 75% & 95% extender.

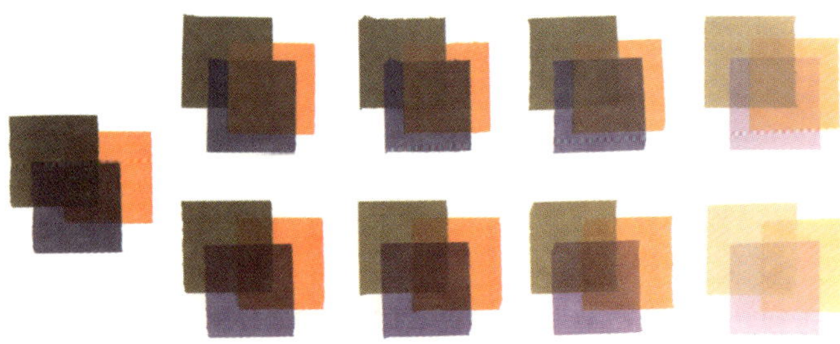

Left centre: full strength orange on purple on brown. Top line: mixed with 25%, 50%, 75% & 95% opaque white. Bottom line: mixed with 25%, 50%, 75% & 95% extender.

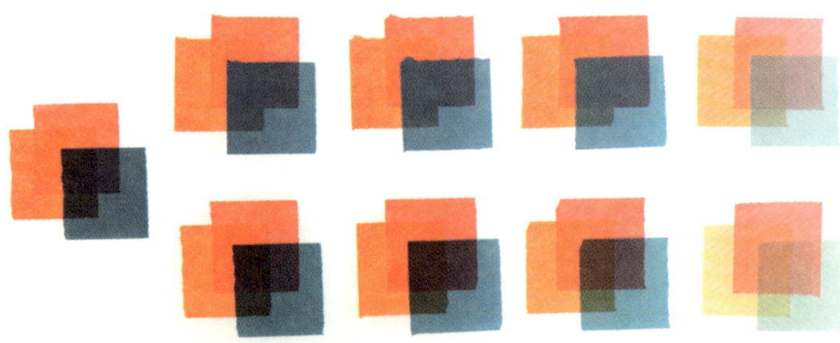

Left centre: full strength turquoise on red on orange. Top line: mixed with 25%, 50%, 75% & 95% opaque white. Bottom line: mixed with 25%, 50%, 75% & 95% extender.

Making ink swatches

I love ink swatching. I could happily spend hours (and have) mixing colours and getting to know my inks and their potential. Colour association is subjective, the same colour will mean different things to different people and can evoke a range of feelings within an image. So, spending the time to mix the correct colour, rather than just trusting a pre-mixed colour, is important.

I was taught this adage about inks: 'It is a sin to use straight from the tin' – I don't *entirely* agree with it, but it does make us consider our colour choices. When it comes to black, the colour I use most, I never use it straight from the tin and instead always choose to mix my own shade. I have a swatch chart of fourteen black ink mixes which I made years ago as a teaching tool; from a distance they are relatively difficult to discriminate between, but when viewed up close they are vastly different. When I would ask a student what kind of black they wanted to print with they would often reply in a blasé fashion that they didn't mind, but after showing them the chart they would have a clear opinion on the shade of black they wanted.

When producing a colour swatch, it is useful to create your 'draw down' of ink along the edge of your paper so you can hold it up against a second swatch to compare. An ink draw down swatch will give you an idea of the colour of ink in solid tones, but it is not an accurate representation without a tap swatch. The tap swatch is important for seeing the lighter diffusions of the ink that will print in your light tonal areas.

Consider the colour of the paper you are swatching on and how it will affect the ink colours. Keep note of your ink recipes, mixing as accurately as you can. Keep your swatches for reference for future prints, if you like a colour, or if you're making a series of prints, you may need to recreate it.

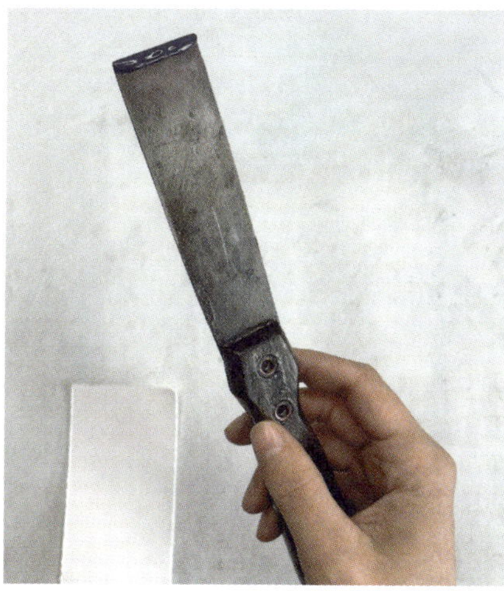

1. Collect a bead of ink along the edge of your push knife.

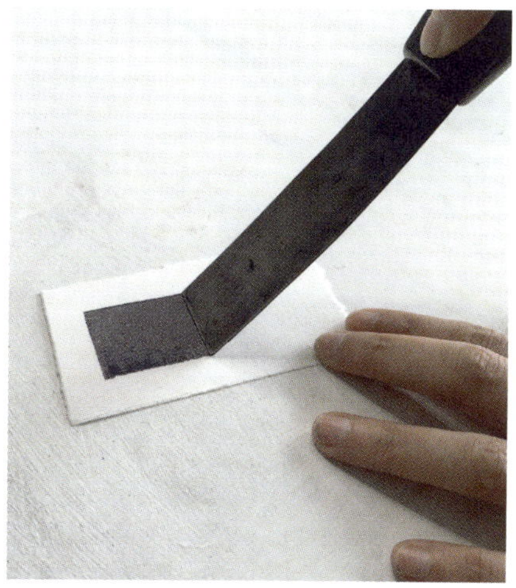

2. With firm pressure, drag the ink bead down the piece of paper.

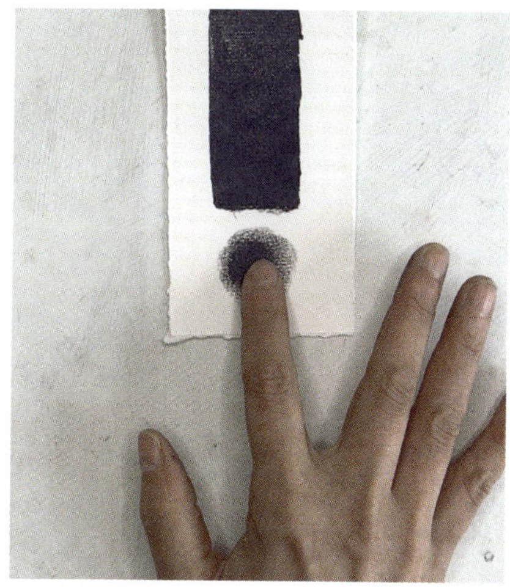

3. Tap a small amount of ink in a circle, spreading the ink thinly.

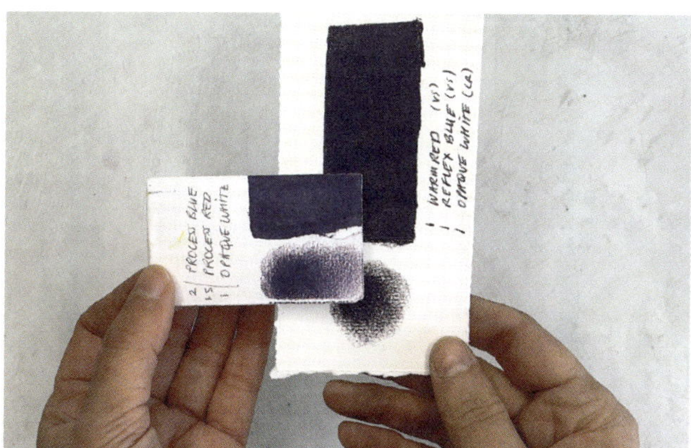

4. Keep a note of your ink recipes for future colour swatch comparisons.

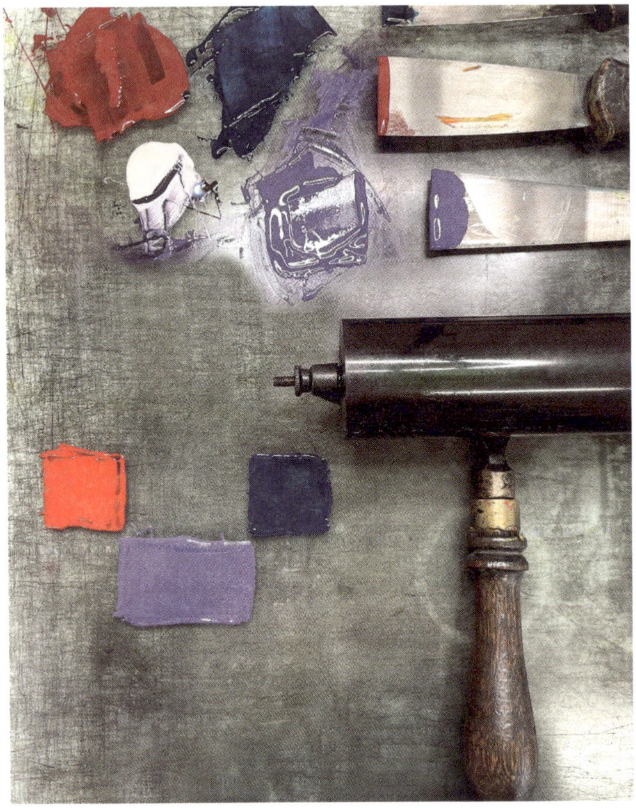

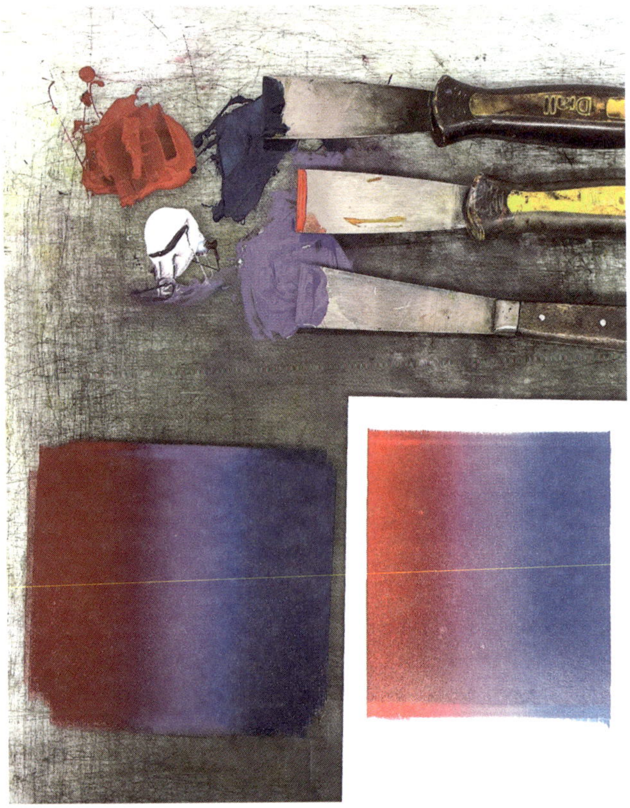

Ink blends

Using ink blends is a useful way of combining multiple colours in one layer using one roller. An ink blend is used to give a gradual transition of colours along the roller. To hold two different colours on one roller and ink two separate areas of the same plate is known as a 'split fountain'.

For colour blends using a wide roller, where the blend is required to be subtle and gradual, pre-mix ratios of the colours you're using and distribute them over the inking slab. For a narrow area of blend, move the roller side to side minimally, but for wider blended areas, move the roller further side to side.

There are a few things to consider when planning an ink blend. The viscosities of the different colour inks will need to be the same to allow for ease of mixing, so modify the inks if needed. Similarly, keep the same level of ink along the entire roller. If there is a heavier build-up of ink in one section it will transfer unevenly.

Consider the size of the blend area when spreading out the ink, in relation to where the colours are needed to be aligned to on the plate. The ink blend being transferred is on the roller, not on the ink slab, so keep your desired blend within the size of your roller and test on scrap paper if necessary. It is easy to widen the blend too far when rolling out the ink on the ink slab. You can draw a guide to put underneath your ink slab (if you can see through it) to visually remind you where the colours need to be.

Lastly, you will be used to charging your roller by rolling it top to bottom and then left to right to fully coat the roller. Only roll in one direction with a blend roll or you will ruin the blend! I can admit that I have ruined a blend roll like this on many occasions, simply by forgetting and rolling in both directions out of habit. When this happens, you will have to clean the ink off your roller and slab and roll out fresh ink into your blend.

RIGHT TOP
Selected ink colours, carefully spread out on an inking slab ready to be blended.

RIGHT
Resulting ink blend on the slab and the roller, with test roll on scrap paper.

Hand tinting your prints

Hand tinting/colouring is a way to make subtle changes to your prints without needing to apply another printed layer. Hand tinting adds a special element to a print which shows the trace of personal human interaction. It can be used as a way to make each print in an edition individual, or to test out ideas on unfinished prints. Your prints which seem to be *unsuccessful* are great prints to test out hand tinting on, especially prints which are pale. The prints which have printed too lightly have the most untouched space between the ink marks and so will hold the watercolours in these spaces.

As the ink we print with in lithography is oil-based it means it won't be damaged by painting water-based colours over it. You can use watercolour paint, drawing ink, or dilute gouache for hand tinting. Similarly, you can soak and stretch the prints beforehand without worrying that the prints will be damaged by the water. The water-based colour will sit in the gaps between the ink but not on top of the ink as the oil-based ink will reject the water-based paint. Once again, we are exploiting the fact that water and oil repel each other! Undiluted gouache or acrylic paint will have a more prominent impact on the prints as these paints have more opacity and can sit on top of the oil-based ink.

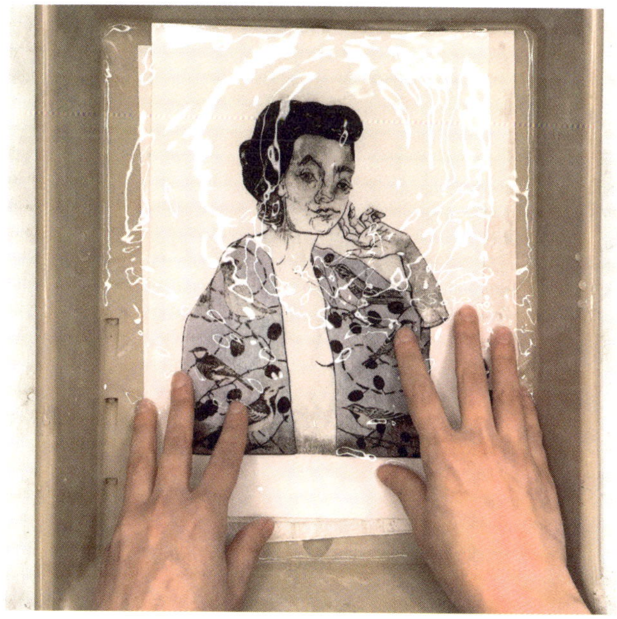

1. Soak prints for 10 minutes in a bath or tray of cold water. When removed, allow them to sit for a few minutes.

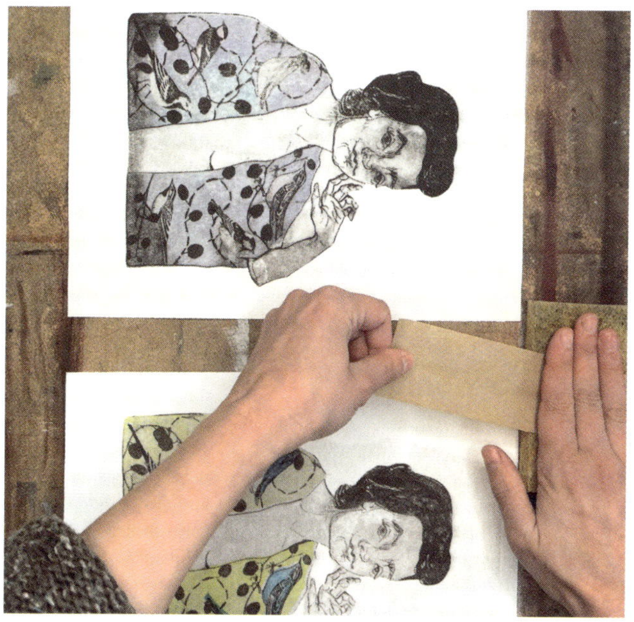

2. Blot off excess surface water with a clean sponge and then attach to a prepared board using strips of dampened gum tape.

Hand tinting *(continued)*

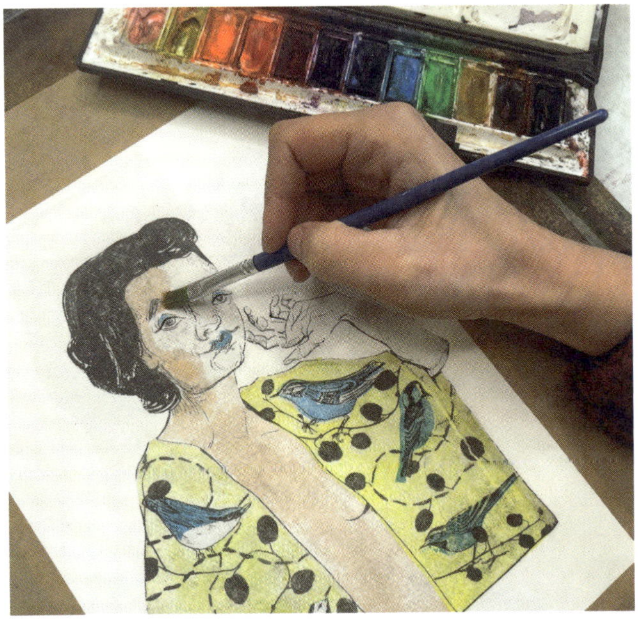

3. Once prints are completely dry and stretched flat, use inks or watercolours to add colourful details.

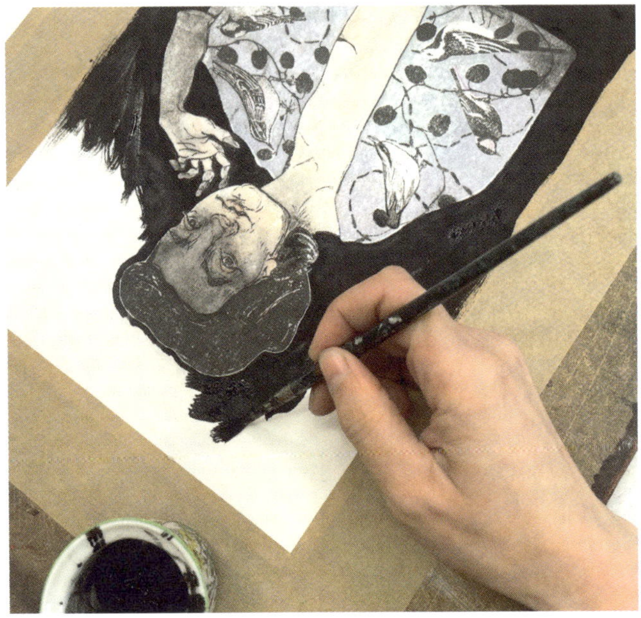

4. Add more drastic colour changes using gouache or acrylic paints which have more opacity.

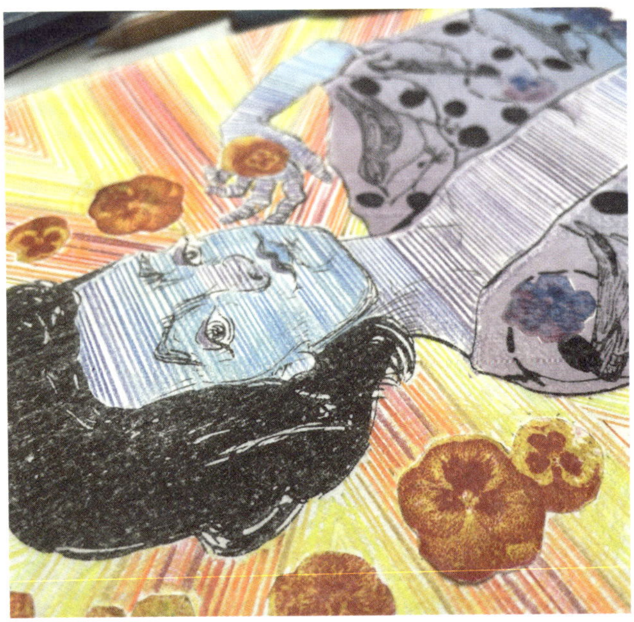

5. Coloured pencils and other dry media can be used on dry prints without the need for stretching.

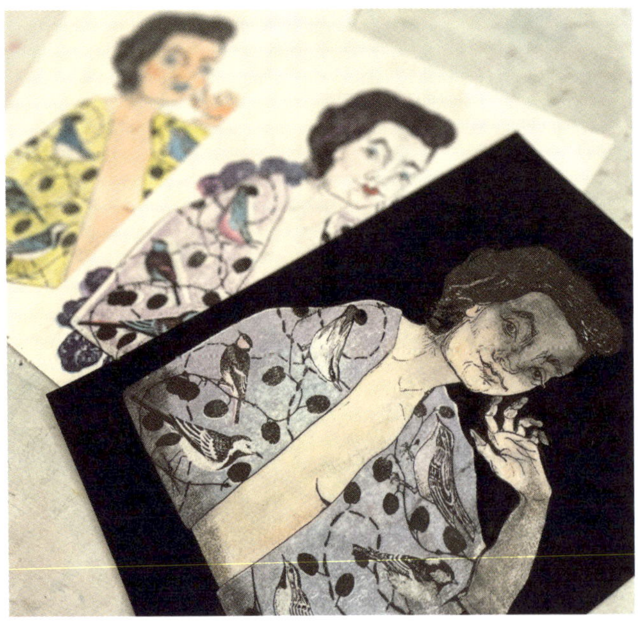

6. Hand colouring can be used to make each print in an edition unique, or to test out ideas for future work.

Incorporating chine collé

Chine collé is a method used to attach thin, lightweight papers to stronger heavyweight paper, *during* the printing process. The term 'chine collé' translates from French as '*China glued*' and it refers to the thin Chinese papers which were originally used when the process was first developed. The process is used to back prints made on thin lightweight paper to strengthen them, especially for ease with display, or to add interesting details and surfaces to a print, underneath the layer of ink.

You can use a variety of glues with chine collé, for example, glue stick, rice paste glue, wheat paste glue or dilute PVA. The glues need to be tacky enough to attach the paper to the print but not so tacky that it won't let go of the paper. The glue also needs to be viscous enough that it will not saturate the paper and bleed through to the front of the print.

There are two methods for applying chine collé: one uses wet paste during printing, and one uses dry pre-pasted paper which requires preparation before printing. Cutting up and aligning very small pieces of wet chine collé paper onto a print is very fiddly. The chine collé paper pieces are easier to handle when they are dry, so the pre-pasted method is useful for fiddly pieces. However, the pre-pasted method can only be used with glues like rice paste glue and wheat paste glue, where the tackiness can be reignited with a little dampening.

MAKING WHEAT PASTE GLUE

It's easy to make your own wheat paste glue on the hob. In a saucepan, start by adding 1 tbsp of cold water to 1 tbsp of plain flour and whisk to a smooth paste. Then add 3 tbsp of cold water and mix so the paste is smooth. Now, start to heat the saucepan and continually whisk until the paste begins to boil and thicken, then add 1 tsp of salt. When the paste reaches a custard-like consistency, remove it from the heat and allow it to cool completely. It will keep for up to 4 weeks in an airtight container in the fridge.

METHOD 1

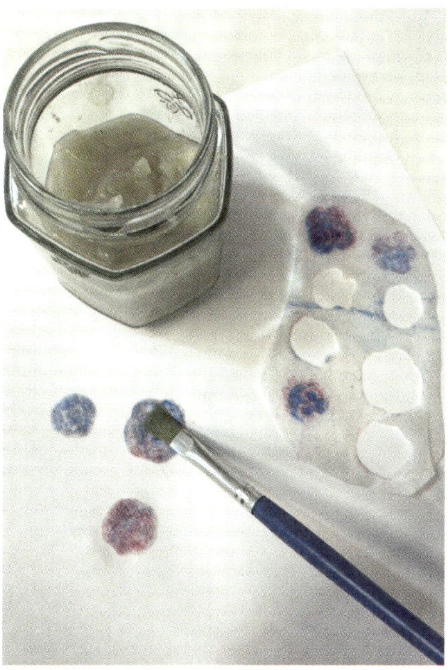

1. Apply paste to the back of the papers and allow it to dry for a minute, but remain tacky.

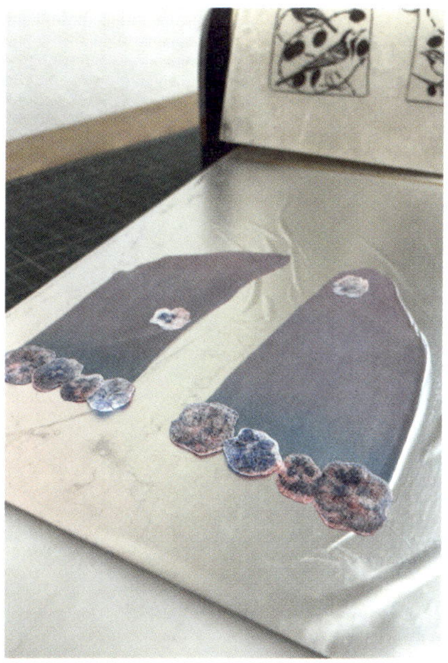

2. Place chine collé pieces face down onto a printing plate, with glue side facing upwards.

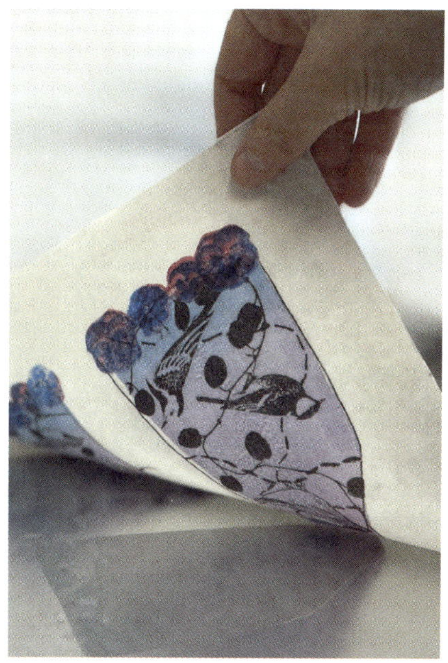

3. The chine collé papers will transfer to the print under the pressure of the press, during the printing process.

METHOD 2

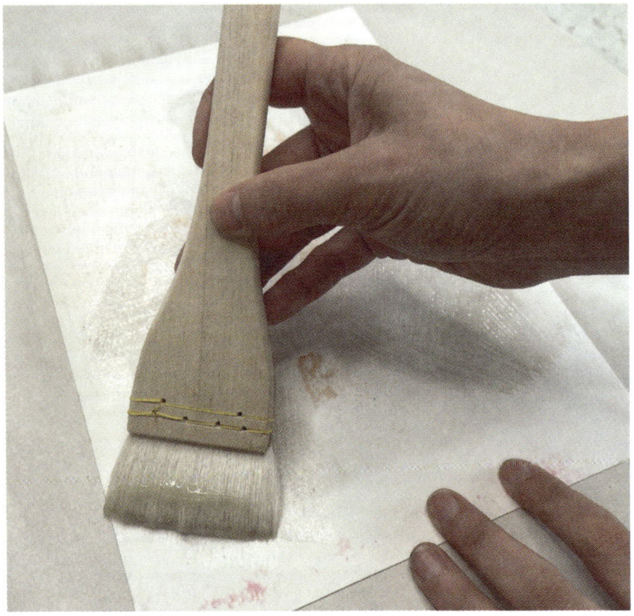

1. To prepare coated chine collé papers, paint on two coats of paste glue to the back of prints, allowing them to dry between coats.

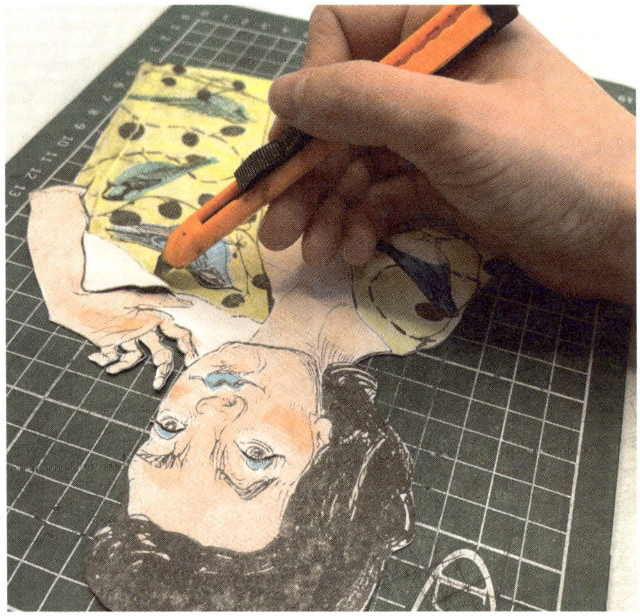

2. Once dried, use a scalpel to cut around the part of the paper you want to transfer, retaining the fiddly details.

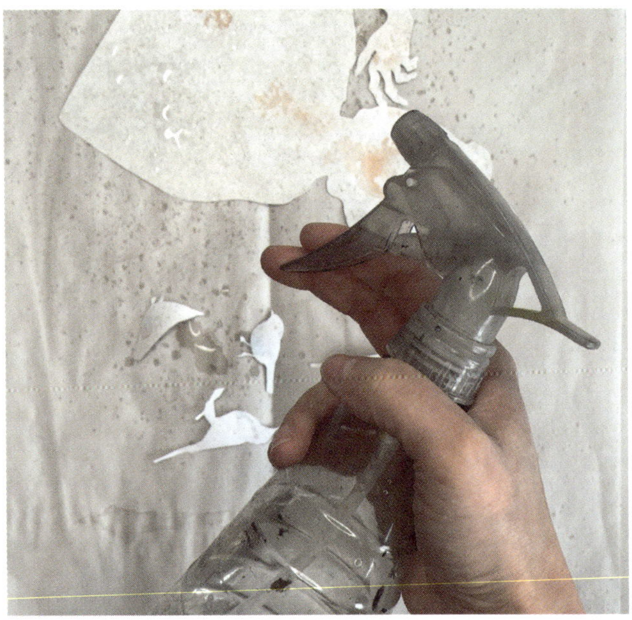

3. Before printing, the papers will need to be misted with a little water to re-ignite the tackiness.

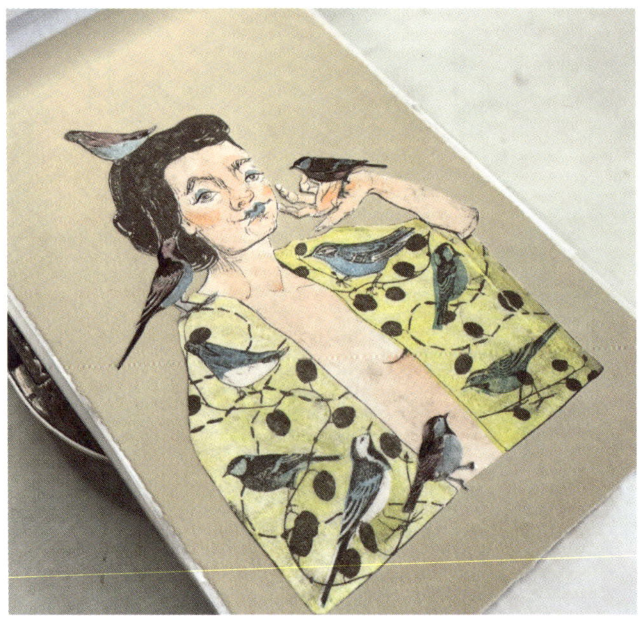

4. This paper lithograph with hand colouring has been cut away from its original background and attached to a sandy coloured backing paper.

Backing lightweight papers

Attaching a print on thin, lightweight or translucent paper to a heavyweight paper makes the print easier to handle and display. It can be easily done by hand or with a press with small prints, but registering larger works can require the help of multiple hands.

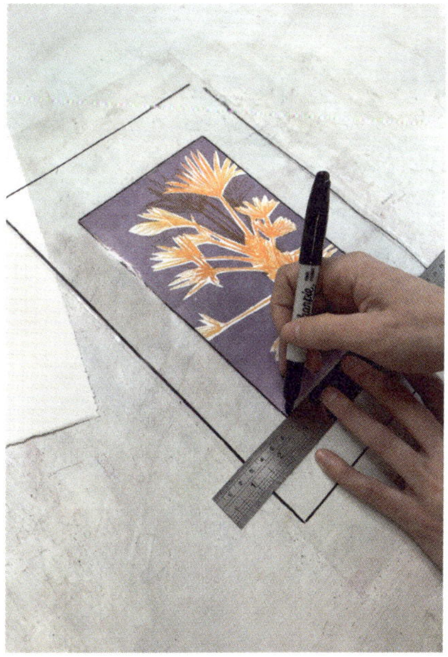

1. Place a piece of thin clean plastic on top of your print and draw around the print and backing paper to make a registration guide.

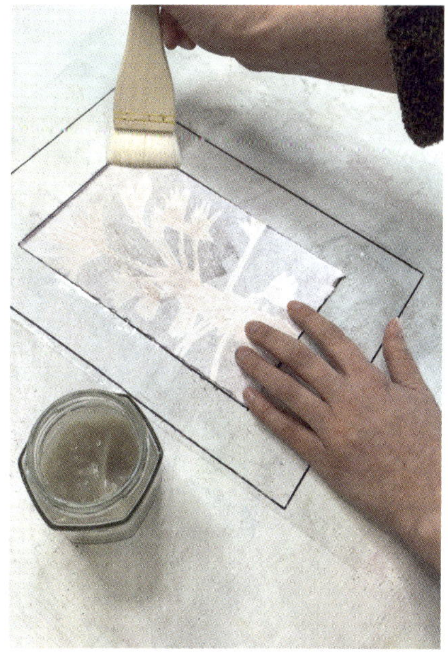

2. Register the print in position on top of the guide and apply wheat paste glue to the back of the print, painting from the middle outwards so the paper doesn't wrinkle.

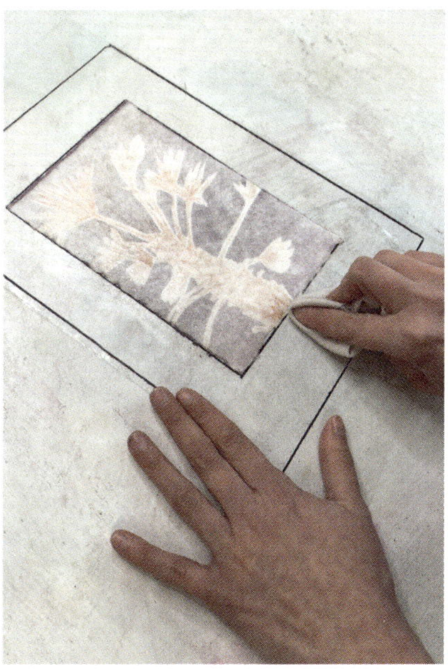

3. Wipe off the excess wheat paste glue from the edges with a clean cloth. Carefully flip over the plastic; the print should stay in place, attached to the plastic.

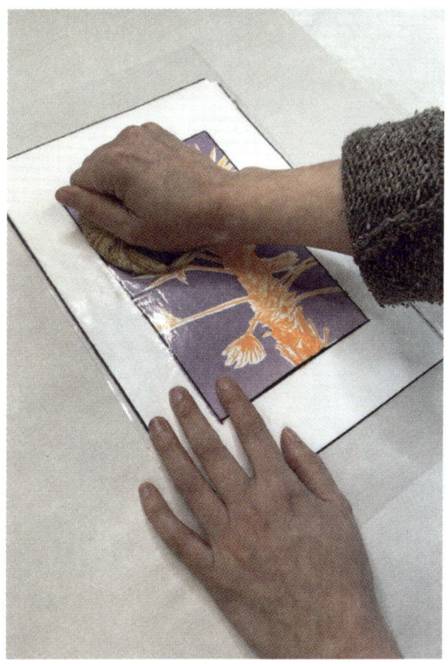

4. Align the registration guide, with attached print, to the backing paper and firmly burnish by hand.

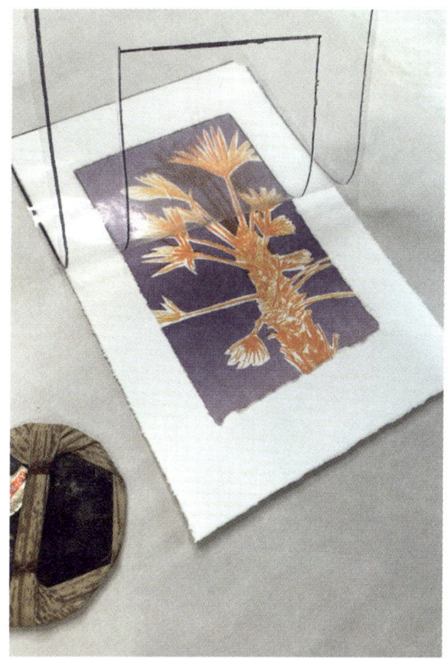

5. Carefully peel back the plastic sheet, leaving the print attached to the backing paper in perfect registration.

CHAPTER 10

Advanced processes

Alternative lithographic processes developed out of a need for ease of accessibility, affordable materials, environmental considerations, and an exploratory mindset which isn't centred around creating large-scale editions. Despite their countless positives there are limitations to the alternative processes, and creating editions is a valuable economic part of being a working artist.

Advanced processes such as stone lithography, metal plate lithography and photoplate lithography offer reliable results and large-scale faithful editions (large scale in terms of matrix size *and* edition size). They also offer opportunities for developing your image making in ways that aren't possible with alternative lithographic processes.

These advanced processes do require specialist equipment and access to expertise that you can only find at a printmaking workshop or college/university. Joining a printmaking workshop is a fantastic way to expose yourself to new approaches to print by working alongside other artists in a supportive community of printmakers. When you join a printmaking workshop you have access to specialist equipment, technical support, a wealth of expertise from other printmakers and technical staff, and importantly, you become part of a community. These printmaking communities are a vital part of keeping many printmaking processes alive and continuing the dissemination of arts education.

FACING PAGE
A lithography photoplate being inked on an offset press, by a BA Fine Art Printmaking student at Brighton University.

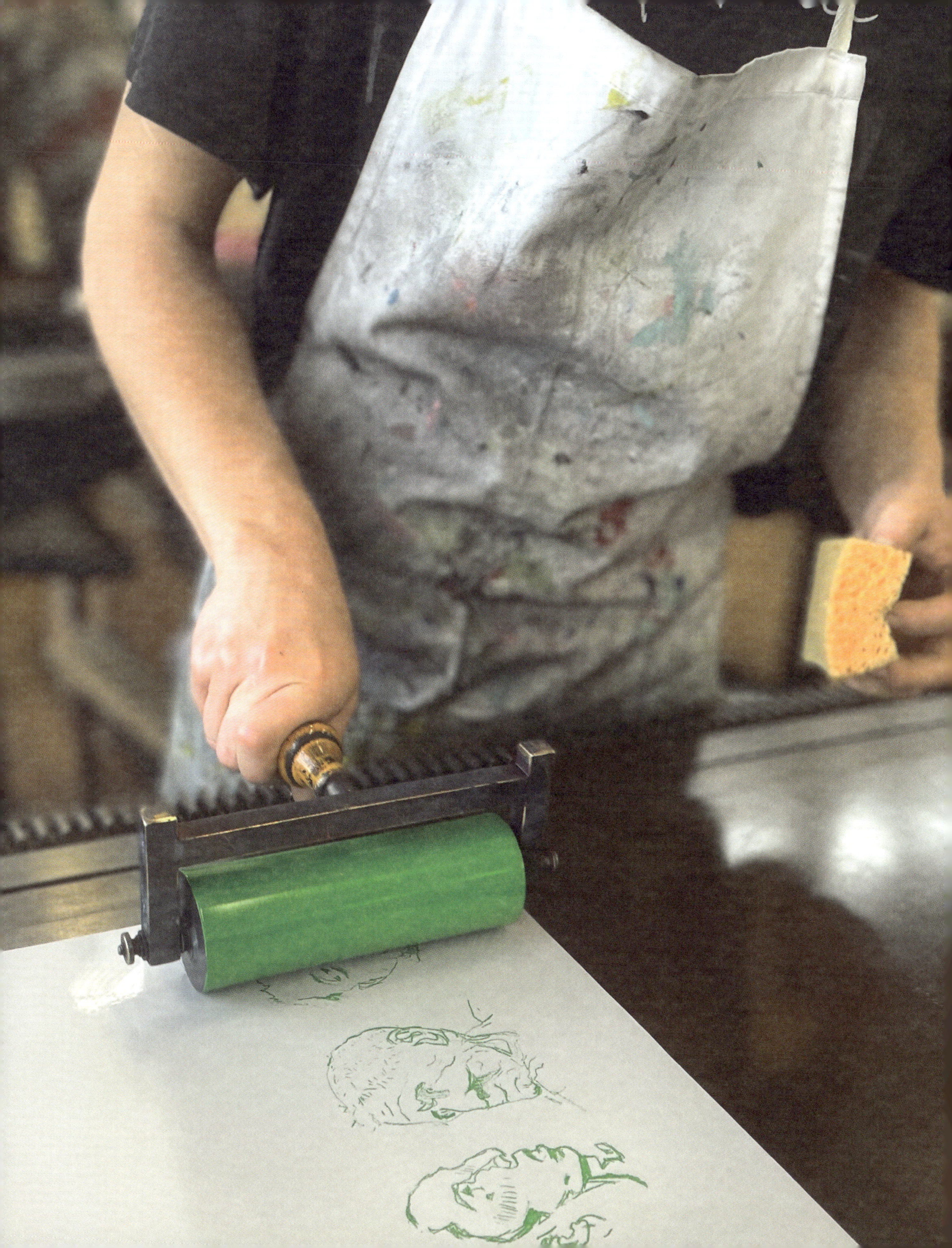

Photoplate lithography

The image making with photoplate lithography differs from traditional lithography as grease is not the important factor. The image is created as a positive film which is exposed to the light-sensitive plate. The darkest tones are created where the light has been blocked with drawing materials of highest level of opacity, rather than highest levels of greasiness. A variety of drawing materials can be used, which allows for a broad range of innovative marks that can't be achieved with traditional lithography. The use of photographic positives is also a key feature, wherein a photographic image is printed straight onto film to be exposed onto the plate. There is also space for creativity and experimentation with the effects of the exposure on the plate.

Working on a positive film, rather than directly onto the matrix, creates a disconnection between artist and matrix. I adore the haptic nature of drawing on stone and plate, and the collaboration with the matrix itself. It's this tactile quality of the lithographic process that draws me to it, and so the additional step of exposing an image to a plate feels like a barrier between myself and the plate, putting the artwork at a distance. This is a personal preference that I hold, and which isn't a problem for many artists.

Compared to working on stone, not having to worry about complicated etching for different materials is a huge bonus. The ease, speed, affordability and reliability of the photoplate process is fantastic; another bonus is that the photoplates are made from aluminium, so they can be recycled once the lithographic coating is removed.

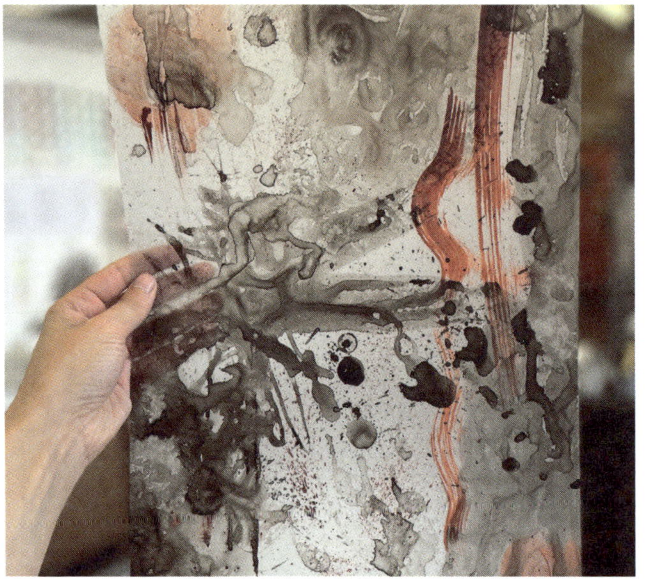

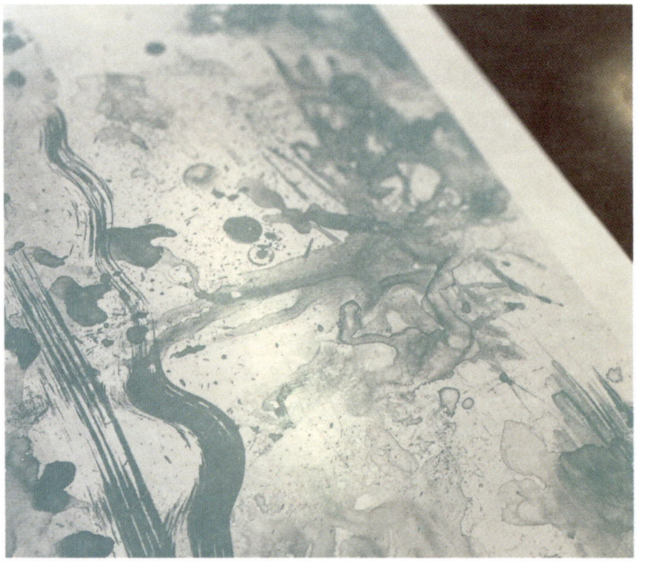

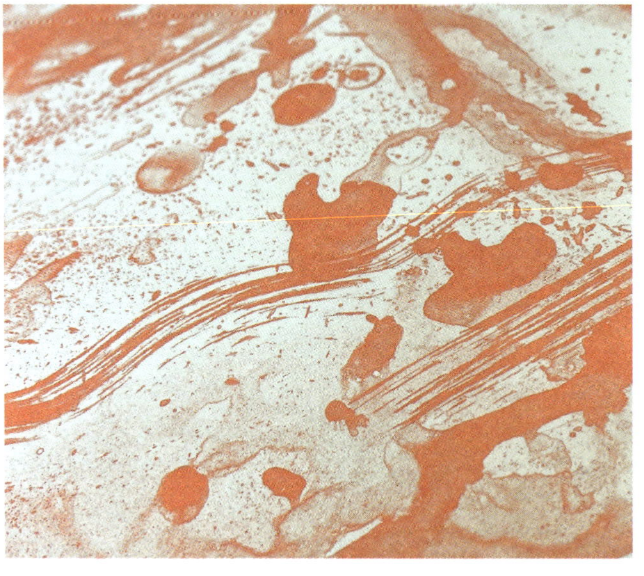

TOP
A photoplate positive drawn on marks resist, showing a variety of different marks and delicate range of tones.

MIDDLE
The exposed photoplate. Note the solid areas and darkest tones where red ink has been used as the drawing material.

BOTTOM
The resulting print has retained near-perfect detail, capturing the finest marks and depth of tonality.

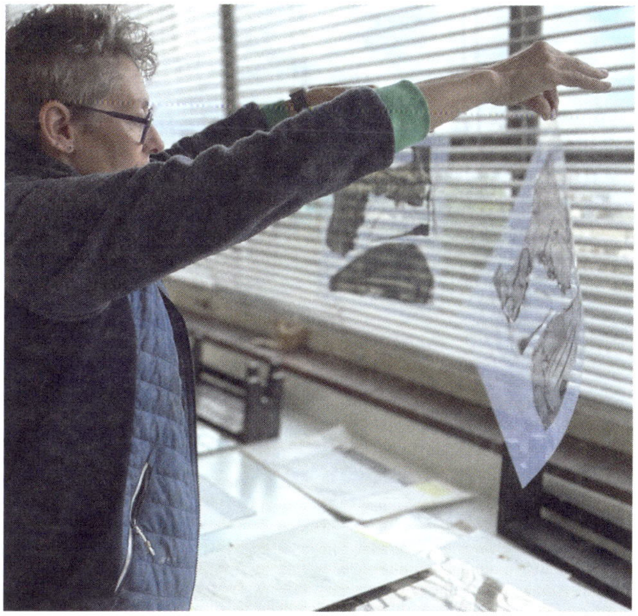

1. Heike Roesel, lithography technical demonstrator at Brighton University, checking the opacity of the positives against the light in the workshop.

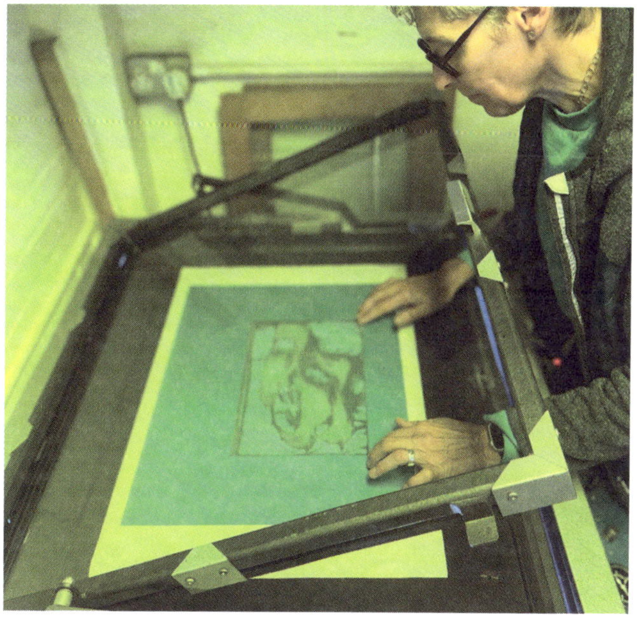

2. The exposure unit at Brighton University. Lithography photoplates arrive pre-coated in an oleophilic light-sensitive emulsion.

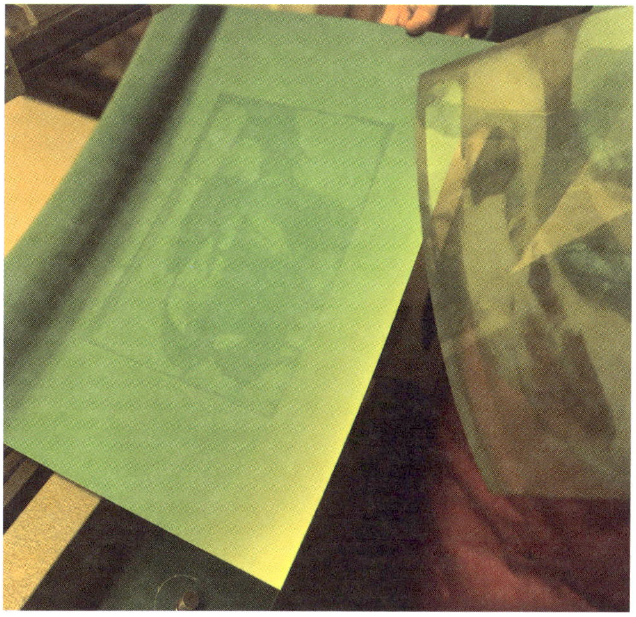

3. After exposure, the non-image area of the plate, which was unprotected by the positive, has lightened where the UV light has made contact with it.

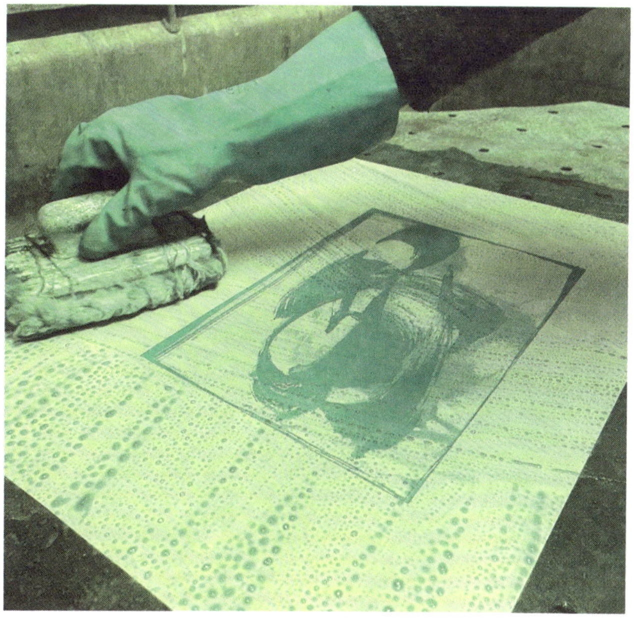

4. Applying a developer to the plate removes the photosensitive coating that has been affected by the UV light.

Photoplate lithography *(continued)*

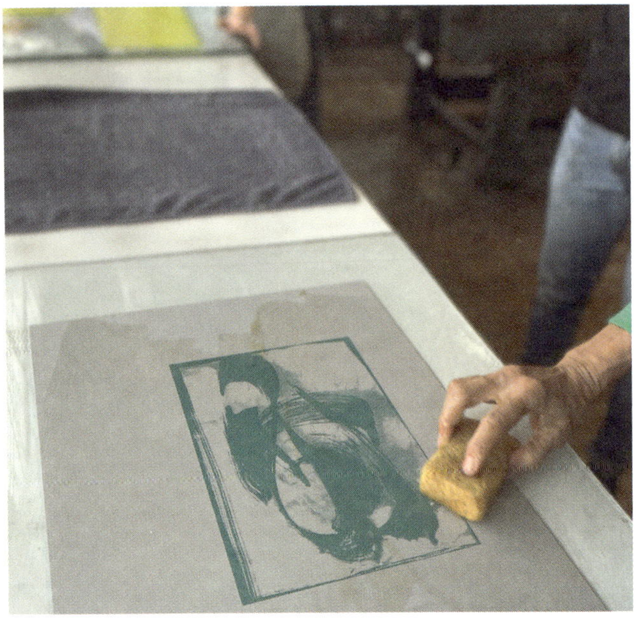

5. A layer of synthetic gum arabic is applied to the plate to protect and strengthen the water receptivity of the plate.

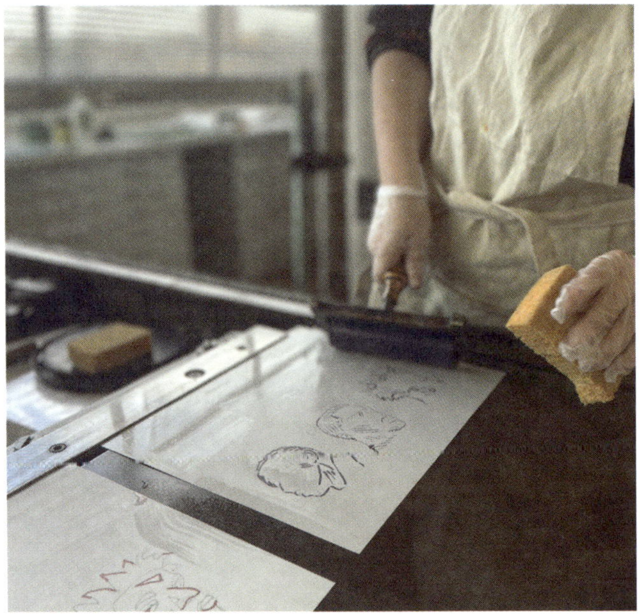

6. Plates are inked in registered position on the press using a specialist fount solution to dampen the plates.

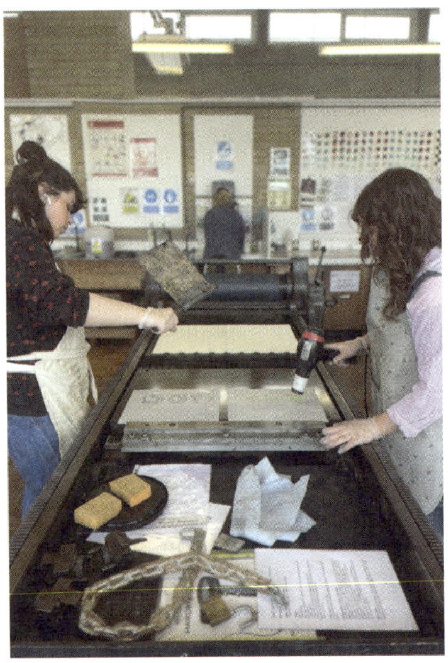

7. Student printmakers at Brighton University dry their plates with the traditional leather fan, and hairdryers.

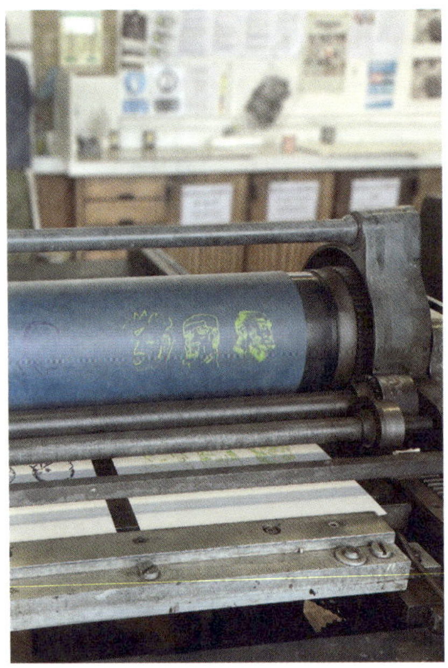

8. On an offset press, the image is collected from the plate and transferred reflected onto the cylindrical rubber blanket.

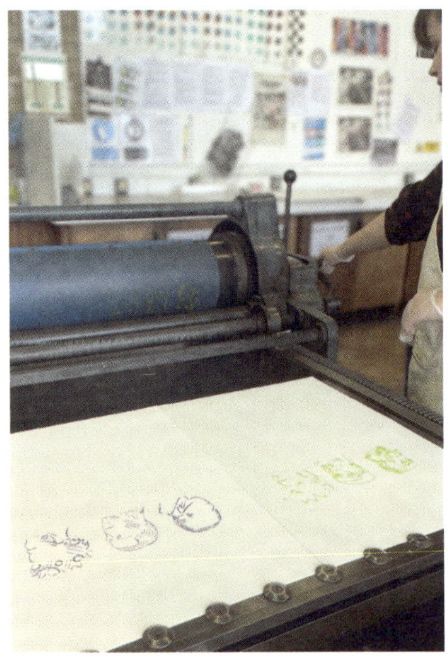

9. The blanket then deposits the ink onto the printing paper the correct way around.

Metal plate lithography

The approach to working on zinc and aluminium plates is similar to that of working on stone. The plates are prepared with a graining process which leaves the metal with a velvet surface of pores to hold the drawing material. The same drawing materials are used on metal plates as stones and there is a freedom in their transportability which doesn't inhibit the drawing process like it can with stone. The plates are etched in the same way, but using different chemicals. Aluminium tends to be more water-loving, which can cause problems with image loss, and they are prone to problems with oxidising. Zinc on the other hand is notoriously prone to scumming as it is more grease-loving. Metal plates have a limited life span when compared to stone, but storing twenty plates is much easier than storing twenty stones. Another huge bonus for using both metal plates and photoplates is that they can be printed on an etching press, so specialist lithographic presses are not needed.

BELOW
Lee Turner, *Checks 16-413*, 16 ⅝ x 16 ⅝in, 2016. Original lithograph hand printed in 72 colours from 6 photo-litho plates.

TOP
Aluminium lithography plate and proof on the press at Hole Editions, Lee Turner's print shop.

BOTTOM
Lee Turner's hand-drawn aluminium lithograph plate for *nine small boys' names*.

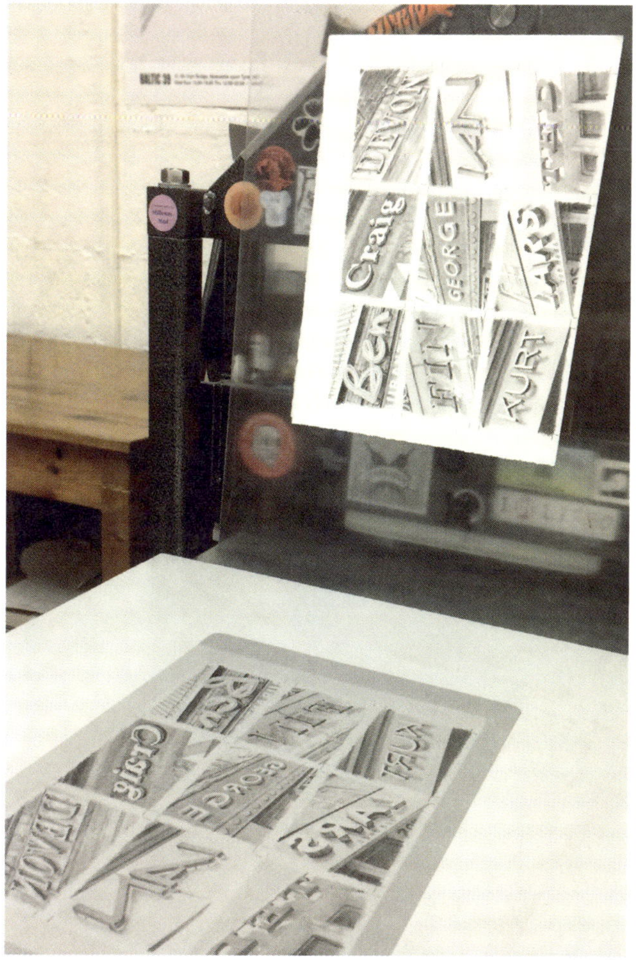

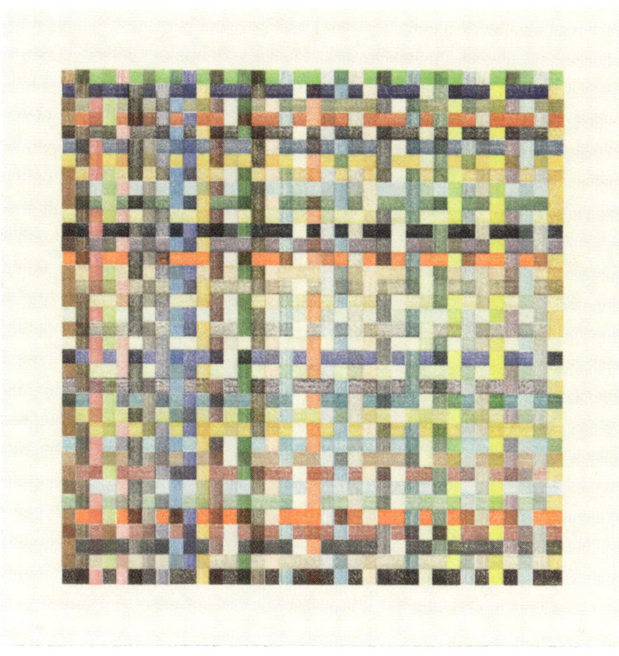

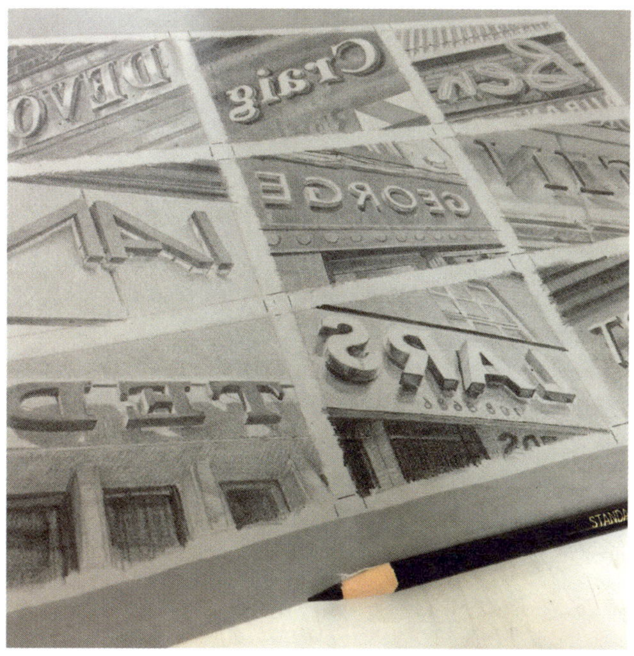

Lee Turner (UK)

holeeditions.co.uk

Lee Turner is an artist and master printer. He owns Hole Editions, a fine art collaborative print workshop in Newcastle upon Tyne, specialising in hand lithography.

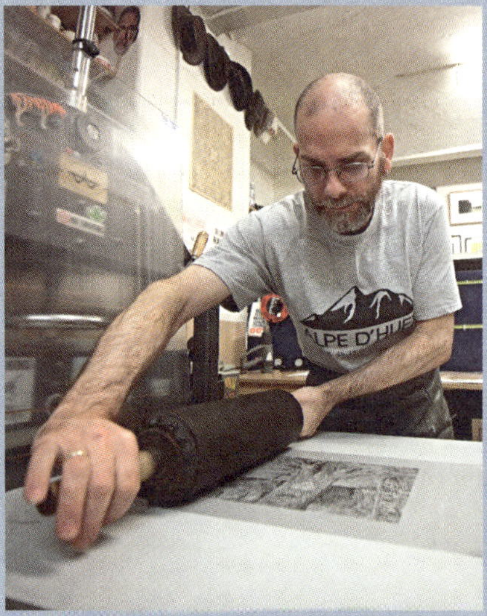

(Photograph by David Lawson)

Wow! I've been pulling lithographs for thirty years. It was on the Foundation Course at Doncaster College that Graham Firth invited a few of us down into the printmaking workshops to teach us the bones of lithography. There was a basic step-by-step guide. Stones were grained with sand. Registration with holes drilled in the stones and drawing pins through the paper. The electric press gobbled up the press bed as we rode the pressure lever over the wedged stones. Results were crude but I was fascinated.

In 2002 I headed over to Albuquerque to take up a place on the Printer Training Program at Tamarind Institute to learn from the masters, the people who wrote the book on litho. I was a sponge, soaking up all the knowledge that they could give. They really do give you a litho love buzz. The intensity of the course helps create those muscle memories and hopefully the perfect practice, making perfect. I travelled the long way home in 2004 via New Zealand to collaborate on a few projects and then to South Africa to do some edition printing. This helped solidify the idea to me of setting up my own collaborative litho workshop.

Hole Editions began in the spring of 2005. Predominantly we use stones, photo plates and ball grained aluminium plates for the production of contract projects or ones which we publish.

In the quiet times, or when I get the itch, I'll make my own work. Often this is to hone my skills or reacquaint myself with a process. The learning never stops. The work that I make varies, from abstract works to signage or condiments, amongst other things. There is nothing deep and meaningful about the work that I make. I like making lithographs. It is as simple as that. I use the lithographic process which is most fitting or one I want to experiment with.

For example, *Checks 16-413* began as a drawing on tracing paper, as stripes, in thirty-six coloured pencils. This was exposed onto multiple photo plates and split with masks. Interestingly, each colour holds the UV light back differently. These plates and others were further modified by exposing other masks to be able to print checks, in seventy-two colours. The fun part was inking up. It was a real challenge to manage the rollouts of twelve colours at a time.

FACING PAGE
Lee Turner, *JGBRR*, 13 5⁄16 x 11 3⁄16in, 2021. Four-colour original lithograph hand printed from three photo-litho plates and one keystone.

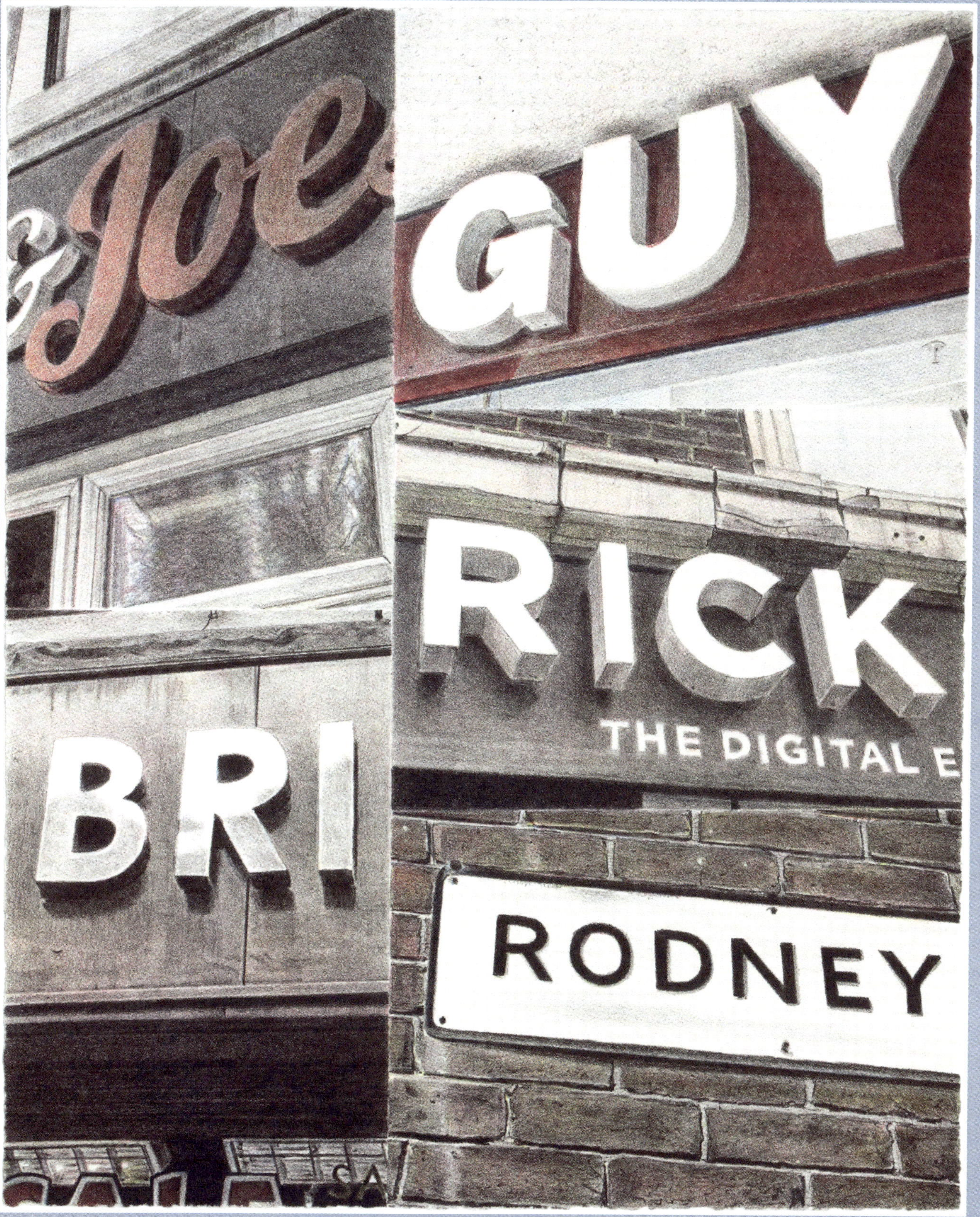
Joe
GUY
RICK
THE DIGITAL E
BRI
RODNEY

CHAPTER 11

Cleaning up

Cleaning up your workspace doesn't need to be a headache, and it doesn't need to create more mess. It's good practice to keep your inking area contained, so that when you're cleaning up, you don't have to chase ink around the studio. Cleaning up as soon as you have finished is always advisable: the longer you leave the ink the harder it will be to clean, and you may need to use harsh solvents to remove it. Never leave your rollers coated in ink for prolonged periods, as the ink will damage the rollers as it dries.

FACING PAGE
Always wear gloves when cleaning up to protect your hands. As lithographic printing ink is highly pigmented it can stain skin and clothes.

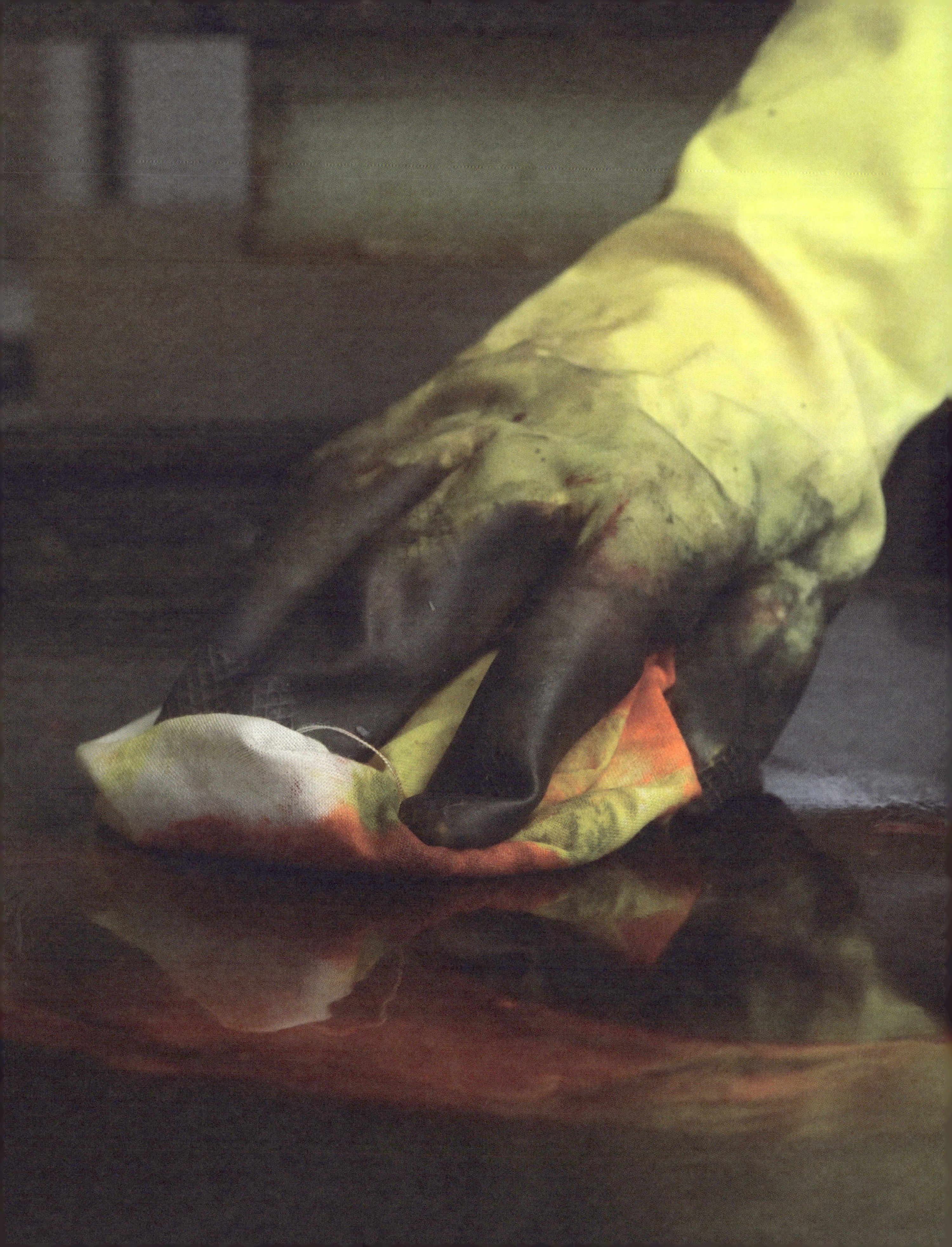

Lithography requires oil-based ink as it resists water, so it should go without saying that we can't use water to clean up the ink. Vegetable oil, citrus-based cleaners like Zest-it and solvents are what you need. If you're working from home or you don't have much ventilation, you will need to consider what substances you use. Many odourless solvents are available, and you often only need to use a small amount, but I recommend using simple vegetable oil as much as possible. It is cheap, works well, and is much better for your health and the environment.

Old cotton sheets and old T-shirts work brilliantly as rags, as they are soft and absorbent fabrics that won't leave lint on your equipment. Store your rags in a rag bin and re-use them until they are saturated in ink, then throw them away. You will be surprised how much ink a rag can hold.

HAND WASHING

Once you've finished printing you will need to give your hands a good wash to get rid of any ink traces. Make yourself a pot of cheap and eco-friendly hand scrub and keep it by the sink to easily remove stubborn ink from your hands.

Fill a jar 80% full with granulated sugar, then top it up with washing-up liquid. You can also add a few drops of essential oils for a nice scent, and a little vegetable oil to aid lubrication. Once this has been absorbed, add a little more washing-up liquid if needed and give it a stir. Rub over dry hands to remove the ink and then lather with a little water to clean off.

Materials and equipment needed when cleaning up after lithographic printing.

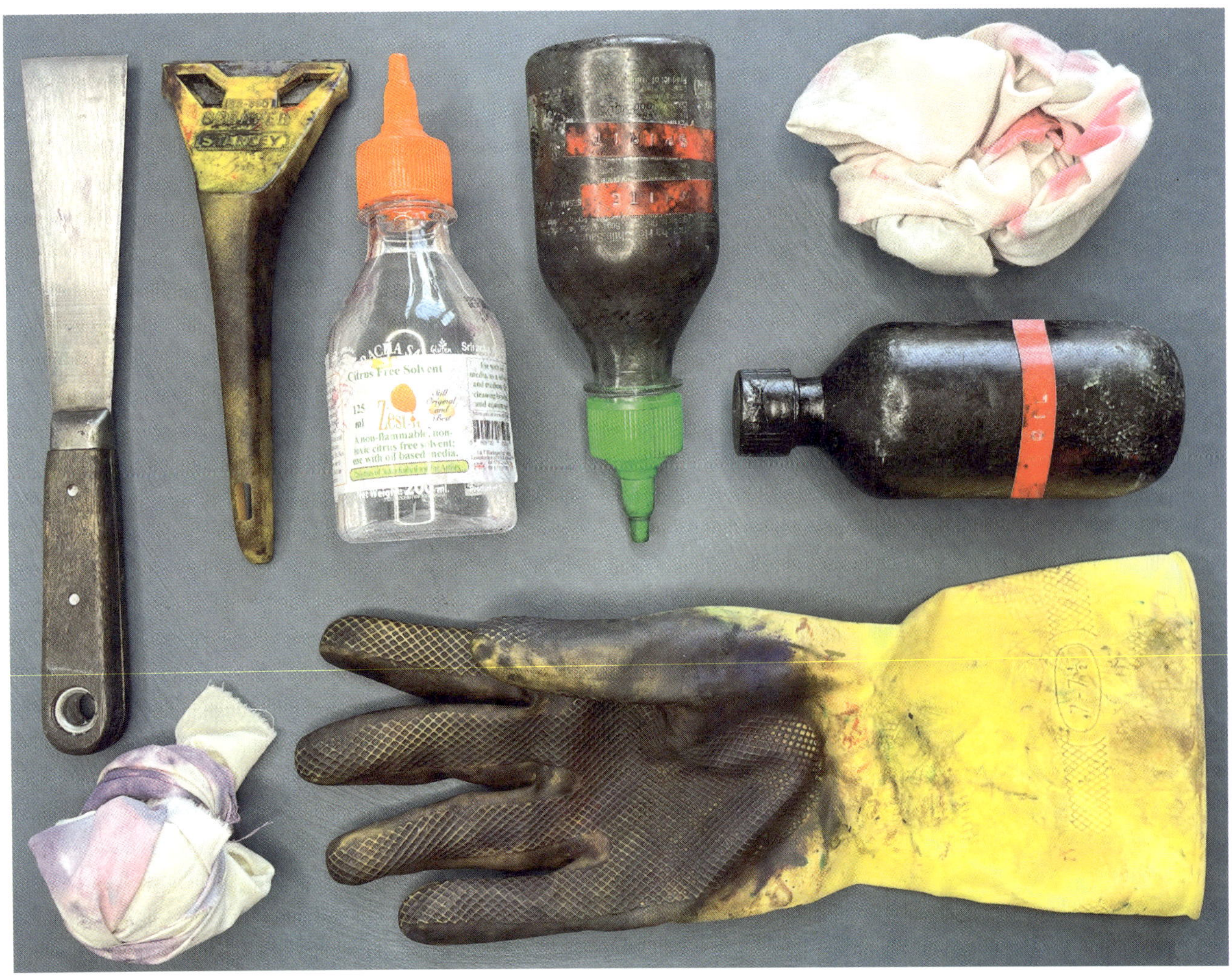

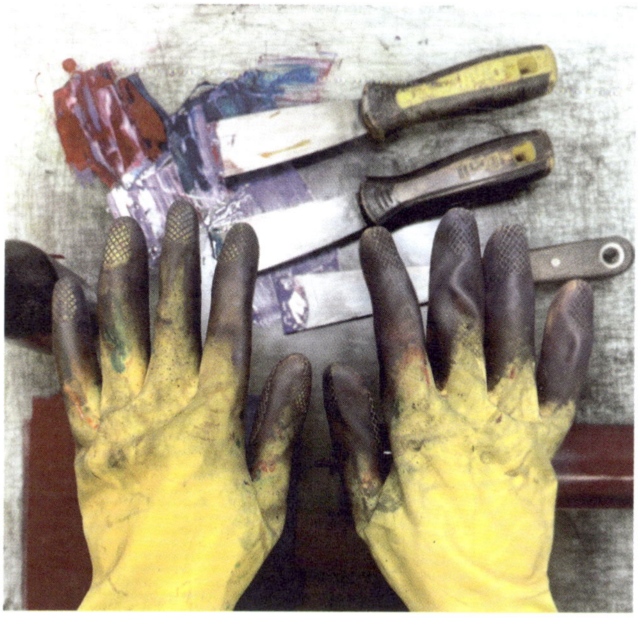

1. Always remember to put your gloves on before starting to clean up, to protect your hands from ink and harsh solvents.

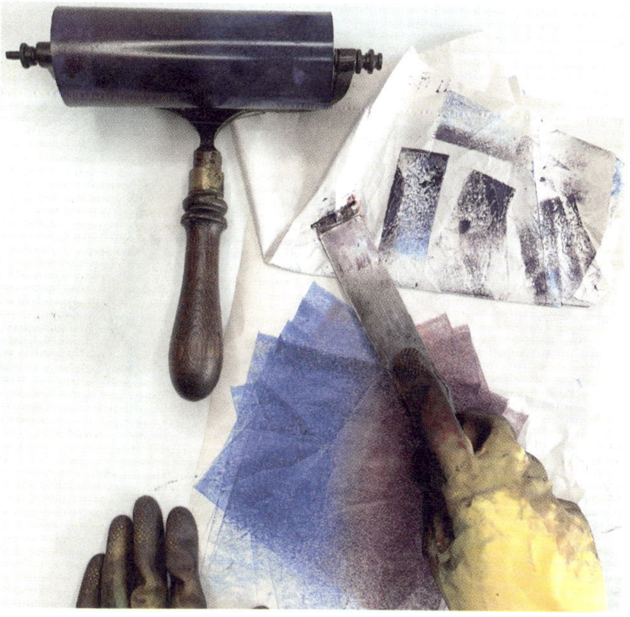

2. Scrape the excess ink onto scrap paper, if you're not storing it, and roll off excess ink from the roller onto scrap paper.

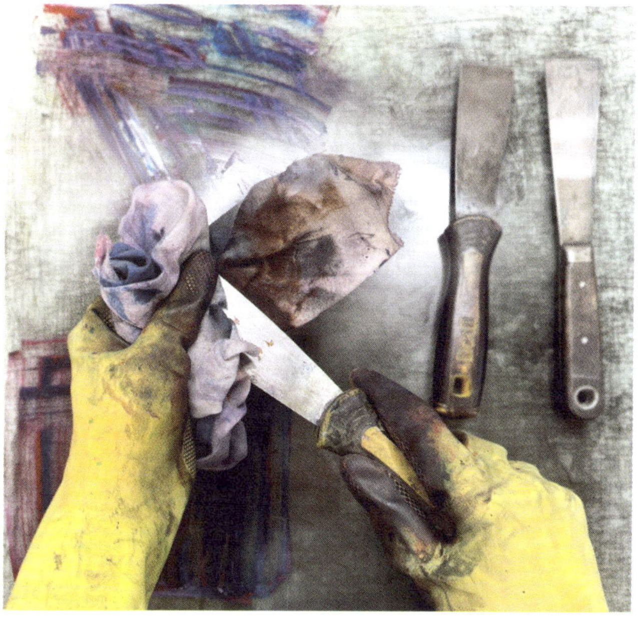

3. Loosen all the remaining ink with vegetable oil and a push knife. Then clean the push knives with a rag, remembering their edges.

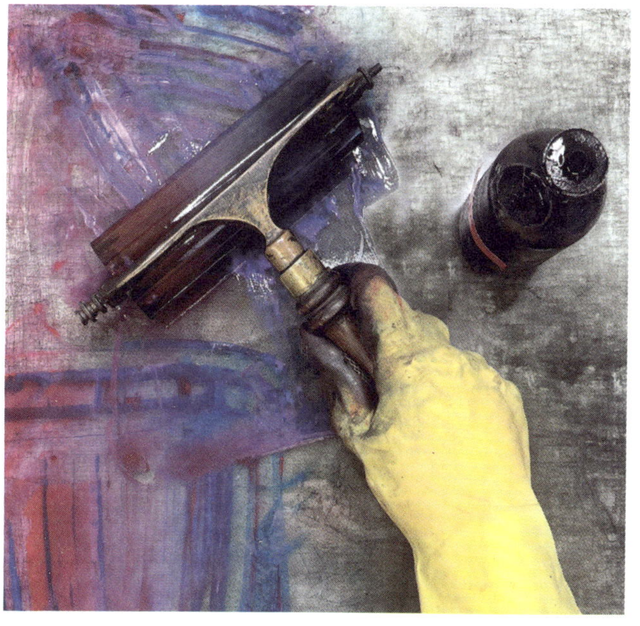

4. Loosen all the ink on the roller by rolling it around in the oil on your inking surface.

Cleaning up *(continued)*

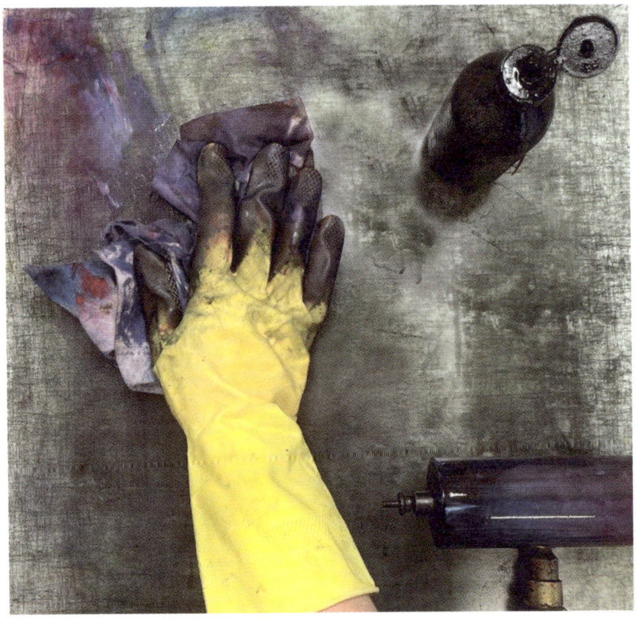

5. Use a rag to collect the ink from your inking surface. Keep turning to a clean area of the rag until it's saturated.

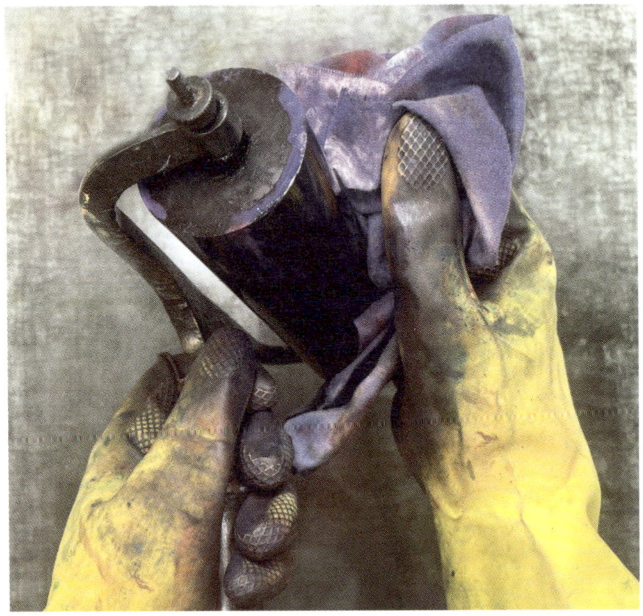

6. Wipe off the ink from your roller with a rag, remembering the edges of the roller. Use a little solvent if necessary.

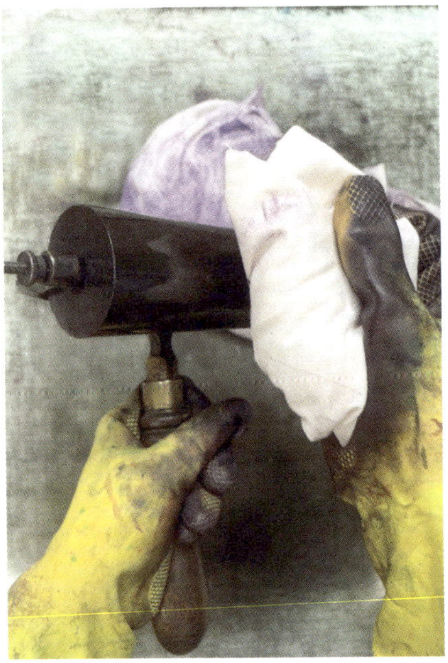

7. Use a fresh clean rag to check for any remaining ink on the roller. If using solvent, finish with a wipe of oil to remove all solvent and protect the roller.

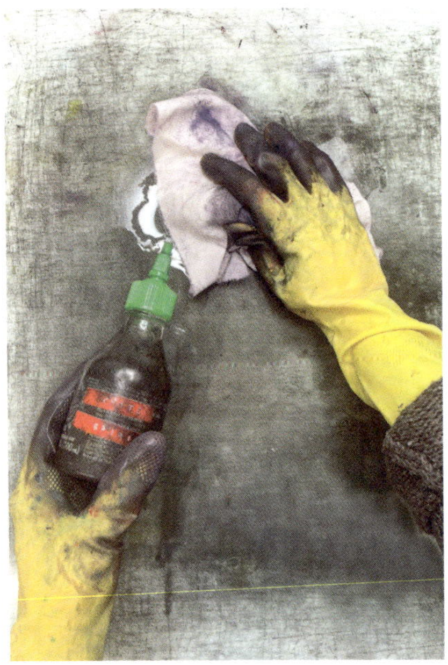

8. Wipe down your inking surface with a little solvent and a rag to remove any traces of oil.

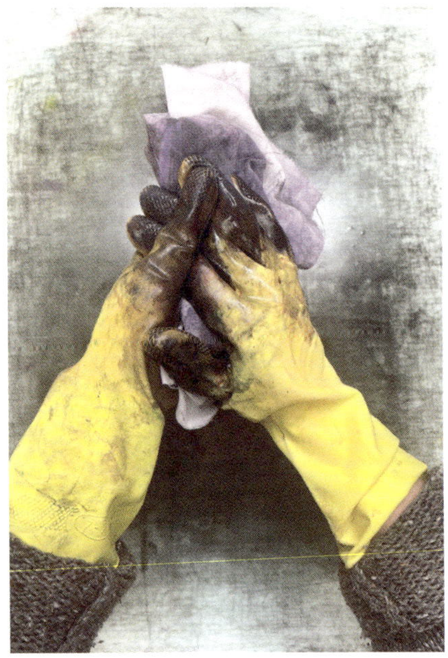

9. Finally, clean your gloves with oil and a rag. Even disposable gloves can be used many times if cleaned with oil.

Storing your ink

Using your push knife, scrape up your printing ink and fold it into a packet to re-use another time. I don't recommend storing the ink that has been rolled out as it is likely contaminated by gum and stray dirt, and don't store inks if you've added driers to them. After printmaker Simon Burder of Oaks Editions recommended using the inner bags of cereal packets to store ink, due to their sturdy nature, I use nothing else! You can also use foil or greaseproof paper for your ink packets. Make a note of the ink recipe and include a draw down sample as reference, so that you can match the colour if you need to mix more ink in the future.

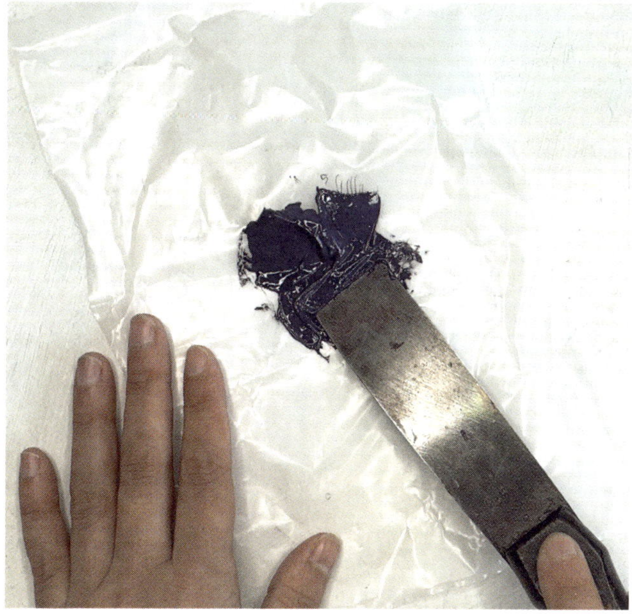

1. Transfer your printing ink to the centre of your ink packet using a push knife.

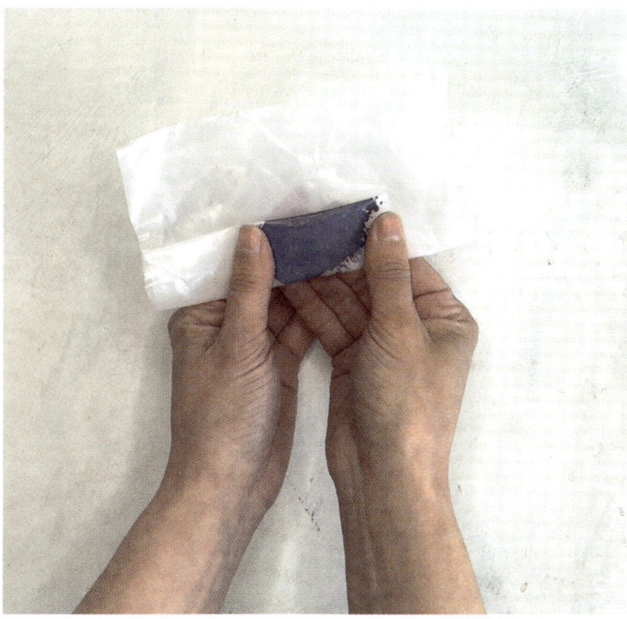

2. Fold over the packet and squash to remove any air, then tape tightly closed.

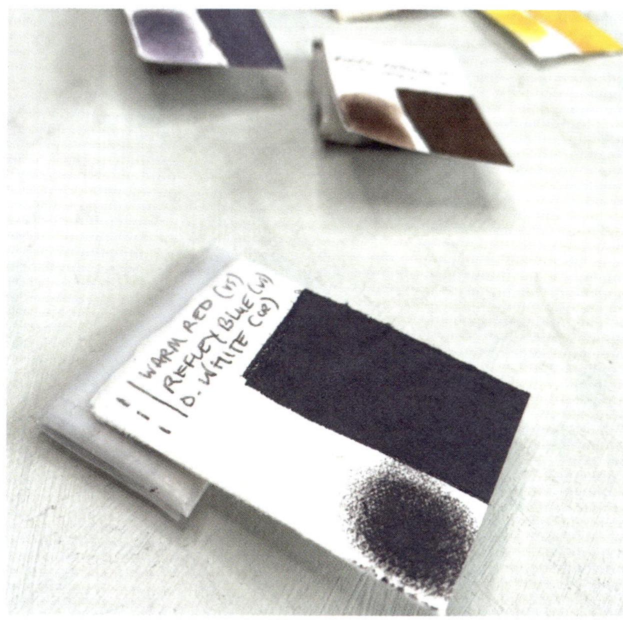

3. Add your draw down sample and recipe notes to identify the ink packet.

CHAPTER 12

Professional practice

When you are printing editions with hopes to sell them, there is admin involved. Keeping good track of the whereabouts of your prints is a valuable aspect of professional practice. You may be selling an edition of prints on various online stores, with galleries or your own website, and simultaneously have some of the same edition framed in multiple exhibitions. You don't want to be rummaging around your plan chest drawers desperately hoping to find a print from an edition that had just sold online, knowing that you can't print any more.

FACING PAGE
The most important thing to remember when handling prints is to have clean hands to protect the prints.

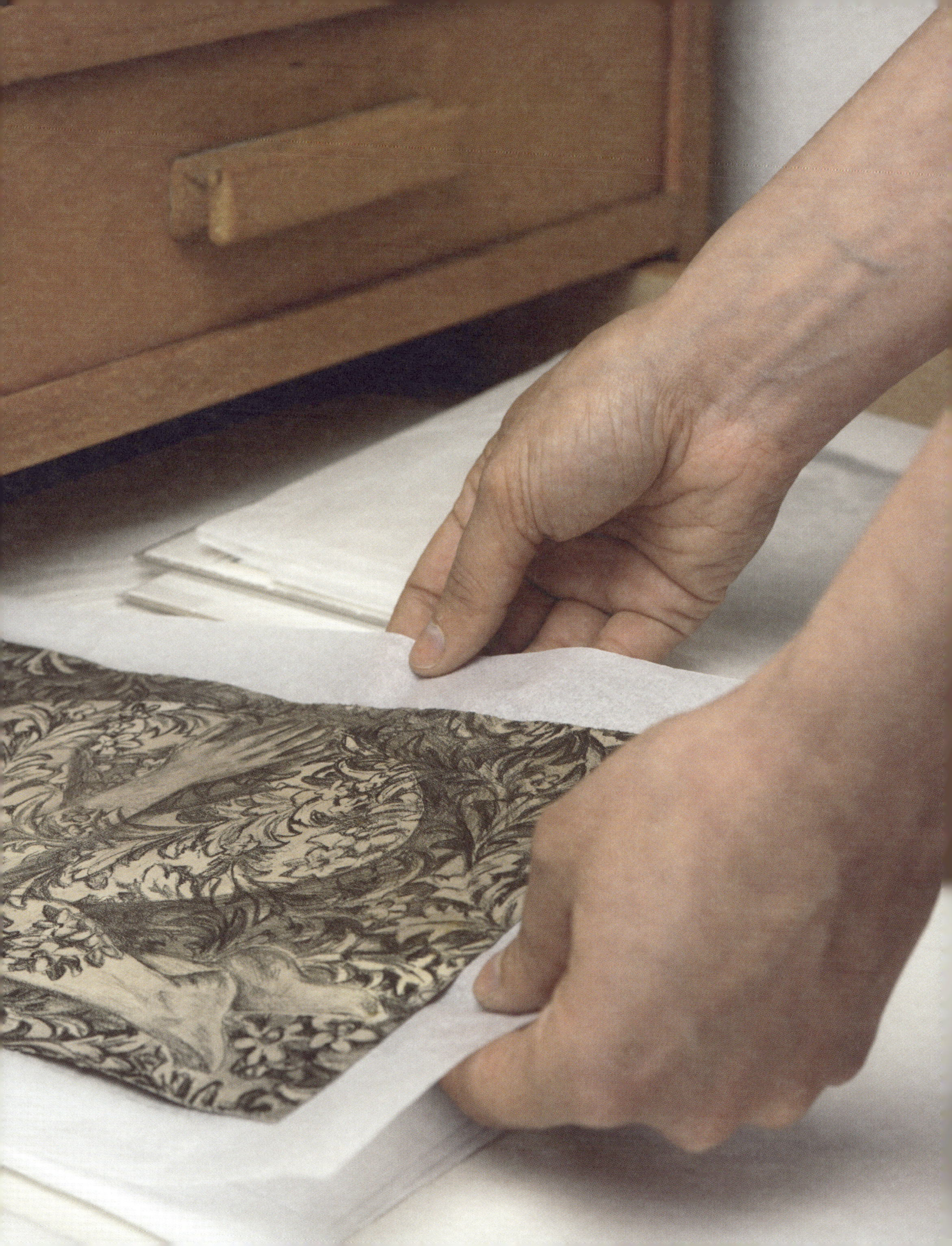

Keeping good records

The admin side of printmaking is very important but doesn't need to be too time consuming. Simply make yourself a spreadsheet, a record of the prints, and importantly, *keep it updated*. Include in your record all the important information about the edition: the edition size, the number of proofs, the paper used, the inks used, the date it was printed, the locations of the prints and details of the sales. Don't expect yourself to just remember or recognise this information, because after a while you won't. Once you have a system in place it is easy to add another print edition to that system and update it when a print sells.

Handling and storing prints

When it comes to handling prints, the first thing to remember is to use *clean hands*. Damaging prints with mucky fingerprints is careless and will devalue your work. Store your prints flat, wrapped in tissue paper or glassine to protect them while they're being stored. You don't want to have to tear into your print packet just to identify what the print is, so keep a print-out of the record of the edition attached to the packet. Prints stored in drawers may see a slight change in ink colour, but they will adjust back to normal when they are back in daylight.

When you are displaying prints in a browser, use compostable plastic sleeves/cellophane to protect the prints. Many galleries won't accept prints that aren't wrapped in compostable plastic: it's just as affordable and there really is no need for excess plastic nowadays. Consider the backing board you are using as well, as this should be acid-free/pH neutral. Your prints could stay wrapped for a long time, so don't risk damage to them.

Taking good care and accounting of your prints is professional practice and will make your life easier. It shows a level of professionalism that will give galleries and buyers faith in you as an artist.

FACING PAGE
Plan chest drawer with print editions stored in tissue paper packets, with print edition record attached.

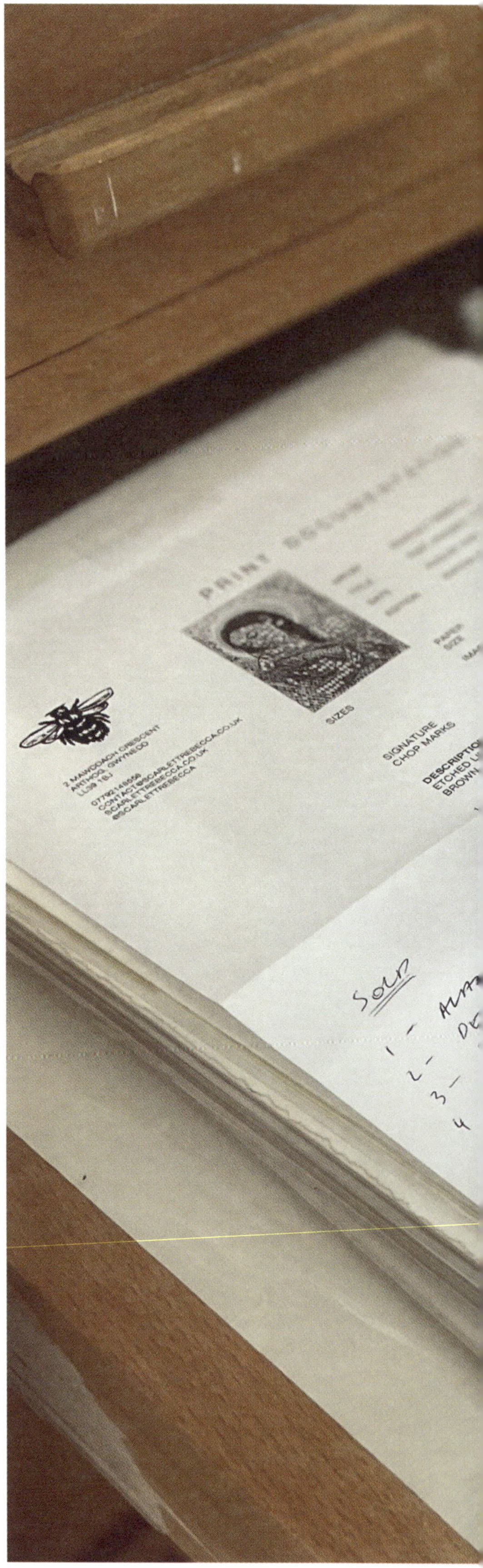

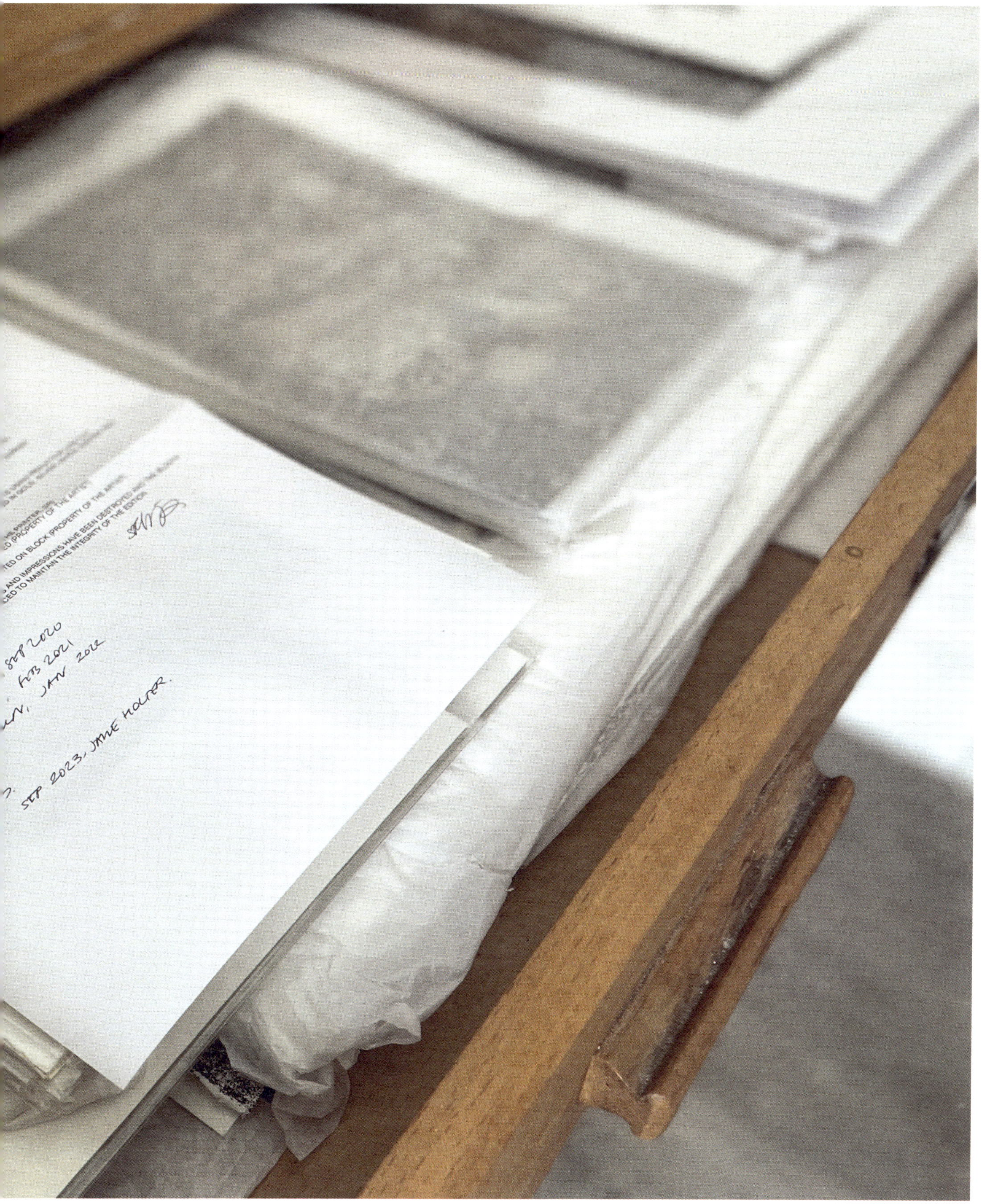

Print annotations

The annotations on prints are used to communicate important information about the prints, such as the edition size, so your buyers can trust what they're getting. There is an assumption with some annotations that the printer is not also the artist, as historically an artist would be working with a master printer to publish an edition of prints. If this is the case you will see the printer's chop marks, their embossed sigil, alongside the artist's signature.

Traditionally the artist's signature is signed at the bottom right, the title is in the centre and the annotations are found on the bottom left. For full bleed prints these are often written on the back of the print.

#/# Denotes the number of prints in the edition and which number in the edition that print is (1/8 denotes that this is the first print from an edition of 8).

TP Trial proof: used to denote that these prints include an element of exploration, for example to test a different colour. These can be numbered in states (T.P. iii denotes the third trial state of a print before reaching the final edition state).

AP Artist proof: a number of prints are often kept back from the edition number for the artist. AP is often used to denote exploratory prints when printed by the artist, rather than by a master printer.

PP Printer's proof: a print gifted to the printer if they are not also the artist.

VE Variable edition: denotes that each print in the edition will have characteristics that are slightly different, alongside the repeated motif.

BAT *Bon à Tirer* – translating as 'good to print' – a print used as a quality gauge for the subsequent prints to match up to in order to form part of the edition. Not included in the final numbered edition.

Framing prints

There are many ways to mount and frame prints, and the display of artwork is very subjective. Sometimes an artist will include instructions on how they believe their artwork should be framed, but if the buyer doesn't agree with that, they can of course frame it however they like. The important thing to consider is the archival quality of the framing materials. If an artwork is framed without using archival quality boards and tapes, over time it can show signs of ageing and foxing (stains from mould or contaminants) and can affect the longevity of your image. It is also recommended to use anti-reflective glass to ensure clarity of your print without reflections obstructing the image. Using UV protective glass/conservation glass will protect your prints from damage by sunlight and ensure the longevity of the artwork.

Print edition annotations on various prints, always on the bottom left corner of the print.

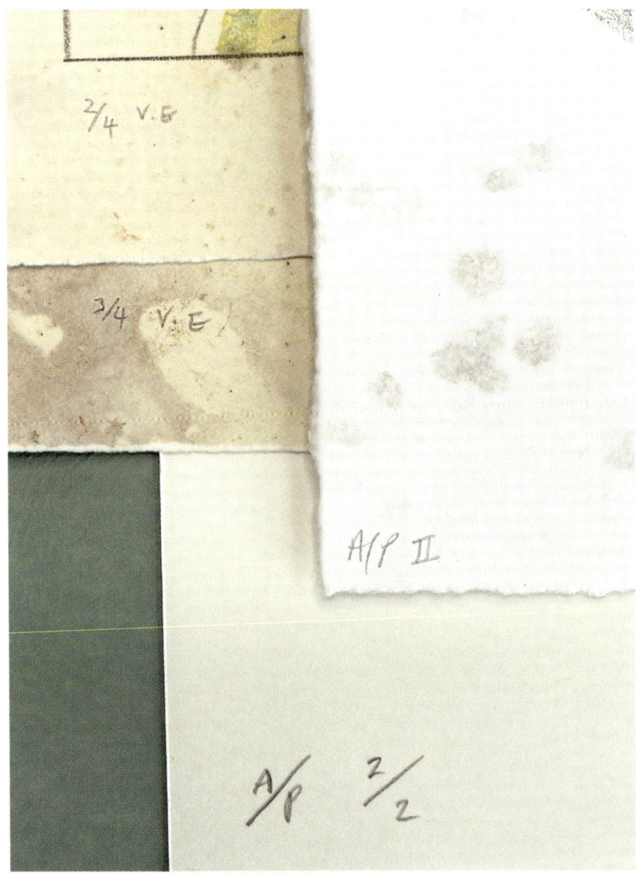

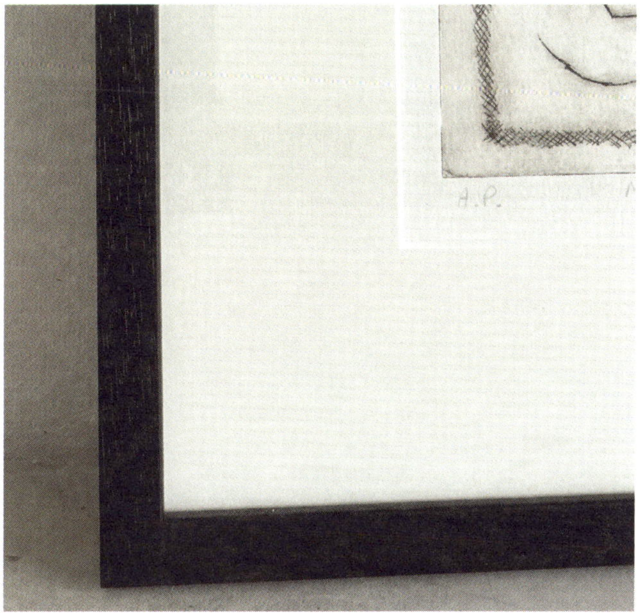

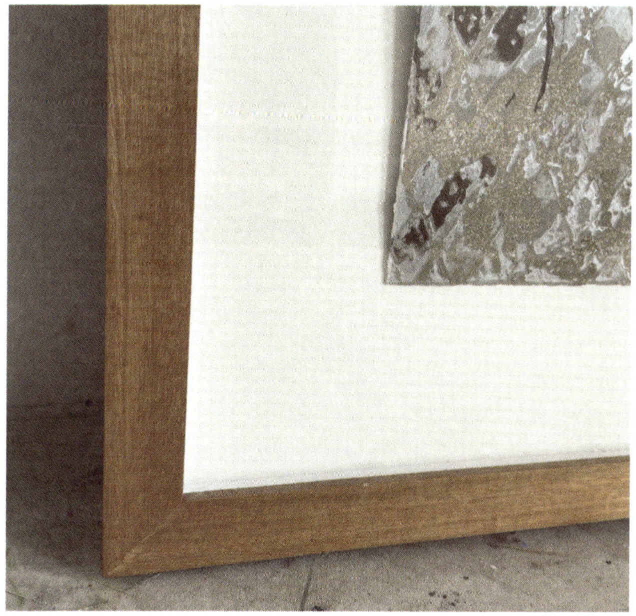

1. Framing with a single or double *window mount* is the most common way of displaying prints. The mount sets the image back from the glass and includes the annotations within the mount. Everything beyond the margin of the window is covered by the mount.

2. For full-bleed, unconventionally shaped prints or non-flat prints, *float mounting* is often chosen as the framing option. The print is displayed resting on the surface of the mount, set back from the glass, allowing a slight shadowing to occur.

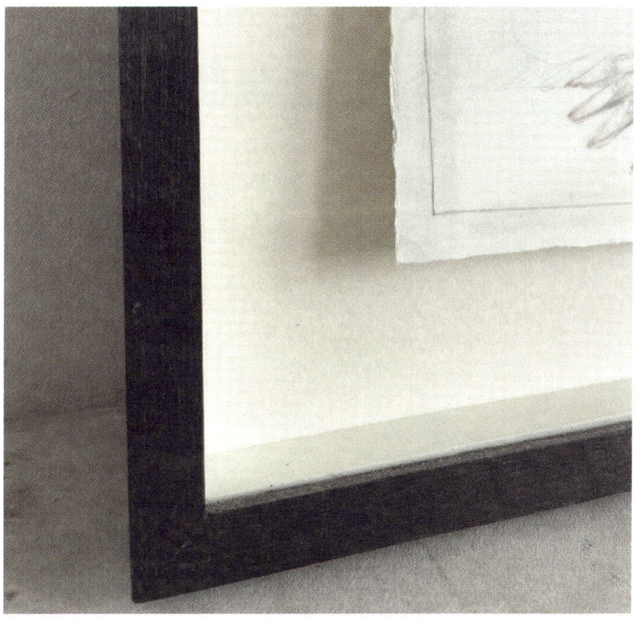

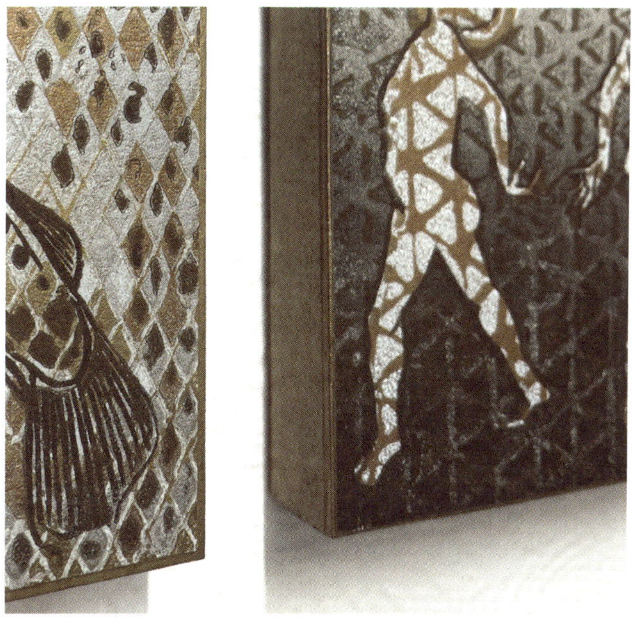

3. *Shadow float mounting* has the addition of a piece of foam board behind the artwork to set it apart from the background mount, increasing the floating effect. This requires a deeper frame to accommodate the extra space.

4. A print can sometimes be *block mounted* when a traditional frame is not suitable. The print is attached to a block and often varnished rather than protected with glass. The print can then be hung as it is, or can be tray framed.

SUPPLIERS

UK

Handprinted
handprinted.co.uk
@handprinteduk
Affordable printmaking supplies.

Intaglio Printmaker
intaglioprintmaker.com
@intaglioprintmaker
Specialist printmaking supplies.

Hawthorn Printmaker Supplies
hawthornprintmaker.com
@hawthorn_printmaker
Affordable specialist printmaking supplies.

Lawrence
lawrence.co.uk
@artshophove
Specialist printmaking supplies.

Jackson's Art Supplies
jacksonsart.com
@jacksons_art
Mid- to low-budget printmaking and general art materials.

Great Art
greatart.co.uk
@greatart_UK
Mid- to low-budget printmaking and general art materials.

L. Cornelissen & Son
cornelissen.com
@l.cornelissen_and_son
Fine art and printmaking supplies.

Cass Art
cassart.co.uk
@cassart1984
General art materials.

Seawhite
seawhite.co.uk
@seawhiteofbrighton
Low-budget and wholesale art materials.

John Purcell Paper
johnpurcell.net
@johnpurcellpaper
Specialist and printmaking paper supplies.

RK Burt & Company Ltd
rkburt.co.uk
@rkburtco
Specialist and printmaking paper supplies.

Two Rivers Paper
tworiverspaper.com
@tworiverspaper
Specialist handmade paper supplies.

Harry F Rochat Ltd
harryrochat.com
@rochat_printing_presses
Manufacturing, servicing and removal of printing presses.

AMR Press
amrloganpress.co.uk
@letterpress.today
Restoration, servicing and removal of printing presses.

RS Components
uk.rs-online.com/web/
@WeAreRSGroup
Maintenance, tools and PPE supplies.

Printmaking Services
printmakingservices.co.uk
@printmakingservices
Restoration, servicing and removal of printing presses.

EUROPE

Gerstaecker (Germany)
gerstaecker.de
@gerstaeckerverlag
General art supplies.

Le Géant des Beaux-Arts (France)
geant-beaux-arts.fr
@le_geant_des_beaux_arts
General art supplies.

Polymetaal (Netherlands)
polymetaal.nl
Specialist printmaking supplies and presses.

Joop Stoop (France)
joopstoop.com
@joopstoopparis
Specialist printmaking supplies.

BOESNER (Across Europe)
boesner.com
@boesner_deutschland
General art supplies.

USA

McClain's Printmaking Supplies
imcclains.com
@mcclains.printmaking.supplies
Specialist (relief) printmaking supplies.

Blick
dickblick.com
@blickartmaterials
Mid- to low-budget general art supplies.

Graphic Chemical & Ink Co.
graphicchemical.com
@graphicchemicalinkco
Specialist printmaking supplies.

Takach Press
takachpress.com
@takachpress
Specialist printmaking supplies and presses.

PRINT WORKSHOPS (UK and Ireland)

Edinburgh Printmakers (Edinburgh)
edinburghprintmakers.co.uk

Glasgow Print Studio (Glasgow)
glasgowprintstudio.co.uk

Northern Print (Newcastle)
northernprint.org.uk

Hole Editions (Newcastle)
holeeditions.wordpress.com

West Yorkshire Print Workshop (Mirfield)
wypw.org

Birmingham Printmakers (Birmingham)
birminghamprintmakers.org

Leicester Print Workshop (Leicester)
leicesterprintworkshop.com

Gloucester Print Coop (Gloucester)
gpchq.co.uk

Bip-Art (Brighton)
bip-art.co.uk

Handprinted (Bognor Regis)
handprinted.co.uk

Omega Printmakers (Portsmouth)
omegaprintmakers.com

Curwen Study Centre (Suffolk)
curwenprintstudy.co.uk

Norwich Printmaking Hub (Norwich)
norwichprintmakinghub.com

Digswell Arts (Hertfordshire)
digswellarts.org

Dekkle (Baldock)
dekkle.com

Oaks Editions (London)
oaksfineart.co.uk

Art Academy (London)
artacademy.ac.uk

East London Printmakers (London)
eastlondonprintmakers.co.uk
Ochre Print Studio (Guildford)
ochreprintstudio.co.uk

Lemonade Press (Bristol)
thelemonadepress.co.uk

Spike Island (Bristol)
spikeisland.org.uk

Aberystwyth Printmakers (Aberystwyth)
aberystwythprintmakers.org.uk

Print Haus (Cardiff)
theprinthaus.org

Regional Print Centre (Wrexham)
regionalprint.org.uk

Belfast Print Workshop (Belfast)
bpw.org.uk

Seacourt Printmakers (Bangor, Northern Ireland)
seacourt-ni.org.uk

Graphic Studio Dublin (Dublin)
graphicstudiodublin.com

Creative Spark (Dundalk)
creativespark.ie

Cork Printmakers (Cork)
corkprintmakers.ie

Limerick Printmakers (Limerick)
limerickprintmakers.com

FEATURED ARTISTS

SCARLETT REBECCA
scarlettrebecca.co.uk
patreon.com/scarlettrebecca
@scarlettrebecca

BRIAN WAGNER
hedgebitch.com
@hedgebitch

VALERIE SYPOSZ
valeriesyposz.com
@valeriesyposz

KATHRYN DESFORGES
kathryndesforges.co.uk
@kathryn_desforges_studio

MARY DALTON
marydalton.co.uk
@m_dalton_print

MINA RAKIDŽIĆ
behance.net/minarakidzic
@ra_mina

SUE JARMAN
suejarman.co.uk
@sue_jarman

LEE TURNER
holeeditions.wordpress.com
@holeeditions

INDEX

A
acetone 70
advanced processes 168–176
annotations 186

B
bleed print. 56–59
blends 162
Brighton University 169–172
brayers *see rollers*

C
calendaring 32
carbon paper 50
carving 73–74, 83, 107–108
chine collé 130, 165–166, 167
cleaning 61, 121, 144, 176–181
CMYK 125, 145–148, 160
collage 115–117
colour
  colour printing 55–59, 80–84, 106–108, 121, 125–130, 145–152
  colour mixing 118, 121, 159–160, 161, 162
conté pencil/crayon 80, 106
crayons 20, 95
Curwen Studio, The 11

D
Dalton, Mary 88, 110–111
Delacroix Eugéne 11
Desforges, Kathryn 86–87
draw down 161, 181
drawing materials 20
driers 22
dry roll 60, 153
drying prints 27

E
editioning 186
equipment 18–27
extender 21, 108, 160

F
foil lithography 36–63
fount solution 134, 141
framing 186–187
French chalk 27, 73, 96, 140

G
gum Arabic 14, 27, 50, 52, 66, 74, 97, 118, 122, 140
gum Arabic transfer *see paper plate lithography*
gum paper 100–103
gum resist 71, 80, 95, 137

H
halftone 125, 145–146
hand burnishing/printing 22, 26, 48, 76–78, 85, 120, 143
hand tinting/colouring 130, 163–164
hand-scrub. 179
handling prints 184
Heritage Crafts 13

I
inks
  printing inks 21, 30–31, 159–160, 161
  preparation 30–31
ink blends 160, 162

J
Jarman, Sue 154–155
jigsaw printing 125–130, 151

K
Kindness, John 158
kitchen lithography *see foil lithography*

L
lino lithography 88–111
linocut 7, 90, 107–108
lithino *see lino lithography*
lo-shu 103–105

M
magnesium carbonate 21
marbling 149
masks 129, 151–152
materials
  materials & equipment 18–27
  drawing materials 20
  foil lithography 39
  wood lithography 68
  lino lithography 92
  paper plate lithography 115
  polyester plate lithography 136
  cleaning up 178
metal-plate lithography 11, 134, 173
modifiers 21–22, 30, 141
moire pattern 145
mokulito *see wood lithography*
monotype 7, 54–59, 129
mounting
  mounting lightweight prints 167
  frame mounts 186–187
muddying (colour) 82, 97
multi-layer printing 55–59, 80–84, 125, 106–108, 125–130, 147–152

O
offset
  offset ink 21
  offset press 25, 172
oil 21, 45–46, 52, 118, 178

P
paper
  paper types 22, 24, 160
  tearing paper 32
  soaking/dampening paper 33, 163
  paper stretch
  transfer paper 50, 100–103
paper plate lithography 112–133
photo editing 117, 126–127, 145–146
photocopy transfer 70
photographic imagery 70, 145–148, 170
photoplate lithography 170–172
photoshop 117, 126–127, 145–146
polyester plate lithography 7, 134–155
PPE 26, 150, 178
preparing to print 28–35
print annotations 186
print records 184
printing
  foil lithography 47–49
  wood lithography 75–78
  lino lithography 97–99
  paper plate lithography 118–124
  polyester plate lithography 141–143
printing press 25, 35
processing
  foil lithography 45
  wood lithography 73–74
  lino lithography 96–97
  polyester plate lithography 140–141
professional practice 182–187

R
Rakidžić, Mina 132–133
Re-using plates 79, 82, 83, 100, 144
Redon, Odilon 12
reduction print 80–84
registration 34, 84, 136, 147
roller lines (tramlines) 109, 153
rollers 26

S

sanding 69, 79, 82, 93, 100, 106
salt wash 150–151
scraper bar 15
scumming 99, 109, 118, 141, 153
Senefelder, Alois 11
soap 43, 60, 72, 79
sponges 27
stone lithography 11, 13–15, 16–17, 173
storing
- storing ink 181
- storing plates 50, 144
- storing prints 184

studio 27, 30
sundries 27
swatching 160–161
Syposz, Valerie 62–63

T

T and bar registration 34
tack reducer 21
Tamarind Institute, The 13, 16, 174
toner 20, 70, 112, 116, 150
Toulouse-Lautrec, Henri de 12
transfer paper 50, 100–103
transparent white/base 21, 108, 160
troubleshooting
- foil lithography 60–61
- wood lithography 85
- lino lithography 109
- paper plate lithography 131
- polyester plate lithography 153

T

Turner, Lee 20, 173, 174–175
tusche 20–21, 71, 80–83, 94, 138–139, 150

V

viscosity 55, 162

W

Wagner, Brian 16 – 17
wheat paste glue 165
wood lithography 64–87
woodcut 83–84
working outside 50

First published in 2025 by
The Crowood Press Ltd
Ramsbury, Marlborough
Wiltshire SN8 2HR

enquiries@crowood.com
www.crowood.com

This impression 2025

British Library Cataloguing-in-Publication Data
A catalogue record for this book is available from the British Library.

For product safety-related questions contact productsafety@crowood.com.

ISBN 978 0 7198 4500 0

Cover design by Sergey Tsvetkov
Cover image and photography on pages 2, 4, 9, 19, 29, 37, 65, 89, 113, 135, 157, 177, 183 and 184 by Jake Spicer

Scarlett Rebecca Tierney has asserted her right under the Copyright, Designs and Patents Act 1988 to be identified as the author of this work

Designed and typeset by maru studio G.K.
Printed and bound in India by Parksons Graphics Pvt. Ltd.,

Acknowledgements
This book is dedicated to all the printmakers who generously share their wealth of expertise with the world; there are no secrets with printmakers, they really are the best folks.

I'd like to thank Heike Roesel and everyone at Brighton University for allowing me to photograph their fantastic printmaking workshops. Huge thanks also go to Handprinted for the generous donation of materials for this book. Especial thanks go to Wayne Case for nurturing my love of lithography and encouraging my curiosity.

Above all, my heartfelt thanks go to Jake for his unbridled support and for courageously helping me move ridiculously heavy lithography presses wherever they need to go.